REGISTRUM SACRUM ANGLICANUM

STUBBS

HENRY FROWDE, M.A.

PUBLISHER TO THE UNIVERSITY OF OXFORD

LONDON, EDINBURGH, AND NEW YORK

Registrum Sacrum Anglicanum

AN ATTEMPT TO EXHIBIT THE

COURSE OF EPISCOPAL SUCCESSION IN ENGLAND

FROM THE

RECORDS AND CHRONICLES OF THE CHURCH

BY

WILLIAM STUBBS

BISHOP OF OXFORD

SECOND EDITION

WITH AN APPENDIX OF INDIAN, COLONIAL, AND MISSIONARY CONSECRATIONS
COLLECTED AND ARRANGED BY E. E. HOLMES
HONORARY CANON OF CHRIST CHURCH

Oxford

AT THE CLARENDON PRESS

M DCCC XCVII

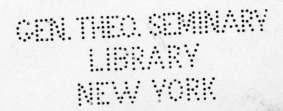

Oxford
PRINTED AT THE CLARENDON PRESS
BY HORACE HART, M.A.
PRINTER TO THE UNIVERSITY

PREFACE

THIS Book is offered as a contribution to Ecclesiastical History in the departments of Biography and exact Chronology. Its position in relation to the first of these, though humble, is sufficiently obvious: in regard to the latter it seems to require some apology. This must be found in the fact that it occupies and confines itself to a distinct ground not solely or exclusively appropriated by any similar work, and so is not intended to supersede the labour or to disparage the arrangement of any former collectors. A short notice of the sources of the information contained in it will suffice.

And, first, with regard to the Saxon period. This portion of the Record has been constructed from a comparison of the Ancient Lists of Bishops with the scanty memoranda of the Anglo-Saxon Chronicle, Simeon of Durham, Florence of Worcester, and the Annotators. The results of this comparison have been carefully tested by the signatures of the Charters printed in Kemble's *Codex Diplomaticus*, and additional light has been thrown on them by the Profession Rolls at Canterbury: these valuable evidences, which are available up to the end of the fourteenth century, are the written declarations of obedience to the Metropolitical Church which were made by each Bishop at his consecration.

The later portion of the Record, from the consecration of Parker downwards, is an abstract of the records of the provinces of Canterbury and York, which are lodged at Lambeth, the Vicar-General's office in Doctors' Commons, and at York.

The second or mediaeval portion is a careful compilation, now for the first time attempted, from all the accessible sources. Of these sources a list will be given. A few general remarks on them may not be out of place or useless to students of the same subjects.

And first, as most accessible, stand the Collections towards English Church History, in which class the *Antiquitates* of Parker and Josselin, Godwin *De Praesulibus*, Wharton's *Anglia Sacra*, and Le Neve's *Fasti*, are text-books.

Next, and indispensably necessary to one who would refer to original records, are the unrivalled Manuscript Collections of Henry Wharton at Lambeth. This wonderful man died in 1695, at the age of thirty, having done for the elucidation of English Church History (itself but one of the branches of study in which he was the most eminent scholar of his time) more than any one before or since. Contemporary and apparently in frequent communication with him was Matthew Hutton of Aynho (he died in 1711), whose valuable Collections are in the Harleian Library. They contain, among other transcripts, copies of several volumes of Wharton's MSS.

Bishop Kennett seems to have transcribed and digested the Collections of both these on ecclesiastical subjects, with additions from his own reading. These are in the Lansdowne Collection.

It was at first attempted to construct a Chronological Table from the above authorities, in conjunction with the printed Chronicles. But the many discrepancies of the latter, and the imperfect notes of the Collectors, who not collecting for this branch of the subject in particular, seldom exhausted their authorities or quoted them exactly, determined the editor to have recourse to original documentary evidence, and nowhere, if possible, to commit himself to a statement on second-hand testimony. With this view he has consulted a large number of the Registers and Records of various sees, and as many of the Chronicles preserved in MS. in our National and Academic libraries, as seemed likely to afford any information. With respect to the Chronicles, a list of those from which information was actually gained will be enough. Of the Episcopal Registers to be found in the several Cathedrals, which are of course less accessible, the chief features are these:

Every Bishop kept (and still keeps) a register of all his official acts. The first page generally contains the account of his consecration or appointment; then follow the Bulls and other privileges which he received from the Popes. The bulk of each volume is occupied with the records of institutions to benefices, acts of consistory courts, and lists of persons ordained; to which in many instances important wills are annexed. This may be considered as an adequate description of the general run of registers. There are however frequent exceptions. Those of Canterbury and York contain proceedings with the Suffragans, records of Convocations and Councils, and a vast number of letters on public business. The Register of William of Wykeham is the model of the record of a statesman Bishop, and a most valuable storehouse of notices of public interest, summonses to Parliament, and miscellaneous official and personal acts. Others contain copies of more ancient documents, which were perishing when transcribed, and are now lost. Nor are the materials only worthy of remark; the arrangement also is various: some are patterns of neatness, especially the early ones of York, and those of Winchester generally; others are confused and scanty, the Canterbury ones being by no means the best, which is very unfortunate, considering their importance. Several are lost, among them the larger portion of Cardinal Beaufort's, which seems to have come after his death into the King's hands and may possibly be found some day. It must have contained very much of historical importance at a period not much illustrated by historians, and especially on the subject before us. The condition however of the existing ones is very good, and altogether they form a curious and by no means exhausted mine of information to a careful inquirer.

From these and similar sources the following tables are framed: in most cases the evidence they afford is direct and particular, in some few the date and circumstances have to be derived from indirect indications. These (which are in the text printed in Italics) will be found chiefly during the troubled times of Richard II, when, notwithstanding the statute of Provisors, each appointment of a Bishop received its confirmation at Rome, where most, if not all, of the unrecorded consecrations probably took place: others during the wars of the Roses, and up to the close of the fifteenth century. For the latter period the dates have been fixed with reference (1) to the time at which the licences for consecration were issued by the Convent of Canterbury, which in most cases was during the week preceding the appointed Sunday; (2) to such scattered notices of the filling up of preferments vacated by consecration as could be found in various Registers; and (3) to the computation of the pontifical years of the several Bishops as given in existing Instruments. It is hoped that in all these cases the dates given will be found correct when examined by the light of further evidence. Similar historical and chronological tests have been applied to every date in this portion of the Record, and if the results in some instances are different from those given by older authorities, no particular has been set down without careful calculation and consideration.

The thanks of the Editor are offered to all who have kindly procured him access to Records, especially to Felix Knyvett, Esq., of Lambeth, the Rev. A. P. Stanley and the Hon. D. Finch of

Canterbury, the authorities at the Vicar-General's office and S. Paul's, Mr. Wooldridge of Winchester, Chancellors Harrington of Exeter and Melvill of S. David's, Egerton V. Harcourt, Esq., and the Rev. W. V. Harcourt of York, the Rev. J. Raine, junior, of Durham, the Rev. Geo. Gilbert of Grantham, the Bishop of Carlisle, W. T. Alchin, Esq., and the Deputy Registrars of Worcester, Hereford, Lichfield, Chichester, Rochester, Norwich, Wells, and Salisbury.

It is perhaps necessary to add, that throughout the work the beginning of the year is placed on the first of January.

Navestock, *January* 25, 1858.

POSTSCRIPT

This book, like all other books, has much greater interest for its author than for any one else. That the interest in this case may be disproportionately great, is a matter that concerns my own personal equation, and the special relation of the book to the course of my literary work. I have, I believe, naturally that strong instinct for the investigation of continuities and coincidences which leads men to the study of chronology and genealogy for the pleasure of exercise, an instinct that was favoured by the circumstances of early home education and local association; my first attempts in the direction of research were the collection and arrangement of dates and dynasties. This book is an illustration of the passion and something more. It was published nearly forty years ago, but the collection of the materials had begun at least as early as 1848; it was founded on the examination of the Records of the Church preserved in the Episcopal Registers of the several Dioceses, in the Collections formed by Henry Wharton and Dr. Ducarel at Lambeth, in the manuscript Chronicles in the Bodleian, the British Museum, and at Corpus Christi College, Cambridge, and in the treasures of the Public Record Office. It was published by the Delegates of the University Press on the recommendation chiefly of Dr. Jacobson, then Regius Professor of Divinity, and of Dr. Cardwell, Camden's Reader in History. Four years afterwards, I became the custodian of the Lambeth MSS. in succession to Wharton and Ducarel; in 1863 I was privileged to take part in the publication, under the Master of the Rolls, of the Chronicles and Records at which I had worked in MS.; three years later, as Regius Professor of Modern History, I took up the responsibilities which, as Delegate of the Press and Curator of the Bodleian, had rested on the two patrons of my book; and finally succeeding Bishop Jacobson in the see of Chester, I somehow achieved that combination of objectivity and subjectivity which made me one of the materials for my own manipulation. The book then is an example of continuity and coincidence.

In the capacities which I have noted, I have had abundant opportunity of correcting and revising the work, and it now appears in a form in which it will be more satisfactory and probably more useful. The sacrifice of the tabular arrangement enables me to give distinctly the principal authorities for the several dates, and particular references to the editions of the Chronicles and other records, so many of which have been printed since 1858. That so few important corrections are required is to be ascribed no doubt to the soundness of the work in print and MS., on which I was able from the first to rely with firm confidence. Still the appearance of new authorities has enabled me to fix a few more exact dates. I wish, too, sincerely to thank those kind friends, like Canon Jessopp, who, either of their own accord or at my request, have helped me to improve the form of the book. In particular, Mr. W. H. Stevenson has given me the most valuable assistance in getting the Anglo-Saxon names into some sort of consistency. His help has been invaluable to me; and I must add that wherever a fault is to be found in the nomenclature, it is pretty certain to be a case in which I have neglected his advice. Of the new material for the mediaeval portion of the work more might have been expected than has really come from the research made in the Papal Archives since the accession of Leo XIII; some sidelights, however, have been furnished by the Papal Registers published in the *Bibliothèque de l'École Française* at Rome, as well as from the three volumes of Papal letters which have appeared under the superintendence of the Master of the Rolls. But they have not done much more than supplement and systematize the information furnished in the Vatican MSS. in the British Museum, which I had thoroughly ransacked in 1855. I must, however, acknowledge a real debt to the late Dr. Maziere Brady, who placed in my hands the manuscript results of his research into the Archives at Rome, which were edited in 1876 under the title of *The Episcopal Succession in England, Scotland, and Ireland from* A.D. 1400 *to* 1875.

I may add that, in one of my last conversations with the late Archbishop, he advised me to make an effort to reproduce and continue the book, in preparation for the meeting of the Bishops of the Anglican Communion in Conference this year. In connexion with this recommendation and admonition, I have thought it advisable to add to the volume the carefully collected list of Consecrations of the Indian, Colonial, and Missionary Bishops, which Canon E. E. Holmes has kindly furnished.

As the references to authorities are now given in full in their proper places, it seems unnecessary to reproduce the formal list of books used in the compilation of the work; but I have retained the memorandum of the Episcopal Registers in Diocesan Registries, in the idea that although obviously imperfect, it may be useful to other inquirers.

W. OXON.

CUDDESDON, *May 27, 1897.*

N.B.—In preparing Appendix I, I have had the assistance of many kind friends who are interested, at first hand, in the undertaking. Those who are versed in inquiries of this kind will know that it is impossible to guarantee perfect accuracy in every case, even when systematic Records are available for examination, much more in cases where no such documentary machinery has been completely organized.

I have specially to thank Prebendary Tucker, who has taken much interest in the work, and has helped me in many difficulties and details.

The Archbishop of Ontario, the Bishops of Capetown, Fredericton, Waiapu, Ballarat, and Brisbane, Bishop Abraham, Bishop Hobhouse, Bishop Macrorie, and others, have been most kind in verifying the records of Consecrations which took place out of England, and for which I was originally indebted to the Editors of the *Guardian* and *Crockford's Clerical Directory*. Thanks are also due to the Rev. H. E. Fox, who kindly gave me all the authentic information which the Church Missionary Society could supply; and to Mr. William Roberton, the Edinburgh Chapter Clerk, who has enabled me to quote the authorities given for the consecration of Bishops in Edinburgh. It is almost unnecessary to add that it was through the kindness of Sir John Hassard and Mr. Lee that I was able to examine the Registers at the Vicar-General's Office and at Lambeth.

E. E. HOLMES.

CUDDESDON, *June 9, 1897.*

NOTE

—◆◆—

List of Episcopal and other Registers, used for the Mediaeval portion of the book.

I. CANTERBURY. **1.** Archbishops. Begin 1279.

   (1) Lambeth.

Peckham.	Whittlesey.	Bourchier. (Imperf.)
Winchelsey. (Also	Sudbury.	Morton. (Ditto.)
Lambeth MS. 244.)	Courtenay.	[1] Dean. (Ditto.)
Reynolds.	Arundel.	Warham. (Ditto.)
Mepeham.	Chicheley.	Pole.
Islip.	Stafford.	Cranmer, &c., to
Langham.	Kemp.	Moore.

   (2) Vicar-General's Office, Doctors' Commons. From Sutton to the present time.

  2. Prior and Convent.

   (1) Rolls of professions of obedience made by the Bishops at their consecration, frequently endorsed with the date and circumstances of the consecration.

   (2) Letters of licence to Bishops elect to be consecrated out of the Metropolitical Church, to which the privilege was secured by immemorial usage and charters of S. Thomas and S. Edmund.

   (3) Miscellaneous Letters on the same subject.

   (4) Registers containing copies of the above, and other memoranda.

   (5) Registers of the Acts of the Prior and Convent during vacancies of the see.

Some account of these records is given in the Fifth Report of the Historical MSS. Commission by Mr. Sheppard, 1877.

---

[1] The Editor, when searching in 1857 for the Will of Bishop Wells of Sidon, was so fortunate as to discover the portion of Archbishop Dean's Register which contains the Bulls of his appointment and his proceedings with the Suffragans, in the Book 'Blamyr' in the Prerogative Office. The existence of this fragment appears to have been unknown to Godwin, Wharton, and Le Neve, and had probably never been noticed by antiquaries, although duly entered in the Catalogue of Wills. [An account of it is given by Mr. Challenor Smith in his *Kalendar of the Wills in the Prerogative Court of Canterbury*, 1893 ; pp. xvi–xix.]

II. LONDON. **1.** Bishops. Begin 1306. Abstracts, MSS. Harl. 6955, 6956.

Baldock.	Walden.	Gilbert.	Barons.
Gravesend.	Clifford.	Kemp.	Fitz James.
Sudbury.	Kemp.	Hill.	Tunstall.
Courtenay.	Gray.	Savage.	Stokesley.
Braybrook.	Fitzhugh.	Warham.	Bonner.

2. Dean and Chapter. MSS. Hutton, Harl. 6955, 6956.

III. WINCHESTER. Bishops. Begin 1282.

Pontoise.	Stratford.	Beaufort.	Langton.
Woodlock.	Orlton.	Wainfleet.	Fox.
Sendale.	Edendon.	Courtenay.	Gardiner.
Asser.	Wykeham.		

An elaborate Index of the Winchester Registers made by W. T. Alchin, Esq., of the City of London Library, is now in the Museum Library; and the publication of the Registers themselves is contemplated by the Hampshire Record Society.

IV. ELY. Begin 1336. Abstracts in Cole's MSS., B. M. Add. 5824–5827.

Montacute.	Arundel.	Bourchier.	Alcock.
De Lisle.	Fordham.	Gray.	West.

V. LINCOLN. Abstracts in Hutton's MSS., Harl. 6950–6954. Begin 1217.

VI. LICHFIELD. Bishops. Begin 1296.

Langton.	Skirlaw.	Booth.	Smith.
Northburgh.	Scroop.	Boulers.	Blyth.
Stretton.	Heyworth.	Hales.	

VII. WELLS. Bishops. Stafford, Beckington, and Stillington. The Registers begin in 1309, and there are full Abstracts among the Hutton MSS., Harl. 6964–6968.

VIII. SALISBURY. Bishops. Reg. Neville and Blyth. The Registers begin in 1297. Abstracts, Harl. 6979 and 6980.

IX. EXETER. Bishops. Begin 1257. Abstracts, MSS. Hutton, Harl. 6979–6980. The Registers are now being printed under the editorship of Mr. Hingeston Randolph.

X. NORWICH. Bishops. Begin 1299.

Salmon.	Bateman.	Courtenay.	Lyhert.
Ayermin.	Percy.	Wakering.	Goldwell.
Beck. (Also	Spencer.	Alnwick.	Nykke.
Harl. 3720.)	Tottington.		

XI. WORCESTER. Bishops. Begin 1268.

Giffard.	Bransford.	Clifford.	Gigliis II.
Gainsborough.	Thoresby.	Peverell.	Medicis.
Reynolds.	Brian.	Morgan.	Ghinucci.
Maidstone.	Barnet.	Polton.	Latimer.
Cobham.	Whittlesey.	Bourchier.	Bell.
Orlton.	Lynn.	Carpenter.	Heath.
Montacute.	Wakefield.	Alcock.	Pates.
Hemenhale.	Winchcomb.	Morton.	

XII. HEREFORD. Bishops. Begin 1275.

Cantilupe.	Courtenay.	Spofford.	Audley.
Swinfield.	Gilbert.	Beauchamp.	Castello.
Orlton.	Trevenant.	Boulers.	Mayhew.
Charlton.	Mascall.	Stanbery.	Fox.
Trilleck.	Lacy.	Milling.	Skip.
Charlton.	Polton.		

There are extracts by Mr. Reynolds, registrar, communicated by Adam Ottley to Henry Wharton, MS. Lamb. 585, also Harl. 4056 and 6979.

XIII. CHICHESTER. Bishops. Begin 1397.

Reade.	Story.	Sherborn.	Day.
Praty.	Fitz James.	Sampson.	

XIV. ROCHESTER. Bishops. Begin 1319.

Heath.	Bottlesham.	Brown.	Fitz James.
Sheppey.	Bottlesham.	Wells.	Fisher.
Whittlesey.	Young.	Lowe.	Hilsey.
Trilleck.	Langton.	Savage.	

XV. YORK. **1.** Archbishops.

Gray. (Edited by	Corbridge.	Waldby.	Booth.
Raine, Surtees	Greenfield.	Scroop.	Rotherham.
Soc. 1870.)	Melton.	Bowet.	Savage.
Giffard.	Zouch.	Kemp.	Bainbridge.
Wickwane.	Thoresby.	Booth.	Wolsey.
Romain.	Neville.	Neville.	Lee.
Newark.	Arundel.		

2. Dean and Chapter.

(1) Acta Capituli, from the close of the thirteenth century.

(2) Registrum Magnum Album; a great collection of documents, precedents, and charters. A similar volume of smaller size is in the British Museum; MS. Lansdowne 402.

(3) Register during the vacancies of the see. A copy of part of this in
  MS. Galba, E. 10.

M. Hutton (MSS. 6969–6972) made an imperfect abstract of the York Registers.
Also Dodsworth, Bodl. MS. MS. Cotton, Vitellius, A. 2, contains Constitu-
tiones Eccl. Ebor.

XVI. CARLISLE. Bishops. Begin 1292.
      Halton.   Ross.   Kirkby.   Welton.   Appleby.
  The rest of the Registers before the Reformation are lost. Extracts made at the
  end of the sixteenth century by Bishop Robinson are in MS. Lansdowne 721.

XVII. The Registers of Durham also are mostly lost : nor have the existing ones,
  which were examined very kindly by the Rev. Chancellor Raine, furnished
  any information for the present work. They are those of Kellaw, Bury,
  Hatfield, Langley, Fox, and Tunstall. [Kellaw's Register is printed in
  the Rolls Series, under the title of *Registrum Palatinum*, ed. Hardy, 1873–
  1878.]

XVIII. Those of St. David's, extracts from which are in MS. Tanner, Bodl. 145,
  begin in 1397 ; the other Welsh Cathedrals have few remains of the Records
  before the sixteenth century. Those of Bangor begin 1512, S. Asaph 1538,
  Llandaff 1660.

The *Liber Landavensis*, an ancient Register of Llandaff, is printed by the Welsh
  MSS. Society; (Llandovery, 1840) ; a good account of the contents by
  Haddan is in the *Archaeologia Cambrensis* for July, 1868.

The *Liber Ruber Asavensis* is best known by the extracts in Nichols' *Collectanea
  Topographica et Genealogica*, vol. ii. p. 255 sq.

REGISTRUM SACRUM ANGLICANUM

EPISCOPAL SUCCESSION IN ENGLAND

EPISCOPAL SUCCESSION IN ENGLAND

A. D. **597.** **Augustine,** Archbishop.   Canterbury; d. 604, May 26.

Consecrated at Arles; Bed. *H. E.* i. 27: 'a Germaniarum episcopis;' S. Gregor. *Epp.* lib. viii. ep. 30: by the Archbishop of Arles, Vergilius (not Etherius, as Bede supposed); *H. E.* i. 27.   The bishops to whom S. Gregory commended him were Vergilius of Arles, Etherius of Lyons, Syagrius of Autun, who actively helped, and Desiderius of Vienne; Greg. *Epp.* vi. 53, 54; ix. 108.   The day stated by William Thorn (*Chron. ap. Twysden,* 1760), Nov. 16, was not a Sunday.

A. D. **604.** **Mellitus.**   London; Canterbury, 619; d. 624, Apr. 24.

Consecrated by Augustine; Bed. *H. E.* ii. 3.

A. D. **604.** **Justus.**   Rochester; Canterbury, 624; d. 627, Nov. 10.

Consecrated by Augustine; Bed. *H. E.* ii. 3.

A. D. **604.** **Laurentius.**   Canterbury; d. 619, Feb. 2.

Consecrated by Augustine; Bed. *H. E.* ii. 3.

A. D. **624.** **Romanus.**   Rochester; d. 627.

Consecrated by Justus; Bed. *H. E.* ii. 8.

A. D. **625,** July 21.   **Paulinus,** Archbishop of York; Rochester, 633; d. 644, Oct. 10.

Consecrated by Justus at Canterbury; Bed. *H. E.* ii. 9.

A. D. **627.** **Honorius.**   Canterbury; d. 653, Sept. 30.

Consecrated by Paulinus at Lincoln; Bed. *H. E.* ii. 18.

B 2

A. D. **630. Felix.**   Dunwich ; d. 647, Mar. 8.
Consecrated by Honorius ; Bed. *H. E.* ii. 15.

A. D. **634. Birinus.**   Dorchester, for the West Saxons ; d. 650, Dec. 3.
Consecrated by Asterius (Bishop of Milan) at Genoa ; Bed. *H. E.* iii. 7.

A. D. **635. Aidan.**   Lindisfarne ; d. 651, Aug. 31.
Consecrated by Irish bishops ; Bed. *H. E.* iii. 3.

A. D. **644. Ithamar.**   Rochester.
Consecrated by Honorius ; Bed. *H. E.* iii. 14.

A. D. **647. Thomas.**   Dunwich ; d. 652.
Consecrated by Honorius ; Bed. *H. E.* iii. 20.

A. D. **650. Agilbert.**   Dorchester ; Paris, 664 ; d. 680, Oct. 11.
Consecrated apparently by French bishops ; Bed. *H. E.* iii. 7.

A. D. **651. Finan.**   Lindisfarne ; d. 661, Aug. 31.
Consecrated by Irish bishops ; Bed. *H. E.* iii. 25.

A. D. **652. Berctgils,** surnamed Boniface.   Dunwich ; d. 669.
Consecrated by Honorius ; Bed. *H. E.* iii. 20.

A. D. **654. Cedd.**   Bishop of the East Saxons (London) ; d. 664, Oct. 26.
Consecrated at Lindisfarne by Finan and two other bishops ; Bed. *H. E.*
iii. 22.

A. D. **655,** Mar. 26. **Deusdedit** (Frithona).   Canterbury ; d. 664, July 14.
Consecrated at Canterbury by Ithamar of Rochester ; Bed. *H. E.* iii. 20.

A. D. **655. Damian.**   Rochester.
Consecrated by Deusdedit ; Bed. *H. E.* iii. 20.

A. D. **656. Diuma.**   Bishop of the Mercians and Middle Angles (Lichfield).
Consecrated by Finan of Lindisfarne ; Bed. *H. E.* iii. 21.

A. D. **658. Ceollach.**   Lichfield ; resigned 659.
Consecrated by Finan of Lindisfarne ; Bed. *H. E.* iii. 21.

A. D. **659. Trumhere.**   Lichfield.
Consecrated by Irish bishops ; Bed. *H. E.* iii. 21, 24.

A. D. **661. Colman.** Lindisfarne; resigned 664.
Consecrated by Irish bishops; Bed. *H. E.* iii. 25.

A. D. **662. Jaruman.** Lichfield; d. 667.
Consecrated by Irish bishops; Bed. *H. E.* iii. 24.

A. D. **662. Wine.** Winchester; Dorchester, 663 (?); London, 666.
Consecrated by French bishops; Bed. *H. E.* iii. 7.

A. D. **664. Tuda.** Lindisfarne; d. 664.
Consecrated by South Irish bishops; Bed. *H. E.* iii. 26.

A. D. **664. Ceadda.** Northumbria; York; Lichfield, 669; d. 672. **Mar. 2.**
Consecrated in Wessex by Wine and two British bishops 'adsumtis in societatem ordinationis duobus de Brittonum gente episcopis;' Bed. *H. E.* iii. 28.

A. D. **664. Wilfrid.** Northumbria; York, (Edd. *V. Wilfr.* c. 12) 669–678; and 686–692; Leicester, 692–705; Hexham, 705; d. 709, Oct. 12, or Apr. 24.
Consecrated at Compiègne by Agilbert of Paris and eleven other bishops; Bed. *H. E.* iii. 28; Edd. *V. Wilfr.* c. 12.

A. D. **668,** March 26. **Theodore of Tarsus.** Canterbury; d. 690, Sept. 19.
Consecrated at Rome by Pope Vitalian; Bed. *H. E.* iv. 1.

A. D. **669. Putta.** Rochester; Hereford, 676; d. 688.
Consecrated by Theodore; Bed. *H. E.* iv. 2. *Conc. Hertford,* 673.

A. D. **669. Bisi.** Dunwich.
Consecrated by Theodore; Bed. *H. E.* iv. 5.

A. D. **670. Leutherius.** Winchester; d. 676.
Consecrated by Theodore; Bed. *H. E.* iii. 7; subs. *K. C. D.* vii; *Cart. S.* 25, 30, 43.

A. D. **672. Wynfrid.** Lichfield; dep. 675.
Consecrated by Theodore; Bed. *H. E.* iii. 24; iv. 3. *Conc. Hertf.* 673.

A. D. **673. Baduvine.** Elmham.
Consecrated by Theodore; Bed. *H. E.* iv. 5; *Cart. S.* 85.

A. D. **673. Æcci.** Dunwich.
Consecrated by Theodore ; Bed. *H. E.* iv. 5.

A. D. **675. Sexwulf.** Lichfield.
Consecrated by Theodore ; Bed. *H. E.* iv. 6 ; *Cart. S.* 43, 58, 59.

A. D. **675. Earconuald.** London ; d. 693, Apr. 30 ; subs. 676–692.
Consecrated by Theodore ; Bed. *H. E.* iv. 6 ; *Cart. S.* 43, 50, 55, 56, 81.

A. D. **676. Cuichelm.** Rochester ; res.
Consecrated by Theodore, Bed. *H. E.* iv. 12.

A. D. **676. Haeddi.** (Dorchester ?) ; Winchester (A. D. 683 ?) ; d. 705.
Consecrated by Theodore ; Bed. *H. E.* iv. 12 ; *Cart. S.* 43, 47, 50, 61,
62, 63 ; subs. 676–701.

A. D. **678. Bosa.** York ; d. 705.
Eadhæd. Lindsey, res. 678 ; Ripon (?), 678.
Eata. Hexham, 678–681 ; Lindisfarne, 678–685 ; Hexham,
685–6 ; d. 686, Oct. 26.

These three bishops were consecrated by Theodore at York after the
expulsion of Wilfrid ; Bed. *H. E.* iv. 12 : 'solus ordinavit ;' Edd. *V.
Wilfr.* c. 24 : 'absque consensu cujuslibet episcopi ;' ib. c. 30.

A. D. **678. Gebmund.** Rochester.
Consecrated by Theodore ; Bed. *H. E.* iv. 12 ; *Cart. S.* 85, 99 ; subs.
693, 699.

A. D. **680. Bosel.** Worcester ; res. 691.
Consecrated by Theodore ; Flor. Wig. *M. H. B.* 622 ; *Cart. S.* 57, 58, 59.

A. D. **680. Cuthwine.** Middle Angles, Leicester.
Consecrated by Theodore ; Flor. Wig. *M. H. B.* 622.

A. D. **680. Ethelwine.** Lindsey.
Consecrated by Theodore ; Bed. *H. E.* iv. 12.

A. D. **681. Trumwine.** Abercorn (?), for the Picts.
Consecrated by Theodore ; Bed. *H. E.* iv. 12 ; v. 23.

A. D. **681. Tunberct.** Hexham ; dep. 684.
Consecrated by Theodore ; Bed. *H. E.* iv. 12.

A. D. **685**, March 26. **Cuthbert.** Lindisfarne; d. 687, Mar. 20.
Consecrated by Theodore at York, 'convenientibus ad consecrationem ejus septem episcopis;' Bed. *H. E.* iv. 28.

A. D. **687.** **John** (of Beverley). Hexham; York, 705; d. 721, May 7.
Consecrated by Theodore, Sept. 12; *Hist. Beverlac. Wharton MS.* 585. He lived as bishop thirty-three years, eight months and thirteen days: this computation would fix his consecration, Aug. 25; *V. S. Johan.* (Raine, *Memorials*, i. 525). The calculation is very hazardous, as the period of thirty-three years seems according to Bede to end in 718, which would throw back the consecration to 685 when Eata was still alive. See Raine, *Fasti Eboracenses*, i. 89.

Uncertain date. [**Aetla.** Dorchester; Bed. *H. E.* iv. 23, perhaps as successor of Agilberht or later.]

A. D. **687.** **Eadberct.** Lindisfarne; d. 698, May 6.
'Ordinatus;' Bed. *H. E.* iv. 29.

A. D. **688.** **Tyrhtel.** Hereford.
Ancient Lists; *M. H. B.* 621; Will. Malmesb. *Gesta Pont.* iv. § 163; *Cart. S.* 82, 85, 113; subs. 693.

A. D. **691.** **Headda.** Lichfield.
Ancient Lists; *M. H. B.* 623, 624; *Cart. S.* 76, 111, 113; subs. 693–706.

A. D. **692.** **Oftfor.** Worcester.
Consecrated by Wilfrid; Bed. *H. E.* v. 23; Flor. Wig. i. 42; *Cart. S.* 75, 85; subs. 693.

A. D. **693.** **Suidberct.** Friesland.
Consecrated by Wilfrid; Bed. *H. E.* v. 11.

A. D. **693**, June 29. **Berctuald** (Brihtwald). Canterbury; d. 731, Jan. 8.
Consecrated by Godwin, metropolitan bishop of the Gauls, archbishop of Lyons; Bed. *H. E.* v. 8; subs. 693–706, 716.

A. D. **693.** **Waldhere.** London.
Bed. *H. E.* iv. 11; *Epist. ad Berct.*, Councils, &c., iii. 275; *Cart. S.* 111, 113; subs. 704.

A. D. **693.   Ecgwine.**   Worcester; d. 717, Dec. 30.
'Primate etiam Britanniae consentiente et confirmante;' *Chr. Evesham,*
p. 4; Flor. Wig. i. 43; *Cart. S.* 77.

A. D. **698.   Eadfrith.**   Lindisfarne; d. 721.
Flor. Wig. i. 45.

A. D. **699 × 706.   Tobias.**   Rochester.
Consecrated by Berctwald; Bed. *H. E.* v. 8; Flor. Wig. i. 44; *Cart. S.*
116; subs. 706.

A. D. **705.   Daniel.**   Winchester; res. 744; d. 745.
Consecrated by Berctwald; Bed. *H. E.* v. 18; Bonif. *Epp.* 11, 15, 33,
55, 56; subs. 705-737.

A. D. **705.   Aldhelm.**   Sherborne; d. 709, May 25.
Consecrated by Berctwald; Flor. Wig. 705; Bed. *H. E.* v. 18.

A. D. **693 × 706.   Nothberht.**   Elmham.
Ancient Lists; subs. 706 (?); *Cart. S.* (716) 116.

A. D. **693 × 706.   Eadgar.**   Lindsey.
Bed. *H. E.* iv. 12; subs. 716 (?); electus, 693; *Cart. S.* 82.

A. D. **704 × 706.   Ingwald.**   London; d. 745.
Bed. *H. E.* v. 23; *Cart. S.* (709) 124, 156; subs. 706-737.

A. D. **709.   Fortheri.**   Sherborne.
Bed. *H. E.* v. 18; *Cart. S.* 128, 143, 147, 155, 158; Bonif. *Ep.* 7;
subs. 712-737, 739.

A. D. **709.   Acca.**   Hexham; dep. 733; d. 740, Oct. 20.
Bed. *H. E.* v. 20; *Chr. S.* 710; Sim. Dun. ii. 32.

A. D. **710.   Torhthere.**   Hereford; Fl. Wig. 710 (?).
'Pontifices ex his ternos sancta infula cinxit,
Nomina sunt quorum Wahlstodus, Torthere, Tirhtil.'
Archbp. Cuthbert; W. Malmesb. *G. P.* iv. § 163; *Cart. S.* 146; subs. 727.

A. D. **709 × 711.   Eadberct.**   Selsey.
'Consecratusque est primus episcopus;' Bed. *H. E.* v. 18.

A. D. **717. Wilfrith.** Worcester; d. 745.
Bed. *H. E.* v. 23 ; *Cart. S.* 156 ; subs. 718–743.

A. D. **718. Wilfrith II.** York ; d. 732.
Consecrated by John ; ' ordinato in episcopatum Eboracensem presbytero suo ;' Bed. *H. E.* v. 6.

A. D. **716 × 731. Heatholac.** Elmham.
Bed. *H. E.* v. 23.

A. D. **675 × 731. Æscwulf.** Dunwich (Aldberht, Bede).
Bed. *H. E.* v. 23.

A. D. **709 × 714. Eolla.** Selsey ; d. before 731.
Bed. *H. E.* v. 18 ; subs. 714.

A. D. **721. Aldwine.** Lichfield ; d. 737 ; also called Wor.
Bed. *H. E.* v. 23 ; subs. [716 ?] 727–736.

A. D. **724. Ethelwald.** Lindisfarne ; d. 740.
Bed. *H. E.* v. 23 ; Flor. Wig. ; Sim. Dun. 740.

A. D. **706 × 731. Cyniberct.** Lindsey ; d. 732.
Bed. *H. E.* iv. 12 ; Sim. Dun. 732.

A. D. **727. Aldwulf.** Rochester.
Consecrated by Archbishop Berctwald ; Bed. *H. E.* v. 23 ; *Cart. S.* 159 ; subs. 735–738.

A. D. **727 × 731. Walchstod.** Hereford.
Bed. *H. E.* v. 23 ; *Cart. S.* 155, 163 ; W. Malmesb. *G. P.* iv. § 163.

A. D. **730. Pecthelm.** Whithern ; d. 735.
Bed. *H. E.* v. 23 (primum habet episcopum) ; Bonif. *Ep.* 29.

A. D. **731,** June 10. **Tatwine.** Canterbury ; d. 734, July 30.
Consecrated at Canterbury by Daniel of Winchester, Ingwald of London, Aldwine of Lichfield, and Aldwulf of Rochester ; Bed. *H. E.* v. 23 ; *Chr. S.* 731 ; Flor. Wig. 731.

A. D. **733. Alwig.** Lindsey; d. 750.

> Consecrated by Archbishop Tatwine; Sim. Dun. 733; *Cart. S.* 174; subs. 737–747.

A. D. **733. Sigga** or **Sigfrith.** Selsey.

> Consecrated by Archbishop Tatwine; Sim. Dun. 733; *Cart. S.* 174; subs. 737–747.

A. D. **734. Egbert.** York; d. 766, Nov. 19.

> *Chr. S.* 734; Sim. Dun. 735; Bonif. *Epp.* 61, 100.

A. D. **734**, Sept. 8. **Friothoberht.** Hexham; d. 766, Dec. 23.

> Consecrated by Archbishop Egbert of York; Sim. Dun. 734; Cont. Bed. *M. H. B.* p. 288.

A. D. **735. Nothelm.** Canterbury; d. 740, Oct. 17.

> *Chr. S.* 736; Flor. Wig. i. 54; Bonif. *Ep.* 30; subs. 738.

A. D. **735**, Aug. 14. **Friothowald.** Whithern; d. 763, May 7.

> Consecrated at York by Archbishop Egbert; Flor. Wig. i. 54; Sim. Dun. 764; Cont. Bed. p. 288.

A. D. **736. Cuthbert.** Hereford; Canterbury, 740; d. 758, Oct. 26.

> Consecrated by Archbishop Nothelm; Sim. Dun. 736; *Cart. S.* 156, 174; Bonif. *Epp.* 70, 108; subs. 737–758.

A. D. **736. Æthelfrith.** Elmham.

> Consecrated by Archbishop Nothelm; Sim. Dun. 736.

A. D. **736. Herewald.** Sherborne.

> Consecrated by Archbishop Nothelm; Sim. Dun. 736; *Cart. S.* 169, 174; subs. 737–759.

A. D. **737. Hwitta.** Lichfield.

> Sim. Dun. 737; *Cart. S.* 165, 174; subs. 747–749.

A. D. **737. Totta** or **Torhthelm.** Leicester; d. 764.

> Sim. Dun. 737; *Cart. S.* 165, 174; Bonif. *Ep.* 101; subs. 747–758.

A. D. **740. Cynewulf.** Lindisfarne, res. 780; d. 782.

> Sim. Dun. 740; Flor. Wig. i. 54.

A. D. **741.** **Podda.** Hereford.
Consecrated by Archbishop Cuthbert; Flor. Wig. *M. H. B.* 543; *Cart. S.* 174; subs. 747.

A. D. **741.** **Dunn.** Rochester.
Consecrated by Archbishop Cuthbert; *Chr. S.* 741; *Cart. S.* 174; subs. 747.

A. D. **736 × 758.** **Eanfrith.** Elmham.
Subs. 758; *Cart. S.* 326; *K. C. D.* 193.

A. D. **743.** **Milred.** Worcester; d. 775.
Flor. Wig. i. 54; *Cart. S.* 171, 174, 177; Bonif. *Ep.* 108; subs. 743–774.

A. D. **744.** **Hunferth.** Winchester.
Chr. S. 744; Flor. Wig. i. 55; *Cart. S.* 174, 179; subs. 747–749.

A. D. **745.** **Ecgwulf.** London.
See Cont. Bed. 745; *Cart. S.* 174, 177; subs. 747–759.

A. D. **747.** **Eardulf.** Rochester.
Cart. S. 175, 193, 195, 199; Bonif. *Ep.* 120; subs. 747–765.

A. D. **731 × 747.** **Eardred, Eardulf.** Dunwich.
Cart. S. 174; subs. 747.

A. D. **750.** **Eadulf (Aldwulf).** Lindsey.
Sim. Dun. 750, 765; subs. 758.

A. D. **752.** **Hemele.** Lichfield; d. 765.
Sim. Dun. 765; *Cart. S.* 183.

A. D. **754.** **Cyneheard.** Winchester.
Chr. S. 754; Bonif. *Epp.* 110, 121; subs. 755–759.

A. D. **747 × 758.** **Hecca (Acca).** Hereford.
Subs. 758; *Cart. S.* 326; *K. C. D.* 193.

—— **Cuthwine.** Dunwich.
Ancient Catalogues.

A. D. **759**, Sept. 29.   **Bregowine.**   Canterbury ; d. 765, Aug. 25.
  Chr. S. 754, 762 ; *Cart. S.* 190–195 ; Bonif. *Ep.* 113.

A. D. **763**, July 17.   **Pehtwine.**   Whithern ; d. 776, Sept. 19.
  Consecrated at 'Aelfetee' by Archbishop Egbert of York ; *Chr. S.* 763,
  776 ; Sim. Dun. 764, 777.

A. D. **764.   Eadbert.**   Leicester.
  Sim. Dun. 764 ; *Cart. S.* 209, 231 ; subs. 764–781.

A. D. **765.   Cuthfrith.**   Lichfield.
  Sim. Dun. 765 ; subs. 767.

A. D. **747 × 765.   Aluberht.**   Selsey.
  Catalogues.

A. D. **747 × 765.   Osa** or **Oswald.**   Selsey.
  Cart. S. 198, 206, 208 ; subs. 765, 772.

A. D. **759 × 772.   Sigheah** or **Wigheah.**   London.
  Cart. S. 208 ; subs. 772.

A. D. **758 × 770.   Ceadda** (**Headda**).   Hereford.
  Subs. 770 ; *Cart. S.* 206 (?).

A. D. **766**, Feb. 2.   **Jaenberht.**   Canterbury ; d. 790, Aug. 11.
  Consecrated by Eadbert of Leicester, Cyneheard of Winchester, and
  Ecgwulf of London ; MS. Cotton, Tiberius A. 13 ; Heming (ed.
  Hearne), p. 60 ; *Chr. S.* 763 ; Sim. Dun. 765 ; *Cart. S.* 201, 207,
  221 ; subs. 765–789.

A. D. **767**, Apr. 24.   **Ethelbert** or **Coena.**   York ; d. 780, Nov. 10.
  Chr. S. 766 ; Sim. Dun. 767 ; Bonif. *Epp.* 122, 125.

—— **Alhmund.**   Hexham ; d. 781, Sept. 7.
  Consecrated with Ethelbert ; *Chr. S.* 766 ; Sim. Dun. 767, 781.

—— **Aluberht.**
  Consecrated for the Old Saxons, at York ; Sim. Dun. 767 ; *Vit. S. Liud-geri*, Pertz, i. 407.

A. D. **767**, Apr. 24. **Ceolwulf.** Lindsey; d. 796.
> Consecrated at the same time; Sim. Dun. 765, 767, 796; *Cart. S.* 213, 230; Council, 786; subs. 767–794.

A. D. **768. Berhthun.** Lichfield.
> *Cart. S.* 209, 213, 214, 223, 226; subs. 772–777.

A. D. **768. Hadwine.** Machui (Mayo); d. 773.
> Sim. Dun. 768, 773.

A. D. **765 × 772. Diora.** Rochester.
> *Cart. S.* 209, 227, 242; subs. 772–781.

A. D. **772. Aldberht (Eadberht).** London.
> Council, 786; subs. 772–786.

A. D. **773. Leuferth.** Mayo.
> Sim. Dun. 773.

A. D. **775. Weremund.** Worcester.
> *Cart. S.* 226; Flor. Wig. 775.

A. D. **777. Tilhere.** Worcester.
> *Cart. S.* 216, 230; Flor. Wig. 778; subs. 777–780.

A. D. **777. Aldberht.** Hereford.
> *Cart. S.* 223; electus, 230, 242; subs. 777–781.

A. D. **777**, June 15. **Æthilberht.** Whithern; Hexham, 789; d. 797, Oct. 16.
> Consecrated at York by Archbishop Ethelbert; *Chr. S.* 777; Sim. Dun. 777; Alcuin, *Ep.* 88; Council, 786.

A. D. **766 × 778. Æthelmod.** Sherborne.
> *Cart. S.* 242; Council, 786; subs. 774–789.

A. D. **766 × 774. Æthelheard.** Winchester.
> Ancient Catalogues.

A. D. **766 × 774. Ecgbald.** Winchester.
> *Cart. S.* 242; subs. 774–781.

—— **Aldberht.** Dunwich.
> Ancient Catalogues.

A. D. **779. Hygberht.** Lichfield; Archbishop of Lichfield, 786–801.
Electus, *Cart. S.* 230, 239, 240, 242; cf. Council, 786; subs. electus, 779; as archbishop, 786–801.

A. D. —. **Ecglaf.** Dunwich.
Ancient Catalogues.

A. D. **770 × 780. Gislhere.** Selsey.
Cart. S. 237, 241; subs. 780, 781.

A. D. **758 × 781. Æthelwulf.** Elmham.
Cart. S. 242; subs. 781.

A. D. **— × 781. Heardred.** Dunwich.
Cart. S. 242; Council, 786; subs. 781–789.

A. D. **780 or 778. Eanbald I.** York; d. 796, Aug. 10.
Consecrated during his predecessor's lifetime; *Chr. S.* 779, 780; Sim. Dun. 780, 796; Alcuin, *Ep.* 70; Alc. *Hist. Ebor.* v. 1515 sq.; Council, 786.

A. D. **781,** Oct. 2. **Tilbert.** Hexham; d. 789.
Consecrated at Wulfswell by Archbishop Eanbald; Sim. Dun. 781; Council, 786.

A D. **781. Hygbald.** Lindisfarne; d. 802, May 25.
Consecrated at Sockburn by Archbishop Eanbald; *Chr. S.* 780; Sim. Dun. 780, 781; *Hist. Dun.* i. 50; Alcuin, *Epp.* 4, 24, 25, 81, 201; Council, 786.

A. D. **781. Heathored.** Worcester; d. 798.
Cart. S. 240, 241, 242; Council, 786; subs. 781–798.

A. D. **781 × 785. Unwona.** Leicester.
Council, 786; subs. 786–789.

A. D. **781 × 785. Dudd.** Winchester.
Ancient Catalogues.

A. D. **781 × 785. Cyneberht.** Winchester.
Alcuin, *Ep.* 130; Council, 786; subs. 786–801.

A. D. **781 × 785. Tota.** Selsey.
Council, 786 ; subs. 786.

A. D. **781 × 785. Esne.** Hereford.
Council, 786 ; subs. 786.

A. D. **781 × 785. Wærmund.** Rochester.
Council, 786 ; subs. 786–803.

A. D. **781 × 785. Alcheard.** Elmham.
Alcuin, *Ep.* 230 ; Council, 786 ; subs. 786–811.

A. D. **786. Aldulf.** Mayo.
Consecrated at Corbridge by Archbishop Eanbald, Tilbert of Hexham,
and Hygbald of Lindisfarne ; Sim. Dun. 786 ; Council, 786.

A. D. **787–788. Ceolmund.** Hereford.
Subs. 788–793 ; *Cart. S.* 254–265.

A. D. **787–789. Wiohthun.** Selsey.
Subs. 789–805 ; *Cart. S.* 255.

A. D. **787–789. Eadgar.** London.
Subs. 789 ; *Cart. S.* 255.

A. D. **790. Ælfhun, Aelhun.** Dunwich ; d. 797.
Chr. S. 797 ; subs. 790–793.

A. D. **791, July 17. Bealdwulf.** Whithern.
Consecrated at Hearrahaleh, by Eanbald of York and Æthelbert of
Hexham ; *Chr. S.* 791 ; Sim. Dun. 791.

A. D. **793, July 21. Æthelheard.** Canterbury.
Chr. S. 790 ; Sim. Dun. 791 ; Alcuin, *Epp.* 28, 84, 85, 171, 172, 190,
219, 248 ; subs. 793–805.

A. D. **789 × 793. Coenwalh (Kenwalch).** London.
Subs. 793 ; *Cart. S.* 267 (?).

A. D. **793. Denefrith.** Sherborne.
Consecrated by Æthelheard ; Profession (anon.), Cleop. E. 1 ; *Ang. Sac.*
i. 79 ; *Reg. Cant.* 1 ; subs. 794–796.

A. D. **793.   Eadbald.**   London ; departed from the land, 796.
  Chr. S. 794–6.

A. D. **796.   Heathoberht.**   London ; d. 801.
  Subs. 798–799.

A. D. **793 × 798.   Utel.**   Hereford.
  Subs. 798–799.

A. D. **796.   Eadulf.**   Lindsey.
  Electus, 796 ; Profession [Eboracensis ? interpolated] to Æthelheard, *Text.*
  Roff. p. 248 ; Cleop. E. 1 ; *Reg. Cant.* ; *Cart. S.* 358 ; subs. 796–836.

A. D. **796**, Aug. 14.   **Eanbald II.**   York.
  Consecrated at Sockburn by Ethelbert of Hexham, Higbald of Lindis-
  farne, and Beadwlf of Whithern ; *Chr. S.* 796 ; Sim. Dun. 796 ; Alcuin,
  Epp. 36, 70, 72, 73, 74, 82, 149, 167, 171, 172, 173, 174.

A. D. **797**, Oct. 29.   **Heardred.**   Hexham.
  Consecrated by Eanbald of York, and Higbald of Lindisfarne, at
  'Uduford' ; *Chr. S.* 797 ; Sim. Dun. 797.

A. D. **798.   Tidferth.**   Dunwich.
  Chr. S. 797 ; *Cart. S.* 358 ; Profession to Æthelheard, *Text. Roff.*
  Hearne, p. 256 ; Cleop. E. 1 ; Alcuin, *Ep.* 230 ; subs. 798–816.

A. D. **798.   Deneberht.**   Worcester ; d. 822.
  Consecrated by Æthelheard ; Flor. Wig. ; *Cart. S.* 358 ; subs. 801–817 ;
  Profession, *Text. Roff.* Hearne, p. 251 ; Cleop. E. 1.

A. D. **796 × 801.   Wigberht.**   Sherborne.
  Flor. Wig. ; *Chr. S.* 812 × 814 ; *Cart. S.* 358 ; subs. 801–816.

A. D. **801 × 803.   Aldwlf.**   Lichfield (Bishop, not Archbishop).
  Subs. 803–814.

A. D. **800.   Wulfhard.**   Hereford.
  Profession to Æthelheard, *Text. Roff.* Hearne, p. 253 ; Cleop. E. 1 ; *Reg.*
  Cant. 1 ; *Cart. S.* 358, 370 ; subs. 801–822.

A. D. **800. Eanberht.** Hexham.

> Consecrated at Ettingaham by Archbishop Eanbald; Sim. Dun. 800; *Chr. S.* 806.

A. D. **802. Alhmund.** Winchester.

> Subs. 803–805.

A. D. **802. Osmund.** London.

> Subs. 803–805.

A. D. **802. Werenberht.** Leicester.

> Subs. 803–814.

A. D. **803,** June 11. **Egbert.** Lindisfarne.

> Consecrated at Bigwell, by Archbishop Eanbald, Eanberht of Hexham, and Baldwlf of Whithern; *Chr. S.* 803; *Hist. Dunelm.* i. 52.

A. D. **803–804. Beornmod.** Rochester.

> Consecrated by Æthelheard; Profession, *Text. Roff.* Hearne, p. 258; *Ang. Sac.* i. 79; Cleop. E. 1; *Reg. Cant.*; *Chr. S.* 801; *Cart. S.* 358; subs. 805–842.

A. D. **805** (Aug. 3). **Wulfred.** Canterbury.

> Wulfred's consecration took place in the Council of Acle, which was held in August, 805; the following bishops being present: Aldulf, Werenberht, Deneberht, Eadulf, Wulfhard, Alheard, Tidferth, Osmund, Alhmund, Wiohthun, Wigberht, and Beornmod. In a note in the copies of Professions in *MS. Cotton*, Cleopatra E. 1, the day is given as 'July 21, 803'; the year must be corrected, as in the chronicle, from which in some old copy the note may have been taken. Wulfred is described on Aug. 6 (Kemble, *C. D.* No. 190) 'in solio archiepiscopatus sedenti'; and Aug. 1, 811, is in the sixth year of his pontificate (ib. no. 195). In a charter in the *Cart. S.* (no. 321), dated at Acle in the year of Æthelheard's death; Wulfred signs 'Ego Wulfredus electus.' The charter K. C. D. 190 (*Cart. S.* 322) is dated 'in VII[as] Kal. Aug. die sabbati quo transfiguratus est Christus'; this would be July 26.

A. D. **806. Tidferth.** Hexham.

> See *Chr. S.* 806.

A. D. **805 × 811. Ethelwulf.** Selsey.

> *Cart. S.* 358; subs. 811–816.

A. D. **805 × 811.   Ethelnoth.**   London.
>   Subs. 811–816 ; *Cart. S.* 358 ; Profession to Wulfred, *Text. Roff.*
>   Hearne, p. 260 ; Cleop. E. 1 ; *Reg. Cant.*

A. D. **805 × 811.   Wigthegn.**   Winchester ; d. 836.
>   Subs. 811–828 ; *Cart. S.* 358 ; Profession to Wulfred, *Text. Roff.*
>   Hearne, p. 261 ; Cleop. E. 1 ; *Reg. Cant.*

A. D. after **808.   Wulfsige** or **Wulfwig.**   York ; d. before 837.
>   See Letter of Ecgred of Lindisfarne to him ; Councils, iii. 615.

A. D. **811 × 814.   Sibba.**   Elmham.
>   *Cart. S.* 358 ; subs. 814–816.

A. D. **815.   Herewine.**   Lichfield.
>   Consecrated by Wulfred ; subs. 816, 817 ; Profession, *Text. Roff.* Hearne,
>   p. 245 ; Cleop. E. 1 ; *Reg. Cant.* ; cf. *Cart. S.* 358.

A. D. **816.   Hrethun.**   Leicester.
>   Consecrated by Wulfred ; *Cart. S.* 358, 370 ; subs. 816–839 ; Profession,
>   *Text. Roff.* Hearne, p. 246 ; Cleop. E. 1 ; *Reg. Cant.*

A. D. **816 × 824.   Hunferth.**   Elmham.
>   Consecrated by Wulfred ; Profession, *Text. Roff.* Hearne, p. 263 ; Cleop.
>   E. 1 ; *Reg. Cant.*

A. D. **818.   Ethelwald.**   Lichfield ; d. 828 or 831.
>   *Chr. S.* 828 ; *Cart. S.* 370 ; subs. 822–825.

A. D. **816 × 824.   Ceolberht.**   London.
>   Profession to Wulfred, *Reg. Cant.* ; subs. 824–839.

A. D. **816 × 824.   Cœnred.**   Selsey.
>   Subs. 824–838.

A. D. **816 × 824.   Weremund.**   Dunwich.
>   Subs. 824.

A. D. **821.   Heathored.**   Lindisfarne.
>   Flor. Wig. i. 65 ; *Hist. Dunelm.* i. 52.

A. D. **822. Eadbert.** Worcester.
Consecrated by Wulfred ; Flor. Wig. i. 65 ; subs. 822–845 ; Profession (Heahberht , *Reg. Cant.* ; *Cart. S.* 370.

A. D. **824. Beonna.** Hereford.
Electus, 824 ; *Cart. S.* no. 378 ; cf. Profession of Diorlaf, below, p. 21 ; subs. 824, 825.

A. D. **824. Heahstan.** Sherborne ; d. 868.
Chr. S. 868 ; subs. electus, 824, and 824–862.

A. D. **816 × 824. Hunberht.** Elmham ; d. 870, Nov. 20.
Chr. S. ; Sim. Dun. 870 ; subs. 824–838.

A. D. **825. Wilred.** Dunwich.
Electus, 825 ; *Cart. S.* 448 ; subs. 825–845.

A. D. **825. Hereferth.** Winchester ; d. 833 or 836.
Chr. S. 833 ; subs. 825, 826 ; Profession to Wulfred, *Reg. Cant.*

A. D. **828. Humbert.** Lichfield.
Profession to Wulfred ; *Reg. Cant.*

A. D. **825 × 831. Eadulf.** Hereford.
Profession to Wulfred ; *Text. Roff.* p. 262 ; Cleop. E. 1 ; subs. 836.

A. D. **830. Ecgred.** Lindisfarne.
Flor. Wig. i. 68 ; *Hist. Dunelm.* i. 52.

A. D. **832,** June 9. **Feologild** [Swithred, MS. Vesp. B. 6]. Canterbury ; d. 832, Aug. 29.
Chr. S. 829 ; Flor. Wig. i. 68.

A. D. **833,** Aug. 24. **Ceolnoth.** Canterbury ; d. 870, Feb. 4.
Chr. S. 830 ; Flor. Wig. i. 68 ; *Ann. Roff. Ang. Sac.* i. 85.

A. D. **833 × 836. Eadhun.** Winchester.
Profession to Ceolnoth, *Reg. Cant.* ; subs. 836–838.

A. D. **833 × 836. Kynferth.** Lichfield.
Prof. to Ceolnoth, Cleop. E. 1 (naming Aldwulf, Herewin, and Ethelwald as predecessors) ; *Reg. Cant.* ; subs. 836–841.

A. D. **837. Cuthwulf.** Hereford.
   Cart. S. 429 ; subs. 838–857.

A. D. **837. Wigmund.** York.
   Sim. Dun. c. 78 ; *Hist. Arch.* (ed. Raine, ii. 338).

A. D. **838. Berhtred.** Lindsey.
   Consecrated by Ceolnoth ; subs. 839–869 ; Profession, Cleop. E. 1 ; *Ang. Sac.* i. 79 ; *Reg. Cant.*

A. D. **838. Helmstan.** Winchester.
   See Flor. Wig. i. 69 ; subs. 834–844 ; Profession to Ceolnoth, *Reg. Cant.*

A. D. **839 × 840. Aldred.** Leicester.
   Subs. 841 (?) ; *Cart. S.* 435.

A. D. **840. Ceolred.** Leicester.
   Consecrated by Ceolnoth ; Profession, *Reg. Cant.* ; subs. 840–869 ; *Cart. S.* 428.

A. D. **844. Tatnoth.** Rochester.
   Electus, 844 ; subs. 845 ; see *Cart. S.* 448.

A. D. **841 × 844. Tunberht.** Lichfield ; d. 854.
   Consecrated by Ceolnoth ; Profession, *Text. Roff.* p. 264 ; Cleop. E. 1 ; *Reg. Cant.* ; subs. 844–857.

A. D. **845. Eanberht.** Lindisfarne ; d. 854.
   Flor. Wig. i. 70 ; *Hist. Dunelm.* i. 53.

A. D. **845. Aelhun.** Worcester ; d. 872 (?).
   Flor. Wig. i. 70 ; subs. 845–869.

A. D. — **845. Gutheard.** Selsey.
   Subs. 845–862.

A. D. **852,** Oct. 30. **Swithun.** Winchester ; d. 862, July 2.
   Flor. Wig. i. 69 ; *Chr. S.* 861 ; Prof. to Ceolnoth, *Text. Roff.* p. 269 ; Cleop. E. 1 ; *Reg. Cant.* subs. 858–862 ; 'ordinatio Swithun 4 Kal. Nov,' *MS. Reg.* 15, c. 7.

A. D. **854. Wulfhere.** York ; d. 900.
   Hist. Dunelm. c. 79 ; Sim. Dun. 854 ; *Chron. Mailros,* 892 ; *Chr. Arch.* ii. 338.

A. D. **854. Eardulf.** Lindisfarne ; Chester-le-Street, 883 ; d. 899.
Flor. Wig. i. 70 ; *Hist. Dunelm.* i. 53.

A. D. **839 × 860. Deorwulf.** London.
Consecrated by Ceolnoth ; subs. 860–862 ; Prof. *Text. Roff.* p. 266 ;
Cleop. E. 1 ; *Reg. Cant.*

A. D. **845 × 862. Weremund.** Rochester.
Subs. 860–862.

A. D. **857 × 866. Mucel.** Hereford.
Flor. Wig. ; Catalogue.

A. D. **862. Alfred (Ealhferth).** Winchester.
Consecrated by Ceolnoth ; subs. 867–871 ; Profession, Cleop. E. 1 ; *Reg.
Cant.*

A. D. **857 × 866. Diorlaf.** Hereford.
Consecrated by Ceolnoth ; subs. 866–884 ; Profession, *Text. Roff.* p. 270
(mentioning Cuthwulf, Eadulf, and Beonna, predecessors) ; Cleop. E.
1 ; *Reg. Cant.*

A. D. **857 × 866. Eadbald.** (Mercian See.)
Subs. 866.

A. D. **857 × 866. Wulfsige.** (Mercian See.)
Subs. 866.

A. D. **862 × 868. Cuthwulf.** Rochester.
Subs. 868.

A. D. **862 × 898. Swithulf.** London.
Flor. Wig. and Ancient Catalogues.

A. D. **866 × 869. Eadbert.** (Mercian See.)
Subs. 869–875.

A. D. **868. Heahmund.** Sherborne ; d. 871.
Chr. S. ; subs. 868–870.

A. D. **845 × 870. Ethelwald.** Dunwich.
Profession to Ceolnoth, *Text. Roff.* p. 268 ; Cleop. E. 1.

A. D. **870.**   **Ethelred** (Bishop of Wiltshire, *Chr. S.*).   Canterbury; d. 889, June 30.

Flor. Wig. i. 82; *Chr. S.* 870, 889; subs. 871–882.

A. D. **872.**   **Ethelheah.**   Sherborne.

Subs. 871 × 878.

A. D. **873,** June 7.   **Wereferth.**   Worcester; d. 915.

Consecrated by Archbishop Ethelred; Flor. Wig. i. 90; subs. 873–904.

A. D. **872 × 877.**   **Tunberht.**   Winchester.

Subs. 877.

A. D. **875 × 880.**   **Wulfred.**   (Mercia.)

Subs. 880–888.

A. D. **879.**   **Denewulf.**   Winchester; d. 909.

See *Chr. S.* 909; subs. 882–904.

A. D. **868 × 880.**   **Swithulf.**   Rochester; d. 897.

See *Chr. S.* 897; subs. 880–889.

A. D. **869 × 888.**   **Alheard.**   Dorchester; d. 897.

See *Chr. S.* 897; subs. 888.

A. D. **872 × 889.**   **Wulfsige.**   Sherborne.

Subs. 889–892.

A. D. **888.**   **Cynemund.**   Hereford.

Electus, 888; subs. 888; *Cart. S.* 557.

A. D. **890.**   **Plegmund.**   Canterbury; d. 914, Aug. 2.

Elected A. D. 890, *Chr. S.*; probably received his pall from Formosus, who became Pope in September, 891; see Gervase, *Opp.* ii. 350; R. de Diceto, *Opp.* i. 17; ii. 209; Flor. Wig. i. 108; subs. 895–910.

A. D. **892 × 900.**   **Asser.**   Sherborne.

See *Chr. S.* 909; subs. 900–904.

A. D. **892 × 900.**   **Heahstan.**   London; d. 898.

Chr. S. 898; Flor. Wig. i. 116.

A. D. **898.**   **Wulfsige.**   London.

Subs. 901–910.

A. D. **900. Ethelbald.** York.
Chron. Arch. Ebor. Raine, ii. 255, 339; Sim. Dun.; *Hist.* i. 225.

A. D. **900. Cutheard.** Chester-le-Street; d. 915.
Flor. Wig. i. 116; *Hist. Dunelm.* i. 72.

A. D. **888 × 901. Eadgar.** Hereford.
Subs. 901–930.

A. D. **889 × 901. Wigmund.** (Mercia.)
Subs. 901–909.

A. D. — **Wighelm.** (Possibly Selsey.)
Subs. 904–909

A. D. **897 × 904. Ceolmund.** Rochester.
Subs. 904–909.

A. D. **904 × 909. Ethelwerd.** Sherborne.
To the year 909 belongs the subdivision of the West Saxon sees, and the very ancient story of the consecration of seven bishops at Canterbury, with the apocryphal account of the negotiation of Edward the Elder with Pope Formosus. It would appear quite certain that Edward divided the diocese of Winchester into two, in 909; see Kemble's *C. D.* Nos. 1090, 1092, 1094, 1095. Possibly the rest of Wessex was divided at the same time; from this date the succession in Ramsbury (for Wilts and Berks), Wells, and Crediton begins; and the most ancient tenth-century MS. (Cotton, Tiberius B. 5) assigns the division of the whole to nearly the same period.

The tradition of the consecration of the seven bishops at Canterbury seems as old as the eleventh century, and contains no special improbability, although it would be unwise to risk a positive identification of the persons consecrated. The apocryphal negotiation between Edward and Formosus appears before the end of the tenth century, even in the letter ascribed to Dunstan, on the See of Cornwall (*Crawford Charter*, vii, *Anecdota Oxoniensia*), according to which, seven years having elapsed and bishoprics being vacant, the Pope urged Edward to fill them up, and the subdivision resulted. As Formosus died in 896, four years before Edward became king, and the seven years of desolation ended in 909, the fable is impossible. But as

Plegmund went to Rome in 908 it is probable that some negotiation there, possibly connected with Plegmund's vindication from a connexion with the questionable action of Formosus, may have stimulated him to an improvement in the organization of his province; on this point see W. Malmesb. *G. R.* vol. ii. pref. pp. lv–lx, and the authorities there quoted. The identification of the seven bishops must remain conjectural : the names Frithstan of Winchester, Ethelstan of Ramsbury, Werstan of Sherborn, Athelm of Wells, Eadulf of Crediton, Beornege of Selsey, and Coenulf of Dorchester seem to rest on the authority of Leofric's *Missal*, fo. 1 ; *Reg. Cant.* ; Wilkins, *Conc.* i. 199, 200 ; W. Malmesb. *G. R.* i. 141.

A. D. **909. Frithstan.** Winchester ; res. 931 ; d. 933, Sept. 10.
    Flor. Wig. i. 120 ; subs. 909–929.

Ethelstan. Ramsbury.
    Subs. 910.

Beornege. Selsey.
    Flor. Wig. i. 130 ; subs. 925–929.

Athelm. Wells ; Canterbury, 914 ; d. 923, Jan. 8.
    Flor. Wig. i. 123.

Eadulf. Crediton.
    Subs. 926–934.

Wærstan. Sherborne.
    Hyde Register, p. 20 ; *Crawford Charter*, vii.

Ceolwulf. Dorchester.

A. D. **915. Tilred.** Chester-le-Street.
    Flor. Wig. i. 124 ; *Hist. Dunelm.* i. 74.

A. D. **915. Ethelhun.** Worcester.
    Flor. Wig. i. 123.

A. D. **918. Ethelbald.** Sherborne.
    See Flor. Wig. i. 128.

A. D. **922. Wilferth.** Worcester.
    Flor. Wig. ; *Cart. S.* 641.

Consecrated by Plegmund.

A. D. **914. Wulfhelm.** Wells ; Canterbury, 923 ; d. 942, Feb. 12.
Flor. Wig. i. 123 ; *Cart. S.* ; subs. 923–941.

A. D. **909 × 926. Kynferth.** Rochester.
Subs. 926–931.

A. D. **923. Elfheah.** Wells.
Subs. 930–937.

A. D. **909 × 926. Ella,** or **Elfwin.** Lichfield.
Flor. Wig. i. 131 ; ann. 928 ; subs. 925–935 ; *Liber S. Gall.* (Goldast. *Scr. R. Alamann.*) ii. 157.

A. D. **910 × 926. Heahstan.** London.

A. D. **910 × 926. Theodred.** London.
Subs. 926–951.

A. D. **918 × 926. Sigelm.** Sherborne.
Subs. 925–932 ; *Lib. S. Gall.*

A. D. **909 × 926. Winsige.** Dorchester.
Subs. 926–934 ; *Lib. S. Gall.* ; *Cart. S.* 642, 716.

A. D. **925 × 927. Odo.** Ramsbury ; Canterbury, 942 ; d. 958, June 2.
Subs. 927–941, Abp. 941–958 ; *Lib. S. Gall.*

A. D. **928. Wigred.** Chester-le-Street.
Flor. Wig. i. 131 ; *Hist. Dunelm.* i. 75. [Other suffragans of York are Earnulf, Columban (A. D. 929), Æscbert and Eadward (A. D. 931).]

A. D. **904–928. Rodewald (Hrothward, Lodeward).** York.
Chron. Arch. Ebor. ; Raine, ii. 255, 339 ; subs. 928 ; *Cart. S.* 664.

A. D. **928. Kinewold.** Worcester.
Flor. Wig. i. 131 ; subs. 930–957 ; *Lib. S. Gall.* p. 153.

Anno ab Inc. Domini 928, indictione ii. Keonwald venerabilis episcopus profectus ab Anglis, omnibus monasteriis per totam Germaniam, cum oblatione argenti non modica, et in id ipsum rege Anglorum eadem sibi tradita, visitatis, in Idibus Octobris venit ad monasterium Sancti Galli : quique gratissime a fratribus susceptus et ejusdem patroni nostri festivitatem cum illis celebrando quatuor ibidem dies demoratus est. secundo autem postquam monasterium ingressus est, hoc est in ipso depositionis S. Galli die basilicam intravit, et pecuniam secum copiosam attulit, de qua partem altario imposuit, partem etiam utilitati fratrum donavit. Post haec eo in conventum nostrum inducto, omnis congregatio concessit ei annonam unius fratris, et tandem orationem quam pro quolibet de nostris sive vivente sive vita decedente facere solemus, pro illo facturam perpetualiter promisit. Haec autem sunt nomina quae conscribi jussit vel rogavit : Rex Anglorum Adalstean, Kenowald episcopus, Wigharth, Kenuun, Conrat, Keonolaf, Wundych, Keondrud. (Goldast, *Scr. Alem.* ii. 153.)

Nomina Fratrum Conscriptorum : Hic regis Angliæ et comitum suorum nomina denotata sunt (ibid. 156) :—

Adalsten, Rex ; Wuolfhelmus, Archiep. ; Elwinus, Episc. ; Eotkarus, Episc. ; Wunsige, Episc. ; Sigihelm, Episc. ; Oda, Episc. ; Fridosten, Episc. ; Kenod, Abba ; Albrich, Abba ; Cudret, Erdulf, Fridolef, Wulfhun, Ortgar, Osfred, Elfsie, Adalwerd, Elwin, Adalwin, Berectwin, Wulfilt, Wighart, Conrat, Kenwin, Wudrud, Kenowad, Episc. ; Kenolaf, Keondrud, cum ceteris.

A. D. **930. Tidhelm.** Hereford.

> Subs. 930–934, 937 ; *Cart. S.* 716.

—— **Kinesige.** Berkshire (?).

> Subs. 931–934 ; *Cart. S.* 687–890.

—— **Conan.** Cornwall.

> Subs. 931–939 ; *Crawford Charter,* vii (ed. Napier).

A. D. **931. Wulfhun.** Selsey.

> Subs. 931–940.

A. D. **931. Wulfstan.** York ; d. 956, Dec. 26.

> *Chron. Arch. Ebor.* Raine, ii. 255, 339 ; subs. 931–955.

A. D. **931,** May 29. **Beornstan.** Winchester ; d. 934, Nov. 4.

> *Chr. S.* 931 ; Flor. Wig. i. 131 ; subs. 931–934.

A. D. **933. Ælfred.** Sherborne.

> Flor. Wig. 941 ; subs. 933–943.

A. D. **933. Burhric (Burgric).** Rochester.

> Subs. 934–946.

A. D. **934.** **Elfheah.** Winchester; d. 951, Mar. 12.
Chr. S. 934, 951 ; Flor. Wig. i. 132 ; subs. 934–951.

A. D. **934.** **Ethelgar.** Crediton ; d. 953 (?), Apr. 30.
Subs. 934–953.

A. D. **938.** **Wulfhelm.** Wells.
Subs. 938–955.

A. D. **934 × 939.** **Wulfhelm.** Hereford.
Subs. 934–940.

A. D. **935 × 941.** **Wulfgar.** Lichfield (?).
Subs. 941–948.

A. D. **941.** **Alfric.** Hereford.
Subs. 941–951.

A. D. **943.** **Wulfsige.** Sherborne.
Subs. 943–958.

A. D. **940 × 944.** **Alfred.** Selsey.
Subs. 943–953.

A. D. **942.** **Ælfric.** Ramsbury.
Subs. 944 ; K. C. D. 1151 ; *Cart. S.* 801.

A. D. **944 × 950.** **Oswulf.** Ramsbury ; d. 970.
Subs. 950–970.

A. D. **944.** **Uhtred.** Chester-le-Street.
Flor. Wig. i. 134 ; *Hist. Dunelm.* i. 76.

A. D. **942 × 956.** **Eadulf.** Elmham.
Consecrated by Archbishop Odo ; Prof. *Reg. Cant.* ; subs. 956–964.

A. D. **947.** **Sexhelm.** Chester-le-Street.
Flor. Wig. i. 134 ; *Hist. Dunelm.* i. 77.

A. D. **946 × 949.** **Beorhtsige.** (See unknown.)
Subs. 949–951.

A. D. **950.   Oskytel.**   Dorchester; York, 958; d. 971, Nov. 1.
Chr. S. 971 ; Flor. Wig. i. 137 ; subs. 952–969.

A. D. **951.   Ælfsige Lippe.**   Winchester; Canterbury, 959; d. 959.
Flor. Wig. i. 135 ; subs. 952–958.

A. D. **953.   Elfwold.**   Crediton ; d. 972.
Flor. Wig. i. 135 ; subs. 953–970.

A. D. — × **953.   Leofwin.**   Lindsey; Dorchester, 958.
Subs. 953–965.

A. D. **951 × 953.   Wulfstan.**   London.
See *Cart. S.* 897.

A. D. **951 × 953.   Brihthelm.**   London.
Subs. 953–959.

A. D. **951 × 955.   Daniel.**   Cornwall.
Subs. 955–959.   See the *Crawford Charter*, vii (ed. Napier, p. 19).

A. D. **956.   Brihthelm.**   Wells; d. 973, May 17.
Electus, 956 ; subs. 956–973.   See *Cart. S.* 986.

A. D. **957.   Ealdred.**   Chester-le-Street; d. 968.
Hist. Dunelm. i. 77 ; *Cart. S.* 1044.

A. D. **957.   Dunstan.**   Worcester ; London, 959 ; Canterbury, 960; d. 988,
May 19.
Consecrated by Archbishop Odo at Canterbury ; Flor. Wig. i. 137.

A. D. **958.   Ælfwold.**   Sherborne ; d. 978.
Chr. S. 978 ; subs. 961–975.

A. D. **959 × 967.**   "Tp. R. Eadg."   **Comoere.**   Cornwall.

A. D. **960.   Brihthelm.**   Winchester.
See Flor. Wig. i. 138 ; subs. 960–963.

A. D. **961.   Ælfstan.**   London.
Subs. 961–995 ; *Cart. S.* 1101, 1175.

A. D. **961. Oswald.** Worcester ; York, 972 ; d. 992, Feb. 29.
Consecrated by Dunstan ; Flor. Wig. i. 139, 140 ; subs. 961–991.

A. D. **961–964. Elfstan.** Rochester.
Subs. 964–995.

A. D. **958–963. Ealdhelm.** Selsey.
See Flor. Wig. i. 142, note ; subs. 967–979.

A. D. **963**, Nov. 29. **Æthelwold.** Winchester ; d. 984, Aug. 1.
Consecrated by Dunstan ; *Chr. S.* 963 ; Flor. Wig. i. 140 ; subs. 964–984.

A. D. **964. Winsige.** Lichfield.
Subs. 964–973.

A. D. **951 × 973. Athulf.** Hereford.
Subs. 973–1012.

A. D. **968. Elfsige.** Chester-le-Street ; d. 990.
Consecrated at York by Oskytel ; Flor. Wig. i. 141 ; *Hist. Dunelm.* i. 78.

A. D. —. **Elfric.** Elmham.
—. **Wulfsige.** Cornwall.
Consecrated by Dunstan ; subs. 967–980 ; *Crawford Charter*, vii.

A. D. **970. Elfstan.** Ramsbury ; d. 981.
See Flor. Wig. i. 141 ; subs. 974–980.

A. D. **973. Elfheah.** Lichfield.
Subs. 975–1002.

A. D. **973. Sideman.** Crediton ; d. 977, Apr. 30.
Chr. S. 977 ; Flor. Wig. i. 142, 145 ; subs. 974–975.

A. D. **973. Kineward.** Wells ; d. 975, June 28.
Chr. S. 975 ; Flor. Wig. i. 143, 145 ; subs. 975.

A. D. **963 × 972. Gucan.** Llandaff.
Consecrated by Dunstan, Ethelwold, Elfwold, Oswald, and Brihthelm ;
(A. D. 982 ;) *Lib. Landavensis*, pp. 235, 509.

A. D. **965 × 974. Eadnoth.** Dorchester.
Subs. 975.

A. D. **964 × 975. Theodred.** Elmham.
Subs. 975.

A. D. **975. Sigar.** Wells ; d. 997, June 28.
Subs. 979–995.

A. D. **978-979. Æscwig.** Dorchester.
Subs. 979–1002.

A. D. **977. Elfric.** Crediton.
Subs. 979–985 ; Flor. Wig. 977.

A. D. **978. Æthelsige.** Sherborne.
See *Chr. S.* 978 ; Flor. Wig. i. 146 ; subs. 979–991.

A. D. **980,** May 2. **Æthelgar.** Selsey ; Canterbury, 988 ; d. 990, Feb. 13.
Consecrated by Dunstan ; *Chr. S.* 980 ; subs. 980–988.

A. D. **981. Wulfgar.** Ramsbury.
Chr. S. 981 ; subs. 982–984.

A. D. — × **982. Theodred.** Elmham.
Subs. 982–995.

A. D. **984,** Oct. 19. **Aelfheah, Elphege,** or **Godwin.** Winchester ; Canterbury, 1005 ; d. 1012, Apr. 19.
Consecrated by Dunstan ; *Chr. S.* 984 ; Flor. Wig. i. 147 ; subs. 985–1009.

A. D. **985. Sigeric.** Ramsbury ; Canterbury, 990 ; d. 994, Oct. 28.
See *Chr. S.* 990, 995 ; Flor. Wig. i. 146 ; subs. 985–994.

A. D. **988. Elfwold.** Crediton.
Subs. 988–1008.

A. D. **989. Ordbriht.** Selsey.
Subs. 990–1008.

A. D. **990. Elfric.** Ramsbury; Canterbury, 995; d. 1005, Nov. 16.
Chr. S. 995, 996; Flor. Wig. i. 153; subs. 994–1005.

A. D. **990. Aldhun.** Chester-le-Street; Durham, 995; d. 1018.
Hist. Dunelm. i. 78.

A. D. **992. Wulfsige.** Sherborne.
Subs. 993–1001.

A. D. **992. Aldulf.** Worcester; York, 995; d. 1002, May 6.
Chr. S. 992; Flor. Wig. i. 149; electus Ebor. 995; subs. 994–1001.

A. D. **980 × 993. Ealdred.** Cornwall.
Subs. 989–1002.

A. D. **995 × 1005. Bledri.** Llandaff.
Consecrated by Elfric; R. Diceto, i. 158; *Lib. Landav.* pp. 241, 518.

A. D. **995 × 997. Sigeferth.** Lindsey; d. Apr. 5.
Subs. 997–1004.

A. D. **995. Godwin.** Rochester.
Subs. 995–1046.

A. D. **995. Elfstan.** Elmham.
Subs. 997–1001.

A. D. **996. Wulfstan.** London.
Chr. S. 996; subs. 997–1003.

A. D. **997. Elfwine.** Wells.
Subs. 997, 998.

A. D. **999. Lifing,** alias **Elfstan** and **Ethelstan.** Wells; Canterbury,
1013; d. 1020, June 12.
Subs. 999–1019.

A. D. **1001. Alfgar.** Elmham; res. 1016; d. 1021, Dec. 25.
See *Chr. S.* 1021; subs. 1001–1018.

A. D. **1001. Ethelric.** Sherborne.
Subs. 1002–1009.

A. D. **1002.** **Ælfhelm.** Dorchester.
Subs. 1002–1005.

A. D. **1002 × 1004.** **Godwin.** Lichfield.
Subs. 1004–1008.

A. D. **1003.** **Wulfstan.** Worcester and York ; d. 1023, May 28.
Flor. Wig. i. 156 ; subs. 1004–1022.

A. D. **1004.** **Ælfwine.** London.
Subs. 1004–1012.

A. D. **1005.** **Kenulf.** Winchester ; d. 1006.
Chr. S. 1006 ; Flor. Wig. i. 158.

A. D. **1005.** **Brihtwold.** Ramsbury ; d. 1045.
Chr. S. 1006 ; subs. 1005–1045.

A. D. **1006.** **Ethelwold.** Winchester.
Flor. Wig. i. 158 ; 1007–1012.

A. D. **1006.** **Eadnoth.** Dorchester ; d. 1016, Oct. 19.
Subs. 1012.

A. D. **1009.** **Ælfmer.** Selsey.
Flor. Wig. i. 162, 182 ; subs. 1012–1031.

A. D. **1008 × 1012.** **Eadnoth.** Crediton.
Subs. 1012–1019.

A. D. **1009 × 1012.** **Ethelsige.** Sherborne.
Subs. 1012–1014.

A. D. **1009 × 1012.** **Brihtwy.** Sherborne.

A. D. **1009 × 1012.** **Godwin.** Rochester (above, A. D. 995).
Subs. 1046.

A. D. **1012.** **Ethelstan.** Hereford ; d. 1056, Feb. 10.
Subs. 1012–1052.

A. D. **1013. Ethelwin.** Wells.
> Subs. 1018–1023. See *Ang. Sac.* i. 558.

—— **Brihtwin.** Wells.
> Subs. 1018.

A. D. **1014,** Feb. 16. **Elfwig.** London.
> Consecrated at York ; *Chr. S.* 1014 ; subs. 1015–1035.

A. D. **1016. Ælfsige.** Winchester ; d. 1032.
> Flor. Wig. i. 171 ; subs. 1014–1033.

A. D. **1016. Ethelric.** Dorchester ; d. 1034, Dec. 8.
> *Chr. S.* 1034 ; subs. 1020–1033.

A. D. **1016. Alwin.** Elmham.
> Flor. Wig. i. 183 ; subs. 1019–1022.

A. D. **1016. Leofsige.** Worcester ; d. 1033, Aug. 19.
> Flor. Wig.; *Chr. S.* 1033 ; subs. 1016–1022.

A. D. **1017. Ælfmær.** Sherborne ; d. Sept. 18.
> Subs. 1020–1022. See Thorn, ap. Twysden, c. 1783.

A. D. **1002 × 1018. Burwold.** Cornwall.
> Subs. 1018.

A. D. **1020,** Nov. 13. **Ethelnoth.** Canterbury ; d. 1038, Oct. 29.
> Consecrated at Canterbury by Wulfstan of York ; see Kemble, *Cod. Dipl.* no. 1314 ; *Chr. S.* 1020 ; subs. 1020–1033.

A. D. **1020. Leofgar.** Lichfield.
> Chesterfield, *Ang. Sac.* i. 432.

A. D. **1020. Edmund.** Durham ; d. 1040.
> Consecrated at York by Archbishop Wulfstan ; Flor. Wig. i. 183 ; *Hist. Dunelm.* i. 86.

A. D. **1022. Bernhard** of Scania, Reinhart of Fionia, and Gerbrand of Roskilde.
> Consecrated by Ethelnoth ; see Adam of Bremen ; Pertz, *Scriptores*, ix. 325.

D

A. D. **1023.** **Elfric.** York; d. 1051, Jan. 22.

Consecrated at Canterbury by Ethelnoth; *Chr. S.* 1023; Flor. Wig. i. 184; subs. 1033–1049.

A. D. **1023.** **Brihtwy.** Sherborne.

Subs. 1023–1045.

A. D. **1026.** **Brihtmær.** Lichfield; d. 1039.

Chesterfield, *Ang. Sac.* i. 432; subs. 1026–1033.

A. D. **1027.** **Lyfing.** Crediton; Worcester, 1038; Cornwall (?); d. 1046, March 23.

Subs. 1027–1045.

A. D. **1027,** Oct. 1. **Joseph.** Llandaff.

Consecrated at Canterbury by Ethelnoth; *Lib. Landav.* pp. 241, 518; Diceto, i. 171.

A. D. **1027.** **Merewit.** Wells.

Chr. S. 1033; W. Malmesb. *Hist. Glast.* ed. Gale, p. 323; subs. 1031–1032.

A. D. **1023 × 1030.** **Elfric.** Elmham; d. 1038.

Chr. S. 1038.

A. D. **1032.** **Ælfwin.** Winchester; d. 1047, Aug. 29.

Chr. S. 1032; subs. 1033–1046.

A. D. **1032.** **Ethelric.** Selsey; d. 1038, Nov. 3.

Chr. S. 1038; subs. 1032, 1033.

A. D. **1033,** June 11. **Duduc.** Wells; d. 1060, Jan. 18.

'Huic successit Duduco, natione Saxo, iii idus Junii ordinatus;' Giso Well.; Hunter, *See of Somerset*, pp. 15, 16.

A. D. **1033.** **Brihteag.** Worcester; d. 1038, Dec. 20.

Chr. S. 1033, 1038; Flor. Wig. i. 189; subs. 1033.

A. D. **1034.** **Eadnoth.** Dorchester; d. 1049.

Flor. Wig. i. 189; subs. 1042–1046.

A. D. **1035.** **Eadsige.** Canterbury, 1038; d. 1050, Oct. 29.

Eadsige is a Bishop in Kent during the life of Archbishop Ethelnoth : Kemble, *C. D.* 1323, 1325, 1327 ; and is associated with the Church of S. Martin, Canterbury : Battely's *Somner*, suppl. pp. 129 sq. ; *Evidentiæ Eccl. Chr.* (Twysden) c. 2223 ; subs. 1035–1050.

A. D. **1035.** **Elfweard.** London ; d. 1044, July 27.

Hist. Evesham (Wharton, *Epp. Lond.* p. 35), ed. Macray, pp. 83–85 ; subs. 1038–1042.

A. D. **1038.** **Elfric.** Elmham.

See *Chr. S.* 1038 ; *K. C. D.* 759.

A. D. **1039.** **Wulfsige.** Lichfield ; d. 1053, Oct.

Flor. Wig. i. 193 ; Chesterfield, *Ang. Sac.* i. 432 ; subs. 1039–1053.

A. D. **1039.** **Grimketel.** Selsey ; Elmham (?) ; d. 1047.

Chr. S. 1038 ; Flor. Wig. i. 192, 193 ; subs. 1042–1046.

A. D. **1041.** **Eadred.** Durham ; d. 1041.

Hist. Dunelm. (ed. Arnold), i. 91.

A. D. **1042,** Jan. 11. **Ethelric.** Durham ; resigned 1056 ; d. 1072, Oct. 15.

Consecrated at York ; *Chr. S.* 1041–2 ; *Hist. Dunelm.* i. 91.

A. D. **1043,** Apr. 3. **Stigand.** Elmham ; Winchester, 1047 ; Canterbury, 1052 ; deposed April 11, 1070 ; d. 1072, Feb. 22.

Consecrated at Winchester ; *Chr. S.* 1043 ; Flor. Wig. i. 193, 199 ; subs. 1046–1065.

A. D. **1044.** **Ealdred.** Worcester ; York, 1061 ; d. 1069, Sept. 11.

Chr. S. 1045 ; Flor. Wig. i. 199 ; subs. 1044–1065.

A. D. **1044.** **Siward,** suffragan for Canterbury ; d. 1048, Oct. 23.

Consecrated by Eadsige ; *Chr. S.* 1044, 1048.

A. D. **1044.** **Robert Champart,** London ; Canterbury, 1051 ; expelled, 1052, Sept. 14 ; d. 1070.

Subs. 1046–1050.

A. D. **1045.** **Herman.** Ramsbury ; Sherborne, 1058 ; d. 1078, Feb. 20.

Chr. S. 1045 ; Flor. Wig. i. 199 ; subs. 1045–1065.

A. D. **1045.** **Elfwold.** Sherborne.
Subs. 1046–1050.

A. D. **1046.** **Leofric.** Crediton (Exeter, 1050); d. 1072, Feb. 10.
'XIII Kal. Maii, Ordinatio Leofrici episcopi:' Kalendar in Leofric's *Missal*; *Chr. S.* 1045, 1047; Flor. Wig. i. 199; subs. 1046–1065.

A. D. **1047.** **Ethelmar.** Elmham.
Flor. Wig. i. 193; subs. 1055.

A. D. **1047.** **Heca.** Selsey; d. 1057.
Chr. S. 1047; Flor. Wig. i. 200; subs. 1050.

A. D. **1050.** **Ulf.** Dorchester; exp. 1052.
Chr. S. 1049; Flor. Wig. i. 203; subs. 1050–1052.

A. D. **1051.** **William.** London; d. 1075.
Consecrated by Archbishop Robert; *Chr. S.* 1051; Flor. Wig. i. 207, 210; subs. 1061–1065.

A. D. **1051.** **Kinsige.** York; d. 1060, Dec. 22.
Chr. S. 1053; Flor. Wig. i. 204.

A. D. **1053.** **Wulfwig.** Dorchester; d. 1067.
Went abroad for consecration: 'quo tempore Anglorum praesules, alii Romam, nonnulli Franciam sacrandi petebant;' Prof. Wulfst. MS. Cleop. E. 1; *Chr. S.* 1053.

A. D. **1053.** **Leofwin.** Lichfield; d. 1067.
Went abroad for consecration; *Chr. S.* 1053; Flor. Wig. i. 211.

A. D. **1053.** **Magswem.** Glasgow.
Consecrated by Kinsige of York; *Chron. Pontiff. Ebor.* (Raine, ii), p. 343.

A. D. **1056.** **Leofgar.** Hereford; d. 1056, June 17.
He was bishop eleven weeks and four days; his consecration would fall in March; *Chr. S.* 1056; Flor. Wig. i. 214.

A. D. **1056,** May 26. **Herewald.** Llandaff; d. 1104, March 6.
Consecrated by Kinsige of York; *Liber Landavensis.* Ralph de Diceto states that the following consecrations of Welsh bishops took place at

Canterbury: Chevelliauc and Libiau of Llandaff, and Lunverd of S. David's, by Archbishop Ethelred, 870–889; Bledri of Llandaff, and Tramerin and Elvod of S. David's, by Elfric, 990–1005; Joseph of Llandaff, and Bleduc of S. David's, by Ethelnoth at Canterbury, 1020–1038; and Herewald of Llandaff by Lanfranc (*Opp*. i. 138, 158, 171). Cf. Hist. MSS. Comm. v. 452; *Lib. Landav.* pp. 255, 535.

A. D. **1056.** **Ethelwin.** Durham; d. 1071.

Chr. S. 1056; Flor. Wig. i. 215; *Hist. Dunelm.* i. 92.

A. D. **1058.** **Ethelric.** Selsey; deposed in 1070; surviving in 1076.

Consecrated by Archbishop Stigand; *Chr. S.* 1056, 1058; Flor. Wig. i. 216, 217.

A. D. **1058.** **Siward.** Rochester; d. 1075.

Consecrated by Stigand; *Chr. S.* 1056, 1058; Flor. Wig. i. 217.

A. D. **1053 × 1060.** **John.** Glasgow.

Consecrated by Kinsige of York; *Chron. Pontiff. Ebor.* (Raine, ii), p. 343.

A. D. **1061,** Apr. 15. **Giso.** Wells; d. 1088; and
Walter. Hereford; d. 1079.

Consecrated at Rome by Pope Nicolas II; *History of the See of Somerset*, Camden Soc. p. 16; Flor. Wig. i. 218.

A. D. **1062,** Sept. 8. **Wulfstan.** Worcester; d. 1095, Jan. 18.

Consecrated at York by Archbishop Ealdred; Flor. Wig. i. 221: 'Ego autem Aldredum Eboracensis ecclesiae antistitem adii;' Prof. *Reg. Cant.*; MS. Cotton, Cleop. E. 1; *Chron. Pont. Ebor.*, p. 347; Flor. Wig. i. 220.

A. D. **1067.** **Remigius.** Dorchester (Lincoln); d. 1092, May 7.

Consecrated by Stigand: 'Ego vero, hujus negotii neque ex toto ignarus nec usquequaque gnarus, ad eum (sc. Stigandum) veni, professionem sibi suisque successoribus feci, curamque episcopalem de manu ipsius me consecrantis accepi;' Prof. *Reg. Cant.*; MS. Cleop. E. 1.

A. D. **1070,** May 30. **Walkelin.** Winchester; d. 1098, Jan. 3.

Consecrated probably at Windsor by Armenfrid, Bishop of Sion: 'Et quia Doruberniae archipraesul depositus est et Eboracensis erat defunctus, jussu regis in octavis Pentecostes ab eodem Armenfrido Sedunensi episcopo ordinatus est Walcelinus;' Flor. Wig. ii. 7.

A. D. **1070.**   **Stigand.**   Selsey (Chichester, 1075); d. 1087.
Flor. Wig. ii. 6.

A. D. **1070.**   **Herfast.**   Elmham (Thetford, 1075); d. 1085 (?).
Profession 'jam sacratus,' to Lanfranc; *Ang. Sac.* i. 80; Flor. Wig. ii. 6.

[The following changes of Episcopal Sees took place shortly after the
Conquest, partly in consequence of a decree of a Council at London in
1075: Sherborne and Ramsbury to Old Sarum, 1075 (to Salisbury,
1219); Wells to Bath, 1088; Selsey to Chichester, 1075; Lichfield to
Chester, 1075; to Coventry, 1095; Dorchester to Lincoln, 1095;
Elmham to Thetford, 1075; to Norwich, 1094.   The see of Crediton
had been removed to Exeter in 1050.]

A. D. **1070,** August 29.   **Lanfranc.**   Canterbury; d. 1089. May 24.
Consecrated at Canterbury by William of London, Walkelin of Winchester,
Giso of Wells, Walter of Hereford, Herman of Sherborne, Siward of
Rochester, Remigius of Dorchester, Herfast of Elmham, and Stigand
of Selsey; Will. Malmesb. *G. P.* § 25 : consecratus est autem a Gisone
Wellensi et Waltero Herefordensi; Flor. Wig. ii. 7; Gervase, ii. 365.

A. D. **1070.**   **Thomas.**   York; d. 1100, Nov. 18.
Consecrated at Canterbury by Lanfranc; W. Malmesb. *G. P.* § 25;
Gervase, ii. 366; Hugo Cantor (ed. Raine, ii), p. 101.

A. D. **1071,** March.   **Walcher.**   Durham; d. 1080, May 14.
Consecrated at Winchester by Thomas of York; letter of Archbishop
Ralph, ap. Twysden, c. 1744; Flor. Wig. ii. 10; Hoveden, i. 126.

A. D. **1072,** April.   **Osbern fitzOsbern.**   Exeter; d. 1103.
Consecrated at London by Lanfranc; Prof. *Reg. Cant.*; *Chr. S. A.*;
Gervase, ii. 366.

A. D. **1072.**   **Peter.**   Lichfield; d. 1085.
Consecrated at Gloucester by Lanfranc; *Chr. S. A.*; Gervase, ii. 366.

A. D. **1073,** Mar. 3.   **Ralph.**   Orkney.
Consecrated at York by Thomas of York, Wulfstan of Worcester, and
Peter of Lichfield; *Chr. S. A.* (ann. 1076); Lanfr. *Epp.* 11 and 12.

A. D. **1074. Patrick.** Dublin ; d. 1084, Oct. 10.
Consecrated at London by Lanfranc ; Prof. *Reg. Cant.* ; *Chr. S. A.* ;
Gervase, ii. 366.

A. D. **1075. Hugh d'Orivalle.** London ; d. 1085, Jan. 12.
Consecrated by Lanfranc ; Prof. *Reg Cant.*

A. D. **1076. Arnost.** Rochester ; d. 1076.
Consecrated at London or Westminster by Lanfranc : Prof. *Reg. Cant.* ;
Chr. S. A. Thomas of York assisting : MS. Domitian A. 5 ; Wilk.
Conc. i. 369 ; Gervase, ii. 366.

A. D. **1077**, March 19. **Gundulf.** Rochester ; d. 1108, Mar. 7.
Consecrated at Canterbury by Lanfranc ; Prof. *Reg. Cant.* ; *Chr. S. A.* ;
Vita Gundulfi ; *Ang. Sac.* ii. 280.

A. D. **1078. Osmund.** Salisbury ; d. 1099, Dec. 3.
Consecrated by Lanfranc ; Prof. *Reg. Cant.*

A. D. **1079**, Dec. 29. **Robert Losinga.** Hereford ; d. 1095, June 26.
Consecrated at Canterbury by Lanfranc ; Flor. Wig. ii. 13 ; Prof. *Reg.*
Cant. ; Gervase, ii. 367.

A. D. **1081**, Jan. 3. **William of S. Carileph.** Durham ; d. 1096, Jan. 1.
Consecrated at Gloucester by Thomas of York, Wulfstan of Worcester,
Osbern of Exeter, Giso of Wells, and Robert of Hereford ; *Chr. S. A.* ;
Flor. Wig. ii. 17 ; *Hist. Dunelm.* i. 119.

A. D. **1085. Donagh ô' Haingly.** Dublin ; d. 1095.
Consecrated at Canterbury by Lanfranc ; Prof. *Reg. Cant.* ; *Chr. S. A.*

A. D. **1086. Robert of Limesy.** Lichfield ; d. 1117, Sept. 1 ; and
      William of Beaufeu. Thetford ; d. 1091.
Consecrated by Lanfranc at Canterbury, 'simul uno die ;' *Chr. S. A.* ;
Prof. *Reg. Cant.* ; Gervase, ii. 367.

A. D. **1086** [Apr. 5 ?]. **Maurice.** London ; d. 1107, Sept. 26.
Consecrated at Winchester by Lanfranc, Thomas of York assisting ; Prof.
Reg. Cant. ; *Chr. S. A.* ; MS. Domitian A. 5.

A. D. **1087.** **Gosfrid.** Chichester; d. 1088, Sept. 25.

Consecrated at Canterbury by Lanfranc; Prof. *Reg. Cant.*; *Chr. S.* A.; Gervase, ii. 367.

A. D. **1088,** July. **John of Tours.** Bath; d. 1122, Dec. 29.

Consecrated at Canterbury by Lanfranc; Prof. *Reg. Cant.*; *Chr. S.* A.; Gervase, ii. 367; Hunter, *Bishopric of Somerset,* p. 21.

A. D. **1091.** **Ralph Luffa.** Chichester; d. 1123, Dec. 24.

Consecrated by Thomas of York; Prof. *Reg. Cant.*; Hugo Cantor, ed. Raine, p. 104 ['die Epiphaniae;' *Ann. Cicestr.* ed. Liebermann, p. 93].

A. D. **1091.** **Herbert Losinga.** Thetford; d. 1119, July 22.

Consecrated by Archbishop Thomas of York; Prof. *Reg. Cant.*; Hugo Cantor, p. 104.

A. D. **1092.** **Hervey.** Bangor; Ely, 1109; d. 1131, Aug. 30.

Consecrated by Thomas, Archbishop of York; Hugo Cantor, p. 104.

A. D. **1093,** Dec. 4. **Anselm.** Canterbury; d. 1109, Apr. 21.

Consecrated at Canterbury by Thomas of York, Maurice of London, Walkelin of Winchester; 'ab omnibus episcopis Angliae:' W. Malmesb. *G. P.* § 49; *Chr. S.* A.; Hugo Cantor, p. 105; Eadmer, *H. N.* p. 42; *Vita Anselmi,* p. 361; Gervase, ii. 373.

A. D. **1094** [Feb. 12]. **Robert Bloett.** Lincoln; d. 1123, Jan. 10.

Consecrated at Hastings by Anselm and seven bishops, during the month spent at Hastings after the Christmas court, before the king sailed for Normandy: Eadmer, *Hist. Nov.* pp. 45–47; the church of Battle Abbey was dedicated Feb. 11 (*Chron. de Bello,* p. 41', 1094: *Chr. S.*; seven bishops being present: Walkelin of Winchester, Ralph of Chichester, Osmund of Salisbury, John of Bath, William of Durham, Roger of Coutances, and Gundulf of Rochester; *Chron. Battle*; Prof. *Reg. Cant.*

A. D. **1096,** Apr. 20. **Samuel ô' Haingly.** Dublin; d. 1121, July 4.

Consecrated at Winchester by Anselm and four bishops; Eadmer, *H. N.* p. 74; Prof. *Reg. Cant.*

A. D. **1096**, June 8. **Gerard.** Hereford ; York, 1101 ; d. 1108, May 21 ; and **Sampson.** Worcester ; d. 1112, May 5.

> Consecrated at S. Paul's, London, by Anselm, Thomas of York, Maurice of London, Gundulf of Rochester, and Herbert of Norwich ; Eadmer, *H. N.* p. 74.

A. D. **1096**, Dec. 28. **Malchus.** Waterford.

> Consecrated at Canterbury by Anselm, Gundulf of Rochester, and Ralph of Chichester ; Eadmer, *H. N.* p. 77.

A. D. **1099**, June 5. **Ranulf Flambard.** Durham ; d. 1128, Sept. 5.

> Consecrated at S. Paul's by Archbishop Thomas of York, on Trinity Sunday ; Sim. Dun. (Twysden, cc. 60, 224) ; *Chron. Arch. Ebor.* Raine, ii. 363 ; *Hist. Dunelm.* i. 138.

A. D. **1101 × 1108.** **Roger of Whitby.** Orkney.

> Consecrated by Archbishop Gerard of York ; *Chron. Arch. Ebor.* ii. 367 ; Hugo Cantor, p. 127.

A. D. **1107**, Aug. 11. **William Giffard.** Winchester ; d. 1129, Jan. 25.

> **Roger.** Salisbury ; d. 1139, Dec. 4.

> **William Warelwast.** Exeter ; d. 1137, Sept. 27.

> **Reinelm.** Hereford ; d. 1115, Oct. 27.

> **Urban.** Llandaff ; d. 1133.

> Consecrated at Canterbury by Archbishop Anselm, Gerard of York, Robert of Lincoln, John of Bath, Herbert of Norwich, Robert of Lichfield, Ralph of Chichester, Ranulf of Durham ; Eadmer, *H. N.* p. 187 ; Flor. Wig. ii. 56 ; Simeon, c. 230 ; *Lib. Landav.* pp. 268, 553.

A. D. **1108**, July 26. **Richard de Belmeis.** London ; d. 1127, Jan. 16.

> Consecrated at Pagham by Archbishop Anselm, William of Winchester, Ralph of Chichester, Roger of Salisbury, and William of Exeter ; Eadmer, *H. N.* p. 108 ; Flor. Wig. ii. 59 ; Simeon, c. 231.

A. D. **1108**, Aug. 9. **Ralph d'Escures.** Rochester; Canterbury, 1114, Apr. 26 ; d. 1122, Oct. 20.

> Consecrated at Canterbury by Anselm, Richard of London, William of Winchester, and Ralph of Chichester; Eadmer, *H. N.* p. 198 ; Flor. Wig. ii. 59 ; Simeon, c. 231.

A. D. **1109**, June 27. **Thomas.** York ; d. 1114, Feb. 24.

> Consecrated at S. Paul's by Richard of London, William of Winchester, Ranulf of Durham, Herbert of Norwich, Ralph of Rochester, and Hervey of Bangor ; Eadmer, *H. N.* p. 210 ; Flor. Wig. ii. 60 ; Simeon, c. 232 ; Hugo Cantor (Raine, ii), p. 125.

A. D. **1109**, Aug. 1. **Turgot.** S. Andrew's ; d. 1115, Aug. 31.

> Consecrated at York by Archbishop Thomas ; Simeon, c. 232 ; Flor. Wig. ii. 60 ; Hugo Cantor, p. 126.

A. D. **1109 × 1114.** **Michael.** Glasgow.

> Consecrated by Archbishop Thomas ; Hugo Cantor, p. 127 ; *Hist. Arch.* p. 371.

A. D. **1109 × 1114.** **Wimund.** Man.

> Consecrated by Archbishop Thomas ; W. Newburgh, i. 24 ; *Hist. Arch.* p. 372.

A. D. **1109 × 1114.** **Ralph Novellus.** Orkney.

> Consecrated by Archbishop Thomas ; Hugo Cantor, p. 127.

A. D. **1115**, June 27. **Theulf.** Worcester ; d. 1123, Oct. 20.

> Consecrated at Canterbury by Archbishop Ralph, Richard of London, John of Bath, Ralph of Chichester, Herbert of Norwich, Hervey of Ely, and Roger of Sarum ; Eadmer, *H. N.* p. 230 ; Flor. Wig. ii. 68 ; Simeon, c. 236.

A. D. **1115**, Sept. 19. **Bernard.** S. David's ; d. 1147.

> Consecrated at Westminster Abbey by Archbishop Ralph, William of Winchester, John of Bath, Robert of Lincoln, Roger of Salisbury, Urban of Llandaff, and Giles of Limerick ; Eadmer, *H. N.* p. 236 ; Flor. Wig. ii. 68.

A. D. **1115**, Dec. 26.   **Geoffrey de Clive.**   Hereford ; d. 1120, Feb. 3 ; and **Ernulf.**   Rochester ; d. 1124, March 15.

> Consecrated at Canterbury by Archbishop Ralph, William of Winchester, Ralph of Chichester, Herbert of Norwich, and Bernard of S. David's ; Eadmer, *H. N.* p. 237 ; Flor. Wig. ii. 68 ; Simeon, c. 237.

A. D. **1119**, Oct. 19.   **Thurstan.**   York ; d. 1140, Feb. 5.

> Consecrated at Rheims by Pope Calixtus II ; Simeon, c. 240. ; Ord. Vit. xii. 21.

A. D. **1120**, April 4.   **David the Scot.**   Bangor ; d. 1139.

> Consecrated at Westminster by Archbishop Ralph, Richard of London, Robert of Lincoln, Roger of Salisbury, and Urban of Llandaff ; Cont. Flor. Wig. ii. 74 ; Eadmer, *H. N.* p. 260.

A. D. **1121**, Jan. 16.   **Richard.**   Hereford ; d. 1127, Aug. 15.

> Consecrated at Lambeth by Archbishop Ralph, Richard of London, Robert of Lincoln, Urban of Llandaff, Bernard of S. David's, and Ernulf of Rochester ; Cont. Flor. Wig. ii. 75 ; Eadmer, *H. N.* p. 291.

A. D. **1121**, March 13.   **Robert Peche.**   Lichfield ; d. 1127, Aug. 22.

> Consecrated at Abingdon by Archbishop Ralph, William of Winchester, William of Exeter, Urban of Llandaff, and Bernard of S. David's ; Eadmer, *H. N.* p. 293 ; Cont. Flor. Wig. ii. 76.

A. D. **1121**, June 12.   **Everard of Montgomery.**   Norwich, dep. 1145 ; d. 1150, Oct. 15.

> Consecrated at Canterbury by Archbishop Ralph, Ernulf of Rochester, Richard of Hereford, and Robert of Lichfield ; Eadmer, *H. N.* p. 294 ; Cont. Flor. Wig. ii. 76.

A. D. **1121**, Oct. 2.   **Gregory.**   Dublin ; d. 1161, Oct. 8.

> Consecrated at Lambeth by Archbishop Ralph, Richard of London, Robert of Lincoln, Roger of Salisbury, David of Bangor, and Everard of Norwich ; Eadmer, *H. N.* p. 298 ; Cont. Flor. Wig. ii. 77.

A. D. **1123**, Feb. 18.   **William of Corbeuil.**   Canterbury ; d. 1136, Nov. 21.

> Consecrated at Canterbury by Richard of London, William of Winchester, Roger of Salisbury, Bernard of S. David's, and Ernulf of Rochester ; *Chr. S.* 1123 ; Cont. Flor. Wig. ii. 77 ; Gervase, ii. 380.

A. D. **1123**, July 22.   **Alexander.**   Lincoln; d. 1148, Feb. 20.

Consecrated at Canterbury by Archbishop William and four bishops; Cont. Flor. Wig. ii. 78; Gervase, ii. 380.

A. D. **1123**, Aug. 26.   **Godfrey.**   Bath; d. 1135, Aug. 16.

Consecrated at S. Paul's by Archbishop William; Flor. Wig. ii. 78; Gervase, ii. 381.

A. D. **1125**, Apr. 12.   **Seffrid Pelochin.**   Chichester; dep. 1145; d. 1151.

Consecrated at Lambeth by Archbishop William, Thurstan of York, Richard of Hereford, Urban of Llandaff, Bernard of S. David's, David of Bangor, and Everard of Norwich; Cont. Flor. Wig. ii. 79; Gervase, ii. 381.

A. D. **1125**, May 24.   **Simon.**   Worcester; d. 1150, Mar. 20; and
                          John.   Rochester; d. 1137, June 22.

Consecrated by Archbishop William, Richard of Hereford, David of Bangor, Godfrey of Bath, and Seffrid of Chichester; Cont. Flor. Wig. ii. 80; Gervase, ii. 381.

A. D. **1127**.   **Robert.**   S. Andrew's.

Consecrated at York by Archbishop Thurstan, Ralph of Durham, Ralph of Orkney, and John of Glasgow; Cotton MS., Titus A. 19; Raine, iii. 51; Cont. Flor. Wig. ii. 89; see Lib. Vit. Eccl. Dun. p. 59.

A. D. **1128**, Jan. 22.   **Gilbert the Universal.**   London; d. 1134, Aug. 10.

Consecrated at Canterbury by Archbishop William, Seffrid of Chichester, and John of Rochester; Cont. Flor. Wig. ii. 89; Gervase, ii. 381.

A. D. **1129**, Nov. 17.   **Henry of Blois.**   Winchester; d. 1171, Aug. 9.

Consecrated at Canterbury by Archbishop William; Cont. Flor. Wig. ii. 91; Gervase, ii. 381; *Chr. S.*

A. D. **1129**, Dec. 22.   **Roger de Clinton.**   Lichfield; d. 1148, Apr. 16.

Consecrated at Canterbury by Archbishop William; Cont. Flor. Wig. ii. 91; Gervase, ii. 381.

A. D. **1131**, June 28.   **Robert de Bethune.**   Hereford; d. 1148, April 16.

Consecrated at Oxford by Archbishop William; Cont. Flor. Wig. (ed. Camden, p. 644); Cont. Flor. Wig. ii. 92; Gervase, ii. 381.

A. D. **1133**, Aug. 6. **Geoffrey Rufus.** Durham; d. 1140, May 6.
Consecrated at York by Thurstan of York ; and

—— **Adelulf.** Carlisle ; d. 1157.
Consecrated at York by Archbishop Thurstan ; John of Hexham (Surtees
Soc.), p. 109 ; *Hist. Dunelm.* p. 62 (ed. Arnold, i. 142).

A. D. **1133 × 1140. Gilaldanus.** Whithern.
Consecrated by Archbishop Thurstan ; *Chron. Arch.* (Raine, ii) p. 385 ;
Profession, ibid. iii. 60.

A. D. **1133**, Oct. 1. **Nigel.** Ely ; d. 1169, May 30.
Consecrated at Lambeth by Archbishop William ; Rich. Eliens. *Ang. Sac.*
i. 619 ; Gervase, ii. 381.

A. D. **1136. Robert.** Bath ; d. 1166, Aug. 31.
Consecrated (?) by Henry of Winchester ; Cont. Flor. Wig. ii. 95.

A. D. **1138**, Dec. 18. **Robert Chichester.** Exeter ; d. 1155, Mar. 28.
Consecrated at Westminster by Alberic, Bishop of Ostia, in a council of
seventeen bishops ; Gervase, i. 107 ; Profession to the future Archbishop ; *Reg. Cant.*

A. D. **1139**, Jan. 8. **Theobald.** Canterbury ; d. 1161, Apr. 18.
Consecrated at Canterbury by Alberic, Bishop of Ostia, 'astantibus et
cooperantibus omnibus fere episcopis Angliae ;' Gervase, ii. 109.

A. D. **1140. Maurice.** Bangor ; d. 1161, Aug. 12 ; and
Uhtred. Llandaff ; d. 1148.
Consecrated by Archbishop Theobald, Robert of Hereford, and Robert
of Exeter ; Cont. Flor. Wig. ii. 124 ; Gervase, ii. 385 ; Professions,
Reg. Cant.

A. D. **1140. Patrick.** Limerick.
Consecrated by Archbishop Theobald ; Profession, *Reg. Cant.*

A. D. **1141. Robert de Sigillo.** London ; d. 1151.
Consecrated by Archbishop Theobald ; Gervase, ii. 385 ; Profession Roll
at Canterbury.

A. D. **1141. Jocelin de Bohun.** Salisbury ; d. 1184, Nov. 18.
Consecrated by Archbishop Theobald ; Prof. *Reg. Cant.*

A. D. **1142.** **Ascelin.** Rochester; d. 1148, Jan. 24.
Consecrated by Archbishop Theobald; Prof. *Reg. Cant.*

A. D. **1143.** **Gilbert.** S. Asaph.
Consecrated at Lambeth by Archbishop Theobald, Robert of London, and Ascelin of Rochester; Prof. *Reg. Cant.*; Gervase, i. 126.

A. D. **1143,** June 20. **William of S. Barbara.** Durham; d. 1152, Nov. 24.
Consecrated at Winchester by Henry of Winchester (legate): septem episcopis astantibus; Cont. Sim. Dun. (ed. Arnold) i. 150, 163; novem episcopis: John of Hexham, ed. Hinde, p. 143; ed. Arnold, ii. 314. Thorn (Twysden, c. 1802) mentions a council at Winchester this year, present: Archbishop Theobald, Jocelin of Salisbury, Robert of London, Alexander of Lincoln, Seffrid of Chichester, Robert of Hereford, Robert of Bath, Roger of Lichfield, William of Durham, Ascelin of Rochester, Simon of Worcester, Adelulf of Carlisle, Uhtred of Llandaff.

A. D. **1143,** Sept. 26. **William Fitz Herbert.** York; d. 1154, June 8.
Consecrated at Winchester by Henry of Winchester (legate), Ralph of Orkney present, representing the church of York; John of Hexham, ed. Arnold, p. 315; cf. W. Newburgh, i. 17.

A. D. **1146.** **William de Turbe.** Norwich; d. 1174, Jan. 17.
Consecrated at Canterbury by Archbishop Theobald; Prof. *Reg. Cant.*; Gervase, i. 130.

A. D. **1147,** Aug. 3. **Hilary.** Chichester; d. 1169, July 19.
Consecrated at Canterbury by Archbishop Theobald, Nigel of Ely, Robert of Bath, and William of Norwich; Prof. *Reg. Cant.*; Gervase, i. 132.

A. D. **1147,** Dec. 7. **Henry Murdac.** York; d. 1153, Oct. 14.
Consecrated at Treves by Pope Eugenius III; J. Hexham, ed Hinde, p. 155.

A. D. **1148,** March 14. **Walter.** Rochester; d. 1182, July 26; and
Nicolas ap Gurgant. Llandaff; d. 1183, July 6.
Consecrated at Canterbury by Archbishop Theobald, Nigel of Ely, Robert of Exeter, and Maurice of Bangor; Prof. *Reg. Cant.*; Gervase, ii. 385.

A. D. **1148**, Sept. 5. **Gilbert Foliot.** Hereford ; London, 1163 ; d. 1187, Feb. 18.

> Consecrated at S. Omer by Archbishop Theobald, Thierri of Amiens, and Nicolas of Cambray ; Prof. *Reg. Cant.* ; Gervase, i. 135.

A. D. **1148**, Dec. 19. **Robert de Chesney.** Lincoln ; d. 1167 ; and

> **David FitzGerald.** S. David's ; d. 1176, May 8.

> Consecrated at Canterbury by Archbishop Theobald, Hilary of Chichester, Walter of Rochester, Gilbert of Hereford, and Patrick of Limerick ; Prof. *Reg. Cant.* ; Gervase, i. 138.

A. D. **1149**, Oct. 2. **Walter Durdent.** Lichfield ; d. 1160, Dec. 7.

> Consecrated at Canterbury by Archbishop Theobald, Robert of London, Walter of Rochester, and Nicolas of Llandaff ; Prof. *Reg. Cant.* ; Gervase, i. 141.

A. D. **1151**, March 4. **John of Pagham.** Worcester ; d. 1158.

> Consecrated at Canterbury by Archbishop Theobald, Hilary of Chichester, and Walter of Rochester ; Prof. *Reg. Cant.* ; Gervase, i. 142.

A. D. **1152**, Feb. 24. **Geoffrey of Monmouth.** S. Asaph ; d. 1154.

> Consecrated at Lambeth by Archbishop Theobald, William of Norwich, and Walter of Rochester ; Prof. *Reg. Cant.* ; Gervase, i. 142.

A. D. **1152**, Sept. 28. **Richard of Belmeis II.** London ; d. 1162, May 4.

> Consecrated at Canterbury by Archbishop Theobald, Hilary of Chichester, Walter of Rochester, and Gilbert of Hereford ; Prof. *Reg. Cant.* ; Gervase, i. 148 ; R. Diceto, i. 295.

A. D. **1153**, Dec. 20. **Hugh de Puiset.** Durham ; d. 1195, Mar. 3.

> Consecrated at Rome by Pope Anastasius IV ; *Chron. Mailros* ; Coldingham (*Script. Dun.*), c. iii. ; Newburgh, i. 26 ; Gervase, i. 157 ; *Hist. Dunelm.* i. 169.

A. D. **1154.** **Richard.** S. Asaph.

> Consecrated by Archbishop Theobald ; Prof. *Reg. Cant.* ; Gervase, ii. 385.

A. D. **1154**, Oct. 10. **Roger of Pont l'Evêque.** York ; d. 1181, Nov. 26.

> Consecrated in Westminster Abbey by Archbishop Theobald, Richard of London, Nigel of Ely, Robert of Bath, William of Norwich, Walter of

Rochester, Gilbert of Hereford, Robert of Lincoln, and John of Worcester; Gervase, i. 158, 159; R. Diceto, i. 298; W. Newburgh, i. 32; *Reg. Cant.* A. 41.

A. D. **1154**, Dec. 19. **Christian.** Whithern; d. 1186, Oct. 7.

Consecrated at Bermondsey by Hugh, Archbishop of Rouen [and Roger of York?]; *Chron. S. Crucis*; *Ang. S.* i. 161; ii. 235.

A. D. **1155**, June 5. **Robert of Warelwast.** Exeter; d. 1160, Mar. 22.

Consecrated at Canterbury by Archbishop Theobald, Nigel of Ely, Jocelin of Salisbury, Hilary of Chichester, and Walter of Rochester; Prof. *Reg. Cant.*; Gervase, i. 162; R. Diceto, i. 301.

A. D. **1158. Alfred.** Worcester; d. 1160, July 31.

Consecrated by Archbishop Theobald, before Palm Sunday, on which day he was inthroned; R. Diceto, ii. 42; *Ann. Theokesb.* p. 48.

A. D. **1160. Godfrey.** S. Asaph; res. 1175.

Consecrated by Archbishop Theobald; Prof. *Reg. Cant.*; Gervase, ii. 385.

A. D. **1161**, before Apr. 18. **Richard Peche.** Lichfield; d. 1182, Oct. 6.

Consecrated at Canterbury by Walter of Rochester; Prof. *Reg. Cant.*; Gervase, i. 168; R. Diceto, i. 305.

A. D. **1162**, before May 4. **Bartholomew.** Exeter; d. 1184, Dec. 15.

Consecrated at Canterbury by Walter of Rochester; Prof. *Reg. Cant.*; Gervase, i. 169; R. Diceto, i. 304.

A. D. **1162**, June 3. **Thomas Becket.** Canterbury; d. 1170, Dec. 29.

Consecrated at Canterbury by Henry of Winchester, Nigel of Ely, Robert of Bath, Jocelin of Salisbury, William of Norwich, Hilary of Chichester, Richard of Lichfield, Bartholomew of Exeter, Robert of Lincoln, Walter of Rochester, Nicolas of Llandaff, David of S. David's, Godfrey of S. Asaph, and Gilbert of Hereford; Gervase, i. 171.

A. D. **1163**, Dec. 22. **Robert of Melun.** Hereford; d. 1167, Feb. 27.

Consecrated at Canterbury by Archbishop Thomas; Prof. *Reg. Cant*; Gervase, i. 176; *Ann. Theokesb.* p. 49.

A. D. **1164**, Aug. 23. **Roger of Gloucester.** Worcester; d. 1179, Aug. 9.
Consecrated at Canterbury by Archbishop Thomas; Prof. *Reg. Cant.*;
Gervase, i. 182; *Ann. Theokesb.* p. 49.

A. D. **1174**, April 7. **Richard** (of Dover). Canterbury; d. 1184, Feb. 16.
Consecrated at Anagni by Pope Alexander III; Gervase i. 247; R. Diceto,
i. 389.

A. D. **1174**, June 23. **Reginald FitzJocelin.** Bath; Canterbury, (elected
Nov. 27) 1191; d. 1191, Dec. 26.
Consecrated at S. Jean de Maurienne by Archbishop Richard and the
Archbishop Peter of Tarentaise; Prof. *Reg. Cant.*; Gervase, i. 251;
R. Diceto, i. 391.

A. D. **1174**, Oct. 6. **Richard of Ilchester.** Winchester; d. 1188, Dec. 22.
   Geoffrey Ridel. Ely; d. 1189, Aug. 21.
   Robert Foliot. Hereford; d. 1186, May 9; and
   John Greenford. Chichester; d. 1180, Apr. 26.
Consecrated at Canterbury by Archbishop Richard, and Reginald of
Bath; Prof. *Reg. Cant.*; Gervase, i. 251; R. Diceto, i. 392.

A. D. **1175**, Oct. 12. **Adam** (Canon of Paris). S. Asaph; d. 1181.
Consecrated at Westminster by Archbishop Richard; Prof. *Reg. Cant.*;
Gervase, i. 255; ii. 398; R. Diceto, i. 402.

A. D. **1175**, Dec. 14. **John of Oxford.** Norwich; d. 1200, June 2.
Consecrated at Lambeth by Archbishop Richard; Prof. *Reg. Cant.*;
Gervase, ii. 398; R. Diceto, i. 403; Cont. Flor. Wig. ii. 155.

A. D. **1176**, Nov. 7. **Peter de Leia.** S. David's; d. 1198, July 16.
Consecrated at Canterbury by Gilbert of London, Walter of Rochester, and
Roger of Worcester; Prof. *Reg. Cant.*; Gervase, i. 260; R. Diceto, i. 415.

A. D. **1177**, May 22. **Guy (Guianus).** Bangor; d. 1190.
Consecrated at Amesbury by Archbishop Richard, Bartholomew of
Exeter, John of Norwich, Reginald of Bath, and Adam of S. Asaph;
Prof. *Reg. Cant.*; Gervase, ii. 398; Ben. Peterb. i. 165; R. Diceto, i. 420.

A. D. **1180**, Aug. 10. **Baldwin.** Worcester; Canterbury, 1185; d. 1190,
Nov. 19.
Consecrated at Lambeth by Archbishop Richard; Prof. *Reg. Cant.*;
Gervase, i. 294; ii. 398; *Ann. Theokesb.* p. 52.

E

A. D. 1180, Nov. 16.   **Seffrid II.**   Chichester; d. 1204, Mar. 17.
Consecrated at Canterbury by Archbishop Richard; Prof. *Reg. Cant.*;
Gervase, i. 295.

A. D. 1182, Dec. 19.   **Waleram.**   Rochester; d. 1184, Aug. 29.
Consecrated at Lisieux by Archbishop Richard; Prof. *Reg. Cant.*;
Gervase, i. 306; R. Diceto, ii. 14.

A. D. 1183, July 3.   **Walter of Coutances.**   Lincoln; Rouen, 1184; d. 1207,
Nov. 16; and
John.   S. Asaph; d. 1186.
Consecrated at Angers by Archbishop Richard; R. Diceto, ii. 15, 20;
33, 145; *Ann. Cestrienses* (ed. Christie), p. 28.

A. D. 1183, Sept. 25.   **Gerard la Pucelle.**   Lichfield; d. 1184, Jan. 13.
Consecrated at Canterbury by Archbishop Richard, Reginald of Bath,
Baldwin of Worcester, Peter of S. David's, and Walter of Rochester;
Prof. *Reg. Cant.*; Gervase, i. 307; R. Diceto, ii. 20.

A. D. 1185, Sept. 29.   **Gilbert Glanville.**   Rochester; d. 1214, June 24.
Consecrated at Canterbury by Archbishop Baldwin, Reginald of Bath,
Peter of S. David's, and Seffrid of Chichester; Prof. *Reg. Cant.*;
Gervase, i. 330, 331; R. Diceto, ii. 38.

A. D. 1186, Aug. 10.   **William Saltmarsh.**   Llandaff; d. 1191; and
William de Vere.   Hereford; d. 1198, Dec. 24.
Consecrated at Lambeth by Archbishop Baldwin; Prof. *Reg. Cant.*;
Gervase, ii. 405; R. Diceto, ii. 41.

A. D. 1186, Sept. 21.   **Hugh of Avalon.**   Lincoln; d. 1200, Nov. 17; and
William of Northall.   Worcester; d. 1190, May 3.
Consecrated at Westminster in S. Catharine's chapel by Archbishop
Baldwin; Prof. *Reg. Cant.*; Gervase, ii. 405; R. Diceto, ii. 42.

A. D. 1186.   **Reiner.**   S. Asaph; d. 1224.
Consecrated by Archbishop Baldwin; Prof. *Reg. Cant.*; Gervase, ii. 405.

A. D. 1186, Oct. 5.   **John the Chantor.**   Exeter; d. 1191, June 1.
Consecrated by Archbishop Baldwin; Prof. *Reg. Cant.*; Gervase, ii. 405;
R. Diceto, ii. 43.

A. D. **1188**, Jan. 31. **Hugh of Nonant.** Lichfield ; d. 1198, Mar. 27.
  Consecrated at Lambeth by Archbishop Baldwin ; Gervase, i. 406 ; Prof.
  Reg. Cant.

A. D. **1189**, Sept. 17. **John.** Whithern ; d. 1209, Apr. 26.
  Consecrated at Pipewell by John of Dublin, Fulmar of Treves, and
  Concord of Enaghdun ; Ben. Pet. ii. 87.

A. D. **1189**, Oct. 22. **Hubert Walter.** Salisbury ; Canterbury, 1193 ; d.
                  1205, July 13 ; and
          Godfrey de Lucy. Winchester ; d. 1204, Sept. 11.
  Consecrated at Westminster in S. Catharine's chapel by Archbishop
  Baldwin ; Prof. *Reg. Cant.* ; R. Diceto, ii. 71 ; Gervase, ii. 405 ; *Ann.
  Margam*, p. 20 ; R. Devizes (ed. Howlett), p. 387.
  The bishops were assembled to hear the quarrel between the Archbishop
  and the monks ; present : Lichfield, S. David's, Rochester, Bath, and
  Durham ; Gervase, i. 464 sq.

A. D. **1189**, Nov. 19. **Bernard.** Ragusa ; administrator of Carlisle, **1203**.
  Consecrated by Pope Clement III at Rome (Bull, Nov. 25) ; Farlati,
  Illyricum Sacrum, vi. 83.

A. D. **1189**, Dec. 31. **William Longchamp.** Ely ; d. 1197, Jan. 31 ; and
          Richard FitzNeal. London ; d. 1198, Sept. 10.
  Consecrated at Lambeth by Archbishop Baldwin ; Prof. *Reg. Cant.* ;
  R. Diceto, ii. 75 ; Gervase, i. 483.

A. D. **1191**, May 5. **Robert FitzRalph.** Worcester ; d. 1193, June 26.
  Consecrated at Canterbury by William of Ely, Godfrey of Winchester,
  Reginald of Bath, Seffrid of Chichester, Gilbert of Rochester, and
  Hugh of Lichfield ; Prof. *Reg. Cant.* ; R. Diceto, ii. 89 ; Gervase, i.
  491 ; *Waverley*, p. 247.

A. D. **1191**, Aug. 18. **Geoffrey.** York ; d. 1212, Dec. 18.
  Consecrated at Tours by Bartholomew, Archbishop of Tours, Henry of
  Bayeux, and eight others : six suffragans of Tours ; R. Diceto, ii. 96.

A. D. **1192**, Sept. 20. **Savaric fitzGeldewin.** Bath ; d. 1205, Aug. 8.
  Consecrated at Rome by Alban, Bishop of Albano ; R. Diceto, ii. 106.

A. D. **1193**, Dec. 12.   **Henry de Soilli.**   Worcester; d. 1195, Oct. 24; and
                   Henry of Abergavenny.   Llandaff; d. 1218, Nov. 12.
    Consecrated at Canterbury by Archbishop Hubert; Gervase, ii. 410;
      Adam of Domerham (ed. Hearne, p. 359).

A. D. **1194**, Feb. 10 x Mar. 29.   **Henry Marshall.**   Exeter; d. 1206, Nov. 1.
    Consecrated by Archbishop Hubert; Prof. *Reg. Cant.* ; Gervase, ii. 410;
      Hoveden, iii. 237, 241.

A. D. **1194**, June 5.   **Herbert le Poor.**   Salisbury; d. 1217, Feb. 6.
    Consecrated at Westminster in S. Catharine's chapel by Archbishop
      Hubert; R. Diceto, ii. 116; Prof. *Reg. Cant.* ; Gervase, i. 527.

A. D. **1195**, Apr. 16.   **Alan.**   Bangor; d. 1196, May 19.
    Consecrated by Archbishop Hubert; Prof. *Reg. Cant.* ; Gervase, ii. 410;
      Ann. Theokesb. p. 55; *Ann. Southwark,* MS. ; *Flores,* ii. 113.

A. D. **1196**, Oct. 20.   **John of Coutances.**   Worcester; d. 1198, Sept. 24.
    Consecrated at Ham Abbey, Stratford, by Archbishop Hubert; Prof.
      Reg. Cant. ; R. Diceto, ii. 146; Gervase, i. 543.

A. D. **1197**, Mar. 16.   **Robert of Shrewsbury.**   Bangor; d. 1213.
    Consecrated at Westminster by Archbishop Hubert; Prof. *Reg. Cant.* ;
      Gervase, ii. 410; *Ann. Southwark,* MS. ; *Flores,* ii. 117.

A. D. **1197**, April 20.   **Philip of Poictou.**   Durham; d. 1208, April 22.
    Consecrated at Rome by Pope Celestine III ; in the Lateran; Colding-
      ham (*Scriptt. Dunelm.*), c. xii.

A. D. **1198**, Mar. 8.   **Eustace.**   Ely; d. 1215, Feb. 3.
    Consecrated in S. Catharine's chapel, Westminster, by Archbishop Hubert
      and nine bishops; R. Diceto, ii. 159; Gervase, i. 551; Cont. Flor.
      Wig. ii. 163.

A. D. **1198**, June 21.   **Geoffrey Muschamp.**   Lichfield; d. 1208, Oct. 6.
    Consecrated at Canterbury by Archbishop Hubert; R. Diceto, ii. 162;
      Gervase, i. 554, 556; ii. 410.   The Bishops of Rochester, Chichester,
      Salisbury, Exeter, and Worcester present. *Epp. Cantuar.* p. 410.

A. D. **1199**, May 23. **William of S. Mere l'Eglise.** London, res. 1221, Jan. 26; d. 1224, Mar. 27.

Consecrated at S. Catharine's, Westminster, by Archbishop Hubert and thirteen bishops. They were assembled for John's coronation : Godfrey of Winchester, John of Norwich, Seffrid of Chichester, Gilbert of Rochester, Savaric of Bath, Henry of Llandaff, Henry of Exeter, Herbert of Salisbury, Eustace of Ely, Geoffrey of Lichfield, Hugh of Lincoln, Philip of Durham, and the Archbishops of Dublin and Ragusa; Hoveden, iv. 90; R. Diceto, ii. 166; Gervase, ii. 410.

A. D. **1200**, June 4. **Mauger.** Worcester; d. 1212, July 1.

Consecrated at S. Peter's, Rome, by Pope Innocent III; R. Diceto, ii. 168.

A. D. **1200**, June 24. **John de Gray.** Norwich; d. 1214, Oct. 18.
                         Giles de Braose. Hereford; d. 1215, Nov. 17.

These two bishops were consecrated in S. Catharine's chapel in West-- minster Abbey by Archbishop Hubert, 'praesentibus pluribus ejus suffraganeis;' the bishops then in council at Westminster being : William of London, Gilbert of Rochester, Reiner of S. Asaph, Henry of Llandaff, Henry of Exeter, Herbert of Sarum, Robert of Bangor, Eustace of Ely, and Geoffrey of Lichfield; R. Diceto, ii. 169; *Ann. Southwark*, MS. Cotton Faustina A. 8.

A. D. **1203**, Aug. 24. **William de Blois.** Lincoln; d. 1206, May 10.

Consecrated at Westminster by William, Bishop of London, Gilbert of Rochester, Henry of Exeter, Savaric of Bath, Herbert of Sarum, Geoffrey of Lichfield, and Giles of Hereford; 'alii episcopi tam Angliae quam Walliae litteras excusatorias archiepiscopo miserunt praeter G. Wintoniensem qui recessit indignans eo quod consecratio episcopi eidem non concederetur;' Prof. *Reg. Cant.*; cf. M. Paris, ii. 484; Girald. Cambr. *Opp*. iii. 304; *Ann. Southwark*, MS.

A. D. **1203**, Dec. 7. **Geoffrey de Henlaw.** S. David's; d. 1214.

Consecrated at Westminster in S. Catharine's chapel by Archbishop Hubert, William of London, Gilbert of Rochester, Henry of Exeter, Mauger of Worcester, William of Lincoln, and Maurice of Cork; Prof. *Reg. Cant.*; Ann. Menevenses, *Ang. Sac*. ii. 650; Gir. Cambr. *Opp*. iii. 324.

A. D. **1204**, July 11. **Simon de Wells.** Chichester; d. 1207.

Consecrated at Westminster by Archbishop Hubert; Prof. *Reg. Cant.*

A. D. **1205**, Sept. 25.   **Peter des Roches.**   Winchester ; d. 1238, June 9.

Consecrated at Rome in St. Peter's by Pope Innocent III ; *Ann. South-wark*, MS. ; *Ann. Winton.* p. 79.

A. D. **1206**, May 28.   **Jocelin.**   Bath ; d. 1242, Nov. 19.

Consecrated in the chapel of S. Mary, Reading, by William, Bishop of London, Herbert of Sarum, John of Norwich, Eustace of Ely, Henry of Exeter, Mauger of Worcester, Simon of Chichester, Geoffrey of Lichfield, Robert of Bangor, Henry of Llandaff, and Reiner of S. Asaph ; Prof. & Letters, *Reg. Cant.* ; *Ann. Southwark*, MS. ; M. Paris, ii. 495.

A. D. **1207**, June 17.   **Stephen Langton.**   Canterbury ; d. 1228, July 9.

Consecrated at Viterbo by Pope Innocent III ; M. Paris, ii. 515.

A. D. **1209**, Dec. 20.   **Hugh de Wells.**   Lincoln ; d. 1235, Feb. 7.

Consecrated by Archbishop Stephen at Melun ; M. Paris, ii. 528 ; Cont. Flor. Wig. ii. 168.

A. D. **1214**, Oct. 5.   **Walter de Gray.**   Worcester ; York, 1216 ; d. 1255, May 1 ; and

        Simon of Apulia.   Exeter ; d. 1223, Sept. 9.

These two bishops were consecrated at Canterbury by Archbishop Stephen, William of London, Peter of Winchester, Reiner of S. Asaph, Eustace of Ely, Jocelin of Bath, and Hugh of Lincoln ; Prof. *Reg. Cant.* ; M. Paris, ii. 581 ; Cont. Gerv. ii. 108.

A. D. **1215**, Jan. 25.   **Richard le Poor.**   Chichester ; Sarum, 1217 ; Durham, 1228 ; d. 1237, Apr. 15 ; and

        William of Cornhill.   Lichfield ; d. 1223, Aug. 19.

The two bishops were consecrated at Reading, 'in capella infirmaria,' by Archbishop Stephen ; Prof. *Reg. Cant.* ; *Ann. Southwark*, MS. ; *Ann. Waverley*, p. 282 ; Cont. Gerv. ii. 109.

A. D. **1215**, Feb. 22.   **Benedict of Sansetun.**   Rochester ; d. 1226, Dec. 18.

Consecrated at Osney, by Archbishop Stephen ; *Ann. Southwark*, MS. ; Prof. *Reg. Cant.* ; Cont. Gerv. ii. 109.

A. D. **1215**, June 21.   **Gervase.**   S. David's ; d. 1229.

Consecrated by the Archbishop at Staines ; *Ann. Southwark*, MS. ; *Ann. Cambr.* p. 72.

A. D. **1215**, June 21.   **Martin**, alias **Caducan**.   Bangor; d. 1241, Apr. 11.

Consecrated at Staines by the Archbishop, *Ann. Southwark*, MS.; *Ann. Wig.* (Jun. 16), p. 404; see *Brut y Tywysogion*, p. 285; Prynn's *Records*, iii. 30; *Ann. Theokesb.* p. 61.

A. D. **1216**, July 3.   **Silvester of Evesham**.   Worcester; d. 1218, July 16.

Consecrated at Perugia by Pope Innocent III; *Ann. Wig.* p. 405; *Ann. Theokesb.* p. 62.

A. D. **1216**, Dec. 18.   **Hugh of Mapenor**.   Hereford; d. 1219, Apr. 13.

Consecrated at Gloucester by Silvester of Worcester, Simon of Meath, Reiner of S. Asaph, Henry of Llandaff, and Gervase of S. David's; *Ann. Wig.* p. 406; *Waverley*, p. 287.

A. D. **1217**, July 2.   **Richard Marsh**.   Durham; d. 1226, May 1.

Consecrated at S. Oswald's, Gloucester, by Walter, Archbishop of York; *Graystanes* (*Scriptt. Dunelm.*), c. 1; *Ann. Waverley*, p. 288.

A. D. **1218**, Jan. 7.   **Ralph of Wareham**.   Chichester; d. 1222, Apr. 15.

Consecrated at Canterbury by William of London, Jocelin of Bath, and Benedict of Rochester; Prof. *Reg. Cant.*; *Registrum Roffense* (ed. Thorpe), p. 56.

A. D. **1218**, Oct. 7.   **William of Blois**.   Worcester; d. 1236, Aug. 18.

Consecrated at Westminster by Archbishop Stephen; Prof. *Reg. Cant.*; *Ann. London.* p. 22.

A. D. **1219**, Feb. 24.   **Hugh of Beaulieu**.   Carlisle; d. 1223, June 4.

Consecrated at York by [Archbishop Walter, and] Robert of Waterford; cf. *Close Rolls*, i. 392.

A. D. **1219**, Oct. 27.   **Hugh Foliot**.   Hereford; d. 1234, July 26; and **William of Goldclive**.   Llandaff; d. 1230, Jan. 28.

Consecrated together at Canterbury by Archbishop Stephen; Prof. *Reg. Cant.*; *Ann. Margam*, p. 16.

A. D. **1220**, Mar. 8.   **John of Fountains**.   Ely; d. 1225, May 6.

Consecrated at Westminster by Archbishop Stephen; M. Paris, iii. 58; *Hist. Eliens. Ang. Sac.* i. 635.

A. D. **1220**.   **Luke Netterville**.   Armagh; d. 1227, Apr. 17.

Consecrated by Archbishop Stephen; Ware, *Armagh*, p. 12.

A. D. **1221**, Apr. 25.   **Eustace Fauconberg.**   London ; d. 1228, Nov. 2.

Consecrated at Westminster in S. Catharine's chapel by Benedict of Rochester, Jocelin of Bath, Richard of Sarum [William of Lichfield, Ralph of Chichester, and John of Ely] ; *Ann. London.* p. 23 ; *Ann. Southwark*, MS. Walt. Covent. ii ; M. Paris, iii. 66 ; Letters in *Reg. Cant.*

A. D. **1222**, May 29.   **Pandulf Masca.**   Norwich ; d. 1226, Sept. 16.

Consecrated at Rome by Pope Honorius III ; *Ann. Waverley*, p. 296 ; *Papal Registers*, i. 88.

A. D. **1224**, Dec. 7 x May 6.   **Walter Mauclerc.**   Carlisle ; res. 1246, July 13 ; d. 1248, Oct. 28.

Consecrated by Archbishop Walter of York ; Raine, iii. 121 ; *Ann. Waverley*, p. 299.

A. D. **1224**, Apr. 14.   **Alexander Stavensby.**   Lichfield ; d. 1238, Dec. 26.

Consecrated at Rome by Pope Honorius III ; *Ann. Southwark*, MS. ; *Ann. Waverley*, p. 299.

A. D. **1224**, Apr. 21.   **William Briwere.**   Exeter ; d. 1244, Oct. 24 ; and
Ralph Neville.   Chichester ; d. 1244, Feb. 1.

Consecrated at Westminster in S. Catharine's chapel by Archbishop Langton ; Prof. *Reg. Cant.* ; Cont. Gerv. ii. 113 ; *Ann. Southwark*, MS. ; *Ann. Waverley*, p. 299.

A. D. **1225**, June 29.   **Geoffrey de Burgh.**   Ely ; d. 1228, Dec. 8 ; and
Abraham.   S. Asaph ; d. 1233.

Consecrated at Westminster by Archbishop Langton ; *Ann. Southwark*, MS. ; *Ann. Waverley*, p. 301 ; *Ann. Wig.* p. 417.

A. D. **1226**, Dec. 20.   **Thomas Blunville.**   Norwich ; d. 1236, Aug. 16.

Consecrated at Westminster in S. Catharine's chapel by Archbishop Langton ; Prof. & Letters in *Reg. Cant.* ; *Ann. Waverley*, p. 302 ; *Ann. Southwark*, MS. [Eight bishops were with the Archbishop at this date ; *Foed.* i. 184.]

A. D. **1227**, May 9.   **Henry Sandford.**   Rochester ; d. 1235, Feb. 24.

Consecrated in the Palace at Canterbury by Archbishop Langton, Peter of Winchester, and William of Exeter ; Edm. Hadenham, *Ang. Sac.* i. 348 ; Cont. Gerv. ii. 115.

A. D. **1229**, May 27. **Robert Bingham.** Salisbury; d. 1246, Nov. 3.
Consecrated at Wilton by Jocelin of Bath, William of Worcester, and Alexander of Lichfield; *Ann. Waverley*, p. 307.

A. D. **1229**, June 10. **Roger Niger.** London; d. 1241, Sept. 29; and **Hugh Norwold.** Ely; d. 1254, Aug. 6.
Consecrated by Jocelin, Bishop of Bath, in the infirmary chapel at Canterbury.

A. D. **1229**, June 10. **Richard le Grant.** Canterbury; d. 1231, Aug. 3.
Consecrated at the high altar at Canterbury by Henry of Rochester; *Chron. Dover*; Cont. Gerv. ii. 128; R. Wendover, ii. 378; M. Paris, iii. 190; *Ann. Waverley*, p. 307.

A. D. **1230**, Dec. 1. **Elias of Radnor.** Llandaff; d. 1240, May 13.
Consecrated at Merton by Archbishop Richard; Prof. *Reg. Cant.*; *Ann. Theokesb.* p. 77.

A. D. **1231**, Feb. 9. **Anselm le Gras.** S. David's; d. 1247.
Consecrated at Canterbury by Archbishop Richard; Prof. *Reg. Cant.*; Cont. Gerv. ii. 128.

A. D. **1234**, April 2. **Edmund Rich.** Canterbury; d. 1240, Nov. 16.
Consecrated at Canterbury by Roger of London, Peter of Winchester, Jocelin of Bath, William of Worcester, William of Exeter, Ralph of Chichester, Henry of Rochester, Robert of Sarum, Hugh of Ely, Luke of Dublin, John of Ferns; *Reg. D. & C. S. Paul's*, i. fol. 18; Cont. Flor. Wig. ii. 176; *Ann. Waverley*, p. 312; *Ann. Lewes*, MS.

A. D. **1234**, Nov. 12. **Ralph of Maidstone.** Hereford; res. 1239, Dec. 17.
Consecrated at Canterbury by Archbishop Edmund; *Ann. Waverley*, p. 316; *Ann. Lewes*, MS.

A. D. **1235**, June 17. **Robert Grosteste.** Lincoln; d. 1253, Oct. 10.
Consecrated at Reading by Archbishop Edmund, Roger of London, Jocelin of Bath, Robert of Sarum, Hugh of Ely, and Ralph of Hereford; Letters in the *Canterbury Register*; *Ann. Wikes*, p. 82; *Ann. Winton.* p. 87; *Ann. Theokesb.* p. 97; *Ann. Elias de Trickingham*, MS. Lambeth, 1106: 'die Sancti Botulfi;' *Papal Letters*, i. 149.

A. D. **1235**, June 17.   **Hugh.**   S. Asaph ; d. 1240.
Consecrated with the Bishop of Lincoln ; Prof. *Reg. Cant.*

A. D. **1235**, Sept. 2.   **Gilbert.**   Whithern ; d. 1253.
Consecrated at York by Archbishop Walter Gray ; *Ann. Mailros,* p. 202.

A. D. **1237**, May 3.   **Walter Cantilupe.**   Worcester ; d. 1266, Feb. 12.
Consecrated at Viterbo by Pope Gregory IX ; *Ann. Wig.* p. 428.

A. D. **1237.   Richard.**   Bangor ; d. 1267.
Consecrated by Archbishop Edmund ; Prof. *Reg. Cant.*

A. D. **1238**, Nov. 21.   **Richard of Wendene (Wendover ?).**   Rochester ;
d. 1250, Oct. 12.
Consecrated in the church of S. Gregory at Canterbury by Archbishop
Edmund and the Bishops of London, Lincoln, Chichester, and Ely ;
Cont. Gerv. ii. 135 ; *Ann. London.* p. 36 ; *Waverley,* p. 319 ; *Flores
Hist.* ii. 226.

A. D. **1239**, Sept. 25.   **William de Raley.**   Norwich ; Winchester, 1244 ;
d. 1250, Sept. 1.
Consecrated at S. Paul's, London, by Archbishop Edmund ; *Ann. Osney,*
p. 86 ; *Waverley,* p. 323 ; *Ann. Wikes,* p. 86 ; M. Paris, iii. 617.

A. D. **1240**, July 1.   **Hugh Pateshull.**   Lichfield ; d. 1241, Dec. 8.
Consecrated at Newark Priory, Guildford, by Archbishop Edmund ;
M. Paris, iv. 31 ; *Ann. Wikes,* p. 88.

A. D. **1240**, Sept. 30.   **Albert of Cologne.**   Armagh ; res. 1247.
Consecrated at Westminster by Walter of Worcester ; M. Paris, iv. 49.

A. D. **1240.   Howel ap Ednevet.**   S. Asaph ; d. 1247.
Consecrated at Boxgrave by Archbishop Edmund ; Letters at Canterbury ;
Wharton, *Bishops of S. Asaph,* pp. 319, 321, 371.

A. D. **1240**, Dec. 23.   **Peter d'Aigueblanche.**   Hereford ; d. 1268, Nov. 27.
Consecrated at S. Paul's, London, by Walter, Bishop of Worcester, the
Archbishop of York, and others ; M. Paris, iv. 75 ; *Chr. Abingdon* ;
Ann. Wikes, p. 88 ; *Wigorn.* p. 432.

A. D. **1241**, June 9. **Nicolas Farnham.** Durham; res. 1249, Feb. 2; d. 1258.

> Consecrated at S. Oswald's, Gloucester, by Walter, Archbishop of York; Graystanes, c. v; *Ann. Winton.* p. 88; *Ann. Wikes* & *Ann. Osney*, p. 88; *Ann. Theokesb.* p. 118.

A. D. **1244**, Sept. 11. **Roger.** Bath; d. 1247, Dec. 21.

> Consecrated at Reading by William of Winchester; *Ann. Winton.* p. 90; *Waverley*, p. 334; Trivet, p. 234; *Ann. Wikes* & *Ann. Osney*, pp. 91, 92; M. Paris, iv. 391.

A. D. **1244**, Oct. 9. **Fulk Bassett.** London; d. 1259, May 20.

> Consecrated at Trinity, Aldgate, by William of Winchester; *Ann. Winton.* p. 90; *Chr. Abingdon.*; *Waverley*, p. 334; *Osney*, p. 92; *Chron. Majorum*, p. 10; M. Paris, iv. 393.

A. D. **1245**, Jan. 15. **Boniface of Savoy.** Canterbury; d. 1270, July 18.

> Consecrated at Lyons by Pope Innocent IV (the Bishops of Hereford and Lincoln were at Lyons); *Ann. Waverley*, p. 335; Cont. Gerv. ii. 202; M. Paris, iv. 425.

A. D. **1245**, Feb. 19. **Walter Suffield.** Norwich; d. 1257, May 18; and **William de Burgh.** Llandaff; d. 1253, June 11.

> Consecrated at Carhow, near Norwich; *Ann. Waverley*, p. 336; Letters in the *Canterbury Register*.

A. D. **1245**, [Feb. 19?]. **Roger Weseham.** Lichfield; res. 1256, Dec. 4; d. 1257, May 20.

> Consecrated at Lyons by Pope Innocent IV; M. Paris, iv. 426.

A. D. **1245**, March 5. **Richard Wych.** Chichester; d. 1253, Apr. 3.

> Consecrated at Lyons by Pope Innocent IV: 'dominica post Cineres;' *Chron. Abingdon.*; *Ann. Wig.* p. 436; M. Paris, iv. 426; *Ann. Waverley*, p. 335.

A. D. **1245**, Oct. 22. **Richard Blondy.** Exeter; d. 1257, Dec. 26.

> Consecrated in the great church at Reading by Fulk, Bishop of London; Letters in *Canterbury Register*; the Archbishop's Commission, &c.; M. Paris, iv. 491.

A. D. **1247**, July 14. **William of York.** Salisbury; d. 1256, Jan. 31.
Consecrated at Wilton by Fulk of London; *Ann. Winton.* p. 91; *Ann. Osney* & *Ann. Wikes*, p. 96; Cautions in *Reg. Cant.*

A. D. **1247**, Oct. 13. **Silvester Everdon.** Carlisle; d. 1254, May 13.
Consecrated at S. Agatha's (Easby) near Richmond; *Chr. Lanercost*, p. 53; *Ann. Wikes*, p. 94; M. Paris, iv. 645.

A. D. **1248**, June 14. **William Button.** Bath; d. 1264, Apr. 3.
Consecrated at Lyons by Pope Innocent IV; Profession in *Reg. Cant.*

A. D. **1248**, July 26. **Thomas Wallensis.** S. David's; d. 1255, July 11.
Consecrated at Canterbury by Robert, Bishop of Lincoln; Profession in *Reg. Cant.*; *Ann. Osney*, p. 97; *Ann. Wikes*, p. 97.

A. D. **1249**, November. **Anian.** S. Asaph; d. 1266.
Consecrated by the bishops Walter of Worcester, Richard of Bangor, and Richard of Meath; *Ann. Wig.* p. 439; Wharton, *Bishops of S. Asaph*, p. 322.

A. D. **1249**, Dec. 5. **Walter Kirkham.** Durham; d. 1260, Aug. 9.
Consecrated at York by Archbishop Walter Gray; *Graystanes*, c. vi.

A. D. **1251**, April 9. **Laurence of S. Martin.** Rochester; d. 1274, June 3.
Consecrated at Lyons by Archbishop Boniface; Ann. Roffen. *Ang. Sac.* i. 350.

A. D. **1254**, Jan. 11. **John de la Ware.** Llandaff; d. 1256, June 30; and
John Bishop. Chichester; d. 1262.
Consecrated at Canterbury by Archbishop Boniface, Fulk of London, Walter of Worcester, and William of Bath; *Ann. Theokesb.* p. 153; Prof. *Reg. Cant.*

A. D. **1254**, May 17. **Henry Lexington.** Lincoln; d. 1258, Aug. 8.
Consecrated at the New Temple in London by Archbishop Boniface, Fulk of London, Walter of Worcester, Walter of Norwich, and William of Bath; Prof. *Reg. Cant.*; *Ann. Winton.* p. 94.

A. D. **1255**, Feb. 7. **Thomas Vipont.** Carlisle; d. 1256, Oct. —; and
Henry. Whithern; d. 1293, Nov. 1.
Consecrated at S. Agatha's, Easby, by Walter, Bishop of Durham; *Ann. Lanercost*, p. 62.

A. D. **1255**, Aug. 15.   **William de Kilkenny.**   Ely; d. 1256, Sept. 22.
   Consecrated at Belley by Archbishop Boniface, Arnold of Tarentaise, and John of Belley : Prof. *Reg. Cant.* ; M. Paris, v. 508.

A. D. **1256**, Mar.   **Richard Carew.**   S. David's; d. 1280, Apr. 1.
   Consecrated at Rome by Pope Alexander IV ; Prof. *Reg. Cant.* ; Ann. Menev. *Ang. Sac.* ii. 650 ; *Papal Letters*, i. 327, 328.

A. D. **1256**, July 23.   **Sewall de Bovill.**   York ; d. 1258, May 10.
   Consecrated at York by Walter of Worcester and Walter of Durham ; *Reg. Magnum Album* at York ; *Ann. Wikes*, p. 110.

A. D. **1257**, Jan. 7.   **William of Radnor.**   Llandaff; d. 1266, Jan. 9.
   Consecrated at S. Paul's by Archbishop Boniface, Walter of Worcester, and Walter of Norwich ; Letters in *Reg. Cant.*

A. D. **1257**, Mar. 11.   **Giles of Bridport.**   Salisbury ; d. 1262, Dec. 13.
   Consecrated at Canterbury by Archbishop Boniface, Walter of Worcester, Walter of Norwich, and William of Bath ; Prof. *Reg. Cant.* ; Cont. Gerv. ii. 205 ; *Ann. Winton.* p. 95.

A. D. **1257**, Oct. 14.   **Hugh Belsham.**   Ely; d. 1286, June 15.
   Consecrated at Viterbo by Pope Alexander IV ; Prof. *Reg. Cant.* ; Gerv. ii. 206 ; *Chron. Dover*, MS. ; Hist. Eliens. *Ang. Sac.* i. 637.

A. D. **1258**, Mar. 10.   **Roger Longespee.**   Lichfield ; d. 1295, Dec. 16.
                    Walter Bronscombe.   Exeter ; d. 1280, July 22.
                    Simon de Wauton.   Norwich ; d. 1266, Jan. 2.
   Consecrated at Canterbury by Archbishop Boniface, Giles of Salisbury, and William of Bath ; Prof. *Reg. Cant.* ; Cont. Gerv. ii. 206 ; Barth. Cotton, p. 137 : *Reg. Bronscombe* at Exeter ; *Ann. Wikes*, p. 118 ; M. Paris, v. 667.

A. D. **1258**, Apr. 14.   **Robert de Chause.**   Carlisle ; d. 1278, Sept.
   Consecrated at Bermondsey by William of Bath and Giles of Sarum ; M. Paris, v. 678.

A. D. **1258**, Sept. 22.   **Godfrey Ludham** or **de Kineton.**   York ; d. 1265, Jan. 12.
   Consecrated at Viterbo by Pope Alexander IV ; M. Paris, v. 718.

A. D. **1258**, Nov. 3. **Richard Gravesend.** Lincoln; d. 1279, Dec. 18.

> Consecrated at Canterbury by Archbishop Boniface, Walter of Worcester, Walter of Exeter, and Simon of Norwich; Prof. *Reg. Cant.*; M. Paris, v. 721; *Ann. Osney*, p. 122.

A. D. **1260**, Feb. 15. **Henry Wengham.** London; d. 1262, July 13.

> Consecrated at S. Mary, Overies, by Archbishop Boniface, Walter of Worcester, Laurence of Rochester, Giles of Sarum, Roger of Lichfield, Walter of Exeter, and Simon of Norwich; Prof. *Reg. Cant.*; Cont. Gerv. ii. 208; *Ann. Wikes*, p. 122; *Ann. Osney*, p. 125; *Chron. Majorum*, p. 44; *Flores*, ii. 443.

A. D. **1260**, May 16. **Aymer of Lusignan.** Winchester; d. 1260, Dec. 4.

> Consecrated 'in curia Romana' (Anagni) by Pope Alexander IV; *Ann. Osney*, p. 125; *Ann. Winton.* p. 98.

A. D. **1261**, Feb. 13. **Robert de Stichill.** Durham; d. 1274, Aug. 4.

> Consecrated at Southwell by Godfrey of York; *Graystanes*, c. vii. p. 45.

A. D. **1262**, Sept. 10. **John Gervais.** Winchester; d. 1268, Jan. 20.

> Consecrated 'in curia Romana' (Montefiascone) by Pope Urban IV; *Chron. Lewes*, MS.; Prof. *Reg. Cant.*

A. D. **1262**, Sept. 24. **Stephen Berksted.** Chichester; d. 1287, Oct. 30.

> Consecrated at Canterbury by Archbishop Boniface, William of Llandaff, and Walter of Exeter; Prof. *Reg. Cant.*; *Ann. Wikes*, p. 133; Cont. Gerv. ii. 214.

A. D. **1263**, May 27. **Henry Sandwich.** London; d. 1273, Sept. 12; and **Walter de la Wyle.** Salisbury; d. 1271, Jan. 3.

> Consecrated at Canterbury by John of Winchester, Walter of Worcester, William of Llandaff, Richard of Lincoln, and Stephen of Chichester; Cont. Gerv. ii. 220; *Ann. Wikes*, p. 133.

A. D. **1265**, Jan. 4. **Walter Giffard.** Bath; York, 1266; d. 1279, Apr. 22.

> Consecrated at Paris in Notre Dame by Peter of Hereford; *Chron. Lewes*, MS.; Prof. *Reg. Cant.*

A. D. **1266**, April 4. **Roger Skerning.** Norwich; d. 1278, Jan. 22.

Consecrated at S. Paul's, London, by the Archbishop of Rages in Media; *Ann. London.* p. 73; *Chron. Dover*, MS.; Cont. Gerv. ii. 244; *Ann. Wikes*, p. 190.

A. D. **1266**, Sept. 19. **Nicolas of Ely.** Worcester; Winchester, 1268; d. 1280, Feb. 12; and

William Bruce. Llandaff; d. 1287, Mar. 19.

Consecrated at Canterbury by Archbishop Boniface; Prof. *Reg. Cant.*; *Ann. London.* p. 75; *Ann. Wig.* p. 456; *Ann. Winton.* p. 104.

A. D. **1267**, after Easter. **William Button.** Bath; d. 1274, Dec. 4.

Consecrated at Farnham by Nicolas of Worcester; Cont. Gerv. ii. 245; *Chron. Dover*, MS.; *Ann. London.* p. 79.

A. D. **1267.** **John.** S. Asaph; d. 1267 or 8.

Consecrated at Canterbury by Archbishop Boniface, Hugh of Ely, and William of Llandaff; Prof. *Reg. Cant.*

A. D. **1267.** **Anian.** Bangor; d. 1305.

Consecrated at Canterbury by Archbishop Boniface, Hugh of Ely, and William of Llandaff; Prof. *Reg. Cant.*

A. D. **1268**, Sept. 23. **Godfrey Giffard.** Worcester; d. 1302, Jan. 26.

Consecrated at Canterbury by Archbishop Boniface; Prof. *Reg. Cant.*; *Ann. London.* p. 78.

A. D. **1268**, Oct. 21. **Anian Schonaw.** S. Asaph; d. 1293, Feb. 5.

Consecrated at Southwark by Archbishop Boniface, and Walter, Bishop of Exeter; Prof. *Reg. Cant.*; Wharton, *Epp. Asav.* p. 324.

A. D. **1269**, June 2. **John Breton.** Hereford; d. 1275, May 12.

Consecrated at Waverley by Nicolas of Winchester, Godfrey of Worcester, Richard of S. David's, William of Bath, William of Llandaff, Walter of Exeter, Walter of Salisbury, and Roger of Lichfield; *Ann. Waverley*, p. 376; *Ann. Winton.* p. 107.

A. D. **1273**, Feb. 26. **Robert Kilwardby.** Canterbury ; Portus, 1278 ;
d. 1279.

> Consecrated at Canterbury by William of Bath, Nicolas of Winchester,
> Hugh of Ely, Walter of Exeter, Godfrey of Worcester, Anian of
> S. Asaph (*Polistorie*, MS.) ; Anian of Bangor (Cont. Gerv. ii. 273) ;
> Laurence of Rochester, Richard of Lincoln, Roger of Lichfield (*Chron.*
> *Maj.* p. 157) ; Roger of Norwich : 'undecim episcopis,' *Rishanger*,
> p. 72. The absentees were London, Hereford, and Chichester ; Salis-
> bury was vacant, S. David's and Llandaff were in the Archbishop's
> company a few days before, and probably were present : cf. Wilkins,
> *Conc.* ii. 24.

A. D. **1274**, Apr. 29. **John Chishull.** London ; d. 1280, Feb. 8.

> Consecrated at Lambeth by Godfrey of Worcester (*Ann. Wikes*, p. 257),
> Anian of S. Asaph (*Chron. Maj.* p. 164) : 'assistentibus etiam pluribus
> aliis episcopis.'

A. D. **1274**, May 13. **Robert Wickhampton.** Salisbury ; d. 1284, Apr. 24.

> Consecrated at Lyons by the Archbishop of Canterbury, and Laurence of
> Rochester ; Letters in the *Canterbury Register* ; *Waverley*, p. 383 ;
> *Ann. Wikes*, p. 258 ; *Ann. Winton.* p. 118.

A. D. **1274**, Oct. 21. **Walter de Merton.** Rochester ; d. 1277, Oct. 27.

> Consecrated by Archbishop Robert at Gillingham ; Prof. *Reg. Cant.* :
> Letters in *Reg. Cant.* ; *Ann. Wikes*, p. 260 ; *Waverley*, p. 117 ; Cont.
> Gerv. ii. 278 ; Ann. Roff. *Ang. Sac.* i. 500 ; *Flores Hist.* iii. 44.

A. D. **1274**, Dec. 9. **Robert of Holy Island.** Durham ; d. 1283, June 7.

> Consecrated at York by Archbishop Walter ; *Graystanes*, c. xiv ;
> *Waverley*, p. 383.

A. D. **1275**, Apr. 7. **Robert Burnell.** Bath ; d. 1292, Oct. 25.

> Consecrated at Merton by Archbishop Robert : Letters at Canterbury ;
> *Ann. Wikes*, p. 263 ; *Waverley*, p. 384 ; Cont. Gerv. ii. 279 ; *Poli-*
> *storie*, MS.

A. D. **1275**, Sept. 8. **Thomas Cantilupe.** Hereford ; d. 1282, Aug. 25.

> Consecrated at Canterbury by Archbishop Robert, John of London, and
> Walter of Rochester ; Cont. Gerv. ii. 280 : 'les autres tous absens,
> dont se ennouya trop lerceveske, et plus charga les veysins de cel elit

eveskes de Gales ne venir ne voloyent ne ens duement excuser ; '
Polistorie, MS. ; Cont. Gerv. ii. 280 ; *Ann. London.* p. 85 ; *Ann. Wikes*,
p. 265.

A. D. **1276**, Mar. 29.   **Gerard Grandison.**   Verdun ; d. 1278.
   Consecrated at Merton by the Archbishop, John of London, Walter of
   Rochester, Robert of Bath, and William of Llandaff ; MS. Gervas.
   (*Opp.* i. p. liii) ; *Litterae Cantuarienses*, iii. 186.

A. D. **1278**, May 29.   **William Middleton.**   Norwich ; d. 1288, Sept. 1 ; and
                      John Bradfield.   Rochester ; d. 1283, Apr. 23.
   Consecrated at Lambeth by Archbishop Robert ; Prof. *Reg. Cant.* ;
   Ann. Roff. *Ang. Sac.* i. 352 ; *Flores*, iii. 50 ; B. Cotton, 157, 395 ;
   Ann. Wikes, p. 276 ; *Ann. Wigorn.* p. 473 ; ·*Waverley*, p. 389.

A. D. **1279**, Feb. 19.   **John Peckham.**   Canterbury ; d. 1292, Dec. 8.
   Consecrated at Rome by Pope Nicolas III ; *Reg. Peckham* ; Cons. Feb.
   26 ; Cont. Gerv. ii. 291 ; MS. Galba, E. 3.

A. D. **1279**, Aug. 27.   **John Darlington.**   Dublin ; d. 1284, Mar. 28.
   Consecrated at Waltham Abbey by Archbishop John, Nicolas of Winchester, Robert of Bath, and William of Norwich ; John Oxenedes,
   p. 232 ; Cont. Flor. Wig. ii. 222 ; *Ann. Wikes*, p. 282 ; Letter in *Reg.
   Peckham*.

A. D. **1279**, Sept. 17.   **William Wickwane.**   York ; d. 1285, Aug. 26.
   Consecrated at Viterbo by Pope Nicolas III ; Stubbs (Raine, ii), p. 407 ;
   Const. Ebor. MS.

A. D. **1280**, Mar. [25 ?].   **Ralph Ireton.**   Carlisle ; d. 1292, Mar. 1.
   Consecrated, in curia Romana, at Rome by Ordonius, Bishop of Tusculum ; *Papal Letters*, Mar. 28, i. 461 ; Bull, Apr. 9 ; Prynn, *Records*,
   iii. 246 ; *Ann. Dunstable*, p. 283.

A. D. **1280**, May 19.   **Oliver Sutton.**   Lincoln ; d. 1299, Nov. 13.
   Consecrated at Lambeth by Archbishop Peckham ; *Reg. Peckham* ; *Ann.
   Lanercost*, p. 103 ; *Waverley*, p. 392 ; *Peterb.* ed. Giles, p. 153 ; *Ann.
   Dunstable*, p. 283.

F

A. D. **1280**, Aug. 11. **Richard Gravesend.** London; d. 1303, Dec. 9.

Consecrated at Coventry by Archbishop Peckham; *Ann. Wikes*, 284; *Ann. Wigorn.* p. 478; Wilkins, *Conc.* ii. 85; *Waverley*, p. 393.

A. D. **1280**, Oct. 6. **Thomas Beck.** S. David's; d. 1293, Apr. 20.

Consecrated at Lincoln by Archbishop Peckham, the Archbishop of Rages, Oliver of Lincoln, Robert of Bath, Hugh of Ely, William of Norwich, Godfrey of Worcester, William of Llandaff, Anian of Bangor, and Anian of S. Asaph; *Reg. Beck*, MS. Harl. 3720; *Lanercost*, p. 105; *Ann. Osney*, p. 286; *Ann. Wikes*, p. 286; *Chron. Peterb.* (ed. Giles) p. 153.

A. D. **1280**, Nov. 10. **Peter Wyvill.** Exeter; d. 1291, Oct. 4.

Consecrated at Canterbury by Richard of London; *Reg. Peckham*, f. 25; *Ann. Wikes*, p. 284; *Ann. Wigorn.* p. 478.

A. D. **1282**, June 14. **John of Pontoise.** Winchester; d. 1304, Dec. 4.

Consecrated at Orvieto by Latinus, Bishop of Ostia; *Reg. Pontoise*; Trivet, p. 306; Prynn, *Records*, iii. 1255, 1261; *Papal Letters*, i. 466.

A. D. **1283**, March 7. **Richard Swinfield.** Hereford; d. 1317, Mar. 15.

Consecrated at Gloucester by Archbishop Peckham; Prof. *Reg. Cant.*; *Waverley*, p. 405; Prynn, iii. 308.

A. D. **1283**, Sept. 26. **Thomas Ingaldesthorp.** Rochester; d. 1291, May 12.

Consecrated at Canterbury by Archbishop Peckham, John of Dublin, Richard of London, and John of Winchester; Cont. Flor. Wig. ii. 229; Cont. Gerv. ii. 292; *Chron. Dover*, MS.; *Flores*, iii. 50; MS. Galba, E. 3.

A. D. **1284**, Jan. 9. **Antony Beck.** Durham; Patriarch of Jerusalem, 1306, May 4; d. 1311, March 3.

Consecrated at York by William, Archbishop of York, Oliver of Lincoln, Robert of Bath, John of Winchester, William of Norwich, Ralph of Carlisle, Henry of Whithern, Thomas of S. David's; *Reg. A. Beck*, MS. Harl. 3720; Stubbs (Raine), p. 407; *Reg. Ebor.* MS. Lansd. 402; *Ann. Osney*, p. 295; *Ann. Wikes*, p. 295; *Graystanes*, c. xviii; Peterb. p. 154.

A. D. **1284**, Oct. 22. **Walter Scammell.** Salisbury; d. 1286, Sept. 25.

Consecrated at Sonning by Archbishop Peckham; *Ann. Wikes*, p. 297; *Ann. Wigorn.* p. 490; *Waverley*, p. 401; *Ann. Dunstable*, p. 315.

A. D. **1286**, Feb. 10. **John Romanus.** Archbishop of York; d. 1296, Mar. 11.

Consecrated at Rome by Latinus, Bishop of Ostia; *Papal Letters*, i. 483, 484; Stubbs (Raine, ii), p. 408; *Const. Ebor.* MS., Vitellius, A. 2.

A. D. **1286**, Sept. 22. **John Kirkby.** Ely; d. 1290, Mar. 26.

Consecrated at Canterbury by Archbishop Peckham; *Polistorie*, MS.; *Ann. Wikes*, p. 308; Cont. Gerv. ii. 293; *Chron. Dover*, MS.

A. D. **1287**, June 1. **Henry Brandeston.** Salisbury; d. 1288, Feb. 11.

Consecrated at Canterbury by Archbishop Peckham, Godfrey of Worcester, Oliver of Lincoln, and Thomas of Rochester; Cont. Gerv. ii. 293; *Ann. Wikes*, p. 309.

A. D. **1288**, Sept. 5. **Gilbert of S. Leofard.** Chichester; d. 1305, Feb. 12.

Consecrated at Canterbury by Archbishop Peckham; Cont. Gerv. ii. 294.

A. D. **1289**, March 20. **Ralph Walpole.** Norwich; Ely, 1299; d. 1302, Mar. 20.

Consecrated at Canterbury by Archbishop Peckham; Cont. Gerv. ii. 294; *Flores*, iii. 69; Barth. Cotton, p. 170; J. Oxenedes, p. 249; *Ann. Wikes*, p. 316.

A. D. **1289**, May 8. **William de la Corner.** Salisbury; d. 1291, Aug. 14.

Consecrated at Canterbury by Archbishop Peckham; Cont. Gerv. ii. 294; *Polistorie*, MS.; *Ann. Wikes*, p. 317.

A D. **1290**, Oct. 1. **William of Louth.** Ely; d. 1298, Mar. 25.

Consecrated at Ely by Archbishop Peckham, Robert of Bath, John of Winchester, Oliver of Lincoln, Ralph of Norwich, William of Sarum, Peter of Exeter, Anian of S. Asaph; MS. Harl. 258; Bodl. L. 58; Gerv. Cont. ii. 296; *Ann. Wikes*, p. 325; J. Oxenedes, p. 253; *Ann. Wigorn.* p. 503; Cont. Flor. Wig. ii. 243; in the parish church of S. Mary, Prof. *Reg. Cant.*

A. D. **1292**, Jan. 6.   **Thomas of Wouldham.**   Rochester; d. 1317, Feb. 28.
Consecrated at Chartham by Archbishop Peckham; Prof. *Reg. Cant.*;
Cont. Gerv. ii. 297; *Flores*, iii. 74; Barth. Cotton, p. 430.

A. D. **1292**, Mar. 16.   **Thomas Button.**   Exeter; d. 1307, Sept. 26; and
              Nicolas Longespee.   Salisbury; d. 1297, May 18.
Consecrated at Canterbury by Archbishop Peckham; Prof. *Reg. Cant.*;
Cont. Gerv. ii. 299; *Polistorie*, MS.; *Ann. Wikes*, p. 332.

A. D. **1292**, Sept. 14.   **John of Halton.**   Carlisle; d. 1324, Nov. 1.
Consecrated at York.   The Bishops at York at the time were Durham,
Whithern, Bath, and Ely : Rot. Scotiae, 20 Edw. I; *Reg. Halton*; *Reg.
Romaine.*

A. D. **1293**, May 17.   **William of March.**   Bath; d. 1302, June 11; and
              Leoline Bromfield.   S. Asaph; d. 1314.
Consecrated at Canterbury by Richard of London, William of Ely,
Thomas of Rochester, and John of Dublin; *Reg. P. & C. Cant.*; *Ann.
Wigorn.* p. 512; Cont. Gerv. ii. 301; *Flores*, iii. 87.

A. D. **1294**, Sept. 12.   **Robert of Winchelsey.**   Archbishop of Canterbury;
d. 1313, May 11.
Consecrated at Aquila by Gerard, Bishop of Sabina; *Reg. Eastry, Cant.*;
Polistorie, MS.; Cont. Gerv. ii. 307.

A. D. **1294**, Oct. 10.   **Thomas Dalton.**   Whithern.
Consecrated at Gedling, Notts, by Archbishop Romaine, John of Carlisle,
and Leoline of S. Asaph; *Reg. Romaine*; MS. Lansd. 402.

A. D. **1296**, Dec. —.   **David Martin.**   S. David's; d. 1328, Mar. 9.
Consecrated at Rome by Hugh, Bishop of Ostia; Prof. *Reg. Cant.*
(Sept. 21); cf. *Papal Letters*, i. 564; and Close Rolls cited, Prynn, iii.
635–769.

A. D. **1296**, Dec. 23.   **Walter Langton.**   Lichfield; d. 1321, Nov. 9.
Consecrated at Cambray by Berard, Cardinal Bishop of Albano; Cont.
Gerv. ii. 314; *Ann. Dunstable*, p. 400; *Reg. Langton*.

A. D. **1297**, Feb. 10. **John of Monmouth.** Llandaff; d. 1323, Apr. 8.

    Consecrated at Canterbury by Archbishop Winchelsey, Thomas of Rochester, David of S. David's, Robert of Clonfert; *Reg. Winchelsey*; Prof. *Reg. Cant.*

A. D. **1297**, Oct. 20. **Simon of Ghent.** Salisbury; d. 1315; Mar. 31.

    Consecrated at Canterbury by Archbishop Winchelsey; Prof. *Reg. Cant.*; *Reg. Eastry*; *Polistorie*, MS.

A. D. **1297. William Hotham.** Dublin; d. 1298, Aug. 30.

    Consecrated at Ghent by Antony, Bishop of Durham; Trivet, p. 364.

A. D. **1298**, June 15. **Henry Newark.** York; d. 1299, Aug. 15.

    Consecrated at York by Antony of Durham, Leoline of S. Asaph, Walter of Lichfield, and Robert of Cork; *Reg. Newark*; Const. Ebor., Vitellius, A. 2; Hemingburgh, ii. 71.

A. D. **1299**, Nov. 15. **John Salmon.** Norwich; d. 1325, July 6.

    Consecrated by Archbishop Winchelsey at Canterbury; *Reg. Winchelsey*.

A. D. **1300**, Feb. 28. **Thomas Corbridge.** York; d. 1304, Sept. 22.

    Consecrated at Rome by Pope Boniface VIII; Const. Ebor., Vitellius, A. 2; Stubbs, p. 411; Hemingburgh, ii. 87.

A. D. **1300**, June 12. **John Dalderby.** Lincoln; d. 1320, Jan. 5.

    Consecrated at Canterbury by Archbishop Winchelsey, Thomas of Rochester, and Simon of Sarum; *Reg. Eastry, Cant.*; *Reg. Dalderby*; Wilkins, *Conc.* ii. 257; Cont. Gerv. ii. 318.

A. D. **1302**, Oct. 28. **Walter Gainsborough.** Worcester; d. 1307, Sept. 17; and

               Robert Orford. Ely; d. 1310, Jan. 21.

    Consecrated at Rome by Leonard, Bishop of Albano; Prof. *Reg. Cant.*; Letter in Thomas's *Worcester*, App. p. 85; Prynn, iii. 919; *Papal Letters*, i. 604.

A. D. **1302**, Nov. 4. **Walter Haselshaw.** Bath; d. 1308, Dec. 11.

    Consecrated at Canterbury by Archbishop Winchelsey; *Reg. Eastry, Cant.*; Cont. Gerv. ii. 319.

A. D. **1305**, May 30.   **Henry Woodlock.**   Winchester; d. 1316, June 28.
Consecrated at Canterbury by Archbishop Winchelsey; *Reg. Eastry, Cant.*; *Ann. London.* p. 137.

A. D. **1305**, Sept. 19.   **John Langton.**   Chichester; d. 1337, June 17.
Consecrated at Canterbury by Archbishop Winchelsey; *Reg. Eastry, Cant.*; *Ann. London.* p. 142.

A. D. **1306**, Jan. 30.   **Ralph Baldock.**   London; d. 1313, July 24; and
William Greenfield.   York; d. 1315, Dec. 6.
Consecrated at Lyons by Cardinal Peter of Sabina; Const. Ebor., Vitellius, A. 2; Stubbs, p. 413; *Ann. London.* p. 144; Hemingburgh, ii. 233; W. Murimuth, p. 8; Prynn, iii. 1048, 1073.

A. D. **1307**, Mar. 26.   **Griffin ap Yorwerth.**   Bangor; d. 1309, May 27.
Consecrated at Carlisle by Bishop Walter of Lichfield; *Reg. Greenfield*; Prof. *Reg. Cant.* (before Peter of Spain, Card.).

A. D. **1308**, Oct. 13.   **Walter Reynolds.**   Worcester; Canterbury, 1313; d. 1327, Nov. 16; and
Walter de Stapledon.   Exeter; d. 1326, Oct. 15.
Consecrated at Canterbury by Archbishop Winchelsey; *Reg. Eastry, Cant.*

A. D. **1309**, Nov. 9.   **John Drokensford.**   Bath; d. 1329, May 9; and
Anian Seys.   Bangor; d. 1328, Jan 26.
Consecrated at Canterbury by Archbishop Winchelsey; *Reg. Eastry, Cant.*

A. D. **1310**, Sept. 6.   **John Keeton.**   Ely; d. 1316, May 14.
Consecrated at Canterbury by Archbishop Winchelsey; *Reg. Eastry, Cant.*

A. D. **1311**, May 30.   **Richard Kellaw.**   Durham; d. 1316, Oct. 9.
Consecrated at York by Archbishop William, John of Carlisle, Thomas of Whithern, and Andrew of Argyle; *Reg. Greenfield*; *Graystanes*, c. 32; *Chron. Lanercost*, p. 215; Hemingburgh, ii. 285; Raine, *Hist. Ebor.* iii. 233.

A. D. **1313**, Oct. 7. **Walter Maidstone.** Worcester ; d. 1317, Mar. 28.

Consecrated, in curia Romana, by Berengarius of Tusculum at Avignon ; *Reg. Maidstone* ; *Papal Letters*, ii. 115.

A. D. **1313**, Nov. 25. **Gilbert Segrave.** London ; d. 1316, Dec. 18.

Consecrated at Canterbury by Henry, Bishop of Winchester; Profession, *Reg. Cant.* ; *Reg. Eastry* ; *Chron. Joh. London.*

A. D. **1315**, Jan. 12. **David ap Blethyn.** S. Asaph ; d. 1352.

Consecrated at Canterbury by Archbishop Walter : Prof. *Reg. Cant.* ; Simon of Sarum assisting : *Reg. Sarum.*

A. D. **1315**, Sept. 28. **Roger Mortival.** Salisbury ; d. 1330, Mar. 14.

Consecrated at Canterbury by the Archbishop, Gilbert of London, Henry of Winchester, and John of Chichester ; *Reg. Mortival* ; Prof. *Reg. Cant.*

A. D. **1316**, Oct. 3. **John Hotham.** Ely ; d. 1337, Jan. 15.

Consecrated at Canterbury by the Archbishop, Thomas of Rochester, and John of Bath ; Prof. *Reg. Cant.* ; *Reg. Drokensford* at Wells.

A. D. **1316**, Oct. 31. **John Sendale.** Winchester ; d. 1319.

Consecrated at Canterbury by the Archbishop ; *Reg. Sendale* ; Prof. *Reg. Cant.*

A. D. **1317**, May 15. **Richard Newport.** London ; d. 1318, Aug. 24.

Consecrated at Canterbury by the Archbishop, Walter of Lichfield, John of Winchester, and Roger of Sarum ; Prof. *Reg. Cant.* ; *Ann. Paulini*, p. 280.

A. D. **1317**, May 22. **Thomas Cobham.** Worcester ; d. 1327, Aug. 27.

Consecrated at Avignon by Nicolas, Bishop of Ostia ; see John of London, MS. ; *Ang. Sac.* i. 533 ; *Ann. Paulini*, p. 280.

A. D. **1317**, May 22. **Adam Orlton.** Hereford ; Worcester, 1327 ; Winchester, 1333 ; d. 1345, July 18.

Consecrated at Avignon by Nicolas, Bishop of Ostia ; *Reg. Orlton.*

A. D. **1317**, Sept. 25.   **William de Melton.**   Archbishop of York ; d. 1340, Apr. 4.

> Consecrated at Avignon by Pope John XXII ; Stubbs (Raine, ii), p. 415 ; MS. Cotton, Vitellius, A. 2 ; *Papal Letters*, ii. 165.

A. D. **1318**, Mar. 26.   **Lewis de Beaumont.**   Durham ; d. 1333, Sept. 24.

> 'Consecratus est . . . apud Westmonasterium :' *Ann. Paulini*, p. 282 ; 'de manibus episcopi Winton. praesentibus cardinalibus et ignotis episcopis quibusdam ;' Rob. Redding, MS. Harl. 685 ; cf. *Graystanes* (*Scriptt. Dunelm.*), c. 38.

A. D. **1319**, Jan. 14.   **Stephen Gravesend.**   London ; d. 1338, Apr. 8.

> Consecrated by the Archbishop, John of Winchester, John of Chichester, Walter of Exeter, John of Bath, and Thomas of Worcester ; Prof. *Reg. Cant.* ; cf. *Ann. Paulini*, p. 284.

A. D. **1319**, Aug. 26.   **Haymo Hethe.**   Rochester ; d. 1352, May 4.

> Consecrated at Avignon by Nicolas, Bishop of Ostia ; W. Dene, *Ang. Sac.* i. 360 ; Prof. *Reg. Cant.* ; *Papal Letters*, ii. 189.

A. D. **1318.**   **John of Eglescliffe.**   Glasgow ; Connor, 1322 ; Llandaff, 1323 ; d. 1347, Jan. 2.

> Provided to Glasgow, July 17, and consecrated at Avignon by Nicolas of Ostia ; Theiner, p. 202 ; *Papal Letters*, ii. 173, 230.

A. D. **1320**, July 20.   **Henry Burghersh.**   Lincoln ; d. 1340, Dec. 4.

> Consecrated at Boulogne-sur-Mer by the bishops John of Norwich, Walter of Exeter, Adam of Hereford, and Ingelram of Terouanne ; *Reg. Cant. Cranbourne* ; cf. *Ann. Paulini*, p. 289 ; Murimuth, p. 31.

A. D. **1320**, Nov. 16.   **Rigaud Asser.**   Winchester ; d. 1323, Apr. 12.

> Consecrated at S. Alban's by Stephen of London, John of Ely, and Haymo of Rochester ; Prof. *Reg. Cant.* ; W. Dene, *Ang. Sac.* i. 361 ; Trokelow, p. 105.

A. D. **1322**, June 27.   **Roger Northburgh.**   Lichfield ; d. 1359, Nov. 22.

> Consecrated at Hales Abbey by the bishops Thomas of Worcester, John of Carlisle, David of S. Asaph, Peter of Corbavia, John of Glasgow, and Robert of Clonfert ; *Reg. Cobham* at Worcester.

A. D. **1323**, June 26. **John Stratford.** Winchester; Canterbury, 1333; d. 1348, Aug. 23.

> Consecrated at Avignon by Vitalis, Bishop of Albano : Birchington, *Ang. Sac.* i. 19 ; by Bertrand, Bishop of Tusculum : *Papal Letters*, ii. 230.

A. D. **1325**, Feb. 24. **John de Ross.** Carlisle; d. 1332.

> Consecrated at Avignon by Bertrand, Bishop of Tusculum ; *Chron. Lanercost,* p. 253 ; *Papal Letters*, ii. 242, 468.

A. D. **1325**, Sept. 15. **William Ayermin.** Norwich; d. 1336, Mar. 27.

> Consecrated at S. Germain des Prés, Paris, by William, Archbishop of Vienne, and the bishops William of Mende, Hugh of Orange, and James of Zagrabia (Agram): Prof. *Reg. Cant.* ; *Reg. Cranbourne.*

A. D. **1327**, Feb. 1. **Simon Wedehall.** Whithern; d. 1355, Mar. 11.

> Consecrated at Westminster by the bishops John of Carlisle, Roger of Lichfield, and John of Llandaff ; *Reg. Melton,* York ; MS. Vesp. c. 16.

A. D. **1327**, March 22. **James Berkeley.** Exeter ; d. 1327, June 24.

> Consecrated at Canterbury by the Archbishop, John of Chichester, and Haymo of Rochester ; Prof. *Reg. Cant.* ; W. Dene, *Ang. Sac.* i. 368 ; Murimuth, p. 52.

A. D. **1327**, Oct. 18. **John Grandison.** Exeter ; d. 1369, July 16.

> Consecrated at Avignon by Peter, Bishop of Praeneste ; Prof. *Reg. Cant.* ; Murimuth, p. 53 ; *Reg. Grandison,* ii. 39–41 (Oliver, p. 76).

A. D. **1327**, Oct. 18. **Thomas Charlton.** Hereford ; d. 1344, Jan. 11.

> Consecrated at Avignon by Peter of Praeneste: 'ibidem cum dicto episcopo Exoniensi ;' Murimuth, p. 58.

A. D. **1328**, June 5. **Simon Mepeham.** Canterbury ; d. 1333, Oct. 12.

> Consecrated at Avignon by Peter of Praeneste ; Cont. Gerv. ii. 324.

A.D. **1328**, June 12. **Henry Gower.** S. David's ; d. 1347 ; and

> **Matthew Englefield.** Bangor ; d. 1357, Apr. 25.

> Consecrated at Canterbury by Stephen of London, John of Bath, and Haymo of Rochester ; Prof. *Reg. Cant.* ; *Reg. Eastry* at Canterbury ; *Reg. Drokensford,* Wells.

A. D. **1329**, Sept. 3.   **Ralph of Shrewsbury.**   Bath and Wells; d. 1363, Aug. 14.

> Consecrated at Canterbury by Archbishop Simon, Haymo of Rochester, and Matthew of Bangor; Prof. in *Reg. Cant.*

A. D. **1330**, July 15.   **Robert Wyvill.**   Salisbury; d. 1375, Sept. 14.

> Consecrated at Woodstock by Henry of Lincoln, Roger of Lichfield, and John of Llandaff: Prof. *Reg. Cant.*; 'apud Botelston in capella domini regis' 'die lunae proxima sequenti facta est eclipsis solis;' *Ann. Paulini*, p. 350.

A. D. **1332**, July 19.   **John Kirkby.**   Carlisle; d. 1352.

> Consecrated by William, Archbishop of York, Lewis of Durham, and Roland of Armagh, at South Burton near Beverley; *Reg. Melton*; Raine, *Memorials*, iii. 251.

A. D. **1333**, Nov. 14.   **Robert Graystanes.**   Durham; deposed 1333.

> Consecrated in the chapel of the Archbishop at York by William, Archbishop, John of Carlisle, and Roland of Armagh; *Reg. Melton*; *Graystanes* (*Scriptt. Dunelm.*\, c. xlix; cf. Murimuth, p. 71.

A. D. **1333**, Dec. 19.   **Richard Aungerville** (of Bury).   Durham; d. 1345, Apr. 14.

> Consecrated at Chertsey Abbey by John, Bishop of Winchester, Elect of Canterbury; Chambre, *Scriptt. Dunelm.* c. i: 'in qua consecratione episcopus Lincolniae fundebat omnes expensas;' cf. Murimuth, p. 71.

A. D. **1334**, May 8.   **Simon Montacute.**   Worcester; Ely, 1337; d. 1345, June 20.

> Consecrated at Thame by Henry of Lincoln, Ralph of Bath, and Robert of Sarum; *Reg. Montacute.*

A. D. **1337**, March 30.   **Antony Beck.**   Norwich; d. 1343, Dec. 19.

> Consecrated at Avignon by Pope Benedict XII; Register of the privileges of Bishop Bek; MS. Harl. 3720.

A. D. **1337**, March 30.   **Thomas Hemenhale.**   Worcester; d. 1338, Dec. 21.

> Consecrated at Avignon by the Pope; Prof. *Reg. Cant.*; *Papal Letters*, ii. 541.

A. D. **1337**, Nov. 30.   **Robert Stratford.**   Chichester; d. 1362, Apr. 9.

> Consecrated at Canterbury by the archbishop John, Adam of Winchester, Haymo of Rochester, and Robert of Sarum; Prof. *Reg. Cant.*; cf. W. Dene, *Ang. Sac.* i. 374.

A. D. **1338**, July 12. **Richard Bintworth.** London; d. 1339, Dec. 8.
> Consecrated at Lambeth by Robert of Chichester, Haymo of Rochester, Roger of Lichfield, Robert of Sarum, Alexander of Dublin : Prof. *Reg. Cant.* ; *Ann. Paulini*, p. 368 ; 'et aliis ibidem existentibus :' cf. W. Dene, *Ang. Sac.* i. 374.

A. D. **1339**, March 21. **Wulstan Bransford.** Worcester; d. 1349, Aug. 6.
> Consecrated at Canterbury by Robert of Chichester : Prof. *Reg. Cant.* ; Murimuth, p. 87. Haymo of Rochester assisted : W. Dene, *Ang. Sac.* i. 374.

A. D. **1340**, March 12. **Ralph Stratford.** London; d. 1354, Apr. 7.
> Consecrated at Canterbury by Archbishop John, Robert of Chichester, Haymo of Rochester, and Robert of Sarum; Prof. *Reg. Cant.* ; W. Dene, *Ang. Sac.* i. 374.

A. D. **1342**, July 7. **Thomas Beck.** Lincoln; d. 1347, Feb. 2.
> Consecrated at Avignon by Pope Clement VI; *Reg. Beck* ; MS. Harl. 3720.

A. D. **1342**, July 7. **William Zouch.** Archbishop of York; d. 1352, July 19.
> Consecrated at Avignon by Pope Clement VI; MS. Vitellius, A. 2 ; Stubbs (ed. Raine, ii. p. 418).

A. D. **1344**, May 23. **William Bateman.** Norwich; d. 1355, Jan. 6.
> Consecrated at Avignon by Pope Clement VI : Murimuth, p. 157. His years change between May 21 and May 28 ; May 23, 1344, was Whitsunday : *Reg. Bateman* ; Murimuth, p. 157.

A. D. **1344**, Aug. 29. **John Trilleck.** Hereford; d. 1360, Nov. 30.
> Consecrated at Waverley Abbey by Ralph of London, Adam of Winchester, Robert of Sarum, and Wulstan of Worcester; *Reg. Trilleck,* Hereford.

A. D. **1345**, July 24. **Thomas de Lisle.** Ely; d. 1361, June 23.
> Consecrated at Avignon ; *Reg. Lisle.*

A. D. **1345**, Aug. 7. **Thomas Hatfield.** Durham; d. 1381, May 8.
> Consecrated by the Archbishop of Canterbury in the chapel at Otford ; Murimuth, p. 172.

A. D. **1346**, May 14.   **William Edendon.**   Winchester ; d. 1366, Oct. 7.

Consecrated at Otford by John, Archbishop of Canterbury, Ralph of London, and Robert of Chichester ; *Reg. Edendon* ; Murimuth, p. 192 ; Birchington, *Vitae Paparum*, MS. Julius, B. 3.

A. D. **1347.**   **John Paschal.**   Llandaff ; d. 1361, Oct. 11.

Consecrated at Avignon ; Prof. *Reg. Cant.* [? previously suff. of Norwich].

A. D. **1347**, July 8.   **Richard FitzRalph.**   Armagh ; d. 1360, Nov. 14.

Consecrated at Exeter by John, Bishop of Exeter, David of S. Asaph, Ralph of Bath, and Robert of Sarum ; *Reg. Grandison* at Exeter ; T. Chesterfield, *Ang. Sac.* i. 443.

A. D. **1347**, Sept. 23.   **John Thoresby.**   S. David's ; Worcester, 1349 ; York, 1352 ; d. 1373, Nov. 6.

Consecrated at Otford by the Archbishop of Canterbury ; Birchington, *Vitae Paparum*, MS. Cotton, Julius, B. 3.

A. D. **1347**, Sept. 23.   **John Gynwell.**   Lincoln ; d. 1362, Aug. 5.

Consecrated on S. Tecla's day with the Bishop of S. David's ; ibid.

A. D. **1349**, July 19.   **Thomas Bradwardin.**   Canterbury ; d. 1349, Aug. 26.

Consecrated at Avignon by Bertrand, Archbishop of Embrun ; Birchington, *Ang. Sac.* i. 42.

A. D. **1349**, Dec. 20.   **Simon Islip.**   Canterbury ; d. 1366, Apr. 26.

Consecrated at S. Paul's, London, by Ralph of London, William of Winchester, and John of S. David's ; *Reg. Islip* ; Birchington, *Ang. Sac.* i. 43 ; cf. W. Dene, *Ang. Sac.* i. 376.

A. D. **1350**, Feb. 14.   **John de S. Paul.**   Dublin ; d. 1362, Sept. 9.

Consecrated at S. Mary's, Southwark, by William of Winchester, John of Worcester, and Caesarius, bishop 'Beatae Mariae de Rosis' ; *Reg. Edendon*, at Winchester.

A. D. **1350.**   **Roger Cradock.**   Waterford ; Llandaff, 1361 ; d. 1382.

Provided Mar. 3 : Avignon ; Theiner, p. 293.

A. D. **1350**, May 2. **William S. Leger.** Meath ; d. 1352, Aug. 24.
> Consecrated at Lambeth by John, Bishop of Worcester, under commission from the Archbishop, April 27 ; *Reg. Islip*, fo. 17.

A. D. **1350**, Sept. 26. **Reginald Brian.** S. David's ; Worcester, 1352 ; d. 1361, Dec. 10.
> Consecrated at Lambeth by John, Bishop of Worcester ; *Reg. Islip* (licence Sept. 23).

A. D. **1352. John Trevor.** S. Asaph ; d. 1357.
> Consecrated at Avignon ; Prof. *Reg. Cant.* ; Profession, Mar. 24, 1353 ; *Reg. Islip*.

A. D. **1352. Thomas Fastolf.** S. David's ; d. 1361, June.
> Consecrated at Avignon by William, Bishop of Tusculum ; provided, Oct. 22 ; Prof. *Reg. Cant.*

A. D. **1353**, March 10. **John Sheppey.** Rochester ; d. 1360, Oct. 19.
> Consecrated at S. Mary's, Southwark, by William of Winchester, John of S. Asaph, and Caesarius, B. M. de Rosis ; *Reg. Edendon* ; *Reg. Sheppey*.

A. D. **1353**, Apr. 21. **Gilbert Welton.** Carlisle ; d. 1362.
> Consecrated at Avignon by Pope Innocent VI ; *Reg. Welton*.

A. D. **1355**, July 12. **Michael Northburgh.** London ; d. 1361, Sept. 9 ; and **Michael Malcolnhagh.** Whithern ; d. 1358.
> Consecrated together at S. Mary's, Southwark, by William of Winchester : ' ascitis et assistentibus sibi venerabilibus patribus domino Caesario ecclesiae Beatae Mariae de Rosis et —— episcopis ; ' *Reg. Edendon*.

A. D. **1356**, Jan. 3. **Thomas Percy.** Norwich ; d. 1369, Aug. 8.
> Consecrated at Waverley Abbey by William of Winchester, Robert of Salisbury, and Robert of Chichester ; *Reg. Edendon* and *Reg. Percy*, Norwich.

A. D. **1357. Leoline ap Madoc.** S. Asaph ; d. 1375.
> Consecrated at Avignon ; provided, July 19 ; *Reg. Islip*.

A. D. **1357. Thomas Ringstead.** Bangor ; d. 1366, Jan. 8.
> Consecrated at Avignon ; provided, Aug. 21 ; *Reg. Islip*.

A. D. **1358**. **Thomas.** Whithern.

> Consecrated at Avignon by Peter, Bishop of Ostia ; Theiner, p. 315 ; (prov. 1358, Dec. 31).

A. D. **1360**, Sept. 27. **Robert Stretton.** Lichfield ; d. 1385, Mar. 28.

> Consecrated at Fulham (?) by Michael, Bishop of London, and John of Rochester ; Birchington, *Ang. Sac.* i. 44 ; *Reg. Islip* (Comm. Sept. 23) ; MS. Julius, B. 3.

A. D. **1361**, Oct. 3. **Lewis Charlton.** Hereford ; d. 1369, June 24.

> Consecrated at Avignon ; *Reg. Charlton.*

A. D. **1362**, Jan. 2. **Adam Houghton.** S. David's ; d. 1389, Feb. 13.

> Consecrated at S. Mary's, Southwark, by William of Winchester, Richard, Archbishop of Nazareth, and Thomas of Lycostomium ; *Reg. Edendon.*

A. D. **1362**, Feb. 6. **William of Whittlesey.** Rochester ; Worcester, 1364 ; Canterbury, 1368 ; d. 1374, June 6.

> Consecrated at Otford by Simon, Archbishop of Canterbury, Richard of Nazareth, and Thomas 'Lamberg' ; *Reg. Whittlesey* ; *Reg. Islip* ; MS. Julius, B. 3.

A. D. **1362**, March 20. **Simon Sudbury.** London ; Canterbury, 1375 ; d. 1381, June 14.

> **John Barnet.** Worcester ; Bath, 1363 ; Ely, 1366 ; d. 1373, June 7.

> **Simon Langham.** Ely ; Canterbury, 1366 ; Card. 1368 ; Bp. Praeneste, 1374 ; d. 1376, July 22.

> Consecrated together at S. Paul's by William of Winchester, Robert of Salisbury, and Adam of S. David's ; *Reg. Edendon.*

A. D. **1362**. **William de Lynn.** Chichester ; Worcester, 1368 ; d. 1373, Nov. 18.

> Consecrated at Avignon ; Profession, Aug. 18, 1362.

A. D. **1363.** **John Swaffham.** Cloyne; Bangor, 1376; d. 1398, June 24.

A. D. **1363,** June 18. **Thomas Appleby.** Carlisle; d. 1395, Dec. 5.
Consecrated at Avignon by Pope Urban V; *Reg. Appleby.*

A. D. **1363,** June 25. **John Bokyngham.** Lincoln; d. 1398, March 10.
Consecrated at Wargrave by William of Winchester, Robert of Sarum,
and John of Ossory; *Reg. Edendon*; Birchington, MS. Julius, D. 3.

A. D. **1364,** May 26. **Thomas Trilleck.** Rochester; d. 1372.
Consecrated at Avignon by Guy, Cardinal Bishop of Portus; *Reg.
Trilleck.*

A. D. **1366.** **Gervas de Castro.** Bangor; d. 1370, Sept. 24.
Consecrated at Avignon; provided, Dec. 11; *Reg. Langham.*

A. D. **1367,** March 7. **John Harewell.** Bath; d. 1386, July.
Consecrated at Bordeaux, in the collegiate church of S. Severinus, by
Elias, Archbishop of Bordeaux, and two other bishops; *Reg. Hare-
well*; Hist. Wellens. *Ang. Sac.* i. 570.

A. D. **1367,** Oct. 10. **William of Wykeham.** Winchester; d. 1404,
Sept. 27.
Consecrated at S. Paul's, London, by Archbishop Simon, Simon of
London, and Robert of Sarum; *Reg. Wykeham*; Birchington, MS.
Julius, D. 3.

A. D. **1369,** Sept. 2. **William Reade.** Chichester; d. 1385, Aug. 18.
Consecrated at Avignon; Chichester Calendar, MS. Ashmole 1146:
'Sept. 2. Consecratio Willelmi episcopi tertii.' Cf. *Collectanea Oxon.*
iii. 222.

A. D. **1370,** March 17. **William Courtenay.** Hereford; London, 1375;
Canterbury, 1381; d. 1396, July 31.
Confirmed at Lambeth, Mar. 19. His pontifical years change between
March 10 and March 20, and he commissions his Vicar-General, March
19, Anno 1°. 1370; *Reg. Courtenay*, Hereford; *Reg. Whittlesey.*

A. D. **1370,** Apr. 21. **Henry Spencer.** Norwich; d. 1406, Aug. 23.
Consecrated at Rome; *Reg. Spencer.*

A. D. **1370**, May 12.   **Thomas Brentingham.**   Exeter; d. 1394, Dec. 23.
> Consecrated at Stepney by Simon of London, Geoffrey of Damascus, and John 'Ayubonensi'; *Reg. Brentingham.*

A. D. **1371.**   **Howel ap Grono.**   Bangor; d. 1372, Feb.
> Consecrated at Avignon; provided, Apr. 21.

A. D. **1372.**   **John Gilbert.**   Bangor; Hereford, 1375; S. David's, 1389; d. 1397, July 28.
> Consecrated at Avignon; provided, Mar. 17.

A. D. **1373**, Feb. 6.   **Thomas Brinton.**   Rochester; d. 1389.
> Consecrated at Avignon; *Reg. Whittlesey.*

A. D. **1374**, Apr. 9.   **Thomas Arundel.**   Ely; York, 1388; Canterbury, 1396; d. 1414, Feb. 19.
> Consecrated at Otford by Archbishop Whittlesey, Simon of London, and Thomas of Rochester; *Reg. Arundel*; *Reg. Whittlesey.*

A. D. **1374**, June 4.   **Alexander Neville.**   York; dep. 1388; d. 1392, May.
> Consecrated at Westminster by Thomas of Durham, William of Winchester, and Thomas of Ely; also 'praesente archiepiscopo Ranensi'; *Reg. Palatinum*, iii. 527; *Reg. Neville.*

A. D. **1374**, Nov. 25.   **John Duncan.**   Sodor and Man; d. 1380.
> Consecrated at Avignon by Simon (Langham), Bishop of Praeneste; *Chron. Mann.* p. 31.

A. D. **1375**, Oct. 28.   **Henry Wakefield.**   Worcester; d. 1395, March 11.
> Consecrated at Hatfield by Thomas of Ely, John of Hereford, and Thomas of Rochester; *Reg. Arundel*, Ely; *Reg. Wakefield.*

A. D. **1375**, Dec. 9.   **Ralph Erghum.**   Salisbury; Bath, 1388; d. 1400, Apr. 10.
> Consecrated at Bruges by Archbishop Simon Sudbury, William of Carpentras, and John of Amiens; *Reg. Erghum*; *Reg. Sudbury.*

A. D. **1376**, May 25.   **William Spridlington.**   S. Asaph; d. 1382, Apr. 9.
> Consecrated at Lambeth by Archbishop Sudbury, John of Bath, and John of Hereford; *Reg. Sudbury.*

A. D. 13.... **William Bottlesham.** 'Nanatensis' in 1382; *Fascic. Zizan.* p. 498; Bethlehem; Rymer, vii. 478. Llandaff, 1386; Rochester, 1389; d. 1400.

A. D. **1382,** Jan. 5. **Robert Braybrooke.** London; d. 1404, Aug. 28; and **John Fordham.** Durham; Ely, 1388; d. 1425, Nov. 19.
Consecrated at Lambeth by Thomas of Exeter, Thomas of Rochester, and John of Bangor; *Reg. Courtenay*; *Reg. Braybrooke*; Chambre (*Scriptt. Dunelm.*), c. 4, p. 144.

A. D. **1382.** **Laurence Child.** S. Asaph; d. 1389, Dec. 27.
Consecrated 'in curia Romana'; provided, June 18; *Reg. Courtenay*.

A. D. **1383,** March 8. **John Colton.** Armagh; d. 1404, May 1.
Consecrated at S. Paul's by Archbishop Courtenay, Thomas of Ely, and John of Hereford; *Reg. Courtenay*.

A. D. **1383,** May 3. **Thomas Rushook.** Llandaff; Chichester, 1385; Kilmore, 1388; d. 1388 or 9.
Consecrated at Blackfriars, London, by Archbishop Courtenay, William of Winchester, Thomas of Exeter, and Thomas of Ely; *Reg. Courtenay*.

A. D. **1385,** July 9. **William ——,** 'Tornacensis.' London (suffragan).
Consecrated at Hadham by Robert of London, Simon of Achonry, and Robert of Sebastopolis; *Reg. Braybrook*.

A. D. **1386,** Jan. 14. **Walter Skirlaw.** Lichfield; Bath, 1386; Durham, 1388; d. 1405, Mar. 24.
Consecrated at Westminster by Archbishop Courtenay, Alexander of York, Robert of London, William of Winchester, Thomas of Exeter, Ralph of Sarum, and Thomas of Llandaff; *Reg. Courtenay*; *Reg. Skirlaw*; Malvern, *Cont. Polychr.* ix. p. 78.

A. D. **1386,** Aug. 19. **Richard le Scrope.** Lichfield; York, 1398; d. 1405, June 8.
Consecrated at Genoa by Pope Urban VI; *Reg. Scrope*.

A. D. **1387.** **Robert Waldby.** Aire in Gascony; Dublin, 1391; Chichester, 1396; York, 1397; d. 1398, Jan. 6.
Gallia Christ. i. 1160; Ware, *Dublin*, p. 9; Bale, *Scriptt.* Cent. vi. pp. 499, 500.

G

A. D. 1388, Sept. 20.   **John Waltham.**   Salisbury; d. 1395, Sept.

Consecrated at Barnwell by Archbishop Courtenay, Robert of London, and William of Winchester; *Reg. Waltham*; *Reg. Courtenay.*

A. D. 1389, June 20.   **Edmund Bromfield.**   Llandaff; d. 1393, June; and **John Trefnant.**   Hereford; d. 1404.

Consecrated at S. Gregory's at Rome by Cosmatus of Bologna, 'I. Verensis,' and Angelo of Castello; *Reg. Trefnant*, Hereford; Malvern, *Cont. Polychron.* ix. 212.

A. D. 1390.   **Richard Metford.**   Chichester; Sarum, 1395; d. 1407.

'Apr. 10: Consecratio venerabilis patris domini Ricardi III^{tii} episcopi Cicestrensis, A. D. 1390;' *Calendar. Cicestr.* MS. Ashmole, 1146; but, as he makes his profession as Electus Confirmatus on May 7, he was probably consecrated May 8; *Reg. Courtenay*; *Cont. Polychron.* ix. 221, 222.

A. D. 1390, May 8.   **Alexander Bache.**   S. Asaph; d. 1395.

Consecrated at Westminster by Archbishop Courtenay; Malvern, *Cont. Polychron.* ix. 235.

A. D. 1393.   **Tideman of Winchcomb.**   Llandaff; Worcester, 1395; d. 1401, June 13.

Royal Assent, Aug. 19: assent in Parliament, Feb. 1394; *Rot. Parl.* iii. 317.

A. D. 1394.   **Robert Reade.**   Waterford; Carlisle, 1396; Chichester, 1397; d. 1415, June.

Provided 1394, Sept. 9.

A. D. 1395, June 20.   **Edmund Stafford.**   Exeter; d. 1419, Sept. 3.

Consecrated at Lambeth by Archbishop Courtenay, Robert of London, and John of Salisbury; *Reg. Stafford.*

A. D. 1395.   **Andrew Barrett.**   Llandaff; d. 1396.

Consecrated at Rome; clericus camerae apostolicae; *MS. Donat.*

A. D. 1395.   **John Trevor.**   S. Asaph; d. 1410, Apr. 10.

Consecrated at Rome; *MS. Donat*; assent in Parliament, Apr. 9; *Rot. Parl.* iii. 407.

A. D. 1396, after July 10.   **John Burghill.**   Llandaff; Lichfield, 1398; d. 1414, May.

Provided, Apr. 12; *Munimenta de Glamorgan*, iv. 305.

A. D. 1397, before Apr. 23. **Thomas Merkes.** Carlisle ; dep. 1399 ; d. 1410.
Profession as 'Thomas Sumestre, ep. Karlelensis,' to Archbishop Scrope ;
Reg. Scrope.

A. D. 1397. **Thomas Peverell.** Ossory ; Llandaff, 1398 ; Worcester,
1407 ; d. 1419, March 2.

A. D. 1397, Nov. 11. **Guy de Mona.** S. David's ; d. 1407, Aug. 31. Day
of consecration given in his register.

A. D. 1398, Feb. 3. **Roger Walden.** Canterbury ; London, 1405 ; d. 1406,
Jan. 6.
Received the pall at High Clere, Feb. 17, from William of Winchester ;
Reg. Wykeham : consecrated 'circa Purificationem B. V. M.' MS. Cotton,
Tiberius, C. 9, and Digby (Bodl.), 201 ; preferment filled up Feb. 6.

A. D. 1398, July 14. **Henry Beaufort.** Lincoln ; Winchester, 1405 ; d.
1447, Apr. 11.
Reg. Beaufort at Lincoln.

A. D. 1400. **Richard Young.** Bangor ; Rochester, 1404 ; d. 1418, Oct.
Consecrated probably at Rome.

A. D. 1400, July 4. **John Bottlesham.** Rochester ; d. 1404, Apr. 17.
Consecrated at Canterbury by Archbishop Arundel, Robert of London,
and Henry of Norwich ; *Reg. Comp. P. & C. Cant.* ; *Reg. Arundel* ;
Reg. Bottlesham.

A. D. 1400, Aug. 15. **William Strickland.** Carlisle ; d. 1419, Aug. 30.
Consecrated at Cawood Castle by Archbishop Richard of York, Lewis of
Volterra, and William Pharensis ; *Reg. Scrope.*

A. D. 1401, Jan. 2. **Roger Appleby.** Ossory ; d. 1404.
Consecrated by Guy of S. David's, William of Tournay, and Thomas
'Constantiensis' ; *Reg. Mona.*

A. D. 1401, Sept. 8. **John Greenlaw.** Bishop of Soltania, suffragan of Bath.
Consecrated, at Bethlehem Hospital without London, by Thomas of
Chrysopolis, John 'Surronensis,' and Thomas of Constantia ; *Reg.
Bowet* ; MS. Hutton.

G 2

A. D. **1401**, Oct. 9.   **Richard Clifford.**   Worcester; London, 1407; d. 1421, Aug. 20.

> Consecrated at S. Paul's by Archbishop Arundel, Robert of London, John of Hereford, Edmund of Exeter, Lewis of Volterra, and Guy of S. David's; *Reg. Arundel*; *Reg. Clifford.*

A. D. **1401**, Nov. 20.   **Henry Bowett.**   Bath; York, 1407; d. 1423, Oct. 20.

> Consecrated at S. Paul's by Archbishop Arundel, Robert of London, John of Hereford, Edmund of Exeter, Richard of Bangor, Thomas of Llandaff, Richard of Worcester, and Lewis of Volterra; *Reg. Arundel.*

A. D. **1404**, July 6.   **Robert Mascall.**   Hereford; d. 1416, Dec. 22.

> Consecrated at Rome; *Reg. Mascall.*

A. D. **1405**, March 29.   **Philip Repingdon.**   Lincoln; res. 1419, Oct. 10.

> Consecrated at Canterbury by Archbishop Arundel, Richard of Worcester, and Lewis of Volterra; *Reg. Arundel.*

A. D. **1406**, Aug. 8.   **Thomas Langley.**   Durham; d. 1437, Nov. 20.

> Consecrated at S. Paul's by Archbishop Arundel, Henry of Winchester, and Richard of Worcester; *Reg. Arundel.*

A. D. **1406**, Sept. 26.   **Nicolas Bubwith.**   London; Sarum, 1407; Bath, 1407; d. 1424, Oct. 27.

> Consecrated at Mortlake by Archbishop Arundel, Henry of Winchester, and Richard of Worcester; *Reg. Arundel*; *Reg. Bubwith.*

A. D. **1407**.   **Robert Hallam.**   Salisbury; d. 1417, Sept. 4.

> Consecrated in Italy by Pope Gregory XII; *Reg. Arundel.*

A. D. **1407**, Oct. 23.   **Alexander Tottington.**   Norwich; d. 1413, April.

> Consecrated at S. Peter's, Gloucester, by Archbishop Arundel, Thomas of Durham, Richard of Worcester, and Robert of Hereford; *Reg. Arundel*; *Reg. Tottington.*

A. D. **1408**, June 17.   **Henry Chicheley.**   S. David's; Canterbury, 1414; d. 1443, Apr. 12.

> Consecrated at Lucca, or Sienna (?), by Pope Gregory XII; *Reg. Chicheley*, S. David's; MS. Tanner, 146; Spencer, *Chicheley*, p. 16.

A. D. **1408**, Aug. 12. **John de la Zouch.** Llandaff; d. 1423; and
> **Benedict Nicholls.** Bangor; S. David's, 1418;
> d. 1433, June 25.

Consecrated probably by Archbishop Arundel; *Reg. Arundel.*

A. D. **1411**, June 28. **Robert Lancaster.** S. Asaph; d. 1433.

> Consecrated at Lincoln by Archbishop Arundel, Philip of Lincoln, and
> William 'Soltoniensis'; *Reg. Arundel.*

A. D. **1413**, Sept. 17. **Richard Courtenay.** Norwich; d. 1415, Sept. 15.

> Consecrated in the chapel in Windsor Park by Archbishop Arundel;
> *Reg. Arundel*; *Reg. Courtenay.*

A. D. **1414.** **John Catterick.** S. David's; Coventry, 1415; Exeter, 1419;
> d. 1419, Dec. 28.

> Consecrated at Bologna by Pope John XXIII; provided, Apr. 27; *Reg. Chicheley.*

A. D. **1415.** **Lewis of Luxemburg.** Terouanne; Rouen, 1436; Ely,
> 1438; d. 1443, Sept. 18.

> Consecrated by Reginald, Archbishop of Rheims; *Gall. Chr.* x. 1564.

A. D. **1415**, June 9. **Stephen Patrington.** S. David's; Chichester, 1417;
> d. 1417, Nov. 22.

> Consecrated at All Saints, Maidstone, by Archbishop Chicheley, Richard
> of London, and Richard of Norwich; *Reg. Chicheley*, fo. 9.

A. D. **1416**, May 31. **John Wakering.** Norwich; d. 1425, Apr. 9.

> Consecrated at S. Paul's by Archbishop Chicheley, Henry of York,
> Richard of London, John of Ely, Philip of Lincoln, Stephen of
> S. David's, Robert of Hereford, John of Lichfield, and Thomas of
> Worcester; *Reg. Wakering*; *Reg. Chicheley*, fo. 11.

A. D. **1417**, Apr. 18. **Edmund Lacy.** Hereford; Exeter, 1420; d. 1455,
> Sept. 18.

> Consecrated at Windsor, 'in capella hospitii domini regis infra castellum
> de Wyndesore, et non in capella collegii,' by Archbishop Chicheley,
> Stephen of S. David's, and Thomas of Worcester; *Reg. Lacy*; *Reg. Chicheley*, fo. 13.

A. D. **1417**, Dec. 12. **John Chandler.** Salisbury; d. 1426, July 16.

Consecrated at Lambeth by Archbishop Chicheley, Thomas of Durham, John of Llandaff, Benedict of Bangor, and Edmund of Hereford; *Reg. Chandler*; *Reg. Chicheley*, fo. 16.

A. D. **1418.** **William Barrow.** Bangor; Carlisle, 1424; d. 1429, Sept. 4.

Consecrated probably at the Council of Constance.

A. D. **1418**, [July 17?]. **Henry de la Ware.** Chichester; d. 1420, June.

Consecrated in Normandy; possibly at Pont de l'Arche; *Reg. Chicheley*.

A. D. **1419**, Dec. 3. **Philip Morgan.** Worcester; Ely, 1426; d. 1435, Oct. 25.

Consecrated in the Cathedral at Rouen; *Reg. Morgan*, Worcester.

—— **John Kemp.** Rochester; Chichester, 1421; London, 1421; York, 1426; Canterbury, 1452; d. 1454, March 22.

Consecrated probably at Rouen at the same time; the Bishops of Arras and Hebron were at Rouen.

A. D. **1420.** **Roger Whelpdale.** Carlisle; d. 1423, Feb. 4.

Consecrated at London by Henry of Winchester; MS. Lansd. 721; Profession, Aug. 21; *Reg. Bowett*.

A. D. **1420**, Apr. 28. **Richard Fleming.** Lincoln; d. 1431, Jan. 25.

Consecrated at Florence; *Reg. Chicheley*, fo. 26; *Reg. Fleming*.

A. D. **1420**, July 21. **Thomas Polton.** Hereford; Chichester, 1421; Worcester, 1426; d. 1433, Aug. 23.

Consecrated at Florence; *Reg. Chicheley* (Prof., Aug. 14).

A. D. **1420**, July 28. **William Heyworth.** Lichfield; d. 1447, March 13.

Consecrated at Fulham by Richard, Bishop of London; *Reg. Heyworth*.

A. D. **1422**, May 24. **Thomas Spofford.** Hereford; res. 1448.

Consecrated at Blackfriars, London, by Henry of Winchester, Thomas of Durham, Philip of Worcester, John of Norwich, and the suffragans of London and Winchester; *Reg. Spofford*.

A. D. **1422**, June 7. **John Langdon.** Rochester; d. 1434, Sept. 30.

Consecrated at Canterbury by Archbishop Chicheley, Philip of Worcester, and John of Dromore; *Reg. Chicheley*, fo. 33; *Reg. Langdon*.

A. D. **1425**, May 27. **John Stafford.** Bath; Canterbury, 1443; d. 1452, May 25.
> Consecrated at Blackfriars, London, [by Henry of Winchester?]; *Reg. Stafford.*

A. D. **1425.** **John Wells.** Llandaff; d. 1440.
> Consecrated at Rome, being Pope's penitentiary; *Reg. Chicheley*, fo. 39.

A. D. **1425.** **John Cliderow.** Bangor; d. 1434.
> Consecrated at Rome, being clerk of the Apostolic Chamber; *Reg. Chicheley*, fo. 39.

A. D. **1426**, May 26. **William Gray.** London; Lincoln, 1431; d. 1436, Feb.
> Consecrated at Leicester, in the church of S. Mary's College, by Archbishop Chicheley; *Reg. Gray*; *Reg. Chicheley*, fo. 41.

A. D. **1426**, June 30. **John Rickingale.** Chichester; d. 1429.
> Consecrated at Mortlake by Archbishop Chicheley; *Reg. Chicheley*, fo. 41.

A. D. **1426**, Aug. 18. **William Alnwick.** Norwich; Lincoln, 1436; d. 1449, Dec. 5.
> Consecrated at Canterbury by Archbishop Chicheley; John Stone, MS.; *Reg. Chicheley*, fo. 42.

A. D. **1427**, Oct. 26. **Robert Neville.** Salisbury; Durham, 1438; d. 1457, July 8.
> Consecrated at Lambeth, in the Great Chapel, by Archbishop Chicheley; *Reg. Neville*; *Reg. Chicheley*, fo. 47.

A. D. **1430**, Apr. 16. **Marmaduke Lumley.** Carlisle; Lincoln, 1450; d. 1450.
> Consecrated at Canterbury, in the chapel of S. Thomas, Eastbridge, by John, Archbishop of York, John of Rochester, and William of Norwich; *Reg. Kemp.*

A. D. **1431**, Feb. 11. **Simon Sydenham.** Chichester; d. 1438.
> Consecrated probably by Cardinal Beaufort; Profession 'post munus' at Lambeth, Feb. 12; *Reg. Chicheley*, Licence, Feb. 4: cf. MS. Ashmole, 1146.

A. D. **1431**, Sept. 16.   **Robert Fitzhugh.**   London; d. 1436, Jan. 15.

Consecrated, in curia Romana, at Foligno, 'in civitate Fulginensi;' *Reg. Fitzhugh.*

A. D. **1433**, Nov. 1.   **John Low.**   S. Asaph; Rochester, 1444; d. 1467.

Consecrated probably by Cardinal Beaufort; *Reg. Chicheley,* fo. 51.

A. D. **1434**, Jan. 31.   **Thomas Rudborne.**   S. David's; d. 1442.

Consecrated at Blackfriars, London; *Reg. Rudborne;* cf. *Reg. Chicheley.*

A. D. **1435**, May 1.   **Thomas Brown.**   Rochester; Norwich, 1436; d. 1445, Dec. 6.

Consecrated at Canterbury by Archbishop Chicheley, Simon of Chichester, and Richard of Ross; *Reg. Brown;* *Reg. Chicheley.*

A. D. **1435**, May 15.   **Thomas Bourchier.**   Worcester; Ely, 1443; Canterbury, 1454; d. 1486, March 30.

Consecrated at Blackfriars by Henry of Winchester, John of York, John of Bath, Robert of Sarum, and John of S. Asaph; *Reg. Bourchier.*

A. D. **1436**, Oct. 28.   **Robert Gilbert.**   London; d. 1448, June 22.

Consecrated at the Carmelites' Church in London by Henry of Winchester; *Reg. Gilbert;* *Reg. Chicheley.*

A. D. **1436**, Nov. 25.   **Thomas Cheriton.**   Bangor; d. 1447, Dec. 23.

Consecrated at London; *Reg. Chicheley.*

A. D. **1437**, March 24.   **William Wells.**   Rochester; d. 1444, February.

Consecrated at Durham House, Westminster, by Archbishop Chicheley, Thomas of Norwich, Marmaduke of Carlisle, and Richard of Ross; *Reg. Wells;* *Reg. Chicheley.*

A. D. **1438**, July 20.   **William Aiscough.**   Salisbury; d. 1450, June 29.

Consecrated at Windsor by Henry of Winchester, John of Bath, Thomas of Norwich, and Thomas of S. David's; *Reg. Aiscough.*

A. D. **1438**, July 27.   **Richard Praty.**   Chichester; d. 1445, August.

Consecrated at Otford by Archbishop Chicheley. *Reg. Praty.*

A. D. **1441**.   **Nicolas Ashby.**   Llandaff; d. 1458.

Profession, May 24; *Reg. Chicheley.*

A. D. **1442**, Aug. 26 × Oct. 2. **William Lindwood.** S. David's; d. 1446, Oct. 21.

> Consecrated at S. Stephen's Chapel, Westminster; *Lindwood's Will*; *Reg. S. Stephen's.*

A. D. **1442. James Blakedon.** Achonry; Bangor, 1453; d. 1464, Oct. 24.

A. D. **1443**, Oct. 13. **Thomas Beckington.** Bath; d. 1465, Jan. 14.

> Consecrated in the old chapel of Eton College by William of Lincoln, William of Salisbury, and Nicolas of Llandaff; *Reg. Beckington.*

A. D. **1444**, March 22. **John Carpenter.** Worcester; d. 1476.

> Consecrated in Eton College Chapel by William of Salisbury, Thomas of Bath, and John of S. Asaph ; *Reg. Carpenter.*

A. D. **1444**, June 14. **Reginald Pecocke.** S. Asaph; Chichester, 1450; dep. 1457, Dec. 4.

> Consecrated at Croydon by Archbishop Stafford, John of Rochester, Thomas of Norwich, Thomas of Bath, and Richard of Ross; *Reg. Stafford.*

A. D. **1444**, Nov. 1. 'Episcopus Lexoviensis,' the Pope's collector in England.

> Consecrated at Lambeth by Archbishop Stafford, Robert of London, and Thomas of Ely; John Stone, MS. C. C. C. C. 417.

A. D. **1446**, Feb. 6. **Adam de Moleyns.** Chichester; d. 1450, Jan. 8.

> Consecrated at Lambeth by Archbishop Stafford; *Reg. Sarum.*

A. D. **1446**, March [20 or 27]. **Walter Lehart.** Norwich; d. 1472, May 17.

> Consecrated at Lambeth by Archbishop Stafford; *Reg. Lehart*, and *Stafford.*

A. D. **1447**, May 7. **John Langton.** S. David's; d. 1447, May 22.

> Consecrated at King's College Chapel, Cambridge, by William of Lincoln; *Reg. Alnwick.*

A. D. **1447**, July 9. **William Booth.** Lichfield; York, 1452; d. 1464, Sept. 12.

> Consecrated at S. Paul's, London, by Robert of London, Thomas of Bath, Walter of Norwich, and the Bishop of S. Asaph [Menevensis, wrongly in the record]; *Reg. D. & C. S. Paul's*; *Reg. Booth.*

A. D. **1447**, July 30.   **William of Waynflete.** Winchester ; d. 1486, Aug. 11.

> Consecrated by Archbishop Stafford at Eton College ; *Reg. Stafford* ; Budden, *Vit. Wainfl. ex Archivis Eton.* ; Rawlinson MS. B. 268, from *Eton Lease Book*, No. 13, folio 2.

A. D. **1447**, Nov. 19.   **John de la Bere.** S. David's ; res. 1460.

> Consecrated by Archbishop Stafford : Profession, 'a vobis consecrandus,' Nov. 13 ; *Reg. Stafford*.

A. D. **1448**, June 23.   **John Stanbery.** Bangor ; Hereford, 1453 ; d. 1474, May 11.

> Consecrated by Archbishop Stafford : Profession, 'a vobis consecrandus,' May 4 ; Licence, June 20 ; *Reg. Stafford*.

A. D. **1449**, Feb. 9.   **Richard Beauchamp.** Hereford ; Salisbury, 1450 ; d. 1481.

> Consecrated at Lambeth by Archbishop Stafford, John of Rochester, Thomas of Bath, John of Worcester, Reginald of S. Asaph, Adam of Chichester, Walter of Norwich, Marmaduke of Carlisle ; *Reg. Beauchamp* ; *Reg. Stafford*.

A. D. **1450**, Feb. 8.   **Thomas Kemp.** d. 1489, Mar. 28.

> Consecrated at York House, Westminster, by John, Archbishop of York, William of Winchester, Thomas of Ely, Thomas of Bath, Walter of Norwich, and Richard of Hereford ; *Reg. Kemp*, London.

A. D. **1450**, Mar. 15.   **Nicolas Close.** Carlisle ; Lichfield, 1452 ; d. 1452.

> Consecrated at York House, Westminster, by Archbishop Kemp of York and Thomas of London ; *Reg. Kemp*, York.

A. D. **1451.**   **Thomas Knight.** S. Asaph ; d. 1471.

> Consecrated probably Feb. 14 [Jan. 27 ; Willis, *S. Asaph*, p. 67].

A. D. **1451**, Feb. 14.   **Reginald Boulers.** Hereford ; Lichfield, 1453 ; d. 1459.

> Consecrated in England by the Bishop John of Rochester ; *Reg. Boulers* at Hereford ; Licence, Jan. 27.

A. D. **1452**, June 18.   **John Chadworth.** Lincoln ; d. 1471, Nov. 23.

> Consecrated in England (?) ; *Reg. Chadworth*.

A. D. **1452**, Nov. 16 × Dec. 18. **William Percy.** Carlisle ; d. 1462.

> Consecrated in the province of York, not in the church of York, under commission from the Archbishop (Nov. 16) to Robert of Durham, Thomas of S. Asaph, John of Lincoln, John of the Isles, and John of Philippopolis ; *Reg. Booth.*

A. D. **1454**, Sept. 8. **William Gray.** Ely ; d. 1478, Aug. 4.

> Consecrated at Mortlake by Archbishop Bourchier, John of Worcester, and Richard of Ross ; *Reg. Gray.*

A. D. **1457**, Sept. 25. **Laurence Booth.** Durham ; York, 1476 ; d. 1480.

> Consecrated at Sherburn in Elmet : Profession, 'a te consecrandus,' Sept. 20 ; Chambre (*Scriptt. Dunelm.*), c. viii ; *Reg. Booth.*

A. D. **1458**, after May 8. **John Hunden.** Llandaff ; res. 1476.

> Fees paid at Rome, June 21 ; Brady, *Ep. Succ.* i. 78 ; temporalities, Aug. 25.

A. D. **1458**, Dec. 3. **George Neville.** Exeter ; York, 1464 ; d. 1476, June 8.

> Consecrated in England ; Licence, Nov. 29.

A. D. **1459**, June 3. **John Arundel.** Chichester ; d. 1477, Oct. 18.

> Consecrated in England ; Licence, May 31.

A. D. **1459**, Nov. 25. **John Hales.** Lichfield ; d. 1490, Dec. 30.

> Consecrated at Coventry, in S. Clement's Chapel, by Archbishop Bourchier ; *Reg. Hales.* Licence, Nov. 11.

A. D. **1460. Robert Tully.** S. David's ; d. 1481.

> Consecrated in England ; Licence, Aug. 28.

A. D. **1462**, Oct. 24. **John Kingscote.** Carlisle ; d. 1463, Nov. 5.

> Consecrated in London (?) ; Profession, Oct. 20 and 28 ; *Reg. Booth.*

A. D. **1464**, June 24. **Richard Scrope.** Carlisle ; d. 1468, May 10.

> Consecrated at York by George of Exeter ; MS. Lansdowne, 721.

A. D. **1465. Richard Edenham.** Bangor ; d. 1496.

> Consecrated in England ; Licence, Mar. 8.

A. D. **1465**, July 7. **John Booth.** Exeter ; d. 1478, Apr. 5.

> Consecrated by Archbishop Bourchier ; Licence, July 2 ; *Reg. Booth.*

A. D. **1466**, Mar. 16.   **Robert Stillington.**   Bath; d. 1491, May.

Consecrated at York House, Westminster, by George, Archbishop of York; *Reg. Stillington.*

A. D. **1468**, Apr. 3.   **Thomas Scott** or Rotherham.   Rochester; Lincoln, 1472; York, 1480; d. 1500, May 29.

Consecrated in England; Licence, March 27; *Reg. Test. Roff.* vol. 3; *Custumale Roffense,* p. 216.

A. D. **1468**, Oct. 2.   **Edward Story.**   Carlisle; Chichester, 1478; d. 1503, Jan. 29.

Consecrated at St. Stephen's, Westminster, by George, Archbishop of York; *Chron. Abbrev.* Caius Coll. MS. p. 12.

A. D. **1471.**   **Richard Redman.**   S. Asaph; Exeter, 1495; Ely, 1501; d. 1505, Aug. 24.

Licence, Oct. 13.

A. D. **1472**, March 15.   **John Alcock.**   Rochester; Worcester, 1476; Ely, 1486; d. 1500, Oct. 1.

Consecrated in England by Archbishop Bourchier; Licence, March 13; *Reg. Test. Roff.* vol. 4; *Cust. Roff.* p. 216.

A. D. **1472**, Oct. 4.   **James Goldwell.**   Norwich; d. 1499, Feb. 15.

Consecrated at Rome, in the church of S. Blaise, by Simon, Bishop of Antibari; John Stone, *Obit. Cant.* MS. C. C. C. C. 417.

A. D. **1474**, Aug. 21.   **Thomas Milling.**   Hereford; d. 1492.

Consecrated at Westminster, in the chapel of S. Mary, by Thomas of London, Richard of S. Asaph, and William (? John) of Ardfert; *Reg. Milling.*

A. D. **1476.**   **John Smith.**   Llandaff; d. 1478, Jan. 29.

Consecrated in England; Licence, July 17.

A. D. **1476**, Sept. 22.   **John Russell.**   Rochester; Lincoln, 1480; d. 1494, Dec. 30.

Consecrated in England; Licence, Sept. 20; *Reg. Test. Roff.* vol. 4.

A. D. **1476**, Sept. 1 x Oct. 12.   **William Dudley.**   Durham; d. 1483, Nov. 24.

Durham *Halmot Book*; temporalities, Oct. 14.

A. D. **1478**, Apr. 26. **Richard Bell.** Carlisle ; res. 1495, Sept. 4.
Consecrated by Edward of Chichester ; Chambre, *Scriptt. Dunelm.* c. ix ; MS. Lansd. 721 ; Brady, i. 102.

A. D. **1478**, Nov. 8. **Peter Courtenay.** Exeter ; Winchester, 1487 ; d. 1492, Sept. 22.
Consecrated at S. Stephen's, Westminster, by Thomas of London ; *Reg. Courtenay.*

A. D. **1478.** **John Marshall.** Llandaff ; d. 1496.
Temporalities, Sept. 18.

A. D. **1479**, Jan. 31. **John Morton.** Ely ; Canterbury, 1486 ; d. 1500, Sept. 15.
Consecrated at Lambeth by Archbishop Bourchier ; Hist. Eliens. *Ang. Sac.* i. 674.

A. D. **1480**, Oct. 1. **Edmund Audley.** Rochester ; Hereford, 1492 ; Sarum, 1502 ; d. 1524, Aug. 23.
Consecrated in England ; Licence, Sept. 18 ; *Custumale Roffense*, p. 217.

A. D. **1482.** **Lionel Wydville.** Sarum ; d. 1484.
Consecrated in England ; Licence, Apr. 17.

A. D. **1482**, July 28. **Richard Martin.** S. David's ; d. 1483.
Consecrated in England ; *Reg. Martin* ; *Reg. Bourchier* (Profession, July 8).

A. D. **1483**, Sept. [7]. **Thomas Langton.** S. David's ; Sarum, 1485 ; Winchester, 1493 ; d. 1501, Jan. 27.
Consecrated by John of Worcester under commission from Archbishop Bourchier dated Sept. 3 ; *Reg. Bourchier.*

A. D. **1484**, May 26. **John Sherwood.** Durham ; d. 1494, Jan. 12.
Consecrated at Rome, in the church of S. Onofrio, by 'Peter Nannetens., Phy. Ariens., and Petr. Nassariens.' ; Brady, *Episcopal Succession*, i. xxi.

A. D. **1485**, Oct. 9. **Hugh Pavy.** S. David's ; d. 1496.
Consecrated in England ; Licence, Sept. 22 ; *Reg. Pavy.*

A. D. **1487**, Jan. 28.   **Robert Morton.**   Worcester; d. 1497, May.

> Consecrated, probably on the Archbishop's inthronement, at Canterbury by Archbishop Morton, John of Ely, Edmund of Rochester, and Thomas of Sarum; Licence, Jan. 24.   See MS. Cotton, Julius, B. 12; Leland, *Coll.* iv. pp. 207, 208.

A. D. **1487**, Apr. 8.   **Richard Fox.**   Exeter; Bath, 1492; Durham, 1494; Winchester, 1501; d. 1528, Sept. 14.

> Consecrated, probably at Norwich, by Archbishop Morton, James of Norwich, and Peter of Winchester; Licence, Apr. 3; see Leland, *Coll.* iv. p. 209.

A. D. **1489**, Nov. 15.   **Richard Hill.**   London; d. 1496, Feb. 20.

> Consecrated at Lambeth by Archbishop Morton, John of Ely, and Edward of Chichester; *Reg. Hill.*

A. D. **1493**, Feb. 3.   **Oliver King.**   Exeter; Bath, 1495; d. 1503, Aug. 29; and **William Smith.**   Lichfield; Lincoln, 1496; d. 1514, Jan. 2.

> Consecrated by Archbishop Morton; Licences, Jan. 31 and Dec. 30.

A. D. **1493**, Apr. 28.   **Thomas Savage.**   Rochester; London, 1496; York, 1501; d. 1507, Sept. 2.

> Consecrated at Lambeth by Archbishop Morton, Richard of London, and Thomas of Pavada; *Reg. Savage.*

A. D. **1494**, Feb. 23.   **John Blyth.**   Sarum; d. 1499, Aug. 23.

> Consecrated at Lambeth by Archbishop Morton; *Reg. Blyth.*

A. D. **1496**, Jan. [17?].   **Michael Deacon.**   S. Asaph; d. 1500.

> Consecrated in England; Licence, Jan. 11.

A. D. **1496**.   **William Senhouse.**   Carlisle; Durham, 1502; d. 1505.

> Provided, Sept. 4, 1495; temporalities, Dec. 11.

A. D. **1496**, Sept. [11?].   **John Ingleby.**   Llandaff; d. 1499.

> Consecrated in England; Licence, Sept. 6.

A. D. **1496**.   **Henry Dean.**   Bangor; Sarum, 1500; Canterbury, 1501, May 26; d. 1503, Feb. 15.

> Provided, July 21; temporalities, Oct. 6.

A. D. **1496**.   **John Arundel.**   Lichfield; Exeter, 1502; d. 1504, Mar. 15; and **John Morgan.**   S. David's; d. 1504.

> Consecrated in England; Licence, Nov. 12.

A. D. **1497**, May 21. **Richard FitzJames.** Rochester ; Chichester, 1503 ; London, 1506 ; d. 1522, Jan. 15.

> Consecrated at Lambeth by Archbishop Morton, John of Llandaff, and Henry of Bangor ; *Reg. FitzJames.*

A. D. **1497**, Sept. 10. **John de Gigliis.** Worcester ; d. 1498, Aug. 25.

> Consecrated at Rome ; *Reg. J. de Gigliis.*

A. D. **1498.** **Silvester de Gigliis.** Worcester ; d. 1521, Apr. 16.

> Consecrated at Rome ; provided, Dec. 24.

A. D. **1499**, Oct. [20]. **Thomas Jane.** Norwich ; d. 1500, September.

> Consecrated in England ; Licence, Oct. 17.

A. D. **1500.** **Thomas Pigott.** Bangor ; d. 1504, Aug. 15.

> Fees paid May 11 ; Brady, i. 82.

A. D. **1500**, Apr. 26. **Miles Salley.** Llandaff ; d. 1516 ; and **David ap Yorwerth.** S. Asaph ; d. 1503.

> Consecrated by Archbishop Morton ; Licences, Mar. 10 and 13.

A. D. **1501**, [Apr. 18]. **Richard Nykke.** Norwich ; d. 1536, Jan. 14.

> Consecrated in England ; Licence, Apr. 17 ; 'Annus xxxii incipit vi⁰. Junii ;' *Reg.*

A. D. **1502.** **Hadrian de Castello.** Hereford ; Bath, 1504–18.

> Provided at Rome, Feb. 14 ; consecrated before May.

A. D. **1502**, Sept. 25. **William Warham.** London ; Canterbury, 1503 ; d. 1532, Aug. 23.

> Consecrated under commission from Archbishop Dean, at Fulham, by Richard of Winchester, John of Exeter, and Richard of Rochester ; cf. Reg. Dean, in *Libr. Blamyr, Reg. Prerog., Reg. Warham.*

A. D. **1503**, Sept. 10 or 17. **Roger Layburn.** Carlisle ; d. 1508.

> Consecrated in England ; MS. Lansd. 721.

A. D. **1503**, Sept. 17. **Geoffrey Blyth.** Lichfield ; d. 1531.

> Consecrated by Richard of Winchester ; *Reg. Blyth* ; *Reg. Cant.*, cited in Richardson's *Godwin*, p. 323 ; Licence, Apr. 28.

A. D. **1504**, Feb. 4. **David ap Owen.** S. Asaph ; d. 1513, February.

> Consecrated by Archbishop Warham ; Licence, Jan. 31 ; *Reg. P. & Cant.* ; Wharton, *Epp. Assav.* p. 356.

A. D. **1504**, Oct. 27.   **Richard Mayew.**   Hereford ; d. 1516, Apr. 18.

Consecrated at Lambeth by Archbishop Warham, William of Lincoln, and Geoffrey of Lichfield ; *Reg. Mayew.*

A. D. **1504**, Nov. 24.   **William Barons.**   London ; d. 1505, Oct. 10 ; and
 John Fisher.   Rochester ; d. 1535, June 22.

Reg. Barons ; *Reg. Fisher* : 'consecratus quoque erat eodem mense die xxiiii reverendissimus dominus Dominus Will. Barons London. episc. per Cantuar. archiep. ac Norvicens. et Lincoliens. episcopos ;' at the end of a MS. of S. Jerome on the canonical epistles, in the Wodhull Library at Thenford, quoted by Churton, *Life of Smyth,* p. 218.

A. D. **1505**, Jan. 5.   **Hugh Oldham.**   Exeter ; d. 1519, June 25.

Consecrated by Archbishop Warham ; *Reg. Oldham* (begins Jan. 12) ; Licence, Dec. 29 ; *Reg. Warham,* fo. 11.

A. D. **1505**, May 11.   **Robert Sherborn.**   S. David's ; Chichester, 1508 ; d. 1536, Aug. 21.

Consecrated by Archbishop Warham ; Licence, Apr. 24 ; *Reg. Warham.* 'Consecratus est in die Pentecostes ;' *Reg. Smith,* Lincoln, quoted by Richardson, *Godwin,* p. 585.

A. D. **1505**.   **John Penny.**   Bangor ; Carlisle, 1509 ; d. 1520.

Consecrated in England ; Licence, Aug. 30.

A. D. **1506**, Nov. 8.   **James Stanley.**   Ely ; d. 1515, March 22.

Consecrated between Nov. 5 and Nov. 13 ; *Foedera,* xiii. 158, 159.

A. D. **1507** [Dec. 12 ?].   **Christopher Bainbridge.**   Durham ; York, 1508 ; d. 1514, July 14.

Temporalities, Nov. 17.

A. D. **1509**, June 17.   **Thomas Skevington.**   Bangor ; d. 1533.

Consecrated at Lambeth by Archbishop Warham, Richard of London, and Richard of Norwich ; *Reg. Warham.*

A. D. **1509**, June 24.   **Thomas Ruthall.**   Durham ; d. 1523, Feb. 4.

Consecrated at York House, Westminster, by Archbishop Bainbridge, Richard of Norwich, and John of Negropont ; *Reg. Bainbridge.*

A. D. **1509**, July 22. **Edward Vaughan.** S. David's; d. 1522.
Consecrated at Lambeth by Richard of London, Richard of Norwich, and John ——— ; *Reg. Warham.*

A. D. **1510**, Jan. 20. **Nicolas Comyn.** Ferns; Waterford, 1519.
Consecrated at S. Paul's, London; Ware's *Ireland*, Ferns, p. 26.

A. D. **1512**, [Dec. 5]. **John. Aviensis.**
Consecrated under commission of Archbishop Warham to Miles of Llandaff; *Reg. Warham*; Licence, Dec. 4.

A. D. **1513**, [Apr. 17]. **Roger Smith.** Lydda; d. 1518.
Consecrated under commission of Archbishop Warham to Miles of Llandaff; *Reg. Warham*; Licence, Apr. 11.

A. D. **1513**, May 29. **Edmund Birkhead.** S. Asaph; d. 1518, April.
Consecrated at Lambeth by Archbishop Warham, Thomas of Durham, and John of Chalcedon; *Reg. Warham.*

A. D. **1513**, July 3. **John Young.** Gallipoli; d. 1526, Mar. 28; and
Richard. Naturensis. Suffragan of Durham.
Consecrated at S. Thomas of Acre, London, by Richard of London; *Reg. FitzJames.*

A. D. **1513**. **John Kite.** Armagh; Thebes, 1521; Carlisle, 1521; d. 1537.
Provided, Oct. 21, 1513.

A. D. **1514**, March 26. **Thomas Wolsey.** Lincoln; York, 1514; d. 1530, Nov. 29.
Consecrated at Lambeth by Archbishop Warham, Richard of London, Richard of Winchester, Richard of Norwich, Hugh of Exeter, and Edmund of S. Asaph; *Reg. Warham.*

A. D. **1514**, Nov. 12. **William Atwater.** Lincoln; d. 1521, Feb. 4.
Consecrated at Lambeth by Archbishop Warham, Richard of London, Richard of Winchester, Hugh of Exeter, Miles of Llandaff, and Edmund of S. Asaph; *Reg. Warham.*

A. D. **1515**, Oct. 7. **Nicolas West.** Ely; d. 1533, Apr. 28.
Consecrated at Lambeth by Archbishop Warham, John of Rochester, and Hugh of Exeter; *Reg. Warham.*

A. D. **1516**, Nov. 30. **Charles Booth.** Hereford ; d. 1535, May 5.
Consecrated at Otford by Archbishop Warham, Richard of Winchester, and Richard of Norwich ; *Reg. Warham* ; *Reg. Booth.*

A. D. **1517**, Mar. 8. **George de Athequa.** Llandaff ; res. 1537.
Consecrated at Blackfriars by Charles of Hereford, John of Gallipoli, and Francis 'Castoriensis' ; *Reg. Warham* ; *Reg. Booth.*

A. D. **1518**, July 11. **Henry Standish.** S. Asaph ; d. 1535, July 9.
Consecrated at Otford by Archbishop Warham, Robert of Chichester, and John of Gallipoli ; *Reg. Warham,* fo. 21.

A. D. **1519**, Nov. 6. **John Voysey.** Exeter ; d. 1554, Oct. 23.
Consecrated at Otford by Archbishop Warham, John of Rochester, and Thomas of Leighlin ; *Reg. Warham,* fo. 22.

A. D. **1521**, May 5. **John Longlands.** Lincoln ; d. 1547, May 7.
Consecrated at Lambeth by Archbishop Warham, John of Rochester, Nicolas of Ely, and John of Exeter ; *Reg. Warham,* fo. 23.

A. D. **1521.** **Julius de Medicis.** Worcester ; res. 1522.
Provided June 7.

A. D. **1522.** **Jerome Ghinucci.** Worcester.
Provided Sept. 26 ; Brady, *Ep. Succ.* i. 49.

A. D. **1522**, Oct. 19. **Cuthbert Tunstall.** London ; Durham, 1530 ; dep. 1552, Oct. 14 ; and 1559, Sept. 28 ; d. 1559, Nov. 18.
Consecrated at Lambeth by Archbishop Warham, Thomas of Durham, and John of Rochester ; *Reg. Tunstall* ; *Reg. Warham.*

A. D. **1523**, Apr. 26. **Richard Rawlins.** S. David's ; d. 1536, Feb. 18.
Consecrated at Lambeth by Archbishop Warham, John of Rochester and John of Lincoln ; *Reg. Warham.*

A. D. **1523**, Dec. 6. **John Clerk.** Bath ; d. 1541, Jan. 3.
Consecrated at Rome ; Cotton MS., Vitellius, B. 5.

A. D. **1524.** **Lozenzo Campegio.** Salisbury.
Provided Dec. 2.

A. D. **1527. Robert King.** Rheon in partibus. Osney, 1541, 1546.

Provided as suffragan of Lincoln, Jan. 7, 1527 ; Brady, *Episc. Succ.* i. 115. The see of Osney founded Sept. 1, 1542, 34 Hen. VIII ; transferred to Christ Church, Oxford, June 9, 1545, 37 Hen. VIII.

A. D. **1530,** Nov. 27. **John Stokesley.** London ; d. 1539, Sept. 8.

Consecrated in the Bishop of London's chapel by John of Lincoln, Henry of S. Asaph, and Richard of S. David's ; *Reg. Stokesley.*

A. D. **1531,** Dec. 3. **Stephen Gardiner.** Winchester ; d. 1555, Nov. 12.

Consecrated in England ; *Reg. Gardiner* (Licence, Nov. 27).

A. D. **1531,** Dec. 10. **Edward Lee.** York ; d. 1544, Sept. 13.

'Reverendissimus pater Edwardus Leius, Ebor. archiepiscopus quinquagesimus octavus consecratus decimo die Decembris, 1531 ;' *Reg. Ebor.*

A. D. **1533,** Mar. 30. **Thomas Cranmer.** Canterbury ; d. 1556, March 21.

Consecrated at S. Stephen's, Westminster, by John of Lincoln, John of Exeter, and Henry of S. Asaph ; *Reg. Cranmer,* fo. 4.

A. D. **1534,** Apr. 19. **Thomas Goodrich.** Ely ; d. 1554, May 10.

        Rowland Lee. Lichfield ; d. 1543, Jan. 24 ; and

        John Salcot or **Capon.** Bangor ; Sarum, 1539 ; d. 1557, Oct. 6.

Consecrated at Croydon by Archbishop Cranmer, John of Lincoln, and Christopher of Sidon ; *Reg. Cranmer,* foll. 87, 156, 162.

A. D. **1535,** Apr. 11. **Nicolas Shaxton.** Salisbury ; res. 1539.

Consecrated at S. Stephen's, Westminster, by Archbishop Cranmer, John of London, and Thomas of Sidon ; *Reg. Cranmer,* fo. 172.

A. D. **1535,** Sept. 26. **Edward Fox.** Hereford ; d. 1538, May 8.

Consecrated at Winchester by Archbishop Cranmer, Stephen of Winchester, and Nicolas of Salisbury ; *Reg. Fox.*

A. D. **1535,** Sept. 26. **Hugh Latimer.** Worcester, res. 1539, July 1 ; d. 1555, Oct. 16.

Consecrated at the same time and place ; see Rymer, *Foedera,* xiv. 553. Latimer's precedence is between Hereford and Rochester ; Wilkins, *Conc.* iii. pp. 809, 822, 831.

A. D. **1535,** Sept. 26. **John Hilsey.** Rochester ; d. 1539.

Consecrated at the same time and place ; *Reg. Hilsey.*

A. D. **1536**, March 19.   **George Brown.**   Dublin ; dep. 1554.

Thomas Manning.   Ipswich (suffragan) ; and

John Salisbury.   Thetford (suffragan) ; Sodor and Man, 1571 ; d. 1573.

Consecrated at Lambeth by Archbishop Cranmer, Nicolas of Sarum, and John of Rochester ; *Reg. Cranmer*, foll. 187, 188.

A. D. **1536**, June 11.   **Richard Sampson.**   Chichester ; Lichfield, 1543 ; d. 1554, Sept. 25 ; and

William Rugge or **Repps.**   Norwich ; res. 1550 ; d. Sept. 21.

Consecrated at Lambeth by Archbishop Cranmer, John of Exeter, and John of Bath ; *Reg. Cranmer*, foll. 189–192 ; 208–212. Dr. Sampson 'was consecrated with the Abbot of S. Benet's, now Bishop of Norwich, on Trinity Sunday last ;' *Letters and Papers, Hen. VIII*, vol. x. p. 481.

A. D. **1536**, June.   **William Barlow.**   S. David's ; Bath, 1549–1554 ; Chichester, 1559 ; d. 1569, Dec. 10.

Record not forthcoming ; the date is fixed, by collateral proof, to June 11, 18, or 26. Barlow's precedence is between Norwich (Repps) and S. Asaph (Parfew) ; see Wilkins, *Conc.* iii. 809, 822, 831 ; Bramhall, ed. Haddan, iii. 138–143 and preface.

A. D. **1536**, July 2.   **Robert Parfew.**   S. Asaph ; Hereford, 1554 ; d. 1558, Sept. 22.

Consecrated at Lambeth by Archbishop Cranmer, John of Bangor, and William of Norwich ; *Reg. Cranmer*, fo. 197 ; *Reg. Asav.*

A. D. **1536**, Oct. 22.   **William More.**   Colchester (suffragan) ; d. 1541.

Consecrated in the Lady Chapel, Blackfriars, by John of Rochester, Robert of S. Asaph, and Thomas of Sidon ; *Reg. Cranmer*, fo. 197.

A. D. **1537**, March 25.   **Robert Holdegate.**   Llandaff ; York, 1545–1554 ; d. 1556.

Consecrated in the Lady Chapel, Blackfriars, by John of Rochester, John of Bangor, and Nicolas of Sarum ; *Reg. Cranmer*, fo. 200.

A. D. **1537** [June 17].   **Thomas Sparke.**   Berwick ; d. 1571.

Consecrated by Edward, Archbishop of York ; Profession, 'a te consecrandus ;' *Reg. Lee* ; Rymer, *Foedera*, xiv. 582.

A. D. **1537**, June 24. **Lewis Thomas.** Shrewsbury (suffragan); and

John Bird. Penreth (suffragan); Bangor, 1539; Chester, 1541–1554.

Consecrated at Lambeth by Archbishop Cranmer, John of Rochester, and Robert of S. Asaph; *Reg. Cranmer.*

A. D. **1537**, Aug. 19. **Robert Aldrich.** Carlisle; d. 1556, March 5.

Consecrated in the chapel of the Savoy by John of London, John of Rochester, and Robert of S. Asaph; *Reg. Lee.* See MS. Lansd. 721.

A. D. **1537**, Nov. 4. **Thomas Morley.** Marlborough (suffragan).

Consecrated at Lambeth by Archbishop Cranmer, John of Lincoln, and John of Rochester; *Reg. Cranmer,* fo. 202.

A. D. **1537**, Dec. 9. **Richard Yngworth.** Dover (suffragan); d. 1545; and

John Hodgkin. Bedford (suffragan); d. 1560.

Consecrated at S. Paul's by John of London, John of Rochester, and Robert of S. Asaph; *Reg. Cranmer,* fo. 203.

A. D. **1538**, March 24. **Henry Holbeche.** Bristol; Rochester, 1544; Lincoln, 1547; d. 1551, Aug. 23.

Consecrated at Rochester House, Lambeth, by John of Rochester, Hugh of Worcester, and Robert of S. Asaph; *Reg. Cranmer,* fo. 215.

A. D. **1538**, Apr. 7. **William Finch.** Taunton (suffragan); d. 1559.

Consecrated in the Lady Chapel, Blackfriars, by John of Rochester, Robert of S. Asaph, and William of Colchester; *Reg. Cranmer,* fo. 214.

A. D. **1538** [Dec. 29]. **Robert Sylvester** or **Pursglove.** Hull (suffragan); d. 1579, May 2.

Consecrated by Archbishop Lee. *Foedera,* xiv. 601.

A. D. **1539**, March 23. **John Bradley.** Shaftesbury (suffragan).

Consecrated at S. John's, Southampton, by John of Bangor, John 'Ypolitanensis,' and Thomas of Marlborough; *Reg. Cranmer,* fo. 223.

A. D. **1539** [Aug. 17]. **John Bell.** Worcester; res. 1543, Nov. 17; d. 1556, Aug. 11.

Consecrated by Archbishop Cranmer; *Foedera,* xiv. 643.

A. D. **1539**, Nov. 23.   **John Skip.**   Hereford ; d. 1552, March 30.
    Consecrated at Lambeth by Archbishop Cranmer, William of S. David's,
    and Richard of Dover ; *Reg. Skip.*

A. D. **1540**, Apr. 4.   **Edmund Bonner.**   London ; dep. 1559 ; d. 1569,
            Sept. 5 ; and

        Nicolas Heath.   Rochester ; Worcester, 1543 ;
            York, 1555–9 ; d. 1579.
    Consecrated in the chapel of London House by Stephen of Winchester,
    Richard of Chichester, and John of Hereford ; *Reg. Cranmer*, fo. 259 ;
    Reg. Bonner.

A. D. **1540**, Dec. 19.   **Thomas Thirlby.**   Westminster ; Norwich, 1550 ;
    Ely, 1554–9 ; d. 1570, Aug. 26.
    Consecrated in Henry VII's Chapel by Edmund of London, Nicolas of
    Rochester, and John of Bedford ; *Reg. Thirlby* ; *Reg. Cranmer*, fo. 261.

A. D. **1541**, May 29.   **William Knight.**   Bath ; d. 1547, Sept. 29.
    Consecrated in the Bishop of Bath's chapel in the Minories by Nicolas
    of Rochester, Richard of Dover, and John of Bedford ; *Reg. Cranmer*,
    fo. 269.

A. D. **1541.**   **Richard Pates.**   Worcester.
    Provided July 8 ; acted as Bishop 1554–1559.

A. D. **1541**, Sept. 25.   **John Wakeman.**   Gloucester ; d. 1549.
    Consecrated at Croydon by Archbishop Cranmer, Edmund of London,
    and Thomas of Westminster ; *Reg. Cranmer*, fo. 271.

A. D. **1541**, Oct. 23.   **John Chamber.**   Peterborough ; d. 1556.
    Consecrated at Peterborough by Thomas of Ely, Robert of Down, and
    Thomas of Philadelphia [the commission is to the Bishops of Ely,
    Lincoln, and Norwich] ; *Reg. Cranmer*, fo. 270.

A. D. **1542**, Feb. 19.   **Arthur Bulkeley.**   Bangor ; d. 1553, March 14.
    Consecrated in the chapel of the Dean of S. Paul's by John of Salisbury,
    William of S. David's, and John of Gloucester ; *Reg. Cranmer*, fo. 278.

A. D. **1542**, June 25.   **Paul Bush.**   Bristol ; res. 1553 ; d. 1558, Oct. 11.
    Consecrated at Hampton by Nicolas of Rochester, Thomas of West-
    minster, and John of Bedford ; *Reg. Cranmer*, fo. 285.

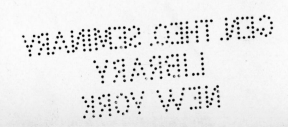

A. D. **1543**, May 6. **George Day.** Chichester; d. 1556, Aug. 11.
Consecrated by Archbishop Cranmer; *Foedera*, xiv. 785.

A. D. **1545**, May 3. **Antony Kitchin.** Llandaff; d. 1563, Oct. 31.
Consecrated in Westminster Abbey by Thomas of Westminster, Thomas of Sidon, and Lewis of Shrewsbury; *Reg. Cranmer*, fo. 310.

A. D. **1545.** **Richard Thornden.** Dover (Suffragan); d. 1557.
No record; but see below in the List of Suffragans.

A. D. **1546**, Feb. 14. **Henry Man.** Sodor and Man; d. 1556, Oct. 19.
Consecrated at S. Paul's by Edmund of London, Thomas of Sidon, and John of Bedford [commission given to Paul of Bristol; *Foedera*, xv. 86]; *Reg. Bonner*.

A. D. **1547**, Sept. 25. **Nicolas Ridley.** Rochester; London, 1550; d. 1555, Oct. 16.
Consecrated in the Dean's Chapel, S. Paul's, by Henry of Lincoln, John of Bedford, and Thomas of Sidon; *Reg. Cranmer*, fo. 327.

A. D. **1548**, Sept. 9. **Robert Ferrar.** S. David's; d. 1555, Mar. 30.
Consecrated at Chertsey by Archbishop Cranmer, Henry of Lincoln, and Nicolas of Rochester; present also Thomas of Ely and Thomas of Westminster; *Reg. Cranmer*, 327.

A. D. **1550**, June 29. **John Poynet.** Rochester; Winchester, 1551-3; d. 1556, Aug. 11.
Consecrated at Lambeth by Archbishop Cranmer, Nicolas of London, and Arthur of Bangor; *Reg. Cranmer*, 330.

A. D. **1551**, March 8. **John Hooper.** Gloucester; Worcester, 1552-3; dep. 1554; d. 1555, Feb. 9.
Consecrated at Lambeth by Archbishop Cranmer, Nicolas of London, and John of Rochester; *Reg. Cranmer*, 332.

A. D. **1551**, Aug. 30. **Miles Coverdale.** Exeter, 1551-3; d. 1568.
Consecrated at Croydon by Archbishop Cranmer, Nicolas of London, and John of Bedford; *Reg. Cranmer*, 334.

A. D. **1551**, Aug. 30. **John Scory.** Rochester; Chichester, 1552; Hereford, 1559; d. 1585, June 26.
Consecrated at Croydon by Archbishop Cranmer, Nicolas of London, and John of Bedford; *Reg. Cranmer*, 333; Cranmer's *Letters*, 294.

A. D. **1552**, June 26. **John Taylor.** Lincoln; d. 1554, December.

Consecrated at Croydon by Archbishop Cranmer, Nicolas of London, and John of Rochester; *Reg. Cranmer*, 335.

A. D. **1553**, May 26. **John Harley.** Hereford; d. 1554.

Consecrated at Croydon by Archbishop Cranmer, Nicolas of London, and Robert of Carlisle; *Reg Cranmer*, 335.

A. D. **1554**, Apr. 1. **John White.** Lincoln; Winchester, 1556; d. 1560, Jan. 12.
    James Brooks. Gloucester; d. 1558, Sept. 7.
    Maurice Griffin. Rochester; d. 1558, Nov. 20.
    Gilbert Bourn. Bath; d. 1569, Sept. 10.
    Henry Morgan. S. David's; d. 1559, Dec. 23; and
    George Coates. Chester; d. 1555.

Consecrated at S. Saviour's, Southwark, by Edmund of London, Cuthbert of Durham, and Stephen of Winchester; *Reg. D. & C. Cant.*; *sede vacante* : Machyn's *Diary*, 58.

A. D. **1554**, Oct. 28. **John Hopton.** Norwich; d. 1558.

Consecrated at London House by Edmund of London, Cuthbert of Durham, and Thomas of Ely; *Reg. D. & C. Cant.*

A. D. **1554**, Nov. 18. **Ralph Bayne.** Lichfield; dep. 1559; d. 1559, Nov. 24; and

    John Holyman. Bristol; d. 1558, Dec. 20.

Consecrated at London House by Edmund of London, John of Norwich, and Gilbert of Bath; *Reg. D. & C. Cant.*; Machyn, p. 75.

A. D. **1555**, Sept. 8. **William Glynne.** Bangor; d. 1558, May 21.
    James Turberville. Exeter; dep. 1559; and
    Hugh Curwen. Dublin; Oxford, 1567; d. 1568, Oct.

Consecrated at London House by Edmund of London, Thomas of Ely, and Maurice of Rochester : *Reg. D. & C. Cant.*; Machyn, p. 94.

A. D. **1555.** **Thomas Goldwell.** S. Asaph; dep. 1559.

Provided June 21; Brady, *Ep. Succ.*, i. 86.

A. D. **1556**, March 22. **Reginald Pole.** Canterbury; d. 1558, Nov. 19.

Consecrated at Greyfriars, Greenwich, by Nicolas of York, Edmund of London, Thomas of Ely, Richard of Worcester, John of Lincoln, Maurice of Rochester, and Thomas of S. Asaph; *Reg. Pole*, fo. 3.

A. D. **1556. Cuthbert Scott.** Chester ; dep. 1559, June 21.
> Consecrated by Archbishop Heath of York. Provided July 6 ; Brady,
> *Ep. Succ.* i. 106.

A. D. **1557**, Aug. 15. **Thomas Watson.** Lincoln, dep. 1559, June 26.
> **David Poole.** Peterborough ; dep. 1559 ; and
> **Owen Oglethorpe.** Carlisle ; dep. 1559, June 21.
> Consecrated at Chiswick by Archbishop Heath of York, Thomas of Ely,
> and William of Bangor ; *Reg. Pole*, 10.

A. D. **1557**, Nov. 21. **John Christopherson.** Chichester ; d. 1558.
> Consecrated at London House by Edmund of London, Thomas of Ely,
> and Maurice of Rochester ; *Reg. Pole*, 12.

A. D. **1559**, Dec. 17. **Matthew Parker.** Canterbury ; d. 1575, May 17.
> Consecrated at Lambeth by William Barlow, elect of Chichester, late
> Bishop of Bath and Wells, John, elect of Hereford, late Bishop of
> Rochester, John of Bedford, and Miles, late Bishop of Exeter ; *Reg.
> Parker*, 10.

A. D. **1559**, Dec. 21. **Edmund Grindal.** London ; York, 1570 ; Canter-
> bury, 1576 ; d. 1583, July 6.
> **Richard Cox.** Ely ; d. 1581, July 22.
> **Rowland Meyrick.** Bangor ; d. 1566, Jan. 24 ; and
> **Edwin Sandys.** Worcester ; London, 1570 ; York,
> 1577 ; d. 1588, July 10.
> Consecrated at Lambeth by Archbishop Parker, William of Chichester,
> John of Hereford, John of Bedford ; *Reg. Parker*, 18, 22, 32, 39.

A. D. **1560**, Jan. 21. **Nicolas Bullingham.** Lincoln ; Worcester, 1571 ;
> d. 1576, Apr. 18.
> **John Jewell.** Sarum ; d. 1571, Sept. 23.
> **Thomas Young.** S. David's ; York, 1561 ; d. 1568,
> June 26 ; and
> **Richard Davies.** S. Asaph ; S. David's, 1561 ; d.
> 1581, Nov. 7.
> Consecrated at Lambeth by Archbishop Parker, Edmund of London,
> Richard of Ely, and John of Bedford ; *Reg. Parker*, 46, 50, 54, 59.

A. D. **1560**, March 24.   **Edmund Gheast.** Rochester ; Sarum, 1571 ; d. 1577, Feb. 28.

Gilbert Berkeley. Bath ; d. 1581, Nov. 2 ; and

Thomas Bentham. Coventry ; d. 1579, Feb. 21.

Consecrated at Lambeth by Archbishop Parker, Nicolas of Lincoln, and John of Sarum ; *Reg. Parker*, 63, 69, 74.

A. D. **1560**, July 14. **William Alley.** Exeter ; d. 1570, Apr. 16.

Consecrated at Lambeth by Archbishop Parker, Edmund of London, and Gilbert of Bath ; *Reg. Parker*, 80.

A. D. **1560**, Sept. 1. **John Parkhurst.** Norwich ; d. 1575, Feb. 2.

Consecrated at Lambeth by Archbishop Parker, Gilbert of Bath, and William of Exeter ; *Reg. Parker*, 84.

A. D. **1561**, Feb. 16. **Robert Horne.** Winchester ; d. 1580, June 1 ; and

Edmund Scambler. Peterborough ; Norwich, 1585 ; d. 1594, May 7.

Consecrated at Lambeth by Archbishop Parker, Edmund of London, Thomas of S. David's, and Thomas of Lichfield ; *Reg. Parker*, 88, 92 ; Machyn, 251.

A. D. **1561**, March 2. **John Best.** Carlisle ; d. 1570, May 22 ; and

James Pilkington. Durham ; d. 1576, Jan. 23.

Consecrated at London House by Archbishop Young of York ; Parker, *Antiqq.* ed. Hanau, p. 37 ; Camden's *Annals*, p. 50 ; Flower's *Visitation*, 255 ; Machyn, 252.

A. D. **1561**, May 4. **William Downham.** Chester ; d. 1577, Dec. 3.

Consecrated by Archbishop Young of York ; Parker, *Antiqq.* p. 37 ; Godwin.

A. D. **1561**, May 26. **Thomas Davis.** S. Asaph ; d. 1573.

Consecrated at Croydon by Archbishop Parker, Richard of S. David's, and Edmund of Rochester ; *Reg. Parker*, 100.

A. D. **1562**, Apr. 19. **Richard Cheyney.** Gloucester ; d. 1579, Apr. 25.

Consecrated at Lambeth by Archbishop Parker, Edmund of London, and Edmund of Rochester ; *Reg. Parker*, 109.

A. D. **1566**, May 5.   **Hugh Jones.**   Llandaff; d. 1574, November.
Consecrated at Lambeth by Archbishop Parker, Edmund of London, and
Edmund of Rochester ; *Reg. Parker*, 114.

A. D. **1566**, Oct. 20.   **Nicolas Robinson.**   Bangor; d. 1585, Feb. 13.
Consecrated at Lambeth by Archbishop Parker, Nicolas of Lincoln, and
Edmund of Rochester ; *Reg. Parker*, 118.

A. D. **1567**, March 9.   **Richard Barnes.**   Nottingham (suffragan); Carlisle,
1570; Durham, 1577; d. 1587, Aug. 24.
Consecrated at York by Archbishop Young of York, James of Durham,
and William of Chester ; *Reg. Young*; Le Neve's *Archbishops*, ii. 15.

A. D. **1569**, May 15.   **Richard Rogers.**   Dover (suffragan); d. 1597, May 19.
Consecrated at Lambeth by Archbishop Parker, Edmund of London,
and Edmund of Rochester ; *Reg. Parker*, 122.

A. D. **1570**, May 21.   **Richard Curteis.**   Chichester; d. 1582, August.
Consecrated at Canterbury by Archbishop Parker, Edmund of London,
Robert of Winchester, and Edmund of Rochester ; *Reg. Parker*, 125.

A. D. **1571**, Feb. 24.   **Thomas Cowper.**   Lincoln ; Winchester, 1584; d.
1594, Apr. 29.
Consecrated at Lambeth by Archbishop Parker, Robert of Winchester,
and Nicolas of Worcester ; *Reg. Parker*, 138.

A. D. **1571**, March 18.   **William Bradbridge.**   Exeter; d. 1578, June 27.
Consecrated at Lambeth by Archbishop Parker, Robert of Winchester,
and Nicolas of Worcester. *Reg. Parker*, 140.

A. D. **1572**, March 9.   **Edmund Freke.**   Rochester ; Norwich, 1575 ; Worcester, 1584 ; d. 1591, March 21.
Consecrated at Lambeth by Archbishop Parker, Robert of Winchester,
and Edmund of Sarum ; *Reg. Parker*, 214.

A. D. **1573**, Dec. 13.   **William Hughes.**   S. Asaph ; d. 1600, Nov. 18.
Consecrated at Lambeth by Archbishop Parker, Robert of Winchester,
and Richard of Chichester ; *Reg. Parker*, ii. 5.

A. D. **1575,** Apr. 17.   **William Blethin.**   Llandaff; d. 1590, Oct. 15.

Consecrated at Lambeth by Archbishop Parker, Edwin of London, and Edmund of Rochester ; *Reg. Parker*, ii. 9.

A. D. **1576,** Apr. 15.   **John Piers.**   Rochester ; Sarum, 1577 ; York, 1589 ; d. 1594, Sept. 28 ; and

John Meyrick.   Sodor and Man ; d. 1599.

Consecrated at Lambeth by Archbishop Grindal, Edwin of London, and Robert of Winchester ; *Reg. Grindal*, 17, 18.

A. D. **1577,** March 24.   **John Aylmer.**   London ; d. 1594, June 3.

Consecrated at Lambeth by Archbishop Grindal, Edwin of York, and John of Rochester ; *Reg. Grindal*, 27.

A. D. **1577,** Apr. 21.   **John Whitgift.**   Worcester ; Canterbury, 1583 ; d. 1604, Feb. 29.

Consecrated at Lambeth by Archbishop Grindal, John of London, Robert of Winchester, and Richard of Chichester ; *Reg. Grindal*, 34.

A. D. **1577,** Sept. 29.   **John May.**   Carlisle ; d. 1598, Feb. 15.

Consecrated at Fulham by John of London, William of Chester, John of Rochester, and Richard of Dover ; MS. Wharton, 578 ; Godwin.

A. D. **1578,** March 16.   **John Young.**   Rochester ; d. 1605, Apr. 10.

Consecrated at Lambeth by Archbishop Grindal, John of London, and John of Sarum ; *Reg. Grindal*, 48.

A. D. **1579. Marmaduke Middleton.**   Consecrated to Waterford ; S. David's, 1582 ; dep. 1590 ; d. 1592, Nov. 30.

Cotton's *Fasti Eccl. Hib.*; Ware, *Waterford*, p. 27.

A. D. **1579,** Aug. 2.   **John Wolton.**   Exeter ; d. 1594, March 13.

Consecrated at Croydon by Archbishop Grindal, John of London, and John of Rochester ; *Reg. Grindal*, 53.

A. D. **1579,** Nov. 8.   **William Chaderton.**   Chester ; Lincoln, 1595 ; d. 1608, Apr. 11.

Consecrated at S. Gregory's, by S. Paul's, by Archbishop Sandys of York, John of London, and John of Rochester ; *Reg. Sandys.*

A. D. **1580**, Sept. 18.   **John Watson.**   Winchester; d. 1584, Jan. 23; and
  William Overton.   Lichfield; d. 1609, Apr. 9.

Consecrated at Croydon by Archbishop Grindal, John of London, and John of Rochester; *Reg. Grindal*, 58, 64.

A. D. **1581**, Sept. 3.   **John Bullingham.**   Gloucester; d. 1598, May 20.

Consecrated at Croydon by Archbishop Grindal, John of London, and John of Rochester; *Reg. Grindal*, 70.

A. D. **1584**, Sept. 13.   **Thomas Godwin.**   Bath; d. 1590, Nov. 19.

Consecrated at Lambeth by Archbishop Whitgift, John of London, and John of Rochester; *Reg. Whitgift*, i. 18.

A. D. **1584**, Dec. 6.   **William Wickham.**   Lincoln; Winchester, 1595; d. 1595, June 11.

Consecrated at Lambeth by Archbishop Whitgift, Edmund of Worcester, John of Exeter, and Marmaduke of S. David's; *Reg. Whitgift*, i. 23.

A. D. **1585**, Feb. 7.   **Richard Howland.**   Peterborough; d. 1600, June 23.

Consecrated at Lambeth by Archbishop Whitgift, Thomas of Winchester, John of Exeter, and William of Lincoln; *Reg. Whitgift*, i. 40.

A. D. **1586**, Jan. 30.   **Herbert Westfaling.**   Hereford; d. 1602, March 1.
  Hugh Bellott.   Bangor; Chester, 1595; d. 1596, June 13; and
  Thomas Bickley.   Chichester; d. 1596, Apr. 30.

Consecrated at Lambeth by Archbishop Whitgift, John of London, and John of Sarum; *Reg. Whitgift*, i. 47, 52, 57.

A. D. **1589**, July 27.   **Matthew Hutton.**   Durham; York, 1595; d. 1606, Jan. 15.

Consecrated at York by Archbishop Piers of York, John of Carlisle, and William of Chester; *Reg. Piers*; Le Neve, *Lives of the Archbishops*, ii. 87.

A. D. **1589**, Dec. 14.   **Richard Fletcher.**   Bristol; Worcester, 1593; London, 1595; d. 1596, June 15; and
  John Underhill.   Oxford; d. 1592, May 12.

Consecrated at Lambeth by Archbishop Whitgift, John of London, John of Rochester, and John of Gloucester; *Reg. Whitgift*, i. 62, 70.

A. D. **1591**, Aug. 29. **Gervas Babington.** Llandaff; Exeter, 1595; Worcester, 1597; d. 1610, May 17.

> Consecrated in Croydon Church by Archbishop Whitgift, John of London, and John of Rochester; *Reg. Whitgift*, i. 77.

A. D. **1591**, Dec. 26. **John Coldwell.** Sarum; d. 1596, Oct. 14.

> Consecrated at Lambeth by Archbishop Whitgift, John of London, Thomas of Winchester, Richard of Bristol, and John of Oxford; *Reg. Whitgift*, i. 81.

A. D. **1592**, Nov. 12. **John Sterne.** Suffragan, Colchester; d. 1608.

> Consecrated in Fulham Church by Archbishop Whitgift, John of London, John of Rochester, and Richard of Bristol ; *Reg. Whitgift*, ii. 1.

A. D. **1593**, Feb. 11. **John Still.** Bath ; d. 1608, Feb. 26.

> Consecrated at Lambeth by Archbishop Whitgift, John of London, John of Rochester, and Richard of Worcester ; *Reg. Whitgift*, ii. 13.

A. D. **1593**. **John Thornborough.** Consecrated to Limerick ; Bristol, 1603 ; Worcester, 1616 ; d. 1641, July 3.

> Ware's *Ireland*, Limerick, p. 20.

A. D. **1594**, June 9. **Anthony Rudd.** S. David's ; d. 1615, March 7.

> Consecrated at Lambeth by Archbishop Whitgift, John of Rochester, and Richard of Worcester ; *Reg. Whitgift*, ii. 19.

A. D. **1595**, Jan. 12. **William Redman.** Norwich ; d. 1602, Sept. 25.

> Consecrated at Lambeth by Archbishop Whitgift, Richard of London, John of Rochester, and William of Lincoln ; *Reg. Whitgift*, ii. 31.

A. D. **1595**, Apr. 13. **Tobias Matthew.** Durham ; York, 1606 ; d. 1628, March 29.

> Consecrated at London by Matthew Hutton, Archbishop of York. See Le Neve, *Lives of the Archbishops*, ii. 105 ; Surtees' *Durham*.

A. D. **1595**, July 20. **William Morgan.** Llandaff ; S. Asaph, 1601 ; d. 1604, Sept. 10.

> Consecrated in Croydon Church by Archbishop Whitgift, Richard of London, John of Rochester, and William of Norwich ; *Reg. Whitgift*, ii. 60.

A. D. **1596**, Jan. 25.   **William Day.**   Winchester ; d. 1596, Sept. 20 ; and
    Richard Vaughan.   Bangor ; Chester, 1597 ; London,
        1604 ; d. 1607, March 30.
Consecrated at Lambeth by Archbishop Whitgift, Richard of London,
and John of Rochester ; *Reg. Whitgift*, ii. 65, 71.

A. D. **1596**, June 13.   **Thomas Bilson.**   Worcester ; Winchester, 1597 ;
d. 1616, June 18.
    Consecrated at Lambeth by Archbishop Whitgift, Richard of London,
    William of Winchester, and Richard of Bangor ; *Reg. Whitgift*, ii. 76.

A. D. **1596**, Aug. 15.   **Anthony Watson.**   Chichester ; d. 1605, Sept. 10.
    Consecrated at Lambeth by Archbishop Whitgift, John of Rochester,
    Richard of Bangor, and Thomas of Worcester ; *Reg. Whitgift*, ii. 90.

A. D. **1597**, May 8.   **Richard Bancroft.**   London ; Canterbury, 1604 ;
d. 1610, Nov. 2.
    Consecrated at Lambeth by Archbishop Whitgift, John of Rochester,
    Anthony of S. David's, Richard of Bangor, and Anthony of Chichester ;
    Reg. Whitgift, ii. 82.

A. D. **1598**, July 23.   **Henry Robinson.**   Carlisle ; d. 1616, June 19.
    Consecrated at London House by Richard of London, John of Rochester,
    and Anthony of Chichester ; *Reg. Whitgift*, iii. 6 ; Mason's *Vindiciae*,
    p. 391.

A. D. **1598**, Nov. 12.   **Godfrey Goldsborough.**   Gloucester ; d. 1604,
        May 26.
    William Cotton.   Exeter ; d. 1621, Aug. 26.
    Henry Cotton.   Sarum ; d. 1615, May 7 ; and
    Henry Rowlands.   Bangor ; d. 1616, July 6.
Consecrated at Lambeth by Archbishop Whitgift, Richard of London,
William of Lichfield, and Anthony of Chichester ; *Reg. Whitgift*, iii.
    11, 17, 24, 32.

A. D. **1600**, Feb. 3.   **Martin Heaton.**   Ely ; d. 1609, July 12.
    Consecrated at Lambeth by Archbishop Whitgift, Richard of London,
    William of Lichfield, and Anthony of Chichester ; *Reg. Whitgift*, iii. 37.

A. D. **1600**, Feb.   **George Lloyd.**   Consecrated to Sodor and Man; Chester, 1605; d. 1615, Aug. 1.

> Lindsay, xxxiv.

A. D. **1601**, Apr. 26.   **Thomas Dove.**   Peterborough; d. 1630, Aug. 30.

> Consecrated at Lambeth by Archbishop Whitgift, Richard of London, Thomas of Winchester, Anthony of Chichester, and Martin of Ely; *Reg. Whitgift*, iii. 43.

A. D. **1601**, Nov. 22.   **Francis Godwin.**   Llandaff; Hereford, 1617; d. 1633, Apr. 29.

> Consecrated in Henry VII's chapel by Archbishop Whitgift, Richard of London, William of Lincoln, and John of Bath; *Reg. Whitgift*, iii. 59.

A. D. **1603**, Feb. 20.   **Robert Bennett.**   Hereford; d. 1617, Oct. 25; and

> **John Jegon.**   Norwich; d. 1618, March 13.

> Consecrated at Lambeth by Archbishop Whitgift, Richard of London, John of Rochester, and Anthony of Chichester; *Reg. Whitgift*, iii. 65, 71.

A. D. **1604**, Feb. 12.   **John Bridges.**   Oxford; d. 1618, March 26.

> Consecrated at Lambeth by Archbishop Whitgift, Richard of London, Tobias of Durham, John of Rochester, and Anthony of Chichester; *Reg. Whitgift*, iii. 84.

A. D. **1604**, Dec. 30.   **Richard Parry.**   S. Asaph; d. 1623, Sept. 26.

> Consecrated at Lambeth by Archbishop Bancroft, Richard of London, Tobias of Durham, and Martin of Ely; *Reg. Bancroft*, 21.

A. D. **1605**, Feb. 10.   **John Philips.**   Sodor and Man; d. 1633, Aug. 7.

> Consecrated at London House by Richard of London, Tobias of Durham, Anthony of Chichester, and George of Chester; *Reg. Bancroft*, 22; see Le Neve's *Archbishops*, ii. 107.

A. D. **1605**, March 17.   **Thomas Ravis.**   Gloucester; London, 1607; d. 1609, Dec. 14.

> Consecrated at Lambeth by Archbishop Bancroft, Tobias of Durham, and Anthony of Chichester; *Reg. Bancroft*, 28; see Le Neve's *Archbishops*, ii. 107.

A. D. **1605**, June 30. **William Barlow.** Rochester; Lincoln, 1608; d. 1613, Sept. 7.

> Consecrated at Lambeth by Archbishop Bancroft, Richard of London, Anthony of Chichester, and Thomas of Gloucester; *Reg. Bancroft*, 35.

A. D. **1605**, Nov. 3. **Launcelot Andrewes.** Chichester; Ely, 1609; Winchester, 1619; d. 1626, Sept. 25.

> Consecrated at Lambeth by Archbishop Bancroft, Richard of London, John of Norwich, Thomas of Gloucester, and William of Rochester; *Reg. Bancroft*, 42.

A. D. **1606**, Sept. 7. **William James.** Durham; d. 1617, May 12.

> Consecrated by Archbishop Mathew of York, Richard of London, William of Rochester, and Launcelot of Chichester; Mason's *Vindiciae*, p. 391.

A. D. **1607**, July 12. **Henry Parry.** Gloucester; Worcester, 1610; d. 1616, Dec. 12.

> Consecrated at Lambeth by Archbishop Bancroft, Thomas of London, William of Rochester, and Launcelot of Chichester; *Reg. Bancroft*, 62.

A. D. **1608**, Apr. 17. **James Montague.** Bath; Winchester, 1616; d. 1618, July 20.

> Consecrated at Lambeth by Archbishop Bancroft, Thomas of London, Henry of Sarum, William of Rochester, Launcelot of Chichester, and Henry of Gloucester; *Reg. Bancroft*, 68.

A. D. **1608**, Oct. 9. **Richard Neile.** Rochester; Lichfield, 1610; Lincoln, 1614; Durham, 1617; Winchester, 1628; York, 1632; d. 1640, Oct. 31.

> Consecrated at Lambeth by Archbishop Bancroft, Thomas of London, Launcelot of Chichester, and James of Bath; *Reg. Bancroft*, 83; Camden, *James I*, p. 6.

A. D. **1609**, Dec. 3. **George Abbot.** Lichfield; London, 1610; Canterbury, 1611; d. 1633, Aug. 4; and

>   **Samuel Harsnett.** Chichester; Norwich, 1619; York, 1628; d. 1631, May 25.

> Consecrated at Lambeth by Archbishop Bancroft, Launcelot of Ely, and Richard of Rochester; *Reg. Bancroft*, 96, 102.

A. D. **1610**, Oct. 21.   **John Spottiswoode.**   Glasgow.

> **Andrew Lamb.**   Brechin; and

> **Gavin Hamilton.**   Galloway.

Consecrated at London House by George of London, Launcelot of Ely, and James of Bath; *Reg. Bancroft*, 175; Le Neve, *Archbishops*, i. 91; Spotswood, *History*, p. 514; Keith, *Bishops*, p. 263.

A. D. **1611**, June 9.   **Giles Thompson.**   Gloucester; d. 1612, June 14; and

> **John Buckridge.**   Rochester; Ely, 1628; d. 1631, May 23.

Consecrated at Lambeth by Archbishop Abbot, John of Oxford, Launcelot of Ely, James of Bath, and Richard of Lichfield; *Reg. Abbot*, 13.

A. D. **1611**, Sept. 8.   **John King.**   London; d. 1621, March 30.

Consecrated at Lambeth by Archbishop Abbot, Richard of Lichfield, Giles of Gloucester, and John of Rochester; *Reg. Abbot*, 28.

A. D. **1612**, Sept. 20.   **Miles Smith.**   Gloucester; d. 1624, Oct. 20.

Consecrated at Croydon by Archbishop Abbot, John of London, Richard of Lichfield, and John of Rochester; *Reg. Abbot*, 33; *Reg. Croydon.*

A. D. **1614**, Apr. 3.   **John Overall.**   Lichfield; Norwich, 1618; d. 1619, May 12.

Consecrated at Lambeth by Archbishop Abbot, John of London, James of Bath, Richard of Lincoln, and John of Rochester; *Reg. Abbot*, 45.

A. D. **1615**, July 9.   **Richard Milbourne.**   S. David's; Carlisle, 1621; d. 1624.

Consecrated at Lambeth by Archbishop Abbot, John of London, Launcelot of Ely, John of Rochester, and John of Lichfield; *Reg. Abbot*, 51.

A. D. **1615**, Dec. 3.   **Robert Abbot.**   Sarum; d. 1618, March 2.

Consecrated at Lambeth by Archbishop Abbot, John of London, Launcelot of Ely, and Richard of Lincoln; *Reg. Abbot*, 58; Camden, *James I*, p. 15.

A. D. **1616**, July 7. **Thomas Morton.** Chester; Lichfield, 1619; Durham, 1632; d. 1659, Sept. 22.

> Consecrated at Lambeth by Archbishop Abbot, Christopher of Armagh, John of London, John of Rochester, John of Lichfield, and [Alexander of Caithness?]; *Reg. Abbot*, 66 ; Camden, p. 19.

A. D. **1616**, Nov. 24. **Robert Snowden.** Carlisle; d. 1621, May 15.

> Consecrated at York by Archbishop Mathew of York, William of Durham, Thomas of Chester, and John of Sodor and Man; *Reg. Mathew*; Le Neve, *Archbishops*, ii. 111 ; Lindsay, p. lxi.

A. D. **1616**, Dec. 8. **Arthur Lake.** Bath; d. 1626, May 4 ; and

                Lewis Bayly. Bangor; d. 1631, Oct. 26.

> Consecrated at Lambeth by Archbishop Abbot, Launcelot of Ely, Richard of Lincoln, John of Rochester, and John of Lichfield ; *Reg. Abbot*, 78, 84 ; Camden, p. 22.

A. D. **1617**, Dec. 14. **Nicolas Felton.** Bristol; Ely, 1619; d. 1626, Oct. 5 ; and

                George Monteigne. Lincoln; London, 1621 ; Durham, 1628 ; York, 1628; d. 1628, Nov. 6.

> Consecrated at Lambeth by Archbishop Abbot, Marco Antonio of Spalato, John of London, Launcelot of Ely, John of Rochester, and John of Lichfield ; *Reg. Abbot*, 96, 105 ; Camden, p. 28.

A. D. **1618**, Apr. 19. **Martin Fotherby.** Sarum; d. 1620, March 11.

> Consecrated at Lambeth by Archbishop Abbot, John of London, John of Lichfield, and George of Lincoln ; *Reg. Abbot*, 119 ; Camden, p. 31.

A. D. **1618**, July 12. **George Carleton.** Llandaff; Chichester, 1619; d. 1628, May.

> Consecrated at Lambeth by Archbishop Abbot, John of London, John of Rochester, John of Lichfield, and George of Lincoln ; *Reg. Abbot*, 125.

I 2

A. D. **1619**, May 9.   **John Bridgman.**   Chester; d. 1652.

   John Howson.   Oxford; Durham, 1628; d. 1632, Feb. 6; and

   Rowland Searchfield.   Bristol; d. 1622, Oct. 11.

Consecrated at Lambeth by Archbishop Abbot, John of London, John of Rochester, Thomas of Lichfield, and Arthur of Bath; *Reg. Abbot*, ii. 7, 14, 22.

A. D. **1619**, Oct. 10.   **Theophilus Field.**   Llandaff; S. David's, 1627; Hereford, 1635; d. 1636, June 2.

Consecrated at Lambeth by Archbishop Abbot, John of London, John of Rochester, Richard of S. David's, and George of Derry; *Reg. Abbot*, ii. 41; Camden, p. 50.

A. D. **1620**, July 9.   **Robert Townson.**   Sarum; d. 1621, May 15.

Consecrated at Lambeth by Archbishop Abbot, John of Rochester, Thomas of Lichfield, Nicolas of Ely, and George of Lincoln; *Reg. Abbot*, 49; Camden, p. 59.

A. D. **1621**, Nov. 11.   **John Williams.**   Lincoln; York, 1641; d. 1650, March 25.

Consecrated at Westminster Abbey by George of London, John of Worcester, Nicolas of Ely, John of Oxford, and Theophilus of Llandaff; *Reg. Abbot*, ii. 62; Camden, p. 75.

A. D. **1621**, Nov. 18.   **John Davenant.**   Sarum; d. 1641, Apr. 20.

   Valentine Carey.   Exeter; d. 1626, June 10; and

   William Laud.   S. David's; Bath, 1626; London, 1628; Canterbury, 1633; d. 1645, Jan. 10.

Consecrated at London House by George of London, John of Worcester, Nicolas of Ely, George of Chichester, John of Oxford, and Theophilus of Llandaff; *Reg. Abbot*, ii. 69, 74, 79; Camden, p. 75; Laud's *Diary*, p. 4.

A. D. **1621**, Dec. 2.   **James Ussher.**   Meath; Armagh, 1625; Carlisle, 1642; d. 1656, March 21.

Consecrated at S. Peter's, Drogheda, by Christopher of Armagh, Thomas of Kilmore, Robert of Down and Connor, and Theophilus of Dromore; Cotton's *Fasti*; Ware, *Meath*, p. 26.

A. D. **1622**, Dec. 18. **William Murray.** Kilfenora ; Llandaff, 1627 ; d. 1640, February.

> Consecrated at S. Patrick's, Dublin, by Launcelot of Dublin, James of Meath, and Roland of Clonfert ; Cotton's *Fasti* ; Ware, *Fenabore*, p. 55.

A. D. **1623**, March 23. **Robert Wright.** Bristol ; Lichfield, 1632 ; d. 1643, August.

> Consecrated at Lambeth by Archbishop Abbot, Launcelot of Winchester, John of Lincoln, and Valentine of Exeter ; *Reg. Abbot*, ii. 85 ; Camden, p. 81.

A. D. **1624**, Feb. 15. **John Hanmer.** S. Asaph ; d. 1629, July 23.

> Consecrated at Lambeth by Archbishop Abbot, John of Worcester, Thomas of Lichfield, Theophilus of Llandaff, and William of S. David's ; *Reg. Abbot*, ii. 90 ; Laud's *Diary*, p. 10.

A. D. **1624**, Sept. 26. **Richard Senhouse.** Carlisle ; d. 1626, May 6.

> Consecrated at York by Archbishop Mathew of York, Richard of Durham, Thomas of Lichfield, and John of Chester : *Reg. Mathew.*

A. D. **1625**, March 6. **Godfrey Goodman.** Gloucester ; dep. 1640 ; d. 1656, Jan. 19.

> Consecrated at Lambeth by Archbishop Abbot, George of London, John of Rochester, Theophilus of Llandaff, and John of Lincoln ; *Reg. Abbot*, ii. 96.

A. D. **1626**, Dec. 3. **Francis White.** Carlisle ; Norwich, 1629 ; Ely, 1631 ; d. 1638, February.

> Consecrated at Durham House by Richard of Durham, John of Rochester, John of Oxford, Theophilus of Llandaff, and William of Kilfenora ; *Reg. Mathew.*

A. D. **1627**, Dec. 23. **Joseph Hall.** Exeter ; Norwich, 1641 ; d. 1656, Sept. 8.

> Consecrated at London House by George of London, Richard of Durham, John of Rochester, John of Oxford, Theophilus of S. David's, and William of Kilfenora ; *Reg. Abbot*, ii. 114.

A. D. **1628**, Aug. 24.   **Richard Montagu.**   Chichester ; Norwich, 1638 ; d. 1641, Apr. 13.

> Consecrated in Croydon Chapel by Archbishop Abbot, William of London, Richard of Winchester, John of Ely, and Francis of Carlisle ; *Reg. Abbot*, ii. 145 ; Hacket's *Williams*, p. 68 ; Laud's *Diary*, p. 43.

A. D. **1628**, Sept. 7.   **Leonard Mawe.**   Bath ; d. 1629, Sept. 2 ; and

> **Walter Curll.**   Rochester ; Bath, 1629 ; Winchester, 1632 ; d. 1647.

> Consecrated in Croydon Chapel by Richard of Winchester, John of Ely, and Francis of Carlisle ; *Reg. Abbot*, ii. 151, 156.

A. D. **1628**, Oct. 19.   **Richard Corbett.**   Oxford ; Norwich, 1632 ; d. 1635, July 28.

> Consecrated at Lambeth by Archbishop Abbot, John of Durham, John of Ely, Francis of Carlisle, and William of Llandaff ; *Reg. Abbot*, ii. 162.

A. D. **1629**, March 15.   **Barnabas Potter.**   Carlisle ; d. 1642, January.

> Consecrated at Ely House by Archbishop Harsnett of York ; Lindsay's *Mason*, p. lxiv ; Wood, *Ath. Oxon.* ii. 6.

A. D. **1629**, Sept. 20.   **John Owen.**   S. Asaph ; d. 1651, Oct. 15.

> Lindsay's *Mason*, p. lxv ; Wood, *Ath. Oxon.* i. 628.

A. D. **1630**, Feb. 7.   **John Bowle.**   Rochester ; d. 1637, Oct. 9.

> Consecrated at Lambeth by Archbishop Abbot, Samuel of York, Theophilus of S. David's, and Walter of Rochester ; *Reg. Abbot*, iii. 17.

A. D. **1630**, Oct. 24.   **William Piers.**   Peterborough ; Bath, 1632 ; d. 1670, April.

> Consecrated in Croydon Chapel by Archbishop Abbot, Richard of Winchester, Theophilus of S. David's, Richard of Oxford, and Walter of Rochester ; *Reg. Abbot*, iii. 23.

A. D. **1632**, March 4.   **David Dolben.**   Bangor ; d. 1633, Nov. 27.

> Consecrated at Lambeth by Archbishop Abbot, William of London Theophilus of S. David's, and Francis of Ely ; *Reg. Abbot*, iii. 32.

A. D. **1632**, June 10.   **John Bancroft.**   Oxford ; d. 1641, February.

> Consecrated at Lambeth by Archbishop Abbot, Theophilus of S. David's, Francis of Ely, William of Llandaff, and John of Rochester ; *Reg. Abbot*, iii. 45.

A. D. **1633**, Feb. 10.   **Augustine Lindsell.**   Peterborough ; Hereford, 1634 ; d. 1634, Nov. 6 ; and
> > **George Coke.**   Bristol ; Hereford, 1636 ; d. 1646, Dec. 10.

> Consecrated at Lambeth by Archbishop Abbot, Thomas of Durham, Theophilus of S. David's, Robert of Lichfield, Francis of Ely, John of Rochester, and John of Oxford ; *Reg. Abbot*, iii. 83, 90.

A. D. **1633**, Oct. 27.   **William Juxon.**   London ; Canterbury, 1660 ; d. 1663, June 4.

> Consecrated at Lambeth by Archbishop Laud, Richard of York, Francis of Ely, William of Llandaff, John of Rochester, and John of Oxford ; *Reg. Laud*, i. 18.

A. D. **1634**, Feb. 16.   **Edmund Griffith.**   Bangor ; d. 1637, May 26.

> Consecrated at Lambeth by Archbishop Laud, William of London, Francis of Ely, William of Llandaff, John of Oxford, and Augustine of Peterborough ; *Reg. Laud*, i. 26.

A. D. **1634**, March 9.   **William Forster.**   Sodor and Man ; d. 1635.

> Consecrated at Winchester House, Southwark, by Archbishop Neile of York, Francis of Ely, and Augustine of Peterborough ; *Reg. Neile.*

A. D. **1634**, May 18.   **Francis Dee.**   Peterborough ; d. 1638, Oct. 8.

> Consecrated at Lambeth by Archbishop Laud, William of London, Theophilus of S. David's, Francis of Ely, and William of Llandaff ; *Reg. Laud*, i. 39.

A. D. **1635**, March 8.   **Matthew Wren.**   Hereford ; Norwich, 1635 ; Ely, 1638 ; d. 1667, Apr. 24.

> Consecrated at Lambeth by Archbishop Laud, Richard of York, Walter of Winchester, Francis of Ely, Joseph of Exeter, and William of Llandaff ; *Reg. Laud*, i. 44.

A. D. **1635**, June 10.   **Richard Parr.**   Sodor and Man ; d. 1643.

> Consecrated at Winchester House, Southwark, by Archbishop Neile of York, Francis of Ely, and William of Llandaff ; *Reg. Neile.*

A. D. **1636**, Feb. 28. **Roger Mainwaring.** S. David's ; d. 1653, July 1.

Consecrated at Lambeth by Archbishop Laud, William of London, Theophilus of Hereford, Francis of Ely, and William of Llandaff ; *Reg. Laud*, i. 57 ; *Diary*, p. 53.

A. D. **1637**, Jan. 15. **Robert Skinner.** Bristol ; Oxford, 1641 ; Worcester, 1663 ; d. 1670, June 14.

Consecrated at Lambeth by Archbishop Laud, William of London, Francis of Ely, John of Oxford, and Matthew of Norwich ; *Reg. Laud*, i. 66.

A. D. **1637**, Sept. 3. **William Roberts.** Bangor ; d. 1665, Aug. 12.

Consecrated in Croydon Chapel by Archbishop Laud, William of London, Francis of Ely, William of Bath, and John of Oxford ; *Reg. Laud*, ii. 29.

A. D. **1638**, Jan. 14. **John Warner.** Rochester ; d. 1666, Oct. 14.

Consecrated at Lambeth by Archbishop Laud, William of London, Walter of Winchester, John of Oxford, and William of Bangor ; *Reg. Laud*, ii. 72.

A. D. **1638**, June 17. **Brian Duppa.** Chichester ; Sarum, 1641 ; Winchester, 1660 ; d. 1662, March 26.

Consecrated at Lambeth by Archbishop Laud, Thomas of Durham, Robert of Lichfield, John of Oxford, and Matthew of Ely ; *Reg. Laud*, ii. 46.

A. D. **1639**, Jan. 13. **John Towers.** Peterborough ; d. 1649, Jan. 10.

Consecrated at Lambeth by Archbishop Laud, William of London, Walter of Winchester, Matthew of Ely, and John of Rochester ; *Reg. Laud*, ii. 52.

A. D. **1640**, March 29. **Morgan Owen.** Llandaff ; d. 1645, March 4.

Consecrated at Lambeth by Archbishop Laud, William of London, Walter of Winchester, Matthew of Ely, and John of Rochester ; *Reg. Laud*, ii. 58.

A. D. **1641**, Dec. 19. **John Prideaux.** Worcester ; d. 1650, July 19.

Consecrated in Henry VII's Chapel by Archbishop Williams of York, William of London, Walter of Winchester, and Robert of Lichfield ; *Reg. Laud*, ii. 70.

A. D. **1642**, Feb. 6. **Thomas Winniffe.** Lincoln ; d. 1654, Sept. 19 ; and
Henry King. Chichester ; d. 1669, Sept. 30.

Consecrated at Fulham by William of London, Walter of Winchester
John of Rochester, and John of Worcester ; *Reg. Laud*, ii. 84, 92.

A. D. **1642**, [June 26 ?]. **Thomas Westfield.** Consecrated to Bristol ; d. 1644,
June 25.

See Hardy's Le Neve, i. 216.

A. D. **1642**, May 15. **Ralph Brownrigg.** Exeter ; d. 1659, Dec. 7.

Consecrated in Henry VII's Chapel by Archbishop Williams of York,
William of London, Thomas of Durham, and Henry of Chichester ;
Reg. Laud, ii. 99.

A. D. **1644**, Apr. 28. **Accepted Frewen.** Lichfield ; York, 1660 ; d. 1664,
March 28.

Consecrated at Magdalen College, Oxford, by Archbishop Williams of
York, Walter of Winchester, Robert of Oxford, Brian of Sarum, John
of Peterborough, and John of Rochester ; Wood, *Ath. Oxon.* ii. 64 ;
Dugdale's *Diary*, p. 65. Wood mentions Worcester instead of Rochester.

A. D. [**1644**, August]. **Thomas Howell.** Bristol ; d. 1646.

Consecrated at Oxford by Archbishop Ussher of Armagh ; Wood, *Ath.
Oxon.* ii. 656. He did homage at Christ Church, March 23, 1645 ;
Dugdale, p. 78.

A. D. **1660**, Oct. 28. **Gilbert Sheldon.** London ; Canterbury, 1663 ; d.
1677, Nov. 9.

Humfrey Henchman. Sarum ; London, 1663 ; d.
1675, Oct. 7.

George Morley. Worcester ; Winchester, 1662 ; d.
1684, Oct. 29.

Robert Sanderson. Lincoln ; d. 1663, Jan. 29 ;
and

George Griffith. S. Asaph ; d. 1666, Nov. 28.

Consecrated in Henry VII's Chapel by Brian of Winchester, Accepted of
York, Matthew of Ely, John of Rochester, and Henry of Chichester ;
Reg. Juxon, fo. 208 ; Pepys' *Diary*, i. 269.

A. D. **1660**, Dec. 2.   **William Lucy.**   S. David's; d. 1677, Oct. 4.

Hugh Lloyd.   Llandaff; d. 1667, June 7; and

John Gauden.   Exeter; Worcester, 1662; d. 1662, Sept. 20.

Consecrated in Henry VII's Chapel by [Accepted of York,] Gilbert of London, [John of Rochester,] Humfrey of Sarum, George of Worcester, [Brian of Winchester,] and Robert of Lincoln. Lucy, Lloyd, and Gauden are in Juxon's *Register* said to be consecrated on Nov. 18 : but all the seven were consecrated on Dec. 2 ; see Sancroft's Sermon ; Kennett, *Reg.* p. 323, &c.

A. D. **1660**, Dec. 2.   **Richard Sterne.**   Carlisle; York, 1664; d. 1683, June 18.

John Cosin.   Durham; d. 1672, Jan. 15.

Brian Walton.   Chester; d. 1661, Nov. 29; and

Benjamin Laney.   Peterborough; Lincoln, 1663; Ely, 1667; d. 1675, Jan. 24.

Consecrated in Henry VII's Chapel by Accepted of York, Gilbert of London, John of Rochester, Humfrey of Sarum, George of Worcester, [Brian of Winchester, and Robert of Lincoln]; *Reg. Juxon*; *Reg. Frewen*. The Bishops of Winchester and Lincoln are not mentioned among the consecrators in the *York Register*, nor by Kennett; *Register*, p. 323 ; Lindsay, p. lxxv.

A. D. **1661**, Jan. 6.   **Gilbert Ironside.**   Bristol; d. 1671, Sept. 19.

Edward Reynolds.   Norwich; d. 1676, July 28.

Nicolas Monk.   Hereford; d. 1661, Dec. 17; and

William Nicolson.   Gloucester; d. 1672, Feb. 5.

Consecrated in Henry VII's Chapel by Gilbert of London, Accepted of York, John of Durham, Henry of Chichester, Robert of Lincoln, and Benjamin of Peterborough; *Reg. Juxon* [Jan. 13 wrongly]; Kennett, *Reg.*, p. 356.

A. D. **1661**, March 24.   **Samuel Rutter.**   Sodor and Man; d. 1663, May 30.

Consecrated at Ely House by John of Durham, Matthew of Ely, George of Worcester, Richard of Carlisle, and Brian of Chester; *Reg. Frewen.*

A. D. **1661**, Dec. 15. **James Sharpe.** S. Andrew's.

      Andrew Fairfowl. Glasgow.

      Robert Leighton. Dunblane ; and

      James Hamilton. Galloway.

    Consecrated at Westminster by Gilbert of London, George of Worcester, Richard of Carlisle, and Hugh of Llandaff ; *Reg. Juxon*, 237 ; Kennett, 280.

A. D. **1661**, Dec. 22. **John Hackett.** Lichfield ; d. 1670, Oct. 28.

    Consecrated at Lambeth by Gilbert of London, Henry of Chichester, Humfrey of Sarum, George of Worcester, and William of Gloucester ; *Reg. Juxon*, 275 ; Kennett, *Reg.* 587.

A. D. **1662**, Feb. 9. **Herbert Croft.** Hereford ; d. 1691, May 18.

    Consecrated at Lambeth by Gilbert of London, Henry of Chichester, Humfrey of Sarum, George of Worcester, and William of Gloucester ; *Reg. Juxon*, 283 ; Kennett, p. 626.

A. D. **1662**, Feb. 9. **Henry Fern.** Chester ; d. 1662, March 16.

    Consecrated at Ely House ; Kennett, p. 644 ; *Kingdom's Intelligencer*, No. 7.

A. D. **1662**, May 11. **George Hall.** Chester ; d. 1668, Aug. 23.

    Consecrated at Ely House by Archbishop Frewen of York, John of Durham, Matthew of Ely, Robert of Oxford, Henry of Chichester, and Richard of Carlisle ; *Reg. Frewen* ; Kennett, p. 684.

A. D. **1662**, July 20. **Seth Ward.** Exeter ; Sarum, 1667 ; d. 1689, Jan. 6.

    Consecrated at Lambeth by Gilbert of London, George of Winchester, Henry of Chichester, Humfrey of Sarum, and William of Gloucester ; *Reg. Juxon*, 302 ; Kennett, p. 733.

A. D. **1662**, Nov. 30. **John Earle.** Worcester ; Sarum, 1663; d. 1665, Nov. 17.

    Consecrated in Henry VII's Chapel by Gilbert of London, George of Winchester, Henry of Chichester, Humfrey of Sarum, and William of Gloucester ; *Reg. Juxon*, 309 ; Kennett, p. 823.

A. D. **1663**, May 10.   **Joseph Henshaw.**   Peterborough ; d. 1679, March 9.

> Consecrated at Lambeth by Gilbert of London, George of Winchester, Henry of Chichester, and Humfrey of Sarum ; *Reg. Juxon*, 326.

A. D. **1663**, May 20 (?).   **William Fuller.**   Limerick ; Lincoln, 1667 ; d. 1675, Apr. 22.

> Consecrated at Christ Church, Dublin, by Michael of Dublin, John of Clogher, Robert of Ferns, and Edward of Cork ; Cotton's *Fasti*, &c. ; Ware, *Limerick*, p. 21.

A. D. **1663**, July 5.   **Isaac Barrow.**   Sodor and Man ; S. Asaph, 1670 ; d. 1680, June 24.

> Consecrated in Henry VII's Chapel by John of Durham, Humfrey of Sarum, Richard of Carlisle, and George of Chester ; *Reg. Frewen*.

A. D. **1663**, Dec. 20.   **William Paul.**   Oxford ; d. 1665, May 24.

> Consecrated at Lambeth by Archbishop Frewen of York, Humfrey of London, George of Winchester, and Henry of Chichester ; *Reg. Juxon*, 376.

A. D. **1664**, July 10.   **Edward Rainbow.**   Carlisle ; d. 1684, March 26.

> Consecrated in Henry VII's Chapel by Archbishop Sheldon and others ; *Reg. Rainbow* ; Wood, *Ath. Oxon.* i. 861 ; Lindsay, p. lxvi.

A. D. **1665**, Dec. 3.   **Walter Blandford.**   Oxford ; Worcester, 1671 ; d. 1675, July 16.

> Consecrated at New College, Oxford, by Humfrey of London, William of Gloucester, and Seth of Exeter ; Wood, *Ath. Oxon.* ii. 677.

A. D. **1665**, Dec. 31.   **Alexander Hyde.**   Sarum ; d. 1667, Aug. 22.

> Consecrated at New College, Oxford, by Archbishop Sheldon, George of Winchester, William of Gloucester, Joseph of Peterborough, Walter of Oxford, and William of Limerick ; Wood, *Ath. Oxon.* ii. 668.

A. D. **1666**, July 1.   **Robert Morgan.**   Bangor ; d. 1673, Sept. 1.

> Consecrated at Lambeth by Archbishop Sheldon, Humfrey of London, George of Winchester, and William of Limerick ; *Reg. Juxon*, 385.

A. D. **1666**, Nov. 25. **John Dolben.** Rochester ; York, 1683 ; d. 1686, Apr. 11.

> Consecrated at Lambeth by Archbishop Sheldon, Richard of York, Humfrey of London, George of Winchester, Benjamin of Lincoln, and John of Lichfield ; *Reg. Sheldon*, 6.

A. D. **1667**, Aug. 24. **Francis Davies.** Llandaff ; d. 1675, March 14.

> Consecrated at Lambeth by Archbishop Sheldon, Humfrey of London, Benjamin of Ely, and John of Rochester ; *Reg. Sheldon*, 18.

A. D. **1667**, Oct. 13. **Henry Glemham.** S. Asaph ; d. 1670, Jan. 17.

> Consecrated at Lambeth by Archbishop Sheldon, George of Winchester, Benjamin of Ely, Seth of Sarum, and William of Lincoln ; *Reg. Sheldon*, 40.

A. D. **1667**, Nov. 3. **Antony Sparrow.** Exeter ; Norwich, 1676 ; d. 1685, May 19.

> Consecrated at Lambeth by Archbishop Sheldon, George of Winchester, Benjamin of Ely, William of Gloucester, Seth of Sarum, Robert of Bangor, and William of Lincoln ; *Reg. Sheldon*, 47.

A. D. **1668**, Nov. 15. **John Wilkins.** Chester ; d. 1672, Nov. 19.

> Consecrated at Ely House by John of Durham, Benjamin of Ely, and Seth of Sarum ; Wood, *Ath. Oxon.* ii. 371 ; Evelyn, *Diary*, ii. 35, adds Canterbury and Rochester.

A. D. **1670**, March 6. **Peter Gunning.** Chichester ; Ely, 1675 ; d. 1684, July 6.

> Consecrated at Lambeth by Archbishop Sheldon, Richard of York, Humfrey of London, George of Winchester, Benjamin of Ely, Seth of Sarum, John of Rochester, and Antony of Exeter ; *Reg. Sheldon*, 54.

A. D. **1670**, June 19. **Robert Creighton.** Bath ; d. 1672, Nov. 21.

> Consecrated at Lambeth by Humfrey of London, George of Winchester, Benjamin of Ely, John of Rochester, and William of Lincoln ; *Reg. Sheldon*, 69.

A. D. **1671**, July 2.   **Thomas Wood.**   Lichfield; d. 1692, Apr. 18; and
           Nathaniel Crewe.   Oxford; Durham, 1674; d. 1721,
           Sept. 18.

    Consecrated at Lambeth by Archbishop Sheldon, Humfrey of London,
    Benjamin of Ely, Walter of Worcester, John of Rochester, and William
    of Lincoln; *Reg. Sheldon*, 83, 90.

A. D. **1671**, Oct. 1.   **Henry Bridgman.**   Sodor and Man; d. 1682, May 15.

    Consecrated at Chester by John of Chester, Isaac of S. Asaph, Robert of
    Bangor, and Robert of Clogher; Wood, *Ath. Oxon.* ii. 682; *London
    Gazette*, No. 615.

A. D. **1672**, Feb. 11.   **Guy Carleton.**   Bristol; Chichester, 1679; d. 1685,
July 6.

    Consecrated in Henry VII's Chapel by Archbishop Sterne of York,
    Walter of Worcester, John of Rochester, William of Lincoln, and
    Nathaniel of Oxford; *Reg. Sheldon*, 96.

A. D. **1672**, Nov. 3.   **John Pritchett.**   Gloucester; d. 1681, Jan. 1.

    Consecrated at Lambeth by Archbishop Sheldon, Humfrey of London,
    Benjamin of Ely, John of Rochester, and John of Chester; *Reg.
    Sheldon*, 102.

A. D. **1673**, Feb. 9.   **John Pearson.**   Chester; d. 1686, July 16; and
           Peter Mews.   Bath; Winchester, 1684; d. 1706, Nov. 9.

    Consecrated at Lambeth by Archbishop Sheldon, Humfrey of London,
    John of Rochester, Antony of Exeter, Isaac of S. Asaph, Peter of
    Chichester, Nathaniel of Oxford, and John of Gloucester; *Reg. Sheldon*,
    108; Wood, *Ath. Oxon.* ii. 675; Lindsay, p. lxxviii.

A. D. **1673**, Nov. 16.   **Humfrey Lloyd.**   Bangor; d. 1689, Jan. 18.

    Consecrated at London House by Humfrey of London, George of
    Winchester, Seth of Sarum, John of Rochester, Antony of Exeter,
    and Francis of Llandaff; *Reg. Sheldon*, 116.

A. D. **1674**, Dec. 6.   **Henry Compton.**   Oxford; London, 1675; d. 1713,
July 7.

    Consecrated at Lambeth by Archbishop Sheldon, George of Winchester,
    Seth of Sarum, John of Rochester, Joseph of Peterborough, and Peter
    of Chichester; *Reg. Sheldon*, 123.

A. D. **1675**, Apr. 18.   **Ralph Brideoake.**   Chichester; d. 1678, Oct. 5; and
William Lloyd.   Llandaff; Peterborough, 1679;
Norwich, 1685; dep. 1690, Feb. 1; d. 1710,
Jan. 1.

Consecrated at Lambeth by Archbishop Sheldon, George of Winchester,
Seth of Sarum, Antony of Exeter, Peter of Bath, Guy of Bristol, and
John of Gloucester; *Reg. Sheldon*, 136, 153.

A. D. **1675**, June 27.   **Thomas Barlow.**   Lincoln; d. 1691, Oct. 8.

Consecrated at Ely House by George of Winchester, Seth of Sarum, Peter
of Ely, Peter of Bath, and Guy of Bristol; *Reg. Sheldon*, 146.

A. D. **1675**, Aug. 29.   **James Fleetwood.**   Worcester; d. 1683, July 17.

Consecrated at S. Peter-le-Poor, London, by John of Rochester, Peter of
Ely, Ralph of Chichester, and Thomas of Lincoln; *Reg. Sheldon*, 161.

A. D. **1676**, Feb. 6.   **John Fell.**   Oxford; d. 1686, July 10.

Consecrated at Winchester House, Chelsea, by Henry of London, George
of Winchester, John of Rochester, Peter of Ely, and Ralph of Chichester;
Reg. Sheldon, 176.

A. D. **1676**, Nov. 12.   **Thomas Lamplugh.**   Exeter; York, 1688; d. 1691,
May 5.

Consecrated at Lambeth by Henry of London, Seth of Sarum, John of
Rochester, and Antony of Norwich; *Reg. Sheldon*, 192.

A. D. **1678**, Jan. 27.   **William Sancroft.**   Canterbury; dep. 1690, Feb. 1;
d. 1693, Nov. 24; and
William Thomas.   S. David's; Worcester, 1683;
d. 1689, June 25.

Consecrated at Lambeth by Henry of London, Seth of Sarum, Joseph
of Peterborough, John of Rochester, Peter of Ely, Guy of Bristol,
Thomas of Lincoln, and Thomas of Exeter; *Reg. Sancroft*, 7; Le Neve,
Archbishops, i. 200.

A. D. **1679**, Feb. 9.   **William Gulston.**   Bristol; d. 1684, Apr. 4.

Consecrated at Lambeth by Archbishop Sancroft, Henry of London,
Seth of Sarum, John of Rochester, and Guy of Chichester; *Reg.
Sancroft*, 51.

A. D. **1679**, June 22. **William Beaw.** Llandaff; d. 1706, Feb. 10.

Consecrated at Lambeth by Archbishop Sancroft, Henry of London, Edward of Carlisle, and William of Peterborough; *Reg. Sancroft*, 36.

A. D. **1680**, Oct. 3. **William Lloyd.** S. Asaph; Lichfield, 1692; Worcester, 1699; d. 1717, Aug. 30.

Consecrated at Lambeth by Archbishop Sancroft, Henry of London, John of Rochester, Peter of Ely, and John of Oxford; *Reg. Sancroft*, 43.

A. D. **1681**, March 27. **Robert Frampton.** Gloucester; dep. 1690, Feb. 1; d. 1708, May 25.

Consecrated at All Souls', Oxford, by Archbishop Sancroft, Henry of London, John of Rochester, Peter of Ely, Thomas of Lincoln, and Thomas of Exeter; *Reg. Sancroft*, 50.

A. D. **1683.** **John Lake.** Sodor and Man; Bristol, 1684; Chichester, 1685; d. 1689, Aug. 30.

Consecrated, probably Jan. 7, at London. Confirmed, Jan. 6; *Reg. Sterne.* Licence, Jan. 2; *Reg. Sancroft.*

A. D. **1683**, March 11. **Edward Jones.** Cloyne; S. Asaph, 1692; d. 1703, May 10.

Consecrated at Cashel by Thomas of Cashel, Hugh of Waterford, John of Killaloe, and Simon of Limerick; Cotton's *Fasti.*

A. D. **1683**, Nov. 11. **Francis Turner.** Rochester; Ely, 1684; dep. 1690, Feb. 1; d. 1700, Nov. 2; and

Laurence Womock. S. David's; d. 1686, March 12.

Consecrated at Lambeth by Archbishop Sancroft, Henry of London, Nathaniel of Durham, Seth of Sarum, and William of Peterborough; *Reg. Sancroft*, 75, 82.

A. D. **1684**, June 19. **Thomas Smith.** Carlisle; d. 1702, Apr. 12.

Consecrated at York by Archbishop Dolben of York, Nathaniel of Durham, and John of Sodor and Man; *Reg. Dolben.*

A. D. **1684**, Nov. 2. **Thomas Spratt.** Rochester; d. 1713, May 20.

Consecrated at Lambeth by Archbishop Sancroft, Henry of London, Seth of Sarum, William of Peterborough, Francis of Ely, and Ezekiel of Derry; *Reg. Sancroft*, 102.

A. D. **1685**, Jan. 25. **Thomas Ken.** Bath; dep. 1690, Feb. 1; d. 1711, March 19.

> Consecrated at Lambeth by Archbishop Sancroft, Henry of London, Nathaniel of Durham, William of Peterborough, Francis of Ely, and Thomas of Rochester; *Reg. Sancroft*, 116.

A. D. **1685**, March 15. **Baptist Levinz.** Sodor and Man; d. 1693, Jan. 31.

> Consecrated at Lambeth by Archbishop Sancroft, Henry of London, William of S. Asaph, Francis of Ely, and Alexander of Glasgow; Wharton MS. 578.

A. D. **1685**, Oct. 25. **Thomas White.** Peterborough; dep. 1690, Feb. 1; d. 1698, May 30.

> Consecrated at Lambeth by Archbishop Sancroft, Henry of London, William of S. Asaph, John of Chichester, Francis of Ely, Thomas of Rochester, and James of Dunkeld; *Reg. Sancroft*, 135.

A. D. **1685**, Nov. 8. **Jonathan Trelawney.** Bristol; Exeter, 1689; Winchester, 1707; d. 1721, July 19.

> Consecrated at Lambeth by Archbishop Sancroft, John of York, Henry of London, Nathaniel of Durham, Peter of Winchester, Thomas of Exeter, Francis of Ely, and Thomas of Rochester; *Reg. Sancroft*, 142.

A. D. **1686**, Oct. 17. **John Lloyd.** S. David's; d. 1687, Feb. 13.

> **Samuel Parker.** Oxford; d. 1688, March 20; and
>
> **Thomas Cartwright.** Chester; d. 1689, Apr. 15.

> Consecrated at Lambeth by Archbishop Sancroft, Nathaniel of Durham, William of Norwich, Francis of Ely, and Thomas of Rochester; *Reg. Sancroft*, 148, 156, 161; Cartwright's *Diary*, pp. 5, 6; Luttrell's *Diary*, i. 386.

A. D. **1687**, June 26. **Thomas Watson.** S. David's; dep. 1699; d. 1717, June 3.

> Consecrated at Lambeth by Archbishop Sancroft, Thomas of Rochester, and Thomas of Chester; *Reg. Sancroft*, 170; Cartwright's *Diary*, p. 64.

A. D. **1688**, Oct. 7. **Timothy Hall.** Oxford; d. 1690, Apr. 10.

> Consecrated at Lambeth by Archbishop Sancroft, John of Chichester, and Thomas of Chester; *Reg. Sancroft*, 184.

K

A. D. **1689**, March 31.   **Gilbert Burnet.** Sarum; d. 1715, March 17.

 Consecrated at Fulham by Henry of London, Peter of Winchester, William of Llandaff, and William of S. Asaph; *Reg. Sancroft*, 190. Le Neve adds Lincoln and Carlisle; *Archbishops*, i. 213; Luttrell, i. 516.

A. D. **1689**, June 30.   **Humfrey Humphries.** Bangor; Hereford, 1701; d. 1712, Nov. 20.

 Consecrated at Fulham by Henry of London, Thomas of Carlisle, and Gilbert of Sarum; *Reg. D. & C. Cant.*; *Reg. Sancroft*, 202. Le Neve adds S. Asaph; *Archbishops*, i. 213; Hearne's *Otterbourne*, ii. 725.

A. D. **1689**, Sept. 15.   **Nicolas Stratford.** Chester; d. 1707, Feb. 12.

 Consecrated at Fulham by Henry of London and others; Le Neve, *Archbishops*, i. 227.

A. D. **1689**, Oct. 13.   **Edward Stillingfleet.** Worcester; d. 1699, March 27.

  Simon Patrick. Chichester; Ely, 1691; d. 1707, May 31; and

  Gilbert Ironside. Bristol; Hereford, 1691; d. 1701, Aug. 27.

 Consecrated at Fulham by Henry of London, William of S. Asaph, and Thomas of Rochester; *Reg. D. & C. Cant.* 7, 12, 18.

A. D. **1690**, May 11.   **John Hough.** Oxford; Lichfield, 1699; Worcester, 1717; d. 1743, May 8.

 Consecrated at Fulham by Henry of London, Peter of Winchester, William of Llandaff, William of S. Asaph, Gilbert of Sarum, and Edward of Worcester; *Reg. D. & C. Cant.* 25.

A. D. **1691**, May 31.   **John Tillotson.** Canterbury; d. 1694, Nov. 22.

 Consecrated at Bow Church by Peter of Winchester, William of S. Asaph, Gilbert of Sarum, Edward of Worcester, Gilbert of Bristol, and John of Oxford; *Reg. Tillotson*, 9; Luttrell's *Diary*, ii. 238.

A. D. **1691**, July 5.   **John Moore.** Norwich; Ely, 1707; d. 1714, July 31.

  Richard Cumberland. Peterborough; d. 1718, Oct. 9.

  Edward Fowler. Gloucester; d. 1714, Aug. 26; and

  John Sharpe. York; d. 1714, Feb. 2.

 Consecrated at Bow Church by Archbishop Tillotson, Peter of Winchester, Gilbert of Sarum, Edward of Worcester, Gilbert of Bristol, and Simon of Ely; *Reg. Tillotson*, 24, 33, 42, 51; Luttrell's *Diary*, ii. 260.

A. D. **1691**, Aug. 30. **Robert Grove.** Chichester ; d. 1696, Sept. 25.

Richard Kidder. Bath ; d. 1703, Nov. 26 ; and

John Hall. Bristol ; d. 1710, Feb. 4.

Consecrated at Bow Church by Archbishop Tillotson, Gilbert of Sarum, Edward of Worcester, John of Norwich, and Edward of Gloucester ; *Reg. Tillotson*, 66, 75, 83.

A. D. **1692**, Jan. 10. **Thomas Tenison.** Lincoln ; Canterbury, 1695 ; d. 1715, Dec. 14.

Consecrated at Lambeth by Archbishop Tillotson, Henry of London, Gilbert of Sarum, Edward of Worcester, and Simon of Ely ; *Reg. Tillotson*, 95.

A. D. **1695**, March 10. **James Gardiner.** Lincoln ; d. 1705, March 1.

Consecrated at Lambeth by Archbishop Tenison, Henry of London, Peter of Winchester, William of Lichfield, and Thomas of Rochester ; *Reg. Tenison*, i. 19.

A. D. **1696**, Dec. 13. **John Williams.** Chichester ; d. 1709, Apr. 24.

Consecrated at London by Archbishop Tenison, Henry of London, Peter of Winchester, William of Lichfield, Thomas of Rochester, and Gilbert of Sarum ; *Reg. Tenison*, i. 24.

A. D. **1698**, Jan. 16. **Thomas Wilson.** Sodor and Man ; d. 1755, March 7.

Consecrated in Savoy Chapel by Archbishop Sharpe of York, Nicolas of Chester, and John of Norwich ; *Reg. Sharpe.*

A. D. **1699**, Sept. 24. **William Talbot.** Oxford ; Sarum, 1715 ; Durham, 1721 ; d. 1730, Oct. 10.

Consecrated at Lambeth by Archbishop Tenison, Henry of London, Thomas of Rochester, and John of Norwich ; *Reg. Tenison*, i. 43.

A. D. **1702**, Jan. 4. **John Evans.** Bangor ; Meath, 1715 ; d. 1724, March 2.

Consecrated at Lambeth by Archbishop Tenison, Henry of London, William of Worcester, Gilbert of Sarum, Humfrey of Hereford, and John of Norwich ; *Reg. Tenison*, i. 58.

A. D. **1702**, June 14. **William Nicholson.** Carlisle; Derry, 1718; Cashel, 1727; d. 1727, Feb. 15.

> Consecrated at Lambeth by Archbishop Tenison, Henry of London, John of Norwich, Edward of Gloucester, and John of Bangor; *Reg. Tenison*, i. 134.

A. D. **1703**, Oct. 31. **George Hooper.** S. Asaph; Bath, 1704; d. 1727, Sept. 6.

> Consecrated at Lambeth by Archbishop Tenison, Henry of London, Thomas of Rochester, Simon of Ely, and John of Lichfield; *Reg. Tenison*, i. 68.

A. D. **1704**, July 16. **William Beveridge.** S. Asaph; d. 1708, March 5.

> Consecrated at Lambeth by Archbishop Tenison, Thomas of Rochester, and George of Bath; *Reg. Tenison*, i. 82.

A. D. **1705**, Apr. 29. **George Bull.** S. David's; d. 1710, Feb. 17.

> Consecrated at Lambeth by Archbishop Tenison, Simon of Ely, John of Norwich, and John of Chichester; *Reg. Tenison*, i. 91.

A. D. **1705**, Oct. 21. **William Wake.** Lincoln; Canterbury, 1716; d. 1737, Jan. 24.

> Consecrated at Lambeth by Archbishop Tenison, Henry of London, Gilbert of Sarum, John of Norwich, and John of Chichester; *Reg. Tenison*, i. 100.

A. D. **1706**, June 30. **John Tyler.** Llandaff; d. 1724, July 6.

> Consecrated at Lambeth by Archbishop Tenison, Henry of London, Thomas of Rochester, and John of Bangor; *Reg. Tenison*, ii. 7.

A. D. **1708**, Feb. 8. **Offspring Blackall.** Exeter; d. 1716, Nov. 29; and **Charles Trimnell.** Norwich; Winchester, 1721; d. 1723, Aug. 15.

> Consecrated at Lambeth by Henry of London, Gilbert of Sarum, John of Lichfield, John of Ely, and William of Oxford; *Reg. Tenison*, ii. 33, 41.

A. D. **1708**, Feb. 8. **William Dawes.** Chester; York, 1714; d. 1724, Apr. 30.

> Consecrated in Henry VII's Chapel by Archbishop Sharpe of York, Jonathan of Winchester, Thomas of Rochester, and William of Carlisle; *Reg. Dawes* at Chester; *London Gazette*, No. 4410; Luttrell's *Diary* vi. 265.

A. D. **1708**, June 6.   **William Fleetwood.**   S. Asaph; Ely, 1714; d. 1723, Aug. 4.

    Consecrated at Lambeth by Archbishop Tenison, John of Chichester, William of Oxford, and John of Bangor; *Reg. Tenison*, ii. 49.

A. D. **1709**, Nov. 13.   **Thomas Manningham.**   Chichester; d. 1722, Aug. 25.

    Consecrated at Lambeth by Archbishop Tenison, Henry of London, John of Lichfield, John of Ely, and Charles of Norwich; *Reg. Tenison*, ii. 57.

A. D. **1710**, Nov. 19.   **John Robinson.**   Bristol; London, 1714; d. 1723, Apr. 11; and

    Philip Bisse.   S. David's; Hereford, 1713; d. 1721, Sept. 6.

    Consecrated at Lambeth by Archbishop Tenison, Henry of London, John of Lichfield, and John of Bangor; *Reg. Tenison*, ii. 65, 73.

A. D. **1713**, March 15.   **Adam Ottley.**   S. David's; d. 1723, Oct. 3.

    Consecrated at Lambeth by Henry of London, John of Lichfield, John of Llandaff, Offspring of Exeter, Thomas of Chichester, and Philip of Hereford; *Reg. Tenison*, ii. 90.

A. D. **1713**, July 5.   **Francis Atterbury.**   Rochester; dep. 1723; d. 1733, Feb. 15.

    Consecrated at Lambeth by Jonathan of Winchester, John of Ely, Charles of Norwich, and Adam of S. David's; *Reg. Tenison*, ii. 98.

A. D. **1714**, Apr. 4.   **George Smalridge.**   Bristol; d. 1719, Sept. 27.

    Consecrated at Lambeth by John of London, Jonathan of Winchester, John of Lichfield, and George of Bath; *Reg. Tenison*, ii. 128.

A. D. **1714**, Apr. 4.   **Francis Gastrell.**   Chester; d. 1725, Nov. 14.

    Consecrated at Somerset House by William of York, Philip of Hereford, and Adam of S. David's; *Reg. Dawes.*

A. D. **1715**, Jan. 16.   **Richard Willis.**   Gloucester; Sarum, 1721; Winchester, 1723; d. 1734, Aug. 10.

    Consecrated at Lambeth by Gilbert of Sarum, John of Lichfield, and John of Bangor; *Reg. Tenison*, ii. 146.

A. D. **1715**, Feb. 6.   **John Wynne.**   S. Asaph ; Bath, 1727 ; d. 1743, July 15.
Consecrated at Lambeth by Gilbert of Sarum, John of Lichfield, John of Bangor, and Richard of Gloucester ; *Reg. Tenison*, ii. 156.

A. D. **1715**, May 15.   **John Potter.**   Oxford ; Canterbury, 1737 ; d. 1747, Oct. 10.
Consecrated at Lambeth by Jonathan of Winchester, John of Bangor, William of Lincoln, and Richard of Gloucester ; *Reg. Tenison*, ii. 176.

A. D. **1716**, Feb. 12.   **Edmund Gibson.**   Lincoln ; London, 1723 ; d. 1748, Aug. 4.
Consecrated at Somerset House by Archbishop Wake, John of London, Jonathan of Winchester, Charles of Norwich, and Richard of Gloucester ; *Reg. Wake*, i. 21.

A. D. **1716**, March 18.   **Benjamin Hoadly.**   Bangor ; Hereford, 1721 ; Sarum, 1723 ; Winchester, 1734 ; d. 1761, Apr. 17.
Consecrated at Ely House by Archbishop Wake, Jonathan of Winchester, Charles of Norwich, William of Ely, and Edmund of Lincoln ; *Reg. Wake*, i. 28.

A. D. **1717**, Feb. 24.   **Launcelot Blackburn.**   Exeter ; York, 1724 ; d. 1743, March 23.
Consecrated at Ely House by Archbishop Wake, Jonathan of Winchester, William of Sarum, Charles of Norwich, and William of Ely ; *Reg. Wake*, i. 36.

A. D. **1717**, Nov. 17.   **Edward Chandler.**   Lichfield ; Durham, 1730 ; d. 1750, July 20.
Consecrated at Lambeth by Archbishop Wake, John of Worcester, William of Sarum, and Edmund of Lincoln ; *Reg. Wake*, i. 50.

A. D. **1718**, June 1. **Samuel Bradford.**   Carlisle ; Rochester, 1723 ; d. 1731, May 17.
Consecrated at Lambeth by Archbishop Wake, John of London, Francis of Rochester, and Richard of Gloucester ; *Reg. Wake*, i. 266.

A. D. **1718**, Nov. 9.   **White Kennett.**   Peterborough ; d. 1728, Dec. 19.
Consecrated at Lambeth by Archbishop Wake, John of Worcester, William of Sarum, Charles of Norwich, and Richard of Gloucester ; *Reg. Wake*, i. 57.

A. D. **1719**, Nov. 15. **Hugh Boulter.** Bristol; Armagh, 1724; d. 1742, Sept. 27.

> Consecrated at Lambeth by Archbishop Wake, John of Worcester, William of Sarum, William of Ely, and Richard of Gloucester; *Reg. Wake*, i. 64.

A. D. **1721**, Oct. 8. **Thomas Greene.** Norwich; Ely, 1723; d. 1738, May 18.

> Consecrated at Lambeth by Archbishop Wake, John of London, Charles of Winchester, William of Sarum, and Edmund of Lincoln; *Reg. Wake*, i. 78.

A. D. **1721**, Dec. 3. **Richard Reynolds.** Bangor; Lincoln, 1723; d. 1744, Jan. 15; and

> **Joseph Wilcocks.** Gloucester; Rochester, 1731; d. 1756, Feb. 28.

> Consecrated at Lambeth by Archbishop Wake, Richard of Sarum, Edmund of Lincoln, and White of Peterborough; *Reg. Wake*, i. 104, 113.

A. D. **1722**, Oct. 7. **Thomas Bowers.** Chichester; d. 1724, Aug. 22.

> Consecrated at Lambeth by Archbishop Wake, Charles of Winchester, Richard of Sarum, Edmund of Lincoln, and Thomas of Norwich; *Reg. Wake*, i. 122.

A. D. **1723**, Aug. 11. **William Baker.** Bangor; Norwich, 1727; d. 1732, Dec. 4.

> Consecrated at Croydon by Archbishop Wake, Edmund of London, John of S. Asaph, Benjamin of Hereford, and Richard of Lincoln; *Reg. Wake*, i. 158.

A. D. **1723**, Oct. 13. **John Waugh.** Carlisle; d. 1734, Oct. 29.

> Consecrated at Lambeth by Archbishop Wake, Edmund of London, Richard of Winchester, Samuel of Rochester, and Thomas of Ely; *Reg. Wake*, ii. 16.

A. D. **1723**, Nov. 3. **John Leng.** Norwich; d. 1727, Oct. 26.

> Consecrated at Lambeth by Archbishop Wake, Edmund of London, Richard of Winchester, Launcelot of Exeter, and Samuel of Rochester; *Reg. Wake*, i. 197.

A. D. **1724**, Feb. 2. **Henry Egerton.** Hereford; d. 1746, Apr. 1; and

> **Richard Smallbrooke.** S. David's; Lichfield, 1731; d. 1749, Dec. 22.

Consecrated at Lambeth by Archbishop Wake, Edmund of London, Richard of Winchester, Launcelot of Exeter, and Samuel of Rochester; *Reg. Wake*, i. 207, 217.

A. D. **1724**, Oct. 11. **Edward Waddington.** Chichester; d. 1731, Sept. 8.

Consecrated at Lambeth by Archbishop Wake, Edmund of London, Richard of Winchester, Samuel of Rochester, and Thomas of Ely; *Reg. Wake*, i. 227.

A. D. **1724**, Oct. 18. **William Bradshaw.** Bristol; d. 1732, Dec. 16.

Consecrated at Lambeth by Archbishop Wake, Edmund of London, Richard of Winchester, Samuel of Rochester, and Thomas of Ely; *Reg. Wake*, i. 236.

A. D. **1724**, Dec. 28. **Stephen Weston.** Exeter; d. 1742, Jan. 8.

Consecrated at Lambeth by Archbishop Wake, Edmund of London, Richard of Winchester, John of S. Asaph, and Richard of Lincoln; *Reg. Wake*, i. 246.

A. D. **1725**, Jan. 2. **Robert Clavering.** Llandaff; Peterborough, 1729; d. 1747, July 21.

Consecrated at Lambeth by Archbishop Wake, Edmund of London, Richard of Winchester, John of S. Asaph, and John of Oxford; *Reg. Wake*, i. 256.

A. D. **1726**, Apr. 12. **Samuel Peploe.** Chester; d. 1752, Feb. 21.

Consecrated at S. Margaret's, Westminster, by Archbishop Blackburn of York, William of Durham, John of S. Asaph, and John of Carlisle; *Reg. Wake*, ii. 182.

A. D. **1727**, Dec. 17. **Francis Hare.** S. Asaph; Chichester, 1731; d. 1740, Apr. 26.

Consecrated at Lambeth by Archbishop Wake, John of Bath, Edward of Lichfield, Samuel of Rochester, and Thomas of Ely; *Reg. Wake*, ii. 22.

A. D. **1728**, Feb. 4. **Thomas Sherlock.** Bangor ; Sarum, 1734 ; London, 1748 ; d. 1761, July 18.

> Consecrated at Lambeth by Archbishop Wake, John of Bath, John of Oxford, Edward of Lichfield, and Richard of Lincoln ; *Reg. Wake*, ii. 29.

A. D. **1729**, Oct. 19. **John Harris.** Llandaff ; d. 1738, Aug. 28.

> Consecrated at Lambeth by Archbishop Wake, Edmund of London, Richard of Winchester, Edward of Chichester, and Francis of S. Asaph ; *Reg. Wake*, ii. 45.

A. D. **1731**, Apr. 11. **Elias Sydall.** S. David's ; Gloucester, 1731 ; d. 1733, Dec. 24.

> Consecrated at Ely House by Edmund of London, Richard of Winchester, John of Bath, John of Oxford, and Thomas of Ely ; *Reg. Wake*, ii. 61.

A. D. **1732**, Jan. 23. **Nicolas Claggett.** S. David's ; Exeter, 1742 ; d. 1746, Dec. 8 ; and

> **Thomas Tanner.** S. Asaph ; d. 1735, Dec. 4.

> Consecrated at Lambeth by Archbishop Wake, Edmund of London, Thomas of Ely, Richard of Lincoln, and Joseph of Rochester ; *Reg. Wake*, ii. 92, 100.

A. D. **1733**, Feb. 25. **Robert Butts.** Norwich ; Ely, 1738 ; d. 1748, Jan. 26 ; and

> **Charles Cecil.** Bristol ; Bangor, 1734 ; d. 1737, May 29.

> Consecrated at Bow Church by Edmund of London, Richard of Winchester, Thomas of S. Asaph, and Nicolas of S. David's ; *Reg. Wake*, ii. 109, 117.

A. D. **1735**, Jan. 19. **Martin Benson.** Gloucester ; d. 1752, Aug. 30.

> **Thomas Secker.** Bristol ; Oxford, 1737 ; Canterbury, 1758 ; d. 1768, Aug. 3 ; and

> **George Fleming.** Carlisle ; d. 1747, July 2.

> Consecrated at Lambeth by Edmund of London, John of Oxford, and Joseph of Rochester ; *Reg. Wake*, ii. 153, 163, 199.

A. D. **1736**, July 4.　**Isaac Maddox.**　S. Asaph ; Worcester, 1743 ; d. 1759, Sept. 27.

> Consecrated at Lambeth by Edmund of London, Joseph of Rochester, Henry of Hereford, and Nicolas of S. David's ; *Reg. Wake*, ii. 173.

A. D. **1737**, June 12.　**Thomas Gooch.**　Bristol ; Norwich, 1738 ; Ely, 1748 ; d. 1754, Feb. 14.

> Consecrated at Lambeth by Archbishop Potter, John of Bath, Joseph of Rochester, and Francis of Chichester ; *Reg. Potter*, 32.

A. D. **1738**, Jan. 15.　**Thomas Herring.**　Bangor ; York, 1743 ; Canterbury, 1747 ; d. 1757, March 13.

> Consecrated at Lambeth by Archbishop Potter, Nicolas of S. David's, Robert of Norwich, and Thomas of Oxford ; *Reg. Potter*, 41.

A. D. **1738**, Dec. 3.　**Joseph Butler.**　Bristol ; Durham, 1750 ; d. 1752, June 16.

> Consecrated at Lambeth by Archbishop Potter, Joseph of Rochester, Nicolas of S. David's, and Robert of Ely ; *Reg. Potter*, 68.

A. D. **1739**, Feb. 18.　**Matthias Mawson.**　Llandaff ; Chichester, 1740 ; Ely, 1754 ; d. 1770, Nov. 23.

> Consecrated at Lambeth by Archbishop Potter, Richard of Lincoln, Joseph of Rochester, and Richard of Lichfield ; *Reg. Potter*, 77.

A. D. **1740**, Dec. 28.　**John Gilbert.**　Llandaff ; Sarum, 1749 ; York, 1757 ; d. 1761, Aug. 9.

> Consecrated at Lambeth by Archbishop Potter, Joseph of Rochester, Nicolas of S. David's, and Isaac of S. Asaph ; *Reg. Potter*, 95.

A. D. **1743**, Jan. 2.　**Edward Willes.**　S. David's ; Bath, 1743 ; d. 1773, Nov. 24.

> Consecrated at Lambeth by Archbishop Potter, Richard of Lincoln, Joseph of Rochester, and Thomas of Norwich ; *Reg. Potter*, 114.

A. D. **1743**, Nov. 13.　**Matthew Hutton.**　Bangor ; York, 1747 ; Canterbury, 1757 ; d. 1758, March 19.

> Consecrated at Lambeth by Joseph of Rochester, Nicolas of Exeter, Isaac of Worcester, and Joseph of Bristol ; *Reg. Potter*, 146.

A. D. **1744**, Apr. 1.   **John Thomas.**   Lincoln; Sarum, 1761; d. 1766, July 20.

Samuel Lisle.   S. Asaph; Norwich, 1748; d. 1749, Oct. 3; and

Richard Trevor.   S. David's; Durham, 1752; d. 1771, June 9.

Consecrated at Lambeth by Archbishop Potter, Joseph of Rochester, Nicolas of Exeter, Martin of Gloucester, and Thomas of Norwich; *Reg. Potter*, 169, 180, 190.

A. D. **1746**, May 11.   **James Beauclerk.**   Hereford; d. 1787, Oct. 20.

Consecrated at Lambeth by Archbishop Potter, Martin of Gloucester, Isaac of Worcester, and Richard of S. David's; *Reg. Potter*, 200.

A. D. **1747**, Feb. 8.   **George Lavington.**   Exeter; d. 1762, Sept. 13.

Consecrated at Lambeth by Archbishop Potter, Martin of Gloucester, Joseph of Bristol, and Richard of S. David's; *Reg. Potter*, 209.

A. D. **1747**, Oct. 4.   **John Thomas.**   Peterborough; Sarum, 1757; Winchester, 1761; d. 1781, May 1; and

Richard Osbaldeston.   Carlisle; London, 1762; d. 1764, May 13.

Consecrated at Lambeth by Joseph of Rochester, Joseph of Bristol, and Samuel of S. Asaph; *Reg. Potter*, 219, 231.

A. D. **1748**, Feb. 21.   **Zachary Pearce.**   Bangor; Rochester, 1756; d. 1774, June 29.

Consecrated in Kensington Church by Archbishop Herring, Joseph of Rochester, Martin of Gloucester, and Joseph of Bristol; *Reg. Herring*, 38.

A. D. **1748**, Apr. 24.   **Robert Hay Drummond.**   S. Asaph; Sarum, 1761; York, 1761; d. 1776, Dec. 10.

Consecrated in Kensington Church by Archbishop Herring, Joseph of Rochester, Martin of Gloucester, and John of Llandaff; *Reg. Herring*, 65.

A. D. **1749**, Feb. 12.   **Edward Cressett.**   Llandaff; d. 1755, Feb. 13.

Consecrated in Kensington Church by Archbishop Herring, Richard of Lichfield, James of Hereford, and John of Peterborough; *Reg. Herring*, 100.

A. D. **1749**, Dec. 3. **Thomas Hayter.** Norwich ; London, 1761 ; d. 1762, Jan. 9.

> Consecrated at Lambeth by Archbishop Herring, Joseph of Rochester, Joseph of Bristol, and Richard of S. David's ; *Reg. Herring*, 110.

A. D. **1750**, Feb. 19. **Frederick Cornwallis.** Lichfield ; Canterbury, 1768 ; d. 1783, March 19.

> Consecrated at Lambeth by Archbishop Herring, Joseph of Rochester, Martin of Gloucester, and Thomas of Norwich ; *Reg. Herring*, 121.

A. D. **1750**, Dec. 23. **John Conybeare.** Bristol ; d. 1755, July 13.

> Consecrated at Lambeth by Archbishop Herring, Joseph of Rochester, Thomas of Oxford, and Thomas of Norwich ; *Reg. Herring*, 142.

A. D. **1752**, March 22. **Edmund Keene.** Chester ; Ely, 1771 ; d. 1781, July 6.

> Consecrated at Ely House by Archbishop Herring, Joseph of Durham, Richard of Carlisle, and Frederick of Lichfield ; *Reg. Herring*, 154.

A. D. **1752**, Dec. 10. **James Johnson.** Gloucester ; Worcester, 1759 ; d. 1774, Nov. 26.

> Consecrated at Lambeth by Archbishop Herring, Joseph of Rochester, Matthew of Chichester, and Zachary of Bangor ; *Reg. Herring*, 171.

A. D. **1753**, Jan. 28. **Antony Ellis.** S. David's ; d. 1761, Jan. 16.

> Consecrated at Lambeth by Archbishop Herring, Joseph of Rochester, Isaac of Worcester, and Zachary of Bangor ; *Reg. Herring*, 178.

A. D. **1754**, March 31. **William Ashburnham.** Chichester ; d. 1797, Sept. 4.

> Consecrated at Lambeth by Joseph of Rochester, Matthew of Ely, and Frederick of Lichfield ; *Reg. Herring*, 205.

A. D. **1755**, Apr. 13. **Richard Newcome.** Llandaff ; S. Asaph, 1761 ; d. 1769, June 4.

> Consecrated at Lambeth by Archbishop Herring, Thomas of Oxford, George of Exeter, and Zachary of Bangor ; *Reg. Herring*, 213.

A. D. **1755**, Apr. 27. **Mark Hildesley.** Sodor and Man ; d. 1772, Dec. 7.

> Consecrated at Whitehall by Archbishop Hutton of York, Richard of Durham, Richard of Carlisle, and Edmund of Chester ; *Reg. Herring*, 223.

A. D. **1756**, July 4. **John Hume.** Bristol; Oxford, 1758; Sarum, 1766; d. 1782, June 26; and

John Egerton. Bangor; Lichfield, 1768; Durham, 1771; d. 1787, Jan. 18.

Consecrated at Lambeth by Thomas of Norwich, Zachary of Rochester, Edmund of Chester, and James of Gloucester; *Reg. Herring*, 244, 255.

A. D. **1757**, July 3. **Richard Terrick.** Peterborough; London, 1764; d. 1777, March 29.

Consecrated at Lambeth by Archbishop Hutton, John of Sarum, Thomas of Norwich, and John of Bristol; *Reg. Hutton*, 42.

A. D. **1758**, June 29. **Philip Young.** Bristol; Norwich, 1764; d. 1783, Apr. 23.

Consecrated in Bow Church by Archbishop Secker, Zachary of Rochester, John of Oxford, and Richard of Peterborough; *Reg. Secker*, 30.

A. D. **1760**, Jan. 20. **William Warburton.** Gloucester; d. 1779, June 11.

Consecrated at Lambeth by Archbishop Secker, Richard of Durham, James of Worcester, and Philip of Bristol; *Reg. Secker*, 49.

A. D. **1761**, May 24. **Samuel Squire.** S. David's; d. 1766, May 7.

Consecrated at Lambeth by Archbishop Secker, John of Winchester, Matthew of Ely, Zachary of Rochester, and Robert of S. Asaph; *Reg. Secker*, 68.

A. D. **1761**, Sept. 13. **John Ewer.** Llandaff; Bangor, 1769; d. 1774, Oct. 28.

Consecrated at Lambeth by Archbishop Secker, Zachary of Rochester, Robert of Sarum, and Thomas of Norwich; *Reg. Secker*, 96.

A. D. **1761**, Dec. 28. **John Green.** Lincoln; d. 1779, Apr. 25; and

Thomas Newton. Bristol; d. 1782, Feb. 14.

Consecrated at Lambeth by Thomas of London, John of Winchester, John of Sarum, and Zachary of Rochester; *Reg. Secker*, 153, 164.

A. D. **1762**, March 21. **Charles Lyttelton.** Carlisle; d. 1768, Dec. 22.

Consecrated at Whitehall by Archbishop Drummond of York, Richard of Durham, James of Hereford, and Edmund of Chester; *Reg. Secker*, 189.

A. D. **1762**, Nov. 7.   **Frederick Keppel.**   Exeter; d. 1777, Dec. 27.
> Consecrated at Lambeth by Archbishop Secker, John of Winchester, John of Oxford, Richard of Peterborough, and John of Llandaff; *Reg. Secker*, 199.

A. D. **1764**, July 8.   **Robert Lambe.**   Peterborough; d. 1769, Nov. 3.
> Consecrated at Lambeth by Archbishop Secker, Richard of London, John of Winchester, Matthew of Ely, and Zachary of Rochester; *Reg. Secker*, 226.

A. D. **1766**, June 15.   **Robert Lowth.**   S. David's; Oxford, 1766; London, 1777; d. 1787, Nov. 3.
> Consecrated at Lambeth by Archbishop Secker, Richard of London, Edward of Bath, and Zachary of Rochester; *Reg. Secker*, 235.

A. D. **1766**, Nov. 30.   **Charles Moss.**   S. David's; Bath, 1774; d. 1802, Apr. 13.
> Consecrated at Lambeth by Richard of London, John of Winchester, Edward of Bath, and Zachary of Rochester; *Reg. Secker*, 261.

A. D. **176⌐**, Feb. 12.   **Jonathan Shipley.**   Llandaff; S. Asaph, 1769; d /88, Dec. 9.
> Consecrated at Lambeth by Archbishop Cornwallis, Richard of London, John of Winchester, and Robert of Oxford; *Reg. Cornwallis*, 51.

A. D. **1769**, Feb. 24.   **Edmund Law.**   Carlisle; d. 1787, Aug. 14.
> Consecrated at Whitehall by Archbishop Drummond of York, Richard of Durham, Edmund of Chester, and Philip of Norwich; *Reg. Cornwallis*, 64.

A. D. **1769**, Oct. 1.   **Shute Barrington.**   Llandaff; Sarum, 1782; Durham, 1791; d. 1826, March 25.
> Consecrated at Lambeth by Archbishop Cornwallis, Richard of London, and Zachary of Rochester; *Reg. Cornwallis*, 82.

A. D. **1769**, Dec. 17.   **John Hinchcliffe.**   Peterborough; d. 1794, Jan. 11.
> Consecrated at Lambeth by Archbishop Cornwallis, Richard of London, John of Winchester, and Philip of Norwich; *Reg. Cornwallis*, 93.

A. D. **1771**, Feb. 17.　**William Markham.**　Chester ; York, 1777 ; d. 1807, Nov. 3.

> Consecrated at Whitehall by Archbishop Drummond of York, Richard of Durham, James of Worcester, and Edmund of Carlisle ; *Reg. Cornwallis*, 113.

A. D. **1771**, Sept. 8.　**Brownlow North.**　Lichfield ; Worcester, 1774 ; Winchester, 1781 ; d. 1820, July 12.

> Consecrated at Lambeth by Archbishop Cornwallis, Richard of London, Zachary of Rochester, and William of Chester ; *Reg. Cornwallis*, 135.

A. D. **1773**, Feb. 14.　**Richard Richmond.**　Sodor and Man ; d. 1780, Feb. 4.

> Consecrated at Whitehall by Archbishop Drummond of York, John of Durham, Edmund of Ely, and William of Chester ; *Reg. Cornwallis*, 144.

A. D. **1774**, June 26.　**James Yorke.**　S. David's ; Gloucester, 1779 ; Ely, 1781 ; d. 1808, Aug. 26.

> Consecrated at Lambeth by Archbishop Cornwallis, Richard of London, John of Lincoln, Thomas of Bristol, and Brownlow of Lichfield ; *Reg. Cornwallis*, 160.

A. D. **1774**, Nov. 13.　**John Thomas.**　Rochester ; d. 1793, Aug. 22.

> Consecrated at Lambeth by Archbishop Cornwallis, Richard of London, Philip of Norwich, and Shute of Llandaff ; *Reg. Cornwallis*, 170.

A. D. **1775**, Feb. 12.　**Richard Hurd.**　Lichfield ; Worcester, 1781 ; d. 1808, May 28 ; and

> **John Moore.**　Bangor ; Canterbury, 1783 ; d. 1805, Jan. 18.

> Consecrated at Lambeth by Archbishop Cornwallis, Edmund of Ely, Robert of Oxford, and John of Rochester ; *Reg. Cornwallis*, 193, 204.

A. D. **1777**, Feb. 9.　**Beilby Porteus.**　Chester ; London, 1787 ; d. 1809, May 14.

> Consecrated at Whitehall by Archbishop Markham of York, John of Durham, Edmund of Carlisle, and Shute of Llandaff ; *Reg. Cornwallis*, 225.

A. D. **1777**, May 25.   **John Butler.**   Oxford; Hereford, 1788; d. 1802, Dec. 10.

   Consecrated at Lambeth by Archbishop Cornwallis, Robert of London, William of Chichester, and Philip of Norwich; *Reg. Cornwallis*, 248.

A. D. **1778**, Jan. 25.   **John Ross.**   Exeter; d. 1792, Aug. 14.

   Consecrated at Lambeth by Archbishop Cornwallis, Robert of London, William of Chichester, and John of Oxford; *Reg. Cornwallis*, 256.

A. D. **1779**, May 30.   **Thomas Thurlow.**   Lincoln; Durham, 1787; d. 1791, May 27.

   Consecrated at Lambeth by Archbishop Cornwallis, Edmund of Ely, Philip of Norwich, and Charles of Bath; *Reg. Cornwallis*, 268.

A. D. **1779**, Sept. 19.   **John Warren.**   S. David's; Bangor, 1783; d. 1800, Jan. 27.

   Consecrated at Lambeth by Archbishop Cornwallis, Robert of London, John of Rochester, and Richard of Lichfield; *Reg. Cornwallis*, 287.

A. D. **1780**, March 5.   **George Mason.**   Sodor and Man; d. 1783, Dec. 8.

   Consecrated at Whitehall by Archbishop Markham of York, John of Bangor, Beilby of Chester, and John of Exeter; *Reg. Cornwallis*, 297.

A. D. **1781**, Sept. 16.   **James Cornwallis.**   Lichfield; d. 1824, Jan. 20.

   Consecrated at Lambeth by Archbishop Cornwallis, Robert of London, James of Ely, and John of Rochester; *Reg. Cornwallis*, 333.

A. D. **1781**, Oct. 28.   **Samuel Hallifax.**   Gloucester; S. Asaph, 1789; d. 1790, March 5.

   Consecrated at Lambeth by Archbishop Cornwallis, Philip of Norwich, John of Rochester, and James of Lichfield; *Reg. Cornwallis*, 343.

A. D. **1782**, Apr. 7.   **Lewis Bagot.**   Bristol; Norwich, 1783; S. Asaph 1790; d. 1802, June 4.

   Consecrated at Lambeth by Archbishop Cornwallis, Brownlow of Winchester, Charles of Bath, and Shute of Llandaff; *Reg. Cornwallis*, 352.

A. D. **1782**, Oct. 20.   **Richard Watson.**   Llandaff; d. 1816, July 4.

   Consecrated at Lambeth by Archbishop Cornwallis, Philip of Norwich, and John of Rochester; *Reg. Cornwallis*, 373.

A. D. **1783**, July 6. **Edward Smallwell.** S. David's; Oxford, 1788; d. 1799, June 26; and

Christopher Wilson. Bristol; d. 1792, Apr. 18.

Consecrated at Lambeth by Archbishop Moore, Brownlow of Winchester, Thomas of Lincoln, and John of Bangor; *Reg. Moore*, 43, 52.

A. D. **1784**, Apr. 4. **Claudius Crigan.** Sodor and Man; d. 1813, Apr. 26.

Consecrated at Whitehall by Archbishop Markham of York, John of Rochester, John of Oxford, and John of Exeter; *Reg. Moore*, 63.

A. D. **1787**, Feb. 4. **William White.** Pennsylvania; d. 1836; and

Samuel Provoost. New York; d. 1815.

Consecrated at Lambeth by Archbishop Moore, William of York, Charles of Bath, and John of Peterborough; *Reg. Moore*, 64.

A. D. **1787**, March 11. **George Pretyman.** Lincoln; Winchester, 1820; d. 1827, Nov. 14.

Consecrated at Lambeth by Archbishop Moore, William of Chichester, Shute of Sarum, and Beilby of Chester; *Reg. Moore*, 89.

A. D. **1787**, Aug. 12. **Charles Inglis.** Nova Scotia.

Consecrated at Lambeth by Archbishop Moore, John of Rochester, and Beilby of Chester; *Reg. Moore*, 93.

A. D. **1787**, Nov. 18. **John Douglas.** Carlisle; Sarum, 1791; d. 1807, May 18.

Consecrated at Whitehall by Archbishop Markham of York, Beilby of Chester, John of Oxford, and George of Lincoln; *Reg. Moore*, 104.

A. D. **1787**, Dec. 9. **John Harley.** Hereford; d. 1788, Jan. 9.

Consecrated at Lambeth by Archbishop Moore, Beilby of London, John of Oxford, and John of Bangor; *Reg. Moore*, 127.

A. D. **1788**, Jan. 20. **William Cleaver.** Chester; Bangor, 1800; S. Asaph, 1806; d. 1815, May 15.

Consecrated at Whitehall by Archbishop Markham of York, Thomas of Durham, John of Rochester, and John of Carlisle; *Reg. Moore*, 139.

L

A. D. **1788**, May 11.   **Samuel Horsley.**   S. David's ; Rochester, 1793 ; S. Asaph, 1802 ; d. 1806, Oct. 4.

Consecrated at Lambeth by Archbishop Moore, Beilby of London, Samuel of Gloucester, and Edward of Oxford ; *Reg. Moore*, 169.

A. D. **1789**, June 7.   **Richard Beadon.**   Gloucester ; Bath, 1802 ; d. 1824, Apr. 21.

Consecrated at Lambeth by Archbishop Moore, Beilby of London, John of Peterborough, and Samuel of S. Asaph ; *Reg. Moore*, 190.

A. D. **1790**, June 6.   **George Horne.**   Norwich ; d. 1792, Jan. 17.

Consecrated at Lambeth by Archbishop Moore, Beilby of London, James of Lichfield, and Samuel of St. David's ; *Reg. Moore*, 209.

A. D. **1790**, Sept. 19.   **James Madison.**   Virginia ; d. 1812.

Consecrated at Lambeth by Archbishop Moore, Beilby of London, and John of Rochester ; *Reg. Moore*, 210.

A. D. **1791**, Nov. 6.   **Edward Venables Vernon (Harcourt).**   Carlisle ; York, 1808 ; d. 1847, Nov. 12.

Consecrated at Whitehall by Archbishop Markham of York, Beilby of London, and John of Sarum ; *Reg. Moore*, 238.

A. D. **1792**, Apr. 8.   **Charles Manners Sutton.**   Norwich ; Canterbury, 1805 ; d. 1828, July 21.

Consecrated at Lambeth by Archbishop Moore, John of Peterborough, James of Lichfield, and Richard of Gloucester ; *Reg. Moore*, 247.

A. D. **1792**, June 3.   **Spencer Madan.**   Bristol ; Peterborough, 1794 ; d. 1813, Oct. 8.

Consecrated at Lambeth by Archbishop Moore, Beilby of London, John of Peterborough, and John of Sarum ; *Reg. Moore*, 258.

A. D. **1792**, Dec. 2.   **William Buller.**   Exeter ; d. 1796, Dec. 12.

Consecrated at Lambeth by Archbishop Moore, John of Hereford, Samuel of S. David's, and Richard of Gloucester ; *Reg. Moore*, 268.

A. D. **1794**, Jan. 12.   **William Stewart.**   S. David's ; Armagh, 1800 ; d. 1822, May 6.

Consecrated at Lambeth by Archbishop Moore, Richard of Llandaff, and Richard of Gloucester ; *Reg. Moore*, 292.

A. D. **1794**, May 11. **Henry Reginald Courtenay.** Bristol; Exeter, 1797; d. 1803, June 9.

> Consecrated at Lambeth by Archbishop Moore, Beilby of London, Samuel of Rochester, and Charles of Norwich; *Reg. Moore*, 312.

A. D. **1797**, Apr. 9. **Ffolliot Herbert Walker Cornewall.** Bristol; Hereford, 1803; Worcester, 1808; d. 1831, Sept. 5.

> Consecrated at Lambeth by Archbishop Moore, Beilby of London, James of Lichfield, and Charles of Norwich; *Reg. Moore*, 325.

A. D. **1798**, March 4. **John Buckner.** Chichester; d. 1824, May 2.

> Consecrated at Lambeth by Archbishop Moore, Beilby of London, Samuel of Rochester, and Edward of Carlisle; *Reg. Moore*, 333.

A. D. **1799**, Sept. 1. **John Randolph.** Oxford; Bangor, 1807; London, 1809; d. 1813, July 28.

> Consecrated at Lambeth by Archbishop Moore, Brownlow of Winchester, and Samuel of Rochester; *Reg. Moore*, 334.

A. D. **1800**, June 15. **Henry William Majendie.** Chester; Bangor, 1809; d. 1830, July 9.

> Consecrated at Whitehall by Archbishop Markham of York, Beilby of London, William of S. David's, and John of Oxford; *Reg. Moore*, 364.

A. D. **1801**, Feb. 11. **George Murray.** S. David's; d. 1803, June 3.

> Consecrated at Lambeth by Archbishop Moore, Beilby of London, Richard of Gloucester, and Henry William of Chester; *Reg. Moore*, 372.

A. D. **1802**, June 27. **George Isaac Huntingford.** Gloucester; Hereford, 1815; d. 1832, Apr. 29.

> Consecrated at Lambeth by Archbishop Moore, Beilby of London, Samuel of Rochester, and Richard of Bath; *Reg. Moore*, 394.

A. D. **1802**, Aug. 22. **Thomas Dampier.** Rochester; Ely, 1808; d. 1812, May 13.

> Consecrated at Lambeth by Archbishop Moore, Beilby of London, Brownlow of Winchester, and Richard of Bath; *Reg. Moore*, 415.

A. D. **1803**, March 27.   **George Pelham.**   Bristol ; Exeter, 1807 ; Lincoln, 1820 ; d. 1827, Feb. 7.

> Consecrated at Lambeth by Archbishop Moore, Beilby of London, Brownlow of Winchester, and Samuel of S. Asaph ; *Reg. Moore*, 438.

A. D. **1803**, July 17.   **Thomas Burgess.**   S. David's ; Sarum, 1825 ; d. 1837, Feb. 19 ; and

> **John Fisher.**   Exeter ; Sarum, 1807; d. 1825, May 8.
> Consecrated at Lambeth by Archbishop Moore, Beilby of London, Brownlow of Winchester, and Samuel of S. Asaph; *Reg. Moore*, 450, 462.

A. D. **1805**, Apr. 28.   **Henry Bathurst.**   Norwich ; d. 1837, Apr. 5.

> Consecrated at Lambeth by Archbishop Sutton, Beilby of London, John of Oxford, and Thomas of Rochester ; *Reg. Sutton*, 24.

A. D. **1807**, Feb. 1.   **Charles Moss.**   Oxford ; d. 1811, Dec. 16.

> Consecrated at Lambeth by Archbishop Sutton, John of Bangor, Henry William of Chester, and John of Exeter ; *Reg. Sutton*, 50.

A. D. **1807**, Oct. 4.   **John Luxmoore.**   Bristol ; Hereford, 1808 ; S. Asaph, 1815 ; d. 1830, Jan. 21.

> Consecrated at Lambeth by Archbishop Sutton, James of Ely, and George Isaac of Gloucester ; *Reg. Sutton*, 80.

A. D. **1808**, March 13.   **Samuel Goodenough.**   Carlisle ; d. 1827, Aug. 12.

> Consecrated at Whitehall by Archbishop Harcourt of York, John of Bangor, Henry William of Chester, and John of Sarum ; *Reg. Sutton*, 107.

A. D. **1808**, Oct. 30.   **William Lort Mansel.**   Bristol ; d. 1820, June 27.

> Consecrated at Lambeth by Archbishop Sutton, Brownlow of Winchester, John of Sarum, and Charles of Oxford ; *Reg. Sutton*, 137.

A. D. **1809**, Feb. 12.   **Walker King.**   Rochester ; d. 1827, Feb. 22.

> Consecrated at Lambeth by Archbishop Sutton, John of Bangor, Thomas of S. David's, and Samuel of Carlisle ; *Reg. Sutton*, 156.

A. D. **1810**, Jan. 21.   **Bowyer Edward Sparke.**   Chester ; Ely, 1812 ; d. 1836, Apr. 4.

> Consecrated at Whitehall by Archbishop Harcourt of York, Richard of Bath, Henry William of Bangor, and John of Hereford ; *Reg. Sutton*, 187.

A. D. **1812**, Feb. 23. **William Jackson.** Oxford ; d. 1815, Dec. 2.

Consecrated at Lambeth by Archbishop Sutton, John of London, and William of S. Asaph ; *Reg. Sutton,* 196.

A. D. **1812**, July 5. **George Henry Law.** Chester ; Bath, 1824 ; d. 1845, Sept. 22.

Consecrated at Whitehall by Archbishop Harcourt of York, John of London, Bowyer Edward of Ely, and William of Oxford ; *Reg. Sutton,* 214.

A. D. **1813**, Oct. 3. **William Howley.** London; Canterbury, 1828 ; d. 1848, Feb. 11.

Consecrated at Lambeth by Archbishop Sutton, George Isaac of Gloucester, John of Sarum, and William of Oxford ; *Reg. Sutton,* 222.

A. D. **1813**, Dec. 12. **John Parsons.** Peterborough ; d. 1819, March 12.

Consecrated at Lambeth by Archbishop Sutton, William of London, John of Sarum, and George Henry of Chester ; *Reg. Sutton,* 231.

A. D. **1814**, March 6. **George Murray.** Sodor and Man ; Rochester, 1827 ; d. 1860, Feb. 16.

Consecrated at Whitehall by Archbishop Harcourt of York, George of Exeter, and George Henry of Chester ; *Reg. Sutton,* 240.

A. D. **1815**, July 30. **Henry Ryder.** Gloucester ; Lichfield, 1824 ; d. 1836, March 31.

Consecrated at Lambeth by Archbishop Sutton, William of London, and Walker of Rochester ; *Reg. Sutton,* 268.

A. D. **1816**, March 24. **Edward Legge.** Oxford ; d. 1827, Jan. 27.

Consecrated at Lambeth by Archbishop Sutton, William of London, Henry William of Bangor, and Henry of Norwich ; *Reg. Sutton,* 277.

A. D. **1816**, Aug. 25. **Herbert Marsh.** Llandaff ; Peterborough, 1819 ; d. 1839, May 1.

Consecrated at Lambeth by Archbishop Sutton, William of London, and Edward of Oxford ; *Reg. Sutton,* 287.

A. D. **1819**, May 31. **William Van Mildert.** Llandaff ; Durham, 1826 ; d. 1836, Feb. 21.

Consecrated at Lambeth by Archbishop Sutton, William of London, John of S. Asaph, and Herbert of Peterborough ; *Reg. Sutton,* 302.

A. D. **1820**, July 30.   **John Kaye.**   Bristol; Lincoln, 1827; d. 1853, Feb. 19.

Consecrated at Lambeth by Archbishop Sutton, William of London, George of Exeter, and William of Llandaff; *Reg. Sutton*, 310.

A. D. **1820**, Nov. 12.   **William Carey.**   Exeter; S. Asaph, 1830; d. 1846, Sept. 13.

Consecrated at Lambeth by Archbishop Sutton, William of London, George Henry of Chester, and William of Llandaff; *Reg. Sutton*, 335.

A. D. **1824**, Apr. 11.   **Christopher Bethell.**   Gloucester; Exeter, 1830; Bangor, 1830; d. 1859, Apr. 19.

Consecrated at Lambeth by Archbishop Sutton, William of London, John of S. Asaph, and Bowyer Edward of Ely; *Reg. Sutton*, 353.

A. D. **1824**, June 6.   **Robert James Carr.**   Chichester; Worcester, 1831; d. 1841, Apr. 24.

Consecrated at Lambeth by Archbishop Sutton, William of London, George of Lincoln, and Christopher of Gloucester; *Reg. Sutton*, 361.

A. D. **1824**, June 20.   **Charles James Blomfield.**   Chester; London, 1828; res. 1856; d. 1857, Aug. 5.

Consecrated at Whitehall by Archbishop Harcourt of York, William of London, and William of Exeter; *Reg. Sutton*, 378.

A. D. **1825**, July 24.   **John Banks Jenkinson.**   S. David's; d. 1840, July 7.

Consecrated at Lambeth by William of London, Edward of Oxford, John of Bristol, and Robert James of Chichester; *Reg. Sutton*, 398.

A. D. **1826**, May 21.   **Charles Richard Sumner.**   Llandaff; Winchester, 1827; res. 1869; d. 1874, Aug. 15.

Consecrated at Lambeth by Archbishop Sutton, William of London, Robert James of Chichester, and John Banks of S. David's; *Reg. Sutton*, 416.

A. D. **1827**, March 4.   **Charles Lloyd.**   Oxford; d. 1829, May 31.

Consecrated at Lambeth by Archbishop Sutton, William of London, William of Durham, and Charles James of Chester; *Reg. Sutton*, 431.

A. D. **1827**, March 25.   **Robert Gray.**   Bristol; d. 1834, Sept. 28.

Consecrated at Lambeth by Archbishop Sutton, William of London, William of Durham, and John Banks of S. David's; *Reg. Sutton*, 437.

A. D. **1827**, July 15. **Hugh Percy.** Rochester ; Carlisle, 1827 ; d. 1856, Feb. 5.

> Consecrated at Lambeth by Archbishop Sutton, William of London, Bowyer Edward of Ely, and Robert James of Chichester ; *Reg. Sutton*, 445.

A. D. **1828**, Jan. 13. **Edward Copleston.** Llandaff ; d. 1849, Oct. 14.

> Consecrated at Lambeth by Archbishop Sutton, William of London, Charles Richard of Winchester, and Hugh of Carlisle ; *Reg. Sutton*, 469.

A. D. **1828**, March 9. **William Ward.** Sodor and Man ; d. 1838, Jan. 26.

> Consecrated at Whitehall by Archbishop Harcourt of York, William of London, and George of Rochester ; *Reg. Sutton*, 470.

A. D. **1828**, Sept. 14. **John Bird Sumner.** Chester ; Canterbury, 1848 ; d. Sept. 6, 1862.

> Consecrated at York by Archbishop Harcourt of York, Charles Richard of Winchester, and Christopher of Gloucester ; *Reg. Howley*, 41.

A. D. **1829**, Aug. 23. **Richard Bagot.** Oxford ; Bath, 1845 ; d. 1854, May 15.

> Consecrated at Lambeth by Archbishop Howley, Charles James of London, Charles Richard of Winchester, and George of Rochester ; *Reg. Howley*, 54.

A. D. **1830**, July 11. **James Henry Monk.** Gloucester ; Bristol, 1836 ; d. 1856, June 6.

> Consecrated at Lambeth by Archbishop Howley, Charles James of London, Hugh of Carlisle, and George of Rochester ; *Reg. Howley*, 91.

A. D. **1831**, Jan. 2. **Henry Phillpotts.** Exeter ; d. 1869, Sept. 18.

> Consecrated at Lambeth by Archbishop Howley, Charles James of London, and Robert of Bristol ; *Reg. Howley*, 117.

A. D. **1831**, Oct. 2. **Edward Maltby.** Chichester ; Durham, 1836 ; res. 1856 ; d. 1859, July 3.

> Consecrated at Lambeth by Archbishop Howley, George Henry of Bath, and Robert of Bristol ; *Reg. Howley*, 140.

A. D. **1832**, May 20. **Edward Grey.** Hereford ; d. 1837, June 24.

> Consecrated at Lambeth by Archbishop Howley, Charles James of London, John Banks of S. David's, and Robert of Bristol ; *Reg. Howley*, 154.

A. D. **1834**, Dec. 7.   **Joseph Allen.**   Bristol ; Ely, 1836 ; d. 1845, March 20.
>Consecrated at Lambeth by Archbishop Howley, Charles James of London, Robert James of Worcester, and Edward of Chichester ; *Reg. Howley*, 167.

A. D. **1836**, July 3.   **Samuel Butler.**   Lichfield ; d. 1839, Dec. 4.
>Consecrated at Lambeth by Archbishop Howley, Edward of Durham, John of Lincoln, and Joseph of Bristol ; *Reg. Howley*, 221.

A. D. **1836**, Oct. 2.   **William Otter.**   Chichester ; d. 1840, Aug. 20.
>Consecrated at Lambeth by Archbishop Howley, Charles James of London, and George of Rochester ; *Reg. Howley*, 250.

A. D. **1836**, Nov. 6.   **Charles Thomas Longley.**   Ripon ; Durham, 1856 ; York, 1860 ; Canterbury, 1862 ; d. 1868, Oct. 27.
>Consecrated at York by Archbishop Harcourt of York, Hugh of Carlisle, and John Bird of Chester.   [Told me by the Archbishop himself.]

A. D. **1837**, Apr. 16.   **Edward Denison.**   Sarum ; d. 1854, March 6.
>Consecrated at Lambeth by Archbishop Howley, Charles James of London, Edward of Durham, and Charles Thomas of Ripon ; *Reg. Howley*, 265.

A. D. **1837**, June 11.   **Edward Stanley.**   Norwich ; d. 1849, Sept. 6.
>Consecrated at Lambeth by Archbishop Howley, Charles James of London, John of Lincoln, and John Bird of Chester ; *Reg. Howley*, 281.

A. D. **1837**, Oct. 1.   **Thomas Musgrave.**   Hereford ; York, 1847 ; d. 1860, May 4.
>Consecrated at Lambeth by Archbishop Howley, Charles James of London, Joseph of Ely, and William of Chichester ; *Reg. Howley*, 297.

A. D. **1838**, July 22.   **James Bowstead.**   Sodor and Man ; Lichfield, 1840 ; d. 1843, Oct. 11.
>Consecrated at Lambeth by Archbishop Howley, John of Lincoln, Joseph of Ely, and Thomas of Hereford ; *Reg. Howley*, 303.

A. D. **1839**, June 16.   **George Davys.**   Peterborough ; d. 1864, Apr. 18.
>Consecrated at Lambeth by Archbishop Howley, Charles James of London, John of Lincoln, and John Bird of Chester ; *Reg. Howley*, 318.

A. D. **1840**, March 1.   **Henry Pepys.**   Sodor and Man ; Worcester, 1841 ; d. 1860, Nov. 13.

> Consecrated at Whitehall by Archbishop Harcourt of York, George of Rochester, and James of Lichfield ; *Reg. Howley*, 346.

A. D. **1840**, Aug. 9.   **Connop Thirlwall.**   S. David's ; res. 1874 ; d. 1875, July 27.

> Consecrated at Lambeth by Archbishop Howley, Joseph of Ely, Thomas of Hereford, and James of Lichfield ; *Reg. Howley*, 360.

A. D. **1840**, Sept. 20.   **Philip Nicholas Shuttleworth.**   Chichester ; d. 1842, Jan. 7.

> Consecrated at Lambeth by Archbishop Howley, George of Rochester, and George of Peterborough ; *Reg. Howley*, 375.

A. D. **1841**, May 30.   **Thomas Vowler Short.**   Sodor and Man ; S. Asaph, 1846 ; res. 1870 ; d. 1872, Apr. 13.

> Consecrated at Whitehall by Archbishop Harcourt of York, Charles James of London, and Charles Thomas of Ripon ; *Reg. Howley*, 394.

A. D. **1841**, Oct. 17.   **George Augustus Selwyn.**   New Zealand ; Lichfield, 1867 ; d. 1878, Apr. 11.

> Consecrated at Lambeth by Archbishop Howley, Charles James of London, John of Lincoln, and William Hart of Barbadoes ; *Reg. Howley*, 400. .

A. D. **1842**, Feb. 27.   **Ashhurst Turner Gilbert.**   Chichester ; d. 1870, Feb. 21.

> Consecrated at Lambeth by Archbishop Howley, John of Lincoln, and Edward of Llandaff ; *Reg. Howley*, 417.

A. D. **1843**, Dec. 3.   **John Lonsdale.**   Lichfield ; d. 1867, Oct. 19.

> Consecrated at Lambeth by Archbishop Howley, Charles James of London, Charles Richard of Winchester, and Ashhurst Turner of Chichester ; *Reg. Howley*, 475.

A. D. **1845**, May 4.   **Thomas Turton.**   Ely ; d. 1864, Jan. 7.

> Consecrated at Lambeth by Archbishop Howley, Charles James of London, John of Lincoln, George of Rochester, Thomas of Hereford, John of Lichfield, and William Hart Coleridge ; *Reg. Howley*, 502.

A. D. **1845**, Nov. 30. **Samuel Wilberforce.** Oxford; Winchester, 1869; d. 1873, July 19.

> Consecrated at Lambeth by Archbishop Howley, Charles James of London, Charles Richard of Winchester, and Edward of Sarum; *Reg. Howley*, 548.

A. D. **1847**, Jan. 10. **Walter Augustus Shirley.** Sodor and Man; d. 1847, Apr. 21.

> Consecrated at Whitehall by Hugh of Carlisle, John of Lichfield, and Thomas Vowler of S. Asaph; *Reg. Howley*, 569.

A. D. **1847**, May 23. **Robert John Eden.** Sodor and Man; Bath and Wells, 1854; res. 1869; d. 1870, Apr. 25.

> Consecrated at Whitehall by Hugh of Carlisle, Charles Thomas of Ripon, and Samuel of Oxford; *Reg. Howley*, 573.

A. D. **1848**, Jan. 23. **James Prince Lee.** Manchester; d. 1869, Dec. 24.

> Consecrated at Whitehall by Archbishop Musgrave of York, John Bird of Chester, and Henry of Worcester; *Reg. Howley*, 644.

A. D. **1848**, March 26. **Renn Dickson Hampden.** Hereford; d. 1868, Apr. 23.

> Consecrated at Lambeth by Archbishop Sumner, Edward of Llandaff, Edward of Norwich, and Henry of Worcester; *Reg. Sumner*, 20.

A. D. **1848**, May 14. **John Graham.** Chester; d. 1865, June 15.

> Consecrated at Whitehall by Archbishop Musgrave of York, Edward of Durham, and John of Lincoln; *Reg. Sumner*, 38.

A. D. **1849**, Dec. 2. **Samuel Hinds.** Norwich; res. 1857; d. 1872, Feb. 7.

> Consecrated at Lambeth by Archbishop Sumner, Charles James of London, John of Lincoln, Hugh of Carlisle, James Prince of Manchester, and Renn Dickson of Hereford; *Reg. Sumner*, 67.

A. D. **1849**, Dec. 2. **Alfred Ollivant.** Llandaff; d. 1882, Dec. 16.

> Consecrated at Lambeth by Archbishop Sumner, Charles James of London, John of Lincoln, Hugh of Carlisle, James Prince of Manchester, and Renn Dickson of Hereford; *Reg. Sumner*, 83.

A. D. **1853**, May 5. **John Jackson.** Lincoln; London, 1869; d. 1885, Jan. 6.

> Consecrated in Lambeth Church by Archbishop Sumner, Charles James of London, Charles Richard of Winchester, John of Lichfield, Samuel of Oxford, [George Jehoshaphat of Quebec, and the Bishop McIlvaine of Ohio]; *Reg. Sumner*, 124.

A. D. **1854**, May 14. **Walter Kerr Hamilton.** Salisbury; d. 1869, Aug. 1.

> Consecrated at Lambeth by Archbishop Sumner, Charles Richard of Winchester, Ashhurst Turner of Chichester, Samuel of Oxford, and George Augustus of New Zealand; *Reg. Sumner*, 172.

A. D. **1854**, July 25. **Horace Powys.** Sodor and Man; d. 1877, May 31.

> Consecrated at York by Archbishop Musgrave, Hugh of Carlisle, Charles Thomas of Ripon, and James Prince of Manchester; *Reg. Musgrave*.

A. D. **1856**, Apr. 13. **Henry Montagu Villiers.** Carlisle; Durham, 1860; d. 1861, Aug. 9.

> Consecrated at Whitehall by Archbishop Musgrave of York, Charles Thomas of Ripon, James Prince of Manchester, and John of Chester; *Reg. Sumner*, 227.

A. D. **1856**, Aug. 10. **Charles Baring.** Gloucester and Bristol; Durham, 1861; d. 1879, Sept. 13.

> Consecrated at Lambeth by Archbishop Sumner, Charles Richard of Winchester, Ashhurst Turner of Chichester, and Samuel of Oxford; *Reg. Sumner*, 243.

A. D. **1856**, Nov. 23. **Archibald Campbell Tait.** London; Canterbury, 1868; d. 1882, Sept. 3.

> Consecrated at Whitehall by Archbishop Sumner, Ashhurst Turner of Chichester, John of Lincoln, and Henry Montagu of Carlisle, [also the Bishops of Jamaica and Rupertsland]; *Reg. Sumner*, 271.

A. D. **1857**, Jan. 18. **Robert Bickersteth.** Ripon; d. 1884, Apr. 15.

> Consecrated in Bishopthorpe Church by Archbishop Musgrave of York, Charles Thomas of Durham, James Prince of Manchester, and Henry Montagu of Carlisle; *Reg. Musgrave*.

A. D. **1857**, June 11. **John Thomas Pelham.** Norwich ; res. 1893 ; d. 1894, May 1.

Consecrated in Marylebone Church by Archbishop Sumner, Archibald Campbell of London, Charles Richard of Winchester, Charles of Gloucester, [and Robert of Ripon] ; *Reg. Sumner*, 289.

A. D. **1859**, June 14. **James Colquhoun Campbell.** Bangor ; res. 1890 ; d. 1895, Nov. 9.

Consecrated in Westminster Abbey by Archbishop Sumner, Archibald Campbell of London, Samuel of Oxford, Alfred of Llandaff, Walter Kerr of Sarum, Robert of Capetown, and George of British Columbia, [also bishops of Grahamstown and Argyle] ; *Reg. Sumner*, 385.

A. D. **1860**, May 17. **Joseph Cotton Wigram.** Rochester ; d. 1867, Apr. 6.

Consecrated in Lambeth Church by Archbishop Sumner, Charles Richard of Winchester, Robert of Bath and Wells, Samuel of Oxford, Henry Montagu of Carlisle, John of Lincoln, Edward Hyndman of Sierra Leone ; *Reg. Sumner*, 421.

A. D. **1860**, Nov. 11. **Samuel Waldegrave.** Carlisle ; d. 1869, Oct. 1.

Consecrated at York by Archbishop Longley, Henry Montagu of Durham, and Robert of Ripon ; *Reg. Longley.*

A. D. **1861**, March 25. **Henry Philpott.** Worcester ; d. 1892, Jan. 10.

Consecrated in Lambeth Chapel by Archbishop Sumner, Archibald Campbell of London, and Alfred of Llandaff ; *Reg. Sumner*, 464.

A. D. **1861**, Dec. 15. **William Thomson.** Gloucester and Bristol ; York, 1862 ; d. Dec. 25, 1890.

Consecrated in Lambeth Chapel by Archbishop Sumner, Archibald Campbell of London, and Samuel of Oxford ; *Reg. Sumner*, 491.

A. D. **1863**, March 25. **Charles John Ellicott.** Gloucester and Bristol.

Consecrated in Canterbury Cathedral by Archbishop Longley, Henry of Worcester, Frederick of Sydney, and Charles of Melbourne ; *Reg. Longley*, 71.

A. D. **1864**, March 29. **Edward Harold Browne.** Ely ; Winchester, 1873 ; res. 1890 ; d. 1891, Dec. 18.

Consecrated in Westminster Abbey by Archbishop Longley, Connop of S. David's, and Henry of Worcester ; *Reg. Longley*, 91.

A. D. **1864**, June 29. **Francis Jeune.** Peterborough ; d. 1869, Aug. 21.

> Consecrated in Canterbury Cathedral by Archbishop Longley, Charles Richard of Winchester, John of Lincoln, Charles John of Gloucester, George of Victoria, and Bishop F. R. Nixon ; *Reg. Longley*, 106.

A. D. **1865**, Aug. 24. **William Jacobson.** Chester ; res. 1884 ; d. 1884, July 13.

> Consecrated in York Minster by Archbishop Thomson, Robert of Ripon, and Samuel of Carlisle ; *Reg. Thomson.*

A. D. **1867**, June 11. **Thomas Legh Claughton.** Rochester ; S. Albans, 1877 ; res. 1890 ; d. 1892, July 25.

> Consecrated in Rochester Cathedral by Archbishop Longley, Samuel of Oxford, Walter Kerr of Sarum, Henry of Worcester, Charles of S. Andrews, and Piers Calveley Claughton ; *Reg. Longley*, 145.

A. D. **1868**, June 24. **James Atlay.** Hereford ; d. 1894, Dec. 24.

> Consecrated in Westminster Abbey by Archbishop Longley, Edward Harold of Ely, Charles John of Gloucester, Thomas Legh of Rochester, and George Augustus of Lichfield ; *Reg. Longley*, 179.

A. D. **1868**, Nov. 15. **William Connor Magee.** Peterborough ; York, 1890 ; d. 1891, May 5.

> Consecrated in Whitehall Chapel by Archbishop Thomson of York, Archibald Campbell of London, Samuel of Oxford, Robert of Ripon, and Thomas of Barbadoes ; *Reg. Tait*, 16.

A. D. **1869**, Feb. 24. **Christopher Wordsworth.** Lincoln ; d. 1885, Mar. 20.

> Consecrated in Westminster Abbey by Archbishop Tait, John of London, Samuel of Oxford, Alfred of Llandaff, Edward Harold of Ely, James Colquhoun of Bangor, Thomas Legh of Rochester, George Augustus of Lichfield, Charles John of Gloucester, William Connor of Peterborough, [Charles of S. Andrews and Bishops Macdougall and Ryan] ; *Reg. Tait*, 67.

A. D. **1869**, Oct. 28. **George Moberly.** Salisbury ; d. 1885, July 6.

> Consecrated in Westminster Abbey by Archbishop Tait, John of London, Samuel of Oxford, and William of Chester ; *Reg. Tait*, 97.

A. D. **1869**, Nov. 30.   **Harvey Goodwin.**   Carlisle ; d. 1891, Nov. 25.

Consecrated in York Minster by Archbishop Thomson, Robert of Ripon, Edward Harold of Ely, William of Chester, and James of Hereford ; *Reg. Thomson.*

A. D. **1869**, Dec. 21.   **Frederick Temple.**   Exeter ; London, 1885 ; Canterbury, 1896 ; and

Arthur Charles Hervey.   Bath and Wells ; d. 1894, June 9.

Consecrated in Westminster Abbey by John of London, Connop of S. David's, Henry of Worcester, and Edward Harold of Ely ; *Reg. Tait*, 114.

A. D. **1870**, Jan. 25.   **John Fielder Mackarness.**   Oxford ; res. 1888 ; d. 1889, Sept. 16.

Consecrated in Westminster Abbey by John of London, George Augustus of Lichfield, Edward Harold of Ely, Thomas Legh of Rochester, and George of Sarum ; *Reg. Tait*, 165.

A. D. **1870**, Feb. 2.   **Henry Mackenzie.**   Nottingham (suffragan) ; d. 1878, Oct. 15.

Consecrated at S. Mary's, Nottingham, by John of London, Christopher of Lincoln, George Augustus of Lichfield, James of Hereford, [Charles John of Wellington, and Charles of S. Andrews] ; *Reg. Tait*, 169.

A. D. **1870**, March 25.   **Edward Parry.**   Dover (suffragan) ; d. 1890, Apr. 11.

Consecrated in Lambeth Chapel by John of London, Alfred of Llandaff, and Charles John of Gloucester ; *Reg. Tait*, 191.

A. D. **1870**, March 25.   **James Fraser.**   Manchester ; d. 1885, Oct. 22.

Consecrated in Manchester Cathedral by Archbishop Thomson of York, Robert of Ripon, and William of Chester ; *Reg. Thomson.*

A. D. **1870**, May 8.   **Richard Durnford.**   Chichester ; d. 1895, Oct. 14 ; and

Joshua Hughes.   S. Asaph ; d. 1889, Jan. 21.

Consecrated in Whitehall Chapel by John of London, Samuel of Winchester, George Augustus of Lichfield, Alfred of Llandaff, and Connop of S. David's, [Archbishop Thomson present] ; *Reg. Tait*, 208, 225.

A. D. **1873**, Dec. 14. **James Russell Woodford.** Ely; d. 1885, Oct. 24.

Consecrated in Westminster Abbey by Archbishop Tait, John of London, Edward Harold of Winchester, Robert of Ripon, Thomas Legh of Rochester, and Harvey of Carlisle, [also Christopher of Lincoln, and Bishop Macdougall]; *Reg. Tait*, 285.

A. D. **1874**, March 15. **John Sutton Utterton.** Guildford (suffragan); d. 1879, Dec. 21.

Consecrated in Lambeth Church by John of London, Edward Harold of Winchester, Thomas Legh of Rochester, [and Bishops Ryan and Alford]; *Reg. Tait*, 292.

A. D. **1874**, Aug. 24. **William Basil Tickell Jones.** S. David's; d. 1897, Jan. 14.

Consecrated in Westminster Abbey by Archbishop Tait, John of London, Thomas Legh of Rochester, Joshua of S. Asaph, [and Bishop Kerfoot of Pittsburg]; *Reg. Tait*, 315.

A. D. **1876**, Oct. 22. **James Moorhouse.** Melbourne; Manchester, 1886.

Consecrated in Westminster Abbey by Archbishop Tait, John of London, James of Hereford, and Bishop Perry; *Reg. Tait*, 335.

A. D. **1877**, April 25. **Edward White Benson.** Truro; Canterbury, 1883; d. 1896, Oct. 11.

Consecrated at S. Paul's by Archbishop Tait, John of London, Edward Harold of Winchester, James of Hereford, Christopher of Lincoln, George of Sarum, Frederick of Exeter, James Russell of Ely, Edward of Dover, and Henry of Nottingham; *Reg. Tait*, 357.

A. D. **1877**, July 25. **Anthony Wilson Thorold.** Rochester; Winchester, 1890; d. 1895, July 25.

Consecrated at Westminster by Archbishop Tait, Archbishop Thomson, John of London, Charles of Durham, Edward Harold of Winchester, Thomas Legh of S. Albans, John Fielder of Oxford, James Russell of Ely, William Basil of S. David's, and John Sutton of Guildford; *Reg. Tait.*

A. D. **1877**, Aug. 24. **Rowley Hill.** Sodor and Man; d. 1887, May 27.

Consecrated in York Minster by Archbishop Thomson, Charles of Durham, William of Chester, and Anthony Wilson of Rochester; *Reg. Thomson.*

A. D. **1877**, Dec. 21.   **Edward Trollope.**   Nottingham (suffragan); d. 1893, Dec. 10.

Consecrated at Westminster by Archbishop Tait, Edward Harold of Winchester, Frederick of Sydney, and Bishops P. C. Claughton, Perry, and Anderson ; *Reg. Tait*, 389.

A. D. **1878**, June 24.   **William Dalrymple Maclagan.**   Lichfield ; York, 1891.

Consecrated at S. Paul's by Archbishop Tait, John of London, Edward Harold of Winchester, James of Hereford, Anthony Wilson of Rochester, the Bishops of Sydney, Adelaide, Guiana, Pennsylvania, Ohio, North Carolina, Ontario, and Bishop Harper ; *Reg. Tait*, 443.

A. D. **1879**, April 25.   **Joseph Barber Lightfoot.**   Durham ; d. 1889, Dec. 21.

Consecrated in Westminster Abbey by Archbishop Thomson, John of London, Edward Harold of Winchester, Harvey of Carlisle, James of Manchester, Edward White of Truro, James Russell of Ely, and Rowley of Sodor and Man ; *Reg. Tait*, 443.

A. D. **1879**, July 25.   **William Walsham How.**   Bedford (suffragan) ; Wakefield, 1888.

Consecrated at S. Paul's by Archbishop Tait, John of London, Thomas Legh of S. Albans, Anthony Wilson of Rochester, William Dalrymple of Lichfield, Charles Waldegrave of Gibraltar, the Bishop of Columbia, and Bishop C. R. Alford ; *Reg. Tait*, 452.

A. D. **1880**, June 11.   **John Charles Ryle.**   Liverpool.

Consecrated in York Minster by Archbishop Thomson, Joseph Barber of Durham, William of Chester, and James of Manchester ; *Reg. Thomson.*

A. D. **1882**, June 24.   **Alfred Blomfield.**   Colchester (suffragan) ; d. 1894, Nov. 5.

Consecrated at S. Albans by Archbishop Tait, John of London, Thomas Legh of S. Albans, James Russell of Ely, and William Dalrymple of Lichfield ; *Reg. Tait*, 482.

A. D. **1882**, July 25.   **Ernest Roland Wilberforce.**   Newcastle ; Chichester, 1895.

Consecrated in Durham Cathedral by Archbishop Thomson, Joseph Barber of Durham, Edward Harold of Winchester, Harvey of Carlisle, James Russell of Ely, James of Manchester, Thomas Legh of S. Albans, and John Charles of Liverpool ; *Reg. Thomson.*

A. D. **1882**, Nov. 30. **George Wyndham Kennion.** Adelaide ; Bath and Wells, 1894.

Consecrated at Westminster by John of London, Edward Harold of Winchester, Anthony Wilson of Rochester, William Dalrymple of Lichfield, William Walsham of Bedford, the Bishops of Ballarat and Nelson, and Bishops Short, Ryan, and Hellmuth ; *Reg. Tait.* 488.

A. D. **1883**, Apr. 25. **Richard Lewis.** Llandaff ; and

   George Howard Wilkinson. Truro ; res. 1891 ; S. Andrews, 1893.

Consecrated at S. Paul's by Archbishop Benson, John of London, James Colquhoun of Bangor, James Russell of Ely, William Dalrymple of Lichfield, William Basil of S. David's, Ernest Roland of Newcastle, William Walsham of Bedford, Alfred of Colchester, Allan Becher of Bloemfontein, Edward Ralph of Calcutta, and Bishop Bromby ; *Reg. Benson.*

A. D. **1884**, Apr. 25. **William Stubbs.** Chester ; Oxford, 1889.

Consecrated in York Minster by Archbishop Thomson, Joseph Barber of Durham, Thomas Legh of S. Albans, Harvey of Carlisle, James of Manchester, Rowley of Sodor and Man, John Charles of Liverpool, and Ernest Roland of Newcastle ; *Reg. Thomson.*

A. D. **1884**, May 1. **George Ridding.** Southwell.

Consecrated at S. Paul's by Archbishop Benson, John of London, John Thomas of Norwich, James Russell of Ely, Thomas Legh of S. Albans, John Fielder of Oxford, Christopher of Lincoln, William Dalrymple of Lichfield, and the Bishops of Nottingham and Algoma ; *Reg. Benson.*

A. D. **1884**, July 25. **William Boyd Carpenter.** Ripon.

Consecrated at Westminster by Archbishop Thomson, John of London, Joseph Barber of Durham, Thomas Legh of S. Albans, Anthony Wilson of Rochester, William Dalrymple of Lichfield, John Charles of Liverpool, and Ernest Roland of Newcastle ; *Reg. Benson.*

A. D. **1885**, Apr. 25. **Edward King.** Lincoln ; and

   Edward Henry Bickersteth. Exeter.

Consecrated at S. Paul's by Archbishop Benson, Frederick of London, John Fielder of Oxford, James Russell of Ely, Anthony Wilson of Rochester, Ernest Roland of Newcastle, Edward of Nottingham, William Walsham of Bedford, William Boyd of Ripon, and the Bishop of Pretoria ; *Reg. Benson.*

M

A. D. **1885**, Oct. 28.   **John Wordsworth.**   Salisbury.

> Consecrated at Westminster by Archbishop Benson, Frederick of London, Edward Harold of Winchester, Anthony Wilson of Rochester, George of Southwell, Edward of Lincoln, and Edward of Nottingham ; *Reg. Benson.*

A. D. **1886**, Feb. 2.   **Alwyne Compton.**   Ely.

> Consecrated at S. Paul's by Archbishop Benson, Frederick of London, James of Hereford, Thomas Legh of S. Albans, Edward of Lincoln, Edward Henry of Exeter, and William Walsham of Bedford ; *Reg. Benson.*

A. D. **1887**, Aug. 24.   **John Wareing Bardsley.**   Sodor and Man ; Carlisle, 1892.

> Consecrated in York Minster by Archbishop Thomson, Harvey of Carlisle, and James of Manchester ; *Reg. Thomson.*

A. D. **1888**, Feb. 24.   **Alfred Earle.**   Marlborough (suffragan) ; and
>   **Lovelace Tomlinson Stamer.**   Shrewsbury (suffragan).

> Consecrated at S. Paul's by Archbishop Benson, Frederick of London, William Dalrymple of Lichfield, Edward of Dover, William Walsham of Bedford, and Bishop Bromby ; *Reg. Benson.*

A. D. **1888**, May 22.   **John James Pulleine.**   Penrith (suffragan); Richmond (suffragan), 1889.

> Consecrated in York Minster by Archbishop Thomson, Joseph Barber of Durham, William Boyd of Ripon, and the Bishop of Adelaide ; *Reg. Thomson.*

A. D. **1888**, July 15.   **Francis Henry Thicknesse.**   Leicester (suffragan) ; and
>   **Robert Claudius Billing.**   Bedford (suffragan).

> Consecrated at S. Paul's by Archbishop Benson, Frederick of London, William Connor of Peterborough, William Walsham of Wakefield, Alfred of Marlborough, and the Bishops of Queensland, Springfield, and Tennessee ; *Reg. Benson.*

A. D. **1888**, Nov. 30.   **George Henry Sumner.**   Guildford (suffragan).

> Consecrated at Westminster by Archbishop Benson, Frederick of London, Edward Harold of Winchester, Anthony Wilson of Rochester, Ernest Roland of Newcastle, Alwyne of Ely, Edward of Dover, and the Bishops of Jamaica, Adelaide, and Jerusalem ; *Reg. Benson.*

A. D. **1889**, Feb. 24. **Francis John Jayne.** Chester.

Consecrated in York Minster by Archbishop Thomson, Harvey of Carlisle, William Basil of S. David's, William Boyd of Ripon, John Wareing of Sodor and Man, and John James of Penrith ; *Reg. Thomson.*

A. D. **1889**, March 25. **Alfred George Edwards.** S. Asaph.

Consecrated at Westminster by Archbishop Benson, Frederick of London, Thomas Legh of S. Albans, William Basil of S. David's, Richard of Llandaff, Francis Henry of Leicester, the Bishops of Antigua and Jamaica, and Bishop Mitchinson ; *Reg. Benson.*

A. D. **1889**, June 11. **Robert Jarratt Crosthwaite.** Beverley (suffragan) ;
and
Henry Ware. Barrow-in-Furness (suffragan).

Consecrated in York Minster by Archbishop Thomson, Harvey of Carlisle, John James of Richmond, and Bishop Hellmuth ; *Reg. Thomson.*

A. D. **1889**, Nov. 1. **James Leslie Randall.** Reading (suffragan) ; and
Edward Ash Were. Derby (suffragan).

Consecrated at Westminster by Archbishop Benson, Frederick of London, Harvey of Carlisle, William of Oxford, George of Southwell, Edward of Lincoln, and Bishop Mitchinson ; *Reg. Benson.*

A. D. **1890**, May 1. **Brook Foss Westcott.** Durham.

Consecrated at Westminster by Archbishop Thomson, Edward Harold of Winchester, Harvey of Carlisle, William of Oxford, William Boyd of Ripon, George Howard of Truro, Edward Henry of Exeter, William Walsham of Wakefield, and Bishop Barry ; *Reg. Thomson.*

A. D. **1890**, June 24. **John Wogan Festing.** S. Albans.
Daniel Lewis Lloyd. Bangor ; and
John Lloyd. Swansea (suffragan).

Consecrated at S. Paul's by Archbishop Benson, Frederick of London, Harvey of Carlisle, William Dalrymple of Lichfield, William Basil of S. David's, Richard of Llandaff, the Bishops of Madras, Colchester, Bedford, and Marlborough, and Bishops Campbell, Barry, and Marsden ; *Reg. Benson.*

M 2

A. D. 1890, Oct. 18. **George Rodney Eden.** Dover (suffragan).

Consecrated at Canterbury by Archbishop Benson, Brooke Foss of Durham, Anthony Wilson of Rochester, Charles Waldegrave of Gibraltar, and Bishop Mitchinson ; *Reg. Benson.*

A. D. 1891, Feb. 2. **John James Stewart Perowne.** Worcester.

Consecrated at Westminster by Archbishop Benson, Frederick of London, Arthur of Bath and Wells, Anthony Wilson of Rochester, John Wogan of S. Albans, Alfred of Marlborough, Robert Claudius of Bedford, and Bishop Royston; *Reg. Benson.*

A. D. 1891, Apr. 25. **Mandell Creighton.** Peterborough ; London, 1897 ; and

   Randall Thomas Davidson. Rochester ; Winchester, 1895.

Consecrated at Westminster by Archbishop Benson, Frederick of London, Anthony Wilson of Winchester, Harvey of Carlisle, Alwyne of Ely, William Dalrymple of Lichfield, George of Southwell, William Boyd of Ripon, the Bishops of Colombo and Minnesota, and Bishops Campbell and Barry ; *Reg. Benson.*

A. D. 1891, May 1. **Richard Frederick Lefevre Blunt.** Hull (suffragan).

Consecrated in York Minster by Brooke Foss of Durham, Ernest Roland of Newcastle, John Wareing of Sodor and Man, John James Stewart of Worcester, the Bishops of Beverley and Richmond, and Bishop Bromby; *Reg. Magee.*

A. D. 1891, Sept. 29. **John Gott.** Truro.

   Augustus Legge. Lichfield.

   Henry Bond Bowlby. Coventry (suffragan) ; d. 1894, Aug. 27 ; and

   Huyshe Wolcott Yeatman. Southwark (suffragan).

Consecrated at S. Paul's by Archbishop Benson, Anthony Wilson of Winchester, Harvey of Carlisle, John of Sarum, William Walsham of Wakefield, George of Southwell, John James Stewart of Worcester, Randall Thomas of Rochester, Robert Claudius of Bedford, Lovelace Tomlinson of Shrewsbury, and Bishops Blyth, Mitchinson, and Speechley ; *Reg. Benson.*

A. D. **1892**, March 25.   **Norman Dumenil John Straton.**   Sodor and Man.

> Consecrated in York Minster by Archbishop Maclagan, John Wareing of Carlisle, John Charles of Liverpool, William Walsham of Wakefield, Robert Jarratt of Beverley, and Richard Frederick Lefevre of Hull ; *Reg. Maclagan.*

A. D. **1893**, June 29.   **John Sheepshanks.**   Norwich.

> Consecrated at S. Paul's by Archbishop Benson, Frederick of London, John Charles of Liverpool, William of Oxford, Randall Thomas of Rochester, John Wogan of S. Albans, George Howard of S. Andrews, Robert Claudius of Bedford, the Bishops of Adelaide and Algoma, and Bishop Cheetham ; *Reg. Benson.*

A. D. **1894**, Oct. 18.   **Arthur Thomas Lloyd.**   Thetford (suffragan).

> Consecrated at Westminster by Archbishop Benson, Ernest Roland of Newcastle, John of Norwich, Mandell of Peterborough, George Wyndham of Bath and Wells, James Leslie of Reading, and the Bishop of Honduras ; *Reg. Benson.*

A. D. **1894**, Dec. 28.   **Edmund Arbuthnot Knox.**   Coventry (suffragan); and

> **Henry Frank Johnson.**   Colchester (suffragan).

> Consecrated at S. Paul's by Archbishop Benson, Frederick of London, Augustus of Lichfield, Mandell of Peterborough, Randall Thomas of Rochester, John Wogan of S. Albans, John James Stewart of Worcester, George Wyndham of Bath and Wells, Reginald Stephen of Colombo, and Bishop Mitchinson ; *Reg. Benson.*

A. D. **1895**, March 25.   **John Percival.**   Hereford.

> Consecrated at Westminster by Archbishop Benson, Frederick of London, Mandell of Peterborough, the Bishop of Columbia, and Bishop Barry ; *Reg. Benson.*

A. D. **1895**, Apr. 21.   **George Forrest Browne.**   Stepney (suffragan).

> Consecrated at S. Paul's by Frederick of London, John of Hereford, Mandell of Peterborough, John Wogan of S. Albans, William Walsham of Wakefield, and Henry Frank of Colchester ; *Reg. Benson.*

A. D. **1895**, June 29.   **William Awdry.**   Southampton (suffragan).

Consecrated at S. Paul's by Archbishop Benson, Frederick of London, Mandell of Peterborough, John Wogan of S. Albans, George Henry of Guildford, Huyshe Wolcott of Southwark, Arthur Thomas of Thetford, George Forrest of Stepney, and Bishop Hornby; *Reg. Benson.*

A. D. **1895**, Oct. 18.   **Edward Stuart Talbot.**   Rochester.

Consecrated at Westminster by Archbishop Benson, Randall Thomas of Winchester, George of Southwell, John of Sarum, John of Truro, Augustus of Lichfield, Huyshe Wolcott of Southwark, and the Bishops of Richmond and Mid China; *Reg. Benson.*

A. D. **1896**, Jan. 25.   **Edgar Jacob.**   Newcastle.

Consecrated in York Minster by Archbishop Maclagan, Brooke Foss of Durham, Ernest Roland of Chichester, John Wareing of Carlisle, William Walsham of Wakefield, Robert Jarratt of Beverley, and Richard Frederick Lefevre of Hull; *Reg. Maclagan.*

A. D. **1896**, March 25.   **George Carnac Fisher.**   Southampton (suffragan).

Consecrated at S. Mary's, Lambeth, by Archbishop Benson, Frederick of London, Randall Thomas of Winchester, George Henry of Guildford, and Bishop Barry; *Reg. Benson.*

A. D. **1897**, Feb. 24.   **Edward Carr Glynn.**   Peterborough; and

Robert Edward Trefusis.   Crediton (suffragan).

Consecrated at S. Paul's by Archbishop Temple, Mandell of London, Randall Thomas of Winchester, Ernest Roland of Chichester, Edward Henry of Exeter, Alwyne of Ely, George Wyndham of Bath and Wells, George Forrest of Stepney, and the Bishop of Madagascar; *Reg. Temple.*

A. D. **1897**, May 1.   **John Owen.**   S. David's.

Consecrated at S. Paul's by Archbishop Temple, Mandell of London, Richard of Llandaff, Alfred George of S. Asaph, John of Swansea, and the Bishops of Dunedin and Ontario.   *Reg. Temple.*

APPENDICES

———⸭———

APPENDIX I

INDIAN, COLONIAL, AND MISSIONARY CONSECRATIONS.

PROVINCE OF CANADA.

Nova Scotia.

A.D. **1787**, Aug. 12. CHARLES INGLIS. Consecrated at Lambeth by J. Cantuar., J. Rochester, B. Chester; *Reg. Moore.*

A.D. **1816**, May 19. ROBERT STANSER. Consecrated at Lambeth by C. Cantuar., W. London, G. Exeter, E. Oxford; *Reg. Sutton.*

A.D. **1825**, March 27. JOHN INGLIS. Consecrated at Lambeth by C. Cantuar., W. London, G. Lincoln, W. Llandaff; *Reg. Sutton.*

A.D. **1851**, March 25. HIBBERT BINNEY. Consecrated at Lambeth by J. B. Cantuar., C. J. London, A. T. Chichester, S. Oxford; *Reg. Sumner.*

A.D. **1888**, April 25. FREDERICK COURTNEY. Consecrated at Halifax, N.S., by J. Fredericton, J. T. Ontario, J. W. Quebec, H. T. Kingdon, H. A. Neely, U.S.A.; *Reg. of Prov. of Canada.*

Quebec.

A.D. **1793**, July 7. JACOB MOUNTAIN. Consecrated at Lambeth by J. Cantuar., B. London, J. Bangor, S. S. David's; *Reg. Moore.*

A.D. **1826**, Jan. 1. CHARLES JAMES STEWART. Consecrated at Lambeth by C. Cantuar., W. London, W. Llandaff, C. J. Chester; *Reg. Sutton.*

A.D. **1836**, Feb. 14. GEORGE JEHOSHAPHAT MOUNTAIN. Consecrated at Lambeth by W. Cantuar., C. J. London, C. R. Winchester, J. H. Gloucester; *Reg. Howley.*

A.D. **1863**, June 21. JAMES WILLIAM WILLIAMS. Consecrated at Quebec by F. Montreal, J. Toronto, J. T. Ontario, B. Huron, J. H. Hopkins of Vermont; Queen's Mandate in *Reg. Longley*; *Guardian*, July 15, 1863.

A.D. **1892**, Sept. 18. ANDREW HUNTER DUNN. Consecrated at Montreal by J. T. Ontario, A. Toronto, W. B. Montreal, C. Niagara, H. T. Kingdon, M. S. Huron, F. Nova Scotia, J. L. Milwaukee, U.S.A.; *Reg. of Prov. of Canada*; *Guardian*, Oct. 5, 1892.

Toronto.

A.D. 1839, Aug. 4. JOHN STRACHAN. Consecrated at Lambeth by W. Cantuar., C. J. London, W. Chichester, J. Nova Scotia; *Reg. Howley.*

A.D. 1867, Nov. 1. ALEXANDER NEIL BETHUNE. Consecrated Coadjutor (as Bishop of Niagara), Jan. 25, 1867; *q. v.*

A.D. 1879, May 1. ARTHUR SWEATMAN. Consecrated at Toronto by J. W. Quebec, I. Huron, T. B. Niagara, W. B. Montreal, F. D. Algoma. *Record of Synod of Toronto.*

Fredericton.

A.D. 1845, May 4. JOHN MEDLEY (Metropolitan). Consecrated at Lambeth by W. Cantuar., C. J. London, J. Lincoln, G. Rochester, T. Hereford, J. Lichfield, W. H. Coleridge; *Reg. Howley.*

A.D. 1881, July 10. HOLLINGWORTH TULLY KINGDON (Coadjutor, Fredericton; Bishop of Fredericton, 1892). Consecrated at Fredericton by J. Fredericton, J. W. Quebec, H. Nova Scotia, W. C. Doane, U.S.A., H. A. Neely, U.S.A.; *Reg. of Prov. of Canada.*

Montreal.

A.D. 1850, July 25. FRANCIS FULFORD. Consecrated at Westminster by J. B. Cantuar., E. Sarum, A. T. Chichester, S. Oxford, S. Norwich, J. Toronto; *Reg. Sumner.*

A.D. 1869, Aug. 1. ASHTON OXENDEN (Metropolitan). Consecrated in Westminster Abbey by A. C. Cantuar., J. London, E. H. Ely, T. L. Rochester, G. Columbia, F. T. Labuan, G. Smith, W. J. Trower; *Reg. Tait.*

A.D. 1879, Jan. 25. WILLIAM BENNETT BOND. Consecrated at Montreal by J. Fredericton, J. T. Ontario, H. Nova Scotia, F. D. Algoma, T. B. Niagara, J. W. Quebec; *Reg. of Dioc. Synod of Montreal.*

Huron.

A.D. 1857, Oct. 28. BENJAMIN CRONYN. Consecrated at Lambeth by J. B. Cantuar., C. R. Winchester, H. Nova Scotia, J. Sierra Leone; *Reg. Sumner.*

A.D. 1871, Aug. 24. ISAAC HELLMUTH. Consecrated at London, Ontario, by A. Montreal, J. T. Ontario, A. N. Toronto, S. T. Dunedin, and Bishops of Michigan and Ohio; *Letter from Bishop Hellmuth.*

A.D. 1883, Nov. 30. MAURICE SCOLLARD BALDWIN. Consecrated at Montreal by J. T. Ontario, J. W. Quebec, A. Toronto, W. B. Montreal; *Reg. of Prov. of Canada.*

Ontario.

A.D. 1862, March 25. JOHN TRAVERS LEWIS (Archbishop). Consecrated at Kingston, Canada, by F. Montreal, J. Toronto, G. J. Quebec, B. Huron, S. A. McCoskry of Michigan; *Letter from Archbishop Lewis*; *Guardian*, April 23, 1862.

Algoma.

A.D. 1873, Oct. 28. FREDERIC DAWSON FAUQUIER. Consecrated at Toronto by A. Montreal, A. N. Toronto, J. T. Ontario, I. Huron, J. W. Quebec, A. C. Coxe, U.S.A.; *S.P.G. Record.*

A.D. **1882**, June 29. EDWARD SULLIVAN. Consecrated at Montreal by J. T. Ontario, J. W. Quebec, W. B. Montreal, I. Huron, A. Toronto, A. C. Coxe, U.S.A.; *Reg. of Prov. of Canada.*

A.D. **1897**, Jan. 6. GEORGE THORNELOE. Consecrated at Quebec by W. B. Montreal, H. T. Fredericton, C. Ottawa, F. Nova Scotia, A. H. Quebec, and E. Sullivan (late of Algoma) ; *Reg. of Prov. of Canada.*

Niagara.

A.D. **1867**, Jan. 25. ALEXANDER NEIL BETHUNE (Bishop of Toronto, Nov. 1). Consecrated at Toronto by J. Toronto, B. Huron, J. T. Ontario, S. A. McCoskry, U.S.A., A. C. Coxe, U S.A.; *Reg. of Dioc. Synod of Toronto.*

A.D. **1875**, April 30. THOMAS BROCK FULLER. Consecrated at Hamilton by A. Montreal, F. D. Algoma, I. Huron, J. T. Ontario, A. N. Toronto, and the Bishops of Michigan and Western New York; *Guardian,* May 26, 1875 ; *S. P. G. Record.*

A.D. **1885**, May 1. CHARLES HAMILTON (Bishop of Ottawa, 1896). Consecrated at Fredericton by J. Fredericton, J. W. Quebec, A. Toronto, H. T. Kingdon, H. Nova Scotia, H. A. Neely, U.S.A. ; *Reg. of Prov. of Canada.*

A.D. **1896**, June 24. JOHN PHILIP DU MOULIN. Consecrated at Toronto by J. T. Ontario, C. Ottawa, M. S. Huron, E. Algoma, A. Toronto ; *Reg. of Prov. of Canada.*

Ottawa.

A.D. **1896**. CHARLES HAMILTON. Consecrated Bishop of Niagara, May 1, 1885; *q.v.*

PROVINCE OF RUPERT'S LAND.

Rupert's Land.

A.D. **1849**, May 29. DAVID ANDERSON. Consecrated at Canterbury by J. B. Cantuar., C. J. London, C. R. Winchester, T. V. St. Asaph, S. Oxford, W. H. Coleridge ; *Reg. Sumner.*

A.D. **1865**, June 24. ROBERT MACHRAY (Metropolitan 1875). Consecrated at Lambeth by C. T. Cantuar., A. C. London, E. H. Ely, D. Anderson ; *Reg. Tait.*

Mackenzie River.

A.D. **1884**. WILLIAM CARPENTER BOMPAS, Bishop of Mackenzie River. Consecrated Bishop of Athabasca, 1874; *q. v.*

A.D. **1891**, Nov. 29. WILLIAM DAY REEVE. Consecrated at Winnipeg by R. Rupert's Land, W. C. Saskatchewan and Calgary, A. J. R. Qu'Appelle, W. D. Walker, U.S.A., and the Assistant Bishop of Minnesota ; *C.M.S. Record.*

Moosonee (Hudson's Bay).

A.D. **1872**, Dec. 15. J. HORDEN. Consecrated at Westminster by A. C. Cantuar., J. London, T. L. Rochester, H. Sierra Leone, D. Anderson, V. W. Ryan, P. C. Claughton ; *Reg. Tait.*

A.D. **1893**, Aug. 6. JERVOIS ARTHUR NEWNHAM. Consecrated at Winnipeg by R. Rupert's Land, R. Athabasca, W. C. Saskatchewan, W. D. Walker [North Dakota], U.S.A.; *C.M.S. Record*; *Guardian*, Aug. 6, 1893.

Saskatchewan.

A.D. **1874**, May 3. JOHN MACLEAN. Consecrated at Lambeth by A. C. Cantuar., J. London, J. St. Asaph ; *Reg. Tait.*

A.D. **1887**, Aug. 7. WILLIAM CYPRIAN PINKHAM. Consecrated at Winnipeg by R. Rupert's Land, A. W. Rochester, J. Moosonee, M. S. Huron, A. J. R. Qu'Appelle, R. Athabasca, H. B. Minnesota, U.S.A., W. D. Walker, U.S.A.; *S.P.G. Record*; *Guardian*, Sept. 7, 1887.

Calgary.

A.D. **1888**. W. C. PINKHAM. Consecrated to Saskatchewan, 1887 ; *q. v.*

Qu'Appelle (formerly Assiniboia).

A.D. **1884**, June 24. ADELBERT JOHN ROBERT ANSON (first Bishop of Qu'Appelle). Consecrated in Lambeth Parish Church by E. W. Cantuar., J. London, A. W. Rochester, T. L. S. Albans, W. D. Lichfield, J. Saskatchewan, E. Dover, F. A. R. Nassau, G. F. Ohio, U.S.A.; *Reg. Benson.*

A.D. **1893**, March 25. WILLIAM JOHN BURN. Consecrated in Westminster Abbey by E. W. Cantuar., F. London, D. L. Bangor, C. Christ Church, N.Z., G. H. S. Andrews, A. J. R. Anson, late of Qu'Appelle, J. Mitchinson, late of Barbados ; *Reg. Benson.*

A.D. **1896**, Aug. 30. JOHN GRISDALE. Consecrated at Winnipeg by R. Rupert's Land, R. Athabasca, W. C. Saskatchewan and Calgary, W. D. Mackenzie River, and others ; *Letter from Bishop Grisdale.*

Athabasca.

A.D. **1874**, May 3. WILLIAM CARPENTER BOMPAS. Consecrated at Lambeth by A. C. Cantuar., J. London, J. S. Asaph ; *Reg. Tait.*

A.D. **1884**, Oct. 18. RICHARD YOUNG. Consecrated at Winnipeg by R. Rupert's Land, J. Saskatchewan, A. J. R. Qu'Appelle ; *C.M.S. Record.*

Selkirk.

A.D. **1891**, WILLIAM CARPENTER BOMPAS. Consecrated Bishop of Athabasca, 1874 ; *q. v.* (Bishop of Mackenzie River, 1884).

PROVINCE OF INDIA AND CEYLON.

Calcutta.

A.D. **1814**, May 8. THOMAS FANSHAWE MIDDLETON. Consecrated at Lambeth by C. Cantuar., W. London, G. Lincoln, J. Sarum ; *Reg. Sutton.*

A.D. **1823**, June 1. REGINALD HEBER. Consecrated at Lambeth by C. Cantuar., W. London, J. St. Asaph, W. Llandaff ; *Reg. Sutton.*

A.D. **1827**, June 3. JOHN THOMAS JAMES. Consecrated at Lambeth by C. Cantuar., W. London, W. Durham, J. B. S. David's ; *Reg. Sutton.*

A.D. **1829**, May 17. JOHN MATTHIAS TURNER. Consecrated at Lambeth by W. Cantuar., C. J. London, G. Rochester, J. B. Chester ; *Reg. Sutton.*

A.D. **1832**, April 29. DANIEL WILSON. Consecrated at Lambeth by W. Cantuar., C. J. London, R. Bristol, J. H. Gloucester; *Reg. Howley.*

A.D. **1858**, May 13. GEORGE EDWARD LYNCH COTTON. Consecrated in Westminster Abbey by J. B. Cantuar., A. C. London, C. S. David's, T. V. S. Asaph, S. Oxford, A. Llandaff, W. K. Sarum, F. Montreal, J. Fredericton ; *Reg. Sumner.*

A.D. **1867**, Feb. 2. ROBERT MILMAN. Consecrated at Canterbury by C. T. Cantuar., S. Oxford, J. C. Rochester, F. Montreal, H. L. Dunedin, and the Bishop of Illinois, U.S.A.; *Reg. Longley.*

A.D. **1876**, Nov. 30. EDWARD RALPH JOHNSON. Consecrated in S. Paul's Cathedral by A. C. Cantuar., J. London, E. H. Winchester, T. L. Rochester, H. Carlisle, W. Chester, P. C. Claughton ; *Reg. Tait.*

Madras.

A.D. **1835**, June 14. DANIEL CORRIE. Consecrated at Lambeth by W. Cantuar., H. Lichfield, C. Bangor, H. Carlisle ; *Reg. Howley.*

A.D **1837**, Nov. 19. GEORGE JOHN TREVOR SPENCER. Consecrated at Lambeth by W. Cantuar., S. Lichfield, E. Sarum ; *Reg. Howley.*

A.D. **1849**, Dec. 2. THOMAS DEALTRY. Consecrated at Lambeth by J. B. Cantuar., C. J. London, J. Lincoln, H. Carlisle, J. P. Manchester, R. D. Hereford ; *Reg. Sumner.*

A.D. **1861**, June 29. FREDERICK GELL. Consecrated in Lambeth Chapel by J. B. Cantuar., A. C. London, H. M. Durham, J. Chester, S. Carlisle, F. T. Labuan ; *Reg. Sumner.*

A.D. **1877**, March 11. ROBERT CALDWELL (Assistant Bishop of Madras). Consecrated at Calcutta by E. R. Calcutta, F. Madras, L. G. Bombay, R. S. Colombo ; Queen's Mandate in *Reg. Tait.* (Commission); *S.P.G. Record* ; *Guardian*, April 11, 1877.

A.D. **1877**, March 11. EDWARD SARGENT (Assistant Bishop of Madras). Consecrated at Calcutta by E. R. Calcutta, F. Madras, L. G. Bombay, R. S. Colombo ; *Reg. Tait.* (Commission) ; *S.P.G. Record* ; *Guardian*, April 11, 1877.

Bombay.

A.D. **1837**, Nov. 19. THOMAS CARR. Consecrated at Lambeth by W. Cantuar., S. Lichfield, E. Sarum ; *Reg. Howley.*

A.D. **1851**, Aug. 10. JOHN HARDING. Consecrated at Lambeth by J. B. Cantuar., C. J. London, T. Carr (late of Bombay) ; *Reg. Sumner.*

A.D. **1869**, Jan. 3. HENRY ALEXANDER DOUGLAS. Consecrated in Whitehall Chapel by A. C. Cantuar., S. Oxford, T. L. Rochester ; *Reg. Tait.*

A.D. **1876**, May 1. LOUIS GEORGE MYLNE. Consecrated in S. Paul's Cathedral by A. C. Cantuar., J. London, G. A. Lichfield, J. F. Oxford, C. Lincoln ; *Reg. Tait.*

Colombo.

A.D. **1845**, May 4.　JOHN CHAPMAN.　Consecrated at Lambeth by W. Cantuar., C. J. London, J. Lincoln, G. Rochester, T. Hereford, J. Lichfield, W. H. Coleridge ; *Reg. Howley.*

A.D. **1862.**　PIERS CALVELEY CLAUGHTON.　Consecrated Bishop of St. Helena, 1859 ; *q. v.*

A.D. **1871**, Oct. 28.　HUGH WILLOUGHBY JERMYN.　Consecrated at Lambeth by A. C. Cantuar., T. L. Rochester, A. C. Bath and Wells, P. C. Claughton, V. W. Ryan ; (became Bishop of Brechin, 1875) ; *Reg. Tait.*

A.D. **1875**, Dec. 28.　REGINALD STEPHEN COPLESTON.　Consecrated at Westminster by A. C. Cantuar., J. London, G. A. Lichfield, G. Sarum, J. F. Oxford, Piers C. Claughton ; *Reg. Tait.*

Rangoon.

A.D. **1877**, Dec. 21.　JONATHAN HOLT TITCOMB.　Consecrated at Westminster by A. C. Cantuar., E. H. Winchester, F. Sydney, P. C. Claughton, D. Anderson, C. Perry ; *Reg. Tait.*

A.D. **1882**, May 1.　JOHN MILLER STRACHAN.　Consecrated at Lambeth by A. C. Cantuar., J. London, E. H. Winchester, J. R. Ely, W. W. Antigua, and Bishop Mitchinson ; *Reg. Tait.*

Lahore.

A.D. **1877**, Dec. 21.　THOMAS VALPY FRENCH.　Consecrated at Westminster by A. C. Cantuar., E. H. Winchester, F. Sydney, P. C. Claughton, D. Anderson, C. Perry ; *Reg. Tait.*

A.D. **1888**, Jan. 6.　HENRY JAMES MATTHEW.　Consecrated at Westminster by E. W. Cantuar., W. D. Lichfield, W. W. Bedford, and C. H. Bromby ; *Reg. Benson.*

Travancore and Cochin.

A.D. **1879**, July 25.　JOHN MARTINDALE SPEECHLY.　Consecrated in S. Paul's Cathedral by A. C. Cantuar., J. London, T. L. S. Albans, A. W. Rochester, W. D. Lichfield, G. Columbia, C. W. Gibraltar, C. R. Alford ; *Reg. Tait.*

A.D. **1890**, April 25.　EDWARD NOEL HODGES.　Consecrated at Lambeth by E. W. Cantuar., F. London, A. W. Rochester, P. S. Mauritius, C. R. Alford, T. V. French ; *Reg. Benson.*

Chhota Nagpur.

A.D. **1890**, March 25.　JABEZ CORNELIUS WHITLEY.　Consecrated at Ranchi by E. R. Calcutta, L. G. Bombay, H. J. Lahore, R. S. Colombo, J. M. Rangoon ; *Reg. Benson.*

Lucknow.

A.D. **1893**, Jan. 15.　ALFRED CLIFFORD.　Consecrated at Calcutta by E. R. Calcutta, F. Madras, L. G. Bombay, H. J. Lahore, J. C. Chhota Nagpur, A. Barry, E. N. Travancore and Cochin, J. M. Rangoon, R. S. Colombo ; *S.P.G. Record.*

Tinnevelly.

A.D. **1896**, Oct. 28. SAMUEL MORLEY. Consecrated at Madras by E. R. Calcutta, F. Madras, E. N. Travancore and Cochin ; *Reg. Benson.*

PROVINCE OF NEW ZEALAND.

New Zealand.

A.D. **1841**, Oct. 17. GEORGE AUGUSTUS SELWYN (Primate, 1858). Consecrated at Lambeth by W. Cantuar., C. J. London, J. Lincoln, W. H. Barbados ; *Reg. Howley.*

Auckland.

A.D. **1869**, June 29. WILLIAM GARDEN COWIE, Bishop of Auckland (Primate, 1895). Consecrated at Westminster by A. C. Cantuar., J. London, E. H. Ely, H. Worcester, G. A. Lichfield, G. Columbia, F. T. McDougall, V. W. Ryan ; *Reg. Tait.*

Christ Church.

A.D. **1856**, Aug. 10. HENRY JOHN CHITTY HARPER (Primate, 1869). Consecrated at Lambeth by J. B. Cantuar., C. R. Winchester, A. T. Chichester, S. Oxford ; *Reg. Sumner.*

A.D. **1890**, May 1. CHURCHILL JULIUS. Consecrated at Christ Church by O. Wellington, A. B. Nelson, S. T. Dunedin, E. C. Waiapu, and Bishop Harper; *Letter from Bishop Julius.*

Nelson.

A.D. **1858**, Sept. 29. EDMUND HOBHOUSE. Consecrated in Lambeth Church by J. B. Cantuar., A. C. London, J. Lichfield, S. Oxford ; *Reg. Sumner.*

A.D. **1866**, Aug. 24. ANDREW BURN SUTER. Consecrated at Canterbury by C. T. Cantuar., A. C. London, C. J. Gloucester; *Reg. Longley.*

A.D. **1892**, Feb. 24. CHARLES OLIVER MULES. Consecrated at Wellington by O. Wellington, W. G. Auckland, S. T. Dunedin, E. C. Waiapu, C. Christ Church ; *Guardian*, April 27, 1892 ; *Letter from Bishop Julius.*

Wellington.

A.D. **1858**, Sept. 29. CHARLES JOHN ABRAHAM. Consecrated in Lambeth Church by J. B. Cantuar., A. C. London, J. Lichfield, S. Oxford ; *Reg. Sumner.*

A.D. **1870**, Oct. 9. OCTAVIUS HADFIELD (Primate, 1889). Consecrated at Christ Church by W. G. Auckland, H. J. C. Christ Church, W. Waiapu, A. B. Nelson ; *C.M.S. Record* ; *Guardian*, Jan. 4, 1871.

A.D. **1895**, Jan. 25. FREDERIC WALLIS. Consecrated at Auckland by W. G. Auckland, C. Christ Church, J. Salisbury, C. O. Nelson, C. Melanesia, S. T. Dunedin, W. L. Waiapu ; *Guardian*, March 6, 1895.

Waiapu.

A.D. **1859**, April 3. WILLIAM WILLIAMS. Consecrated at Wellington by G. A. New Zealand, H. J. C. Christ Church, C. J. Wellington, E. Nelson ; *Reg. Sumner*; *Letters Patent* ; *Letter from Bishop Hobhouse* ; *Guardian*, Aug. 3, 1859.

A.D. **1877**, Dec. 9. EDWARD CRAIG STUART. Consecrated at Napier by H. J. C. Christ Church, W. G. Auckland, O. Wellington; (became missionary in Persia, 1894); *C.M.S. Record*; *Letter from Bishop Stuart*.

A.D. **1895**, Jan. 20. WILLIAM LEONARD WILLIAMS. Consecrated at Napier by W. G. Auckland, C. Christ Church, C. O. Nelson, C. Melanesia; *C.M.S. Record*; *Guardian*, March 6, 1895; *Letter from Bishop Williams*.

Melanesia.

A.D. **1861**, Feb. 24. JOHN COLERIDGE PATTESON. Consecrated in S. Paul's, Auckland, by G. A. New Zealand, E. Nelson, C. J. Wellington; Tucker's *Life of Bishop Selwyn*, and *Letter from Bishop Abraham*.

A.D. **1877**, Feb. 18. JOHN RICHARDSON SELWYN. Consecrated at Nelson by H. J. C. Christ Church, A. B. Nelson, W. G. Auckland, O. Wellington, S. T. Dunedin; *Guardian*, May 9, 1877, and *Letter from Bishop Selwyn*.

A.D. **1894**, June 11. CECIL WILSON. Consecrated at Auckland by W. G. Auckland, S. T. Dunedin, C. Christ Church, C. O. Nelson; *Guardian*, Aug. 1, 1894.

Dunedin.

A.D. **1866**, Aug. 24. HENRY LASCELLES JENNER. Consecrated at Canterbury by C. T. Cantuar., A. C. London, G. Gloucester; *Reg. Longley*.

A.D. **1871**, June 4. SAMUEL TARRATT NEVILL. Consecrated at Dunedin by H. J. C. Christ Church, A. B. Nelson, O. Wellington, W. Waiapu; *Guardian*, Oct. 4, 1871 (from *Otago Witness*); *Letter from Bishop Nevill*.

PROVINCE OF NEW SOUTH WALES.

Australia.

A.D. **1836**, Feb. 14. WILLIAM GRANT BROUGHTON (first Bishop of Sydney, 1847). Consecrated at Lambeth by W. Cantuar., C. J. London, C. R. Winchester, J. H. Gloucester; *Reg. Howley*.

Sydney.

A.D. **1847**. WILLIAM GRANT BROUGHTON (Metropolitan). Consecrated Bishop of Australia, Feb. 14, 1836; *q. v.*

A.D. **1854**, Nov. 30. FREDERICK BARKER (Metropolitan). Consecrated at Lambeth by J. B. Cantuar., J. Lichfield, J. Chester, G. Gibraltar; *Reg. Sumner*.

A.D. **1884**, Jan. 1. ALFRED BARRY (Metropolitan). Consecrated at Westminster by E. W. Cantuar., J. London, J. B. Durham, C. Lincoln, A. W. Rochester, E. Dover, E. Algoma, C. Perry; *Reg. Benson*.

A.D. **1890**, June 24. WILLIAM SAUMAREZ SMITH (Metropolitan). Consecrated in S. Paul's Cathedral by E. W. Cantuar., F. London, H. Carlisle, B. W. S. David's, W. D. Lichfield, R. Llandaff, A. Colchester, A. Marlborough, R. C. Bedford, F. Madras, J. C. Campbell (late of Bangor), S. E. Marsden, A. Barry (late of Sydney); *Reg. Benson*.

Newcastle.

A.D. **1847**, June 29. WILLIAM TYRRELL. Consecrated at Westminster by W. Cantuar., C. J. London, C. R. Winchester, J. H. Gloucester, A. T. Chichester, J. Lichfield ; *Reg. Howley.*

A.D. **1880**, May 1. JOSEPH BROWN PEARSON. Consecrated in S. Paul's Cathedral by A. C. Cantuar., J. London, E. H. Winchester, J. Hereford, C. Perry ; *Reg. Tait.*

A D. **1891**. GEORGE HENRY STANTON. Consecrated Bishop of North Queensland, 1878 ; *q. v.*

Goulburn.

A.D. **1863**, March 25. MESAC THOMAS. Consecrated at Canterbury by C. T. Cantuar., H. Worcester, F. Sydney, C. Melbourne ; *Reg. Longley.*

A.D. **1892**, Nov. 1. WILLIAM CHALMERS. Consecrated at Goulburn by W. S. Sydney, S. Ballarat, G. H. Newcastle, S. Riverina, W. T. T. Brisbane, F. F. Melbourne; *Guardian,* Dec. 14, 1892.

Grafton and Armidale.

A.D. **1867**, Feb. 2. WILLIAM COLLINSON SAWYER. Consecrated at Canterbury by C. T. Cantuar., S. Oxford, J. C. Rochester, F. Montreal, H. L. Dunedin, and the Bishop of Illinois ; *Reg. Longley.*

A.D. **1869**, Feb. 24. JAMES FRANCIS TURNER. Consecrated at Westminster by A. C. Cantuar., J. London, S. Oxford, A. Llandaff, E. H. Ely, J. C. Bangor, T. L. Rochester, G. A. Lichfield, F. T. Labuan, C. St. Andrews, V. W. Ryan ; *Reg. Tait.*

A.D. **1894**, May 1. ARTHUR VINCENT GREEN. Consecrated at Melbourne by S. Ballarat, F. F. Melbourne, G. W. Adelaide, G. H. Newcastle, S. Riverina, W. Goulburn ; *Guardian,* June 13, 1894.

Bathurst.

A.D. **1869**, June 29. SAMUEL EDWARD MARSDEN. Consecrated at Westminster by A. C. Cantuar., J. London, E. H. Ely, H. Worcester, G. A. Lichfield, G. Columbia, F. T. McDougall, V. W. Ryan ; *Reg. Tait.*

A.D. **1887**, Oct. 18. CHARLES EDWARD CAMIDGE. Consecrated at Westminster by E. W. Cantuar., A. W. Rochester, J. W. Sodor and Man, C. Perry, S. E. Marsden (late of Bathurst) ; *Reg. Benson.*

Riverina.

A.D. **1884**, May 1. SYDNEY LINTON. Consecrated in S. Paul's Cathedral by E. W. Cantuar., J. London, C. Lincoln, W. D. Lichfield, J. F. Oxford, J. R. Ely, T. L. S. Albans, J. T. Norwich, E. Nottingham, E. Algoma ; *Reg. Benson.*

A.D. **1895**, June 29. ERNEST AUGUSTUS ANDERSON. Consecrated in S. Paul's Cathedral by E. W. Cantuar., F. London, J. W. S. Albans, M. Peterborough, G. F. Stepney, H. W. Southwark, A. T. Thetford, G. H. Guildford, W. B. Hornby ; *Reg. Benson.*

N

DIOCESES NOT YET INCORPORATED IN A PROVINCE.

Tasmania.

A.D. **1842**, Aug. 24. FRANCIS RUSSELL NIXON. Consecrated at Westminster by C. J. London, C. R. Winchester, G. Rochester, A. T. Chichester, W. H. Coleridge; *Reg. Howley.*

A.D. **1864**, June 29. CHARLES HENRY BROMBY. Consecrated at Canterbury by C. T. Cantuar., C. R. Winchester, J. Lincoln, C. J. Gloucester, G. Victoria, F. R. Nixon; *Reg. Longley.*

A.D. **1883**, April 25. DANIEL FOX SANDFORD. Consecrated in S. Paul's Cathedral by E. W. Cantuar., J. London, J. C. Bangor, J. R. Ely, W. B. S. David's, W. D. Lichfield, E. R. Newcastle, W. W. Bedford, A. B. Bloemfontein, E. R. Calcutta, C. H. Bromby; (became Assistant to Bishop of Durham, 1889); *Reg. Benson.*

A.D. **1889**, May 1. HENRY HUTCHINSON MONTGOMERY. Consecrated at Westminster by E. W. Cantuar., A. W. Rochester, W. W. Antigua, J. H. Moosonee, S. T. Ballarat; *Reg. Benson.*

Melbourne.

A.D. **1847**, June 29. CHARLES PERRY. Consecrated at Westminster by W. Cantuar., C. J. London, C. R. Winchester, J. H. Gloucester, A. T. Chichester, J. Lichfield; *Reg. Howley.*

A.D. **1876**, Oct. 22. JAMES MOORHOUSE. Consecrated at Westminster by A. C. Cantuar., J. London, J. Hereford, C. Perry (late of Melbourne); (translated to Manchester, 1886); *Reg. Tait.*

A.D. **1887**, Feb. 24. FIELD FLOWERS GOE. Consecrated at Westminster by E. W. Cantuar., F. London, A. W. Rochester, J. Manchester, H. H. Perth, C. Perry, C. R. Alford, S. E. Marsden; *Reg. Benson.*

Adelaide.

A.D. **1847**, June 29. AUGUSTUS SHORT. Consecrated at Westminster by W. Cantuar., C. J. London, C. R. Winchester, J. H. Gloucester, A. T. Chichester, J. Lichfield; *Reg. Howley.*

A.D. **1882**, Nov. 30. GEORGE WYNDHAM KENNION. Consecrated at Westminster by J. London, E. H. Winton, A. W. Rochester, W. D. Lichfield, W. W. Bedford, S. Ballarat, A. B. Nelson, A. Short, V. W. Ryan, I. Hellmuth; (translated to Bath and Wells, 1894); *Reg. Tait.*

A.D. **1895**, May 23. JOHN REGINALD HARMER. Consecrated at Westminster by E. W. Cantuar., G. W. Bath and Wells, J. Manchester, J. Salisbury, G. R. Dover, J. T. Trinidad, J. R. Selwyn; *Reg. Benson.*

Perth.

A.D. **1857**, July 25. MATTHEW BLAGDEN HALE. Consecrated at Lambeth by J. B. Cantuar., A. C. London, R. Ripon; *Reg. Sumner.*

A.D. **1876**. HENRY HUTTON PARRY. Consecrated Bishop Coadjutor of Barbadoes, 1868; *q. v.*

A.D. **1894**, Oct. 18. CHARLES OWEN LEAVER RILEY. Consecrated at Westminster by E. W. Cantuar., M. Peterborough, G. W. Bath and Wells, E. R. Newcastle, J. Norwich, J. L. Reading, G. A. Honduras; *Reg. Benson.*

Brisbane.

A.D. **1859**, June 14. EDWARD WYNDHAM TUFNELL. Consecrated at Westminster by J. B. Cantuar., A. C. London, S. Oxford, A. Llandaff, W. K. Sarum, R. Capetown, G. Columbia ; *Reg. Sumner.*

A.D. **1875.** MATTHEW BLAGDEN HALE. Consecrated Bishop of Perth, 1857 ; *q. v.*

A.D. **1885**, June 11. WILLIAM THOMAS THORNHILL WEBBER. Consecrated in S. Paul's Cathedral by E. W. Cantuar., F. London, H. Carlisle, W. W. Bedford, E. W. Tufnell, J. Mitchinson ; *Reg. Benson.*

A.D. **1889**, May 1. NATHANIEL DAWES (Coadjutor). Consecrated at Sydney by A. Sydney, J. F. Grafton and Armidale, S. Riverina, W. T. T. Brisbane, F. F. Melbourne, C. E. Bathurst ; *Letter from Bishop Dawes.*

A D. **1895**, Nov. 1. JOHN FRANCIS STRETCH (Coadjutor). Consecrated at Melbourne by W. S. Sydney, F. F. Melbourne, A. V. Grafton and Armidale, S. Ballarat, W. T. T. Brisbane, W. Goulburn ; *Guardian,* Dec. 18, 1895.

Ballarat.

A.D. **1875**, May 1. SAMUEL THORNTON. Consecrated at Westminster by A. C. Cantuar., J. London, C. Melbourne, M. Goulburn ; *Reg. Tait.*

A.D. **1895**, Nov. 1. HENRY EDWARD COOPER (suffragan). Consecrated at Melbourne by W. S. Sydney, F. F. Melbourne, W. Goulburn, A. V. Grafton and Armidale, S. Ballarat ; *Guardian,* Dec. 18, 1895, and *Letter from Bishop of Ballarat.*

North Queensland.

A.D. **1878**, June 24. GEORGE HENRY STANTON (Bishop of Newcastle, 1891). Consecrated in S. Paul's Cathedral by A. C. Cantuar., J. London, E. H. Winchester, J. Hereford, A. W. Rochester, F. Sydney, A. Adelaide, H. J. C. Christ Church, W. P. Guiana, Bishops of Ontario, Pennsylvania, Ohio, and North Carolina ; *Reg. Tait.*

A.D. **1891**, July 25. CHRISTOPHER GEORGE BARLOW. Consecrated at Sydney by W. S. Sydney, J. F. Grafton, G. H. Newcastle; *Letter from Bishop Barlow.*

Rockhampton.

A.D. **1892.** NATHANIEL DAWES. Consecrated Coadjutor Bishop of Brisbane, May 1, 1889 ; *q. v.*

PROVINCE OF SOUTH AFRICA.

Capetown (Metropolitan).

A.D. **1847**, June 29. ROBERT GRAY. Consecrated at Westminster by W. Cantuar., C. J. London, C. R. Winchester, J. H. Gloucester and Bristol, A. T. Chichester, J. Lichfield, H. Edinburgh, M. Goulbourn, P. C. Claughton ; *Reg. Howley.*

A.D. **1874**, May 17. WILLIAM WEST JONES. Consecrated at Westminster by A. C. Cantuar., J. London, E. H. Winchester, J. F. Oxford, J. R. Ely ; *Reg. Tait.*

A.D. **1894**, Sept. 29. ALAN GEORGE SUMNER GIBSON (Coadjutor of Capetown). Consecrated at Capetown by W. W. Capetown, A. B. Grahamstown, H. B.

Pretoria, B. L. S. John's, J. W. Bloemfontein, A. H. Natal and Maritzburg, W. E. Lebombo. *Reg. of Prov. of S. Africa.*

Grahamstown.

A.D. **1853**, Nov. 30. JOHN ARMSTRONG. Consecrated in Lambeth Church by J. B. Cantuar., C. J. London, S. Oxford, J. Lincoln, R. Capetown, W. P. Guiana, A. Adelaide ; *Reg. Sumner.*

A.D. **1856**, Nov. 23. HENRY COTTERILL (became Bishop of Edinburgh, 1872). Consecrated at Whitehall by J. B. Cantuar., A. T. Chichester, J. Lincoln, H. M. Carlisle ; *Reg. Sumner.*

A.D. **1871**, Nov. 30. NATHANIEL JAMES MERRIMAN. Consecrated at Grahamstown by R. Capetown, W. K. Maritzburg, A. B. Bloemfontein ; *Reg. of Prov. of S. Africa* ; *Guardian*, Feb. 7, 1872, from the *Eastern Star.*

A.D. **1883**. ALLAN BECHER WEBB. Consecrated Bishop of Bloemfontein, 1870 ; *q.v.*

Natal.

A.D. **1853**, Nov. 30. JOHN WILLIAM COLENSO (deposed, 1863). Consecrated in Lambeth Church by J. B. Cantuar., C. J. London, S. Oxford, J. Lincoln, R. Capetown, W. P. Guiana, A. Adelaide ; *Reg. Sumner.*

Maritzburg.

A.D. **1869**, Jan. 25. WILLIAM KENNETH MACRORIE. Consecrated at Capetown by R. Capetown, H. Grahamstown, T. E. S. Helena, E. Orange Free State ; *Reg. of Prov. of S. Africa* ; *Guardian*, March 24, 1869 ; *Letter from Bishop Macrorie.*

Natal and Maritzburg.

A.D. **1893**, Sept. 29. ARTHUR HAMILTON BAYNES. Consecrated at Westminster by E. W. Cantuar., F. London, R. T. Rochester, G. Southwell, H. W. Southwark, E. A. Derby, W. P. Guiana, W. K. Macrorie ; *Reg. Benson.*

S. Helena.

A.D. **1859**, June 14. PIERS CALVELEY CLAUGHTON (translated to Colombo, 1862). Consecrated at Westminster by J. B. Cantuar., A. C. London, S. Oxford, W. K. Sarum, A. Llandaff, R. Capetown, G. Columbia ; *Reg. Sumner.*

A.D. **1862**, May 29. THOMAS EARLE WELBY. Consecrated at Lambeth by C. T. Ebor., H. C. London, S. Oxford, A. Llandaff, P. C. Colombo ; *Reg. Sumner.*

Bloemfontein (originally Orange Free State).

A.D. **1863**, Feb. 2. EDWARD TWELLS. Consecrated at Westminster by C. T. Cantuar., S. Oxford, R. Capetown, F. Montreal ; *Reg. Longley.*

A.D. **1870**, Nov. 30. ALLAN BECHER WEBB. Consecrated in S. Andrew's Cathedral, Inverness, by R. Capetown, R. Moray and Ross, T. G. Aberdeen, C. J. Abraham ; *Scottish Guardian*, Dec. 1, 1870 ; *Letter from Bishop Webb.*

A.D. **1886**, March 25. GEORGE WYNDHAM KNIGHT BRUCE. Consecrated in S. Mary's, Whitechapel, by E. W. Cantuar., F. London, R. Llandaff, W. W. Bedford, C. H. Bromby ; *Reg. Benson.*

A.D. **1892**, Sept. 21. JOHN WALE HICKS. Consecrated at Capetown by W. W.

Capetown, A. B. Grahamstown, H. B. Pretoria, B. L. S. John's, G. H. Wilkinson; *Reg. of Prov. of S. Africa*; *Guardian*, Oct. 19, 1892.

Zululand.

A.D. **1870**, May 8. THOMAS EDWARD WILKINSON (Assistant to Bishop of London for North and Central Europe, 1886). Consecrated at Whitehall by W. Ebor., J. London, S. Winchester, G. A. Lichfield, A. Llandaff, C. S. David's ; *Reg. Tait*.

A.D. **1880**, Nov. 30. DOUGLAS McKENZIE. Consecrated at Capetown by W. W. Capetown, W. K. Maritzburg, H. B. Pretoria, A. B. Bloemfontein, N. J. Grahamstown ; *Reg. of Prov. of S. Africa*.

A.D. **1891**, Sept. 29. WILLIAM MARLBOROUGH CARTER. Consecrated in S. Paul's Cathedral by E. W. Cantuar., A. W. Winchester, H. Carlisle, J. Sarum, W. W. Wakefield, G. Southwell, J. J. S. Worcester, R. T. Rochester, R. C. Bedford, L. T. Shrewsbury, G. F. P. Blyth, J. M. Speechly, J. Mitchinson; *Reg. Benson*.

S. John's, Kaffraria.

A.D. **1873**, Nov. 1. HENRY CALLAWAY. Consecrated in S. Paul's Church, Edinburgh, by R. Moray and Ross, A. P. Brechin, H. Edinburgh; *Minutes of Ep. Synod of Scottish Epis. Church*, Nov. 18, 1873 ; *S.P.G. Record*.

A.D. **1883**, Aug. 12. BRANSBY LEWIS KEY (Coadjutor). Consecrated at Umtata by W. W. Capetown, H. S. John's, W. K. Maritzburg, D. McKenzie of Zululand ; (succeeded, 1886) ; *Reg. of Prov. of S. Africa*.

Pretoria.

A.D. **1878**, Feb. 2. HENRY BROUGHAM BOUSFIELD. Consecrated in S. Paul's Cathedral by A. C. Cantuar., J. London, E. H. Winchester, G. Sarum, N. J. Grahamstown, P. C. Claughton ; *Reg. Tait*.

Mashonaland.

A.D. **1891**. GEORGE WYNDHAM KNIGHT BRUCE. Consecrated Bishop of Bloemfontein, March 25, 1886 ; *q. v.*

A.D. **1895**, April 25. WILLIAM THOMAS GAUL. Consecrated at Bloemfontein by W. W. Capetown, B. L. S. John's, H. B. Pretoria, J. W. Bloemfontein ; *Reg. of Prov. of S. Africa*.

Lebombo.

A.D. **1893**, Nov. 5. WILLIAM EDMUND SMYTH. Consecrated at Grahamstown by W. W. Capetown, A. B. Grahamstown, H. B. Pretoria, J. W. Bloemfontein, W. M. Carter of Zululand, B. L. S. John's ; *Reg. Benson (Commission)*; *Guardian*, Dec. 6, 1893 ; *Letter from Bishop Smyth*.

PROVINCE OF THE WEST INDIES.

Jamaica.

A.D. **1824**, July 25. CHRISTOPHER LIPSCOMB. Consecrated at Lambeth by C. Cantuar., W. London, G. Lincoln, W. Llandaff ; *Reg. Sutton*.

A.D. **1843**. AUBREY GEORGE SPENCER. Consecrated Bishop of Newfoundland, 1839 ; *q. v.*

A.D. **1856**, March 24. REGINALD COURTENAY (Coadjutor). Consecrated at Lambeth by J. B. Cantuar., H. Worcester, S. Oxford, A. G. Jamaica; (succeeded, 1872); *Reg. Sumner.*

A.D. **1879**. WILLIAM GEORGE TOZER. Consecrated Bishop of Zanzibar, 1863; *q.v.*

A.D. **1880**, Oct. 28. ENOS NUTTALL (Primate, 1893). Consecrated in S. Paul's Cathedral by A. C. Cantuar., E. H. Winchester, J. London, A. W. Rochester, W. W. Antigua, F. A. R. Nassau, P. C. Claughton, C. Perry, R. Courtenay; *Reg. Tait.*

A.D. **1888**, Nov. 30. CHARLES FREDERICK DOUET (Assistant Bishop). Consecrated at Westminster by E. W. Cantuar., E. H. Winchester, A. W. Rochester, E. R. Newcastle, A. Ely, E. Dover, E. Jamaica, G. W. Adelaide, G. F. Blyth; *Reg. Benson.*

Barbados and the Windward Isles.

A.D. **1824**, July 25. WILLIAM HART COLERIDGE. Consecrated at Lambeth by C. Cantuar., W. London, G. Lincoln, W. Llandaff; *Reg. Sutton.*

A.D. **1842**, Aug. 24. THOMAS PARRY. Consecrated at Westminster by C. J. London, C. R. Winchester, G. Rochester, A. T. Chichester, W. H. Coleridge; *Reg. Howley.*

A.D. **1868**, Nov. 15. HENRY HUTTON PARRY (Coadjutor, Barbados; Perth, W. Aust., 1876). Consecrated at Whitehall by W. Ebor., A. C. London, S. Oxford, R. Ripon, T. Barbados; *Reg. Cant. sede vacante.*

A.D. **1873**, June 24. JOHN MITCHINSON. Consecrated at Canterbury by A. C. Cantuar., J. London, G. A. Lichfield, H. Carlisle, V. W. Ryan; *Reg. Tait.*

A.D. **1882**, May 1. HERBERT BREE. Consecrated at Lambeth Palace Chapel by A. C. Cantuar., J. London, E. H. Winchester, J. R. Ely, W. W. Antigua, J. Mitchinson (late of Barbados); *Reg. Tait.*

British Guiana.

A.D. **1842**, Aug. 24. WILLIAM PIERCY AUSTIN (Primate, 1883). Consecrated at Westminster by C. J. London, C. R. Winchester, G. Rochester, A. T. Chichester, W. H. Coleridge; *Reg. Howley.*

A.D. **1893**, March 25. WILLIAM PROCTOR SWABY. Consecrated at Westminster by E. W. Cantuar., F. London, D. L. Bangor, J. Mitchinson, C. Christ Church, G. H. St. Andrews, A. J. R. Anson; *Reg. Benson.*

Antigua.

A.D. **1842**, Aug. 24. DANIEL GATEWARD DAVIS. Consecrated at Westminster by C. J. London, C. R. Winchester, G. Rochester, A. T. Chichester, W. H. Coleridge; *Reg. Howley.*

A.D. **1858**, Feb. 2. STEPHEN JORDAN RIGAUD. Consecrated at Lambeth by J. B. Cantuar., A. T. Chichester, S. Oxford, A. G. Jamaica; *Reg. Sumner.*

A.D. **1860**, May 17. WILLIAM WALROND JACKSON. Consecrated in Lambeth Church by J. B. Cantuar., C. R. Winchester, S. Oxford, R. J. Bath and Wells, H. M. Carlisle, J. C. Bangor, J. Lincoln, E. H. Sierra Leone; *Reg. Sumner.*

A.D. **1882**, July 25. CHARLES JAMES BRANCH (Coadjutor). Consecrated in Lambeth Palace Chapel by A. C. Cantuar., J. London, A. W. Rochester, W. W. Antigua, H. Barbados ; *Reg. Tait.*

Nassau.

A.D. **1861**, Nov. 24. CHARLES CAULFEILD. Consecrated at Lambeth by J. B. Cantuar., A. C. London, C. R. Winchester ; *Reg. Sumner.*

A.D. **1863**, Nov. 30. ADDINGTON ROBERT PEEL VENABLES. Consecrated at Lambeth by C. T. Cantuar., A. C. London, S. Oxford ; *Reg. Longley.*

A.D. **1878**, June 24. FRANCIS ALEXANDER ROBERT CRAMER-ROBERTS. Consecrated in S. Paul's Cathedral by A. C. Cantuar., J. London, E. H. Winchester, J. Hereford, A. W. Rochester, W. P. Guiana, A. Adelaide, F. Sydney, H. J. C. Christ Church (New Zealand), and the Bishops of Pennsylvania, Ohio, North Carolina, and Ontario ; *Reg. Tait.*

A.D. **1886**, Feb. 24. EDWARD TOWNSON CHURTON. Consecrated at Lambeth Palace Chapel by E. W. Cantuar., J. Hereford, E. Dover, W. W. Bedford, F. A. R. Cramer-Roberts ; *Reg. Benson.*

Trinidad.

A.D. **1872**, June 29. RICHARD RAWLE. Consecrated at Lichfield by G. A. Lichfield, R. Chichester, J. Hereford, C. Lincoln, W. C. Peterborough ; *Reg. Tait.*

A.D. **1889**, March 25. JAMES THOMAS HAYES. Consecrated in Westminster Abbey by E. W. Cantuar., F. London, T. L. S. Albans, W. B. S. David's, R. Llandaff, W. W. Antigua, E. Jamaica, F. H. Leicester, J. Mitchinson ; *Reg. Benson.*

British Honduras.

A.D. **1891**, March 1. HENRY REDMAYNE HOLME. Consecrated at Barbados by E. Jamaica, H. Barbados, J. T. Trinidad, C. J. Branch, C. F. Douet ; *S.P.G. Record.*

A.D. **1893**, Dec. 28. GEORGE ALBERT ORMSBY. Consecrated in S. Mary's, Newington, by E. W. Cantuar., W. W. Capetown, A. W. Winchester, R. T. Rochester, W. Mauritius, H. W. Southwark ; *Reg. Benson.*

COLONIAL DIOCESES AND MISSIONARY BISHOPRICS HOLDING MISSION FROM THE SEE OF CANTERBURY.

Newfoundland.

A.D. **1839**, Aug. 4. AUBREY GEORGE SPENCER (Jamaica, 1843). Consecrated at Lambeth by W. Cantuar., C. J. London, W. Chichester, J. Nova Scotia ; *Reg. Howley.*

A.D. **1844**, April 28. EDWARD FEILD. Consecrated at Lambeth by W. Cantuar., C. J. London, C. Bangor, H. Worcester ; *Reg. Howley.*

A.D. **1867**, Aug. 25.　JAMES BUTLER KNILL KELLY (Coadjutor;—Bishop of New-foundland, 1876; Coadjutor Bishop of Moray and Ross, 1885; Bishop of Moray and Ross, 1886).　Consecrated at Croydon by C. T. Cantuar., T. L. Rochester, W. S. Glasgow and Galloway; *Reg. Longley.*

A.D. **1878**, May 1.　LLEWELYN JONES.　Consecrated in S. Paul's Cathedral by A. C. Cantuar., J. London, J. Hereford, J. B. K. Kelly; *Reg. Tait.*

Gibraltar.

A.D. **1842**, Aug. 24.　GEORGE TOMLINSON.　Consecrated at Westminster by C. J. London, C. R. Winchester, G. Rochester, A. T. Chichester, W. H. Coleridge; *Reg. Howley.*

A.D. **1863**.　WALTER JOHN TROWER.　Consecrated Bishop of Glasgow and Galloway, Sept. 21, 1848, by Bishops W. Skinner of Aberdeen, C. H. Terrot of Edinburgh, A. Ewing of Argyle, and A. P. Forbes of Brechin; *Episc. Minute of Ch. of Scotl.*

A.D. **1868**, May 1.　CHARLES AMYAND HARRIS.　Consecrated at Canterbury by C. T. Cantuar., S. Oxford, T. L. Rochester, W. J. Trower; *Reg. Tait.*

A.D. **1874**, Feb. 1.　CHARLES WALDEGRAVE SANDFORD.　Consecrated in Christ Church Cathedral, Oxford, by A. C. Cantuar., J. London, W. Chester, H. Carlisle, F. Exeter, J. F. Oxford, E. Parry; *Reg. Tait.*

Victoria (Hong Kong).

A.D. **1849**, May 29.　GEORGE SMITH.　Consecrated at Canterbury by J. B. Cantuar., C. J. London, C. R. Winchester, T. V. S. Asaph, S. Oxford, W. H. Coleridge; *Reg. Sumner.*

A.D. **1867**, Feb. 2.　CHARLES RICHARD ALFORD.　Consecrated at Canterbury by C. T. Cantuar., S. Oxford, J. C. Rochester, F. Montreal, H. L. Dunedin, Geo. Smith (Victoria); *Reg. Longley.*

A.D. **1874**, March 15.　JOHN SHAW BURDON.　Consecrated in Lambeth Church by J. London, E. H. Winchester, T. L. Rochester; *Reg. Tait.*

Sierra Leone.

A.D. **1852**, May 30.　OWEN EMERIC VIDAL.　Consecrated at Lambeth by J. B. Cantuar., C. J. London, A. T. Chichester, S. Oxford, R. Capetown; *Reg. Sumner.*

A.D. **1855**, May 17.　JOHN WILLS WEEKS.　Consecrated in Lambeth Church by J. B. Cantuar., C. J. London, C. R. Winchester, S. Oxford; *Reg. Sumner.*

A.D. **1857**, Sept. 21.　JOHN BOWEN.　Consecrated at Lambeth by J. B. Cantuar., G. Peterborough, G. Victoria; *Reg. Sumner.*

A.D. **1860**, Feb. 2.　EDWARD HYNDMAN BECKLES.　Consecrated at Lambeth by J. B. Cantuar., A. C. London, S. Oxford, T. Barbados; *Reg. Sumner.*

A.D. **1870**, Nov. 30.　HENRY CHEETHAM.　Consecrated in S. Paul's Cathedral by A. C. Cantuar., J. London, T. L. Rochester, G. Salisbury; *Reg. Tait.*

A.D. **1883**, Sept. 24.　ERNEST JAMES INGHAM.　Consecrated at Whitehall by W. Ebor., J. London, A. W. Rochester, W. B. S. David's; *Reg. Benson.*

A.D. **1897**, May 27.　JOHN TAYLOR SMITH.　Consecrated in S. Paul's, London, by F. Cantuar., W. B. Ripon, W. L. Waiapu, H. Tugwell, I. Oluwole, C. Phillips, H. Cheetham, P. S. Royston, E. G. Ingham; *Reg. Temple.*

Mauritius.

A.D. **1854**, Nov. 30. VINCENT WILLIAM RYAN. Consecrated at Lambeth by J. B. Cantuar., J. Lichfield, J. Chester, G. Gibraltar; *Reg. Sumner.*

A.D. **1869**, Feb. 24. THOMAS GOODWIN HATCHARD. Consecrated at Westminster by A. C. Cantuar., J. London, S. Oxford, A. Llandaff, E. H. Ely, J. C. Bangor, T. L. Rochester, G. A. Lichfield, F. T. Labuan, C. S. Andrews, V. W. Ryan; *Reg. Tait.*

A.D. **1870**, Nov. 30. HENRY CONSTANTINE HUXTABLE. Consecrated in S. Paul's Cathedral by A. C. Cantuar., J. London, T. L. Rochester, G. Salisbury; *Reg. Tait.*

A.D. **1872**, Dec. 15. PETER SORENSON ROYSTON. Consecrated at Westminster by A. C. Cantuar., J. London, T. L. Rochester, H. Sierra Leone, D. Anderson, V. W. Ryan, P. C. Claughton; *Reg. Tait.*

A.D. **1891**, Feb. 2. WILLIAM WALSH. Consecrated at Westminster by E. W. Cantuar., F. London, A. C. Bath and Wells, A. W. Rochester, J. W. S. Albans, R. C. Bedford, A. Marlborough, P. S. Royston; *Reg. Benson.*

Singapore, Labuan, and Sarawak (originally Labuan).

A.D. **1855**, Oct. 18. FRANCIS THOMAS MACDOUGALL. Consecrated at Calcutta by D. Calcutta, G. Victoria, T. Madras; *Reg. Sumner (Commission)*; *S.P.G. Record.*

A.D. **1869**, June 29. WALTER CHAMBERS. Consecrated at Westminster by A. C. Cantuar., J. London, E. H. Ely, H. Worcester, G. A. Lichfield, G. Columbia, F. T. McDougall, V. W. Ryan; *Reg. Tait.*

A.D. **1881**, May 26. GEORGE FREDERICK HOSE. Consecrated in Lambeth Palace Chapel by A. C. Cantuar., C. J. Gloucester and Bristol, J. S. Asaph, J. T. Ontario, A. Toronto, J. S. Victoria (Hong Kong), F. T. McDougall, P. C. Claughton; *Reg. Tait.*

British Columbia.

A.D. **1859**, Feb. 24. GEORGE HILLS. Consecrated at Westminster by J. B. Cantuar., A. C. London, T. V. S. Asaph, S. Oxford, J. T. Norwich, E. Newfoundland, and the Bishop of West New York; *Reg. Tait.*

A.D. **1893**, March 25. WILLIAM WILLCOX PERRIN. Consecrated at Westminster by E. W. Cantuar., F. London, D. L. Bangor, G. H. S. Andrews, C. Christ Church, A. J. R. Anson, J. Mitchinson; *Reg. Benson.*

New Westminster.

A.D. **1879**, Nov. 1. ACTON WINDEYER SILLITOE. Consecrated at Croydon Parish Church by A. C. Cantuar., J. London, A. W. Rochester, G. Columbia, W. W. Antigua, E. W. Tufnell; *Reg. Tait.*

A.D. **1895**, June 29. JOHN DART. Consecrated in S. Paul's Cathedral by E. W. Cantuar., F. London, M. Peterborough, J. F. S. Albans, G. Southwell, G. H. Guildford, H. W. Southwark, A. T. Thetford, G. F. Stepney, W. B. Hornby; *Reg. Benson.*

Caledonia (British Columbia).

A.D. **1879**, July 25. WILLIAM RIDLEY. Consecrated in S. Paul's Cathedral by A. C. Cantuar., J. London, T. L. S. Albans, A. W. Rochester, W. D. Lichfield, C. W. Gibraltar, G. Columbia, C. R. Alford ; *Reg. Tait.*

Zanzibar and East Africa (originally Zambesi, afterwards Central Africa).

A.D. **1861**, Jan. 1. CHARLES FREDERICK MACKENZIE. Consecrated at Capetown by R. Capetown, J. W. Natal, P. C. S. Helena ; *Guardian*, March 6, 1861.

A.D. **1863**, Feb. 2. WILLIAM GEORGE TOZER. Consecrated at Westminster by C. T. Cantuar., S. Oxford, R. Capetown, F. Montreal ; *Reg. Longley.*

A.D. **1874**, Aug. 24. EDWARD STEERE. Consecrated at Westminster by A. C. Cantuar., J. London, T. L. Rochester, J. S. Asaph ; *Reg. Tait.*

A.D. **1883**, Nov. 30. CHARLES ALAN SMYTHIES. Consecrated in S. Paul's Cathedral by E. W. Cantuar., J. London, H. Carlisle, J. F. Oxford, R. Llandaff, W. W. Bedford, W. G. Tozer ; *Reg. Benson.*

A.D. **1895**, June 29. WILLIAM MOORE RICHARDSON. Consecrated in S. Paul's Cathedral by E. W. Cantuar., F. London, M. Peterborough, J. W. S. Albans, A. T. Thetford, W. B. Hornby, G. F. Stepney, H. W. Southwark, G. H. Guildford ; *Reg. Benson.*

Western Equatorial Africa (originally the Niger District).

A.D. **1864**, June 29. SAMUEL ADJAI CROWTHER. Consecrated in Canterbury Cathedral by C. T. Cantuar., C. R. Winchester, J. Lincoln, C. J. Gloucester, G. Victoria, F. R. Nixon ; *Reg. Longley.*

A.D. **1893**, June 29. JOSEPH SIDNEY HILL. Consecrated in S. Paul's Cathedral by E. W. Cantuar., F. London, J. C. Liverpool, W. Oxford, R. T. Rochester, J. W. S. Albans, R. C. Bedford, G. W. Adelaide, E. Algoma, G. H. Wilkinson, H. Cheetham ; *Reg. Benson.*

A.D. **1893**, June 29. ISAAC OLUWOLE (Coadjutor). Consecrated in S. Paul's Cathedral by E. W. Cantuar., F. London, J. C. Liverpool, W. Oxford, R. T. Rochester, J. W. S. Albans, R. C. Bedford, G. W. Adelaide, E. Algoma, G. H. Wilkinson, H. Cheetham ; *Reg. Benson.*

A.D. **1893**, June 29. CHARLES PHILLIPS (Coadjutor). Consecrated in S. Paul's Cathedral by E. W. Cantuar., F. London, J. C. Liverpool, W. Oxford, R. T. Rochester, J. W. S. Albans, R. C. Bedford, G. W. Adelaide, E. Algoma, G. H. Wilkinson, H. Cheetham ; *Reg. Benson.*

A.D. **1894**, March 4. HERBERT TUGWELL. Consecrated in Lambeth Palace Chapel by E. W. Cantuar., R. T. Rochester, P. S. Royston ; *Reg. Benson.*

Eastern Equatorial Africa.

A.D. **1884**, June 24. JAMES HANNINGTON. Consecrated in Lambeth Church by E. W. Cantuar., J. London, A. W. Rochester, T. L. S. Albans, C. Lincoln, J. F. Oxford, J. R. Ely, W. D. Lichfield, E. Dover, and the Bishops of Nassau, Ohio, and Saskatchewan ; *Reg. Benson.*

A.D. **1886**, Oct. 18. HENRY PERROTT PARKER. Consecrated at S. James', Paddington, by E. W. Cantuar., F. London, H. Carlisle, P. S. Mauritius, H. Cheetham, E. J. Sierra Leone ; *Reg. Benson.*

A.D. **1890**, April 25. ALFRED ROBERT TUCKER. Consecrated in Lambeth Church by E. W. Cantuar., F. London, A. W. Rochester, P. S. Mauritius, T. V. French, C. R. Alford ; *Reg. Benson.*

Likoma (formerly Nyassaland).

A.D. **1892**, Dec. 21. WILFRED BIRD HORNBY. Consecrated in S. Paul's Cathedral by E. W. Cantuar., F. London, A. Ely, J. W. S. Albans, C. A. Smythies, W. K. Macrorie, G. H. Wilkinson, J. R. A. Argyll ; *Reg. Benson.*

A.D. **1895**, June 29. CHAUNCY MAPLES. Consecrated in S. Paul's Cathedral by E. W. Cantuar., F. London, J. W. S. Albans, M. Peterborough, H. W. Southwark, G. H. Guildford, A. T. Thetford, G. F. Stepney, W. B. Hornby ; *Reg. Benson.*

A.D. **1896**, June 29. JOHN EDWARD HINE. Consecrated in S. Matthew's, Bethnal Green, by E. W. Cantuar., E. H. Exeter, J. W. S. Albans, E. S. Rochester, N. Rockhampton, W. T. Mashonaland, W. B. Hornby ; *Reg. Benson.*

Madagascar.

A.D. **1874**, Feb. 2. ROBERT KESTELL KESTELL-CORNISH. Consecrated in S. John's, Edinburgh, by A. P. Brechin, H. Edinburgh, J. J. Aberdeen, W. S. Glasgow ; *Minute of Synod of Ep. Ch. of Scotland* ; *Letter from Bishop Kestell-Cornish.*

Honolulu (Hawaiian Islands).

A.D. **1861**, Dec. 15. THOMAS NETTLESHIP STALEY. Consecrated at Lambeth by J. B. Cantuar., A. C. London, S. Oxford ; *Reg. Sumner.*

A.D. **1872**, Feb. 2. ALFRED WILLIS. Consecrated in Lambeth Palace Chapel by A. C. Cantuar., J. London, S. Winchester, T. L. Rochester ; *Reg. Tait.*

The Falkland Islands.

A.D. **1869**, Dec. 21. WAITE HOCKIN STIRLING. Consecrated at Westminster by J. London, C. S. David's, H. Worcester, E. H. Ely ; *Reg. Tait.*

Mid China (originally North China).

A.D. **1872**, Dec. 15. WILLIAM ARMSTRONG RUSSELL. Consecrated at Westminster by A. C. Cantuar., J. London, T. L. Rochester, H. Sierra Leone, D. Anderson, V. W. Ryan, P. C. Claughton ; *Reg. Tait.*

A.D. **1880**, Oct. 28. GEORGE EVANS MOULE. Consecrated in S. Paul's Cathedral by A. C. Cantuar., J. London, E. H. Winchester, A. W. Rochester, W. W. Antigua, P. C. Claughton ; *Reg. Tait.*

North China.

A.D. **1880**, Oct. 28. CHARLES PERRY SCOTT. Consecrated in S. Paul's Cathedral by A. C. Cantuar., J. London, E. H. Winchester, A. W. Rochester, Bishops of Antigua and Nassau, Bishops Perry, Courtenay, and Piers C. Claughton ; *Reg. Tait.*

Western China.

A.D. **1895**, Oct. 18. WILLIAM WHARTON CASSELLS. Consecrated at Westminster by E. W. Cantuar., R. T. Winchester, J. Salisbury, G. Southwell, J. W. S. Albans, J. Truro, A. Lichfield, J. T. Richmond, H. W. Southwark, G. E. Moule ; *Reg. Benson.*

Corea.

A.D. **1889**, Nov. 1. CHARLES JOHN CORFE. Consecrated at Westminster by E. W. Cantuar., H. Carlisle, F. London, W. Oxford, G. Southwell, E. Lincoln, J. Mitchinson ; *Reg. Benson.*

South Tokyo (originally Japan).

A.D. **1883**, Oct. 18. ARTHUR WILLIAM POOLE. Consecrated in Lambeth Palace Chapel by E. W. Cantuar., A. C. Bath and Wells, E. Dover, T. V. Lahore, R. Caldwell ; *Reg. Benson.*

A.D. **1886**, Feb. 2. EDWARD BICKERSTETH (Bishop of South Tokyo, 1896). Consecrated in S. Paul's Cathedral by E. W. Cantuar., F. London, E. Lincoln, W. W. Bedford, E. H. Exeter, T. L. S. Albans, J. Hereford ; *Reg. Benson.*

Kiu-Shiu (South Japan).

A.D. **1894**, March 4. HENRY EVINGTON. Consecrated in Lambeth Palace Chapel by E. W. Cantuar., R. T. Rochester, P. S. Royston ; *Reg. Benson.*

Osaka (Japan).

A.D. **1896**. WILLIAM AWDRY. Consecrated Bishop of Southampton in S. Paul's Cathedral, 1895, June 29, by E. W. Cantuar., F. London, M. Peterborough, J. W. S. Albans, G. H. Guildford, H. W. Southwark, A. T. Thetford, G. F. Stepney, W. B. Hornby ; *Reg. Benson.*

Hokkaido (Japan).

A.D. **1896**, June 29. PHILIP KEMBALL FYSON. Consecrated in S. Matthew's Church, Bethnal Green, by E. W. Cantuar., E. H. Exeter, J. W. S. Albans, E. S. Rochester, N. Rockhampton, W. T. Mashonaland, W. B. Hornby ; *Reg. Benson.*

Jerusalem and the East.

A.D. **1841**, Nov. 7. MICHAEL SOLOMON ALEXANDER. Consecrated at Lambeth by W. Cantuar., C. J. London, G. Rochester, G. A. New Zealand ; *Reg. Howley.*

A.D. **1846**, July 5. SAMUEL GOBAT. Consecrated at Lambeth by W. Cantuar., C. J. London, J. Lichfield, D. Calcutta ; *Reg. Howley.*

A.D. **1879**, July 25. JOSEPH BARCLAY. Consecrated in S. Paul's Cathedral by A. C. Cantuar., J. London, T. L. S. Albans, A. W. Rochester, W. D. Lichfield, G. Columbia, C. W. Gibraltar, C. R. Alford ; *Reg. Tait.*

A.D. **1887**, March 25. GEORGE FRANCIS POPHAM BLYTH. Consecrated in Lambeth Palace Chapel by E. W. Cantuar., F. London, A. W. Rochester, R. Llandaff, E. Dover, J. T. Ontario, C. Perry ; *Reg. Benson.*

APPENDIX II

TABLES OF THE DATES OF FOUNDATION OF SEES.

Table showing the connexion of the Anglo-Saxon Princes at the time of their conversion to Christianity.

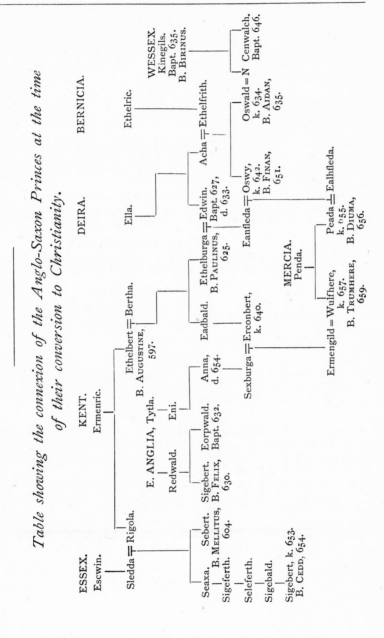

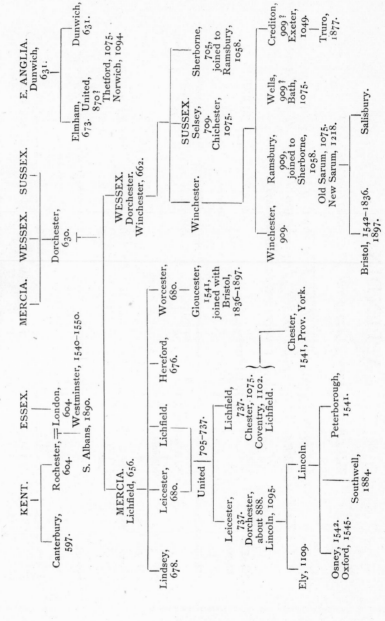

A Chronological view of the formation of the Dioceses of the Province of Canterbury.

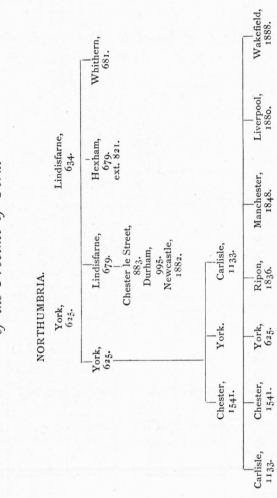

A Chronological view of the formation of the Dioceses
of the Province of York.

NORTHUMBRIA.

York,
625.

Lindisfarne,
634.

York,
625.

Lindisfarne,
679.

Chester le Street,
883.
Durham,
995.
Newcastle,
1882.

Hexham,
679.
ext. 821.

Whithern,
681.

York.

Carlisle,
1133.

Chester,
1541.

York,
625.

Chester,
1541.

Ripon,
1836.

Manchester,
1848.

Liverpool,
1880.

Wakefield,
1888.

Carlisle,
1133.

APPENDIX III

LIST OF ARCHIEPISCOPAL PALLS.

Dates of the Reception of the Pall by the Archbishops of Canterbury, from Lanfranc to Pole.

RECIPIENT.	BISHOPS PRESENTING THE PALL.	RECIPIENT.	BISHOPS PRESENTING THE PALL.
Lanfranc, 1070, at Rome.		John Peckham, 1279, (at Rome).	
Anselm, 1095, June 10, Canterbury.	Walter C. Albano.	Robert Winchelsey, 1294, Sept. 17, (at Aquila).	
Ralph, 1115, June 27, Canterbury.	Anselm the Legate.	Walter Reynolds, 1314, Feb. 13, Chartham.	Walter Worcester.
William de Corbeuil, 1123, May 21, at Rome.	P. Calixtus II.	Simon Mepeham, 1328, June 9, Avignon.	P. John XXII.
Theobald, 1139, April, at Rome.		John Stratford, 1334, April 23, Rue in Ponthieu.	Haymo Rochester.
Thomas Becket, 1162, Aug. 10, Canterbury.		Thomas Bradwardin, died before the ceremony.	
Richard, 1174, April 10, Anagni.	P. Alexander III.	Simon Islip, 1350, Mar. 25, Esher.	William Winchester.
Baldwin, 1185, May 19, Canterbury.		Simon Langham, 1366, Nov. 4, S. Stephen's, Westminster.	John Bath.
Hubert Walter, 1193, Nov. 7, Canterbury.	Gilbert Rochester.	William Whittlesey, 1369, April 19, Lambeth.	William Winchester.
Stephen Langton, June 24, 1207, Viterboc.	P. Innocent III.	Simon Sudbury, inthroned 1376, April 6.	} Thomas Rochester.
Richard le Grant, 1229, Nov. 23.	Henry Rochester.	William Courtenay, 1382, May 6, Croydon.	} Robert London.
Edmund Rich, 1234, April 2, Canterbury.	Roger London.	Thomas Arundel, 1397, Feb. 10, Westminster.	{ Wm. Winchester. Richard Sarum. Robert Chichester.
Boniface, 1244, April 2, (before consecration).	Peter Hereford.		
Robert Kilwardby, 1273, May 8, Tenham.	{ Nic. Winchester. Walter Exeter.		

Recipient.	Bishops presenting the Pall.	Recipient.	Bishops presenting the Pall.
Roger Walden, 1398, Feb. 17, High Clere.	Wm. Winchester.	John Morton, inthr. 1487, Jan. 28.	*John Ely.* *Edmund Rochester.* *Thomas Sarum.* *Robert Worcester.*
Henry Chicheley, 1414, July 29, Sutton Regis.	Henry Winchester. Thomas Norwich.	Henry Dean, 1501, July 20, S. Stephen's, Westminster.	John Lichfield.
John Stafford, 1443, Aug. 23.	William Rochester.	William Warham, 1504, Feb. 2, Lambeth.	Oliver Bath. William Lincoln.
John Kemp, 1452, Sept. 24, Fulham.	Thomas London. Wm. Winchester.	Thomas Cranmer, 1533, Mar. 30 [2].	
[1] Thomas Bourchier, *inthr.* 1455, *Jan.* 25.	*Thomas London.* *William Winchester.* *John Rochester.* *Richard Ross.*	Reginald Pole, 1556, Mar. 25, Bow Church.	Richard Worcester. Thomas Ely.

APPENDIX IV

DATES OF LEGATIONS.

Names of Legates.	Date of Legation.
Archbishop William	1126, January 25.
Henry Winchester	1139, March 1.
Archbishop Theobald	1150 (possibly a year or two earlier).
Archbp. Roger of York	1164, February 27.
Archbp. Thomas Becket	1166, April 24.
Archbishop Richard	1174, April.
Archbishop Baldwin	1186, January 12.
Archbishop Longchamp	1190, June 5.
Archbishop Hubert	1195, March 18.

After this time the Archbishops of Canterbury were, with a few exceptions, considered *Legati nati—ex officio* Legates.

---

[1] The corresponding dates for Archbishops Sudbury, Bourchier, and Morton I have not been able to discover : for the Archbishops of York only in a few instances; these are

John Thoresby, 1353, Mar. 29, from W. Winchester at Esher.
Alexander Neville, 1374, Oct. 10, from the Bishop of Durham at London.
Thomas Arundel, 1388, Sept. 14.
William Booth, 1452, Sept. 24, from Thom. London at Fulham.
George Neville, 1465, Sept. 6, from John Lincoln at York.
Thomas Rotherham, 1480, Sept. 3, at York House.

These dates are of importance, as marking the time at which the plenary power of Metropolitan was assumed by the Archbishops. Between their election and reception of the pall they (usually at least) were restrained from taking even a subordinate part in the consecration of Bishops. Other Bishops however could consecrate without the pall and to the exclusion of the Archbishop; Bishops Edendon and Beaufort are the most eminent instances.

[2] Bull directed to the Archbishop of York and the Bishop of London, and delivered at consecration Mar. 30.

O

APPENDIX V

SUFFRAGAN BISHOPS.

SUFFRAGANS AND BISHOPS IN PARTIBUS.

UNDER the common designation of Suffragan Bishops are comprehended (besides the proper provincial Bishops in their relation to their Metropolitan) all Bishops bearing foreign titles, who have been employed on occasional duties in England, and several who at different periods have been consecrated for the special relief of aged Bishops and overgrown dioceses.   They may be classed as,

1. Suffragans of the Saxon Archbishops consecrated with or without promise of succession.   Without prospect of succession were the Bishops of S. Martin's, who are said to have been the predecessors of the Archdeacons of Canterbury, of whom only two, Eadsige, afterwards Archbishop, and Godwin (subs. Kemble, *C. D.* No. 1338, d. 1061), have left their names : with prospect of succession were Siward (Upsallensis ?), Abbot of Abingdon, and perhaps S. Dunstan.

2. Danish Bishops introduced by Canute and his successors, some of whom survived till the Conquest.

3. Foreign refugee Bishops, employed as vicars by the diocesans.

4. Bishops in partibus, consecrated either for the help of the diocesans, or for the service of the exempt monasteries.

5. Irish Bishops employed in the same way.   See pp. 204–209.

6. French and Scotch Bishops consecrated during the wars of Edward III and the schism of the papacy.

7. Suffragans appointed under the Act 26 Hen. VIII. c. 14.   These will be found above at their proper dates.

The following lists are not by any means complete, nor are they intended as more than an illustration of the ecclesiastical state of England during the periods when the diocesan Bishops were employed principally as statesmen and warriors.   The lists are taken from Henry Wharton's laborious collection (printed by Nichols in 1785), with a few additional names and particulars.

I. Saxon and Danish Bishops.

SIEGFRIED, a Norwegian Bishop of the time of Edgar ; v. *Ang. Sac.* i. p. 603 (Sigidwold natione Graecus) p. ult. ; buried at Glastonbury (W. Malmesb., *Antt. Glaston.*, ed. Gale, p. 325), perhaps the same who is called Bishop of Lindsey.

SIWARD, Abbot of Abingdon, consecrated as coadjutor to Abp. Eadsige, 1044.

RALPH, a cousin of Edward the Confessor, a Norwegian Bishop, Abbot of Abingdon, 1050–1052; Hist. Abingd. *Ang. Sac.* i. p. 167.

OSMUND, consecrated in Poland, went about acting as a Bishop, saying that he had been consecrated at Rome about 1052; Adam of Bremen (Pertz, vii. 340). Possibly this was the Bishop who lived at Ely, and was buried there, between 1066 and 1076 ; see *Liber Eliensis*, i. 220.

CHRISTIERN, came to England with Sweyn in 1070 ; *v. Chr. S.* 1070.

II. Foreign refugee, resigned, and In partibus.

A.D. 1259. AUGUSTINE NOTTINGHAM, Bishop of Laodicea, granted an indulgence to the visitors at the tomb of S. Cuthbert 1259, Nov. 17 ; *Rites of Durham*, p. 134. He was a familiar of Innocent IV, and brother to the Provincial of the Franciscans ; *Mon. Franciscana*, p. 62. Wharton makes him a Suffragan of York, with the date 1310.

A.D. 1266. WILLIAM or GEOFFREY, Archbishop of Edessa, alias Rages in Media. 'Anglicus et tunc temporis in Anglia moram continuans, circumspectus et eloquentia commendabilis ;' Rishanger, p. 54, and note è *Chron. Barnwell*. where he is called GIFREDUS, p. 150. As 'W. Edessanus, archiepiscopus Ragensis,' he has the gift of the deanery of Wimborne, until he can return to his see, 1265, Feb. 12 ; *Mon. Angl.* vi. 1452. Consecrated the Bishop of Norwich in 1266. Consecrated the Prior's Chapel at Bury in 1275 (Willelmo Ragusiae, A.D. 1275) ; Cont. Flor. Wig. ii. 215. Was present at the translation of S. Hugh in 1280 ; Harl. MS. 3720. In 1286 he was Suffragan or Commissary of the Bishop of Norwich, and consecrated the cemetery of the Carmelites 'Lincae'; Bale, Harl. 1819. To him probably belongs the inscription on the wall of a barn at Rhuddlan, formerly the site of a house of Black friars, ' Priez pur l'Alme frere Will. Freney erceveske de Rages :' an effigy of a Bishop with mitre and crozier, described by Mr. H. Burnett of Chester, Apr. 1865. See also Barth. Cotton, p. 157.

A.D. 1287. GILBERT 'HAMMENSIS.' Buried at the Carmelites, Norwich, d. 1287, Oct. 9. Granted forty days' indulgence to all who should attend the preaching of the Carmelites, 1273, 1274, and 1276. He was probably the Bishop 'Hamarensis' in Norway, cons. 1263.

A.D. 1316. DAVID RECREENSIS. Suffragan of York, 1316, Feb. 20 ; receives for salary five marks, 1316, Apr. 9, and in 1317 10 marks.

A.D. 1322. PETER BONONIENSIS, Bishop of Corbavia in Dalmatia (Farlati, iv. 95) ; d. S. Wulstan's day, 1332. Assisted at a consecration in 1322. Consecrated S. Mary's bell at S. Paul's, 1331, Feb. 2; *Ann. Paulin.* p. 353. He dedicated the altar of SS. Peter, Paul, Augustine, and Ethelbert in S. Augustine's, Canterbury, 1325, March 1 ; *Mon. Angl.* i. 120; he had a commission to consecrate at Pynnore in 1322. He died in 1331, and was buried at the Franciscans' church, London. Suffragan of London, Canterbury, and Winchester, 1322–1327.

A.D. 1340. BENEDICT 'CARDICENSIS' (Sardis or Sardica), Prior of the Austin friars of Norwich. Suffragan of Norwich and Winchester, 1333–1346.

A.D. **1340.** JOHN PASCHAL, Bishop of Llandaff, is said to have been a Suffragan of Norwich and Bishop of Scutari; Bale, *Scriptores*, pp. 446, 447. The Bishop of Scutari, however, who at a later date was a Suffragan of Norwich, is called Thomas; and if John was a Suffragan as early as 1340 the name of his see is unknown; see Blomefield's *Norfolk*, iv. 423 (8vo ed.).

A.D. **1340.** GEOFFREY GRANDFELD. Suffragan of Lincoln; probably the Bishop of Ferns (Grosfeld); Ware, *Hibernia*; Bale, *Scriptores*, p. 417.

A.D. **1344.** HUGH, Archbishop of Damascus. Suffragan of York, 1344–1351; see the *Fabric Rolls*, ed. Raine, p. 237. Consecrated a cemetery at Thorp, 1349, Aug. 15. Had a commission to bless the Abbot of Rufford, 1352; *Reg. Zouch.* '1347, Aug. 8. Johannes Episcopus convenit coram Archiepiscopum Cantuariensem Archiepiscopum Damascenum ordinis Heremitarum S. Augustini, qui a Cantabrigia usque ad civitatem Exon: iter faciens episcopalia officia in diocesi Exon: peregerat sine licentia Episcopi, eumque ad confessionem delicti et veniam petendam adegit;' *Reg. Grandison.* 1351, Aug. 2, he accused the Abbot of Byland of breaking into his park at Newstead, and stealing a horse; Rymer, v. 20. This seems to point to some connexion with the abbey at Jervaulx. One Hugh was Abbot there about this time.

A.D. **1348.** RICHARD, Archbishop of Nazareth, elected 1348, Oct. 10. Consecrated at Avignon by Bertrand, Bishop of Sabina, shortly before the issue of the Bull of Provision, 6 Id. Dec.; d. 1366; Ughelli, vii. 773. Assisted at two consecrations in 1362. Suffragan for Canterbury, 1349; Worcester, 1350; London, 1361; and Ely, 1361.

A.D. **1349.** CAESARIUS, 'Episcopus Beatae Mariae de Rosis,' assisted at consecrations 1353 and 1355. Suffragan of Canterbury, Winchester, and S. Albans, 1349. Caesarius has licence to ordain in Bow Church on the vigil of Trinity Sunday, 1349, and to consecrate a cemetery at Sandwich; *Reg. P. and C. Cant.*; Wharton, MS. 582.

A.D. **1350.** ROBERT WORKSOP, Suffragan of York; an Austin friar; buried at Tickhill; Bale, *Scriptt.* p. 429.

A.D. **1353.** THOMAS 'MAGNATIENSIS,' a monk of Miraval, had licence to be consecrated by any Catholic Bishop in S. Mary's, Southwark, 1353, July 26; *Reg. Edendon.* Suffragan of York, 1365; Lichfield, Sede Vacante, 1360; *Ang. Sac.* i. 449; Llandaff, S. V. 1361, Dec. 5; Hereford, S. V. 1361, Apr. 10.

A.D. **1353.** THOMAS WALEYS, Bishop of Lycostomium, a Dominician, has like licence. He assisted at a consecration in 1362, and was perhaps the doctor whose dispute with Pope John XXII, on the Beatific Vision of the Patriarchs, is mentioned by W. Thorne, 2067, and Bale, *Catalogue*, i. 406.

A.D. **1354.** THOMAS SALKELD, Bishop of Chrysopolis. Suffragan of York, 1349–1358. Had a salary of 40 marks per annum for consecrating altars and churches and confirming; *Reg. Zouch.* Commission renewed, 1354, July 11; *Reg. Thoresby.* The king acquits the Bishop of Durham on several charges brought against him by the Bishop of Chrysopolis, 1358, Mar. 2; Rymer, vi. 79. His salary in 1349 was 40 marks, and in 1354 £20.

A.D. **1354.** JOHN WARE 'COMANAGENIENSIS,' consecrated 1354. Suffragan of Exeter, 1355, Dec. 12, to 1386; of Hereford, 1371.

A.D. **1360**. ROBERT 'PRISSINENSIS.' Suffragan of Hereford, 1360; Worcester, 1373–1375; Chichester, S. V. 1362, May 12.

A.D. **1361**. GEOFFREY 'MILIENSIS.' Suffragan of York, 1361–1364.

A.D. **1362**. JOHN LANGEBRUGGE 'BUDUENSIS,' appointed Suffragan of Wells in consequence of the number of unauthorized Bishops who were acting as Suffragans in England, 1362, July 16. Commission renewed, S. V. 1363, Sept. 3; see Wilkins, *Conc.* iii. 49; Maskell, *Mon. Rit.* III. cxxvii.

A.D. **1362**. THOMAS 'LAMBERGENSIS,' assisted at a consecration in 1362. Suffragan of London, 1362.

A.D. **1366**. ROBERT 'LAMBRENSIS.' Suffragan of York, 1366; S. Albans, 1384; Bangor, 1371.

A.D. **1367**. JOHN 'LAMBERGENSIS,' perhaps the same as John Langebrugge. Has a commission to examine the election of the Abbess of Burnham; *Reg. Lincoln.*

A.D. **1370**. GEOFFREY, Archbishop of Damascus, assisted at a consecration in 1370.

A.D. **1370**. JOHN AYOBANENSIS, or AYUBONENSIS, assisted at a consecration in 1370. Suffragan of Canterbury, 1369, Mar. 30. William Ayoboniensis had a commission to consecrate an altar in any church in the Arches Deanery, 1366, Nov. 28. 1380, Mar. 14, 'Johannes episcopus Ayebonensis commorans in hermitagio infra Crepulgate, London:' makes his will—to be buried in the Presbytery of the Conventual Church of Stratford: proved in the Commissary's Court, 1381, Mar. 18.

A.D. **1370**. RICHARD 'SERVIENSIS.' Suffragan of York, 1370–1399. Possibly the person whose tomb was at Wigtoft, with the inscription, 'Priez pur l'Alme Richard de Casterton episcopi Sarum (?)'; Holles, *Lincolnshire Church Notes*, 1642; *Yorkshire County Magazine*, 1893, p. 152.

A.D. **1379**. ROBERT DERLING, Bishop of Dunkeld. Consecrated 1379, Oct. 30, at S. Benedict's, Rome, by Peter, Bishop of Aemonia, or Citta Nuova. Suffragan of York, 1380–1384.

   ** After him appears as Bishop of Dunkeld, Nicolas, Abbot of Pershore; Rector of Beoly, 1396, Dec. 18; Belbroughton, 1411, Mar. 28; Suffragan of Worcester, 1392–1421, and Hereford, 1404. He consecrated part of the buildings and bells at New College, 1400, Oct. 19; Wood, *Hist. Oxon.* ii. 130. Nicolas was succeeded by William Gunwardby, Bishop of Dunkeld; Rector of Houghton Conquest, 1452, Mar. 16; Great Hallingbury, 1440, May 28; Suffragan of Lincoln, 1431, and Ely, 1448–1454; d. 1457. These are omitted in Keith, not having been recognized in Scotland, as neither were John, Bishop of Glasgow, Suffragan of London, 1393–1394; Sarum, 1396; and Robert 'Archiliensis,' Suffragan of Hereford, 1386.

A.D. **1382**. WILLIAM BOTTLESHAM, Bishop 'Navatensis'; possibly of Pavada of Bethlehem, 1385. Translated to Llandaff, 1386; *Fasciculi Zizaniorum* 286, 498.

A.D. **1382**. THOMAS, Bishop of Scutari, dedicated the Carmelite church at Norwich; Blomefield, iv. 423: possibly the Thomas Lodovis, made Bishop of Killala in 1381, or Thomas Orwell, who was Suffragan of Norwich in 1396; see Cotton's *Fasti*, iv. 64.

A.D. **1384.** NICOLAS, Bishop of Christopolis. Suffragan of Wells, 1385–1403; commission renewed, 1403, Nov. 30; Sarum, 1395, Feb. 1, to 1406; Llandaff, 1382.

A.D. **1385.** ROBERT HYNTLESHAM, or HYRTLESHAM, Bishop of Sevastopolis. Suffragan of Norwich; Sarum, 1388–1389. Assisted at a consecration in 1385.

A.D. **1385.** WILLIAM 'TORNACENSIS,' appointed to Tournay during the schism of the Papacy. Consecrated 1385. Assisted at a consecration in 1401. Ordained in London diocese, 1399–1406. See also *Mon. Angl.* ii. 236.

A.D. **1390.** WILLIAM EGMUND 'PRISSINENSIS,' an Austin friar of Stamford. Suffragan of Lincoln. Had a commission to examine the election of the Abbot of S. Mary's, Northampton, 1394, July 31; see Bale, *Scriptores*, p. 515.

A.D. **1390.** OSWALD, Bishop of Whithern, consecrated 1380. Suffragan of York, 1391–1397. Bishop Oswald has a deputation from the Dean and Chapter of York as Suffragan *sede vacante*, 1397, Jan. 18, and ordains in the Franciscan church there, Mar. 17; also the next year after Archbishop Waldby's death, he has a deputation, 1398, Jan. 9; see *Reg. Cap. Ebor.* S. V.; MS. Cotton Galba, E. 10.

A.D. **1390.** WILLIAM NORTHBRUGGE 'PHARENSIS,' consecrated at Rome. He was Rector of Trinity Goodramgate, York, 1400; Nafferton, 1398; warden of the hospital of S. Mary Magdalene at Kynewaldsgrave, 1399; *Mon. Angl.* vi. 650. Suffragan of York, 1390; commission renewed, 1408, Dec. 29; Suffragan of Lichfield, 1385–1387, and Worcester in 1395. He has a commission to consecrate a chapel at Loweswater, 1403, June 30; *York Fabric Rolls*, p. 237.

.D. **1394.** WILLIAM 'BASILIENSIS.' Suffragan of London, 1394–1399.

A.D. **1395.** THOMAS BOTYLER, Bishop of Chrysopolis, assisted at a consecration in 1401. Sub-collector for the crusade against Bajazet in 1399; Rymer, viii. 82. Suffragan of Winchester, 1401; Worcester, 1420.

A.D. **1396.** THOMAS EDWARDSTON, Archbishop, perhaps of Nazareth. Suffragan of Norwich; buried at Clare in Suffolk; d. 1396; *Mon. Angl.* vi. 1598; Bale, *Scriptores*, p. 513. Blomefield (*Hist. Norfolk*) speaks of Thomas Bedingfield, Archbishop of Nazareth.

A.D. **1397.** JOHN SEWALE 'SURRONENSIS,' appointed by bull, 1397, July 20. Has general licence of non-residence, &c., from the Pope, 1399, Oct. 28; *Reg. Arundel.* Assisted at a consecration in 1401. Suffragan of Winchester, 1417–1418; London, 1417–1423; S. Edmund's, 1414; Sarum, 1420–1426; S. David's, 1405. The name is spelled Surrenensis and Cironensis. He was perhaps Bishop of Cyrene.

A.D. **1400.** JOHN LEICESTER, Archbishop of Smyrna, a Carmelite. Rector of Threxton, Norfolk, 1400, Apr. 6. Suffragan of Norwich, 1413, Sept. 17; commission renewed, 1416, June 1, till 1423; of S. Edmund's, 1418; d. 1424, Nov. 6; Weaver.

A.D. **1400.** THOMAS MERKS, alias Sumestre, was translated from Carlisle 'ad Ecclesiam Samastenam, in quâ clerus seu populus Christianus non habetur,' and thence to some unknown see in 1402. He was Rector of Todenham, 1404, Aug. 13. Suffragan of Winchester, 1403–1404. Rector of Sturminster Marshall, 1403. Prebendary of Masham in York Minster, 1401; d. 1409.

A.D. **1400.** THOMAS, Bishop of Constantia in Media, or of Coutances, assisted at a consecration.

A.D. **1401.** JOHN GREENLAW 'SOLTANIENSIS IN MEDIA,' provided 1401, Sept. 20 (Wadding), but consecrated Sept. 8; *Reg. Bowet.* Suffragan of Wells, 1401, Dec., to 1408; York, 1421; Lincoln, 1422; Sarum, 1409. Rector of a mediety of Cotgrave, 1422.

A.D. **1402.** JOHN 'ANCORADENSIS.' Had a commission to purify the cemetery of S. Peter's, Cambridge, 1402, Sept. 7; *Reg. Fordham.* Suffragan of Lincoln, 1420–1432; Ely, 1402; Canterbury, 1424.

A.D. **1407.** JOHN, Bishop of Gallipoli. Suffragan of Sarum, 1407; ordains 1408, Mar. 17.

A.D. **1409.** WILLIAM 'SOLUBRIENSIS' (Selymbria). Suffragan of Sarum, 1409, Jan. 20, to 1417; Exeter, 1415–1416; Winchester, 1407–1417.

A.D. **1410.** MATTHEW, Bishop of Hebron. Suffragan of Hereford, 1410.

A.D. **1411.** WILLIAM SELLERS 'SOLTONIENSIS.' Suffragan of Canterbury. Assisted at a consecration in 1411. Suffragan of Lincoln, 1418. Consecrated Borstall chapel, 1418, Nov. 2. His will ('Saltoniensis') is in Archbishop Chichele's *Register*, dated 1437, Sept. 25; to be buried at S. Clement's, East Cheap.

A.D. **1414.** RICHARD 'KATENSIS.' Suffragan of Sarum, 1414, Feb. 23; ordains 1420–1437; Bath, 1414–1418; Exeter, 1420, Nov. 1; ordains 1417–1433.

A.D. **1423.** JOHN 'STEPHANIENSIS.' Suffragan of Lincoln, 1423–1431; commission renewed, 1431, Sept. 1; Ely, 1424–1443.

A.D. **1423.** JOHN BULLOCK, provided to Ross, in Scotland, 1423, Feb. 1; Brady, i. 143.

A.D. **1426.** ROBERT 'GRADENSIS.' Norwich, 1426, Dec. 22, to 1446, and as late as 1452.

A.D. **1436.** JOHN (BLOXWYCH ?) 'OLENSIS' (Hollensis Islandiae prov. 1427). Vicar of East Ham, 1444, Sept. 17; d. before 1446, June 12. Suffragan of Bath, 1437, Mar. 10, to 1443; Canterbury, 1443, Oct. 5; Exeter, 1442. In 1436, May 28, he was allowed to send John May, captain of the ship *Catherine* of London, to Iceland, to report the condition of his diocese which he had not visited. He seems to have resigned it soon after, and is styled 'nuper Olensis.'

A.D. **1441.** JOHN, Bishop of Philippopolis, provided 1441, July 25; Wadding. Suffragan of York, 1446–1458. He has a commission to consecrate churches, at Burton Pidsea, 1442, Mar. 27; at Monks Fryston, 1444, May 12; at Ribston, 1444, Sept. 4; a burial-ground for the Hospitallers at Ossington, 1445, Dec. 9; a chapel in S. Cuthbert's, York, 1453, Jan. 24; a cemetery for S. Crux, York, 1455, June 4; a basilica and cemetery at Colthorpe, 1458, Aug. 17; *Fabric Rolls*, pp. 238–252.

A.D. **1454.** RODERIC 'ARLATENSIS,' Rector of Buckland Fyllegh. Suffragan of Exeter, 1454, Nov. 8, to 1457.

A.D. **1458.** WILLIAM WESTKARRE, Bishop of Sidon; Black Canon; Prior of Mottisfont. Consecrated the Chrism at Canterbury, 1463, April 14. Suffragan of Winchester, 1457–1486; Canterbury, 1480; Worcester, 1480; Wells, 1459. He was Rector of S. Martin's, Ludgate, 1465–1468; Romney Marsh, S. Mary's, 1468–1473; S. T. P. of S. Mary's College, Oxford; and Commissary of the University, 1442, 1444, 1446.

A. D. **1459.** JOHN 'TINENSIS' (Tenos), Canon regular of S. Austin. Vicar of Devizes. Master of S. John's Hospital at Wells, 1462; d. 1480. Suffragan of Wells, 1459, Oct. 17, to 1479; Exeter, 1461–1462.

A. D. **1471.** HENRY, Bishop of Joppa. Prior of Combwell. Suffragan of Canterbury, 1471. Vicar of Lydd, 1471, Feb. 7; Charryng, 1471, Oct. 24; Lambeth, 1471, Apr. 3. In his will, dated 1474, Apr. 24, and proved 1474, May 25, he left all he had to Combwell Priory.

A. D. **1480.** RICHARD WYCHERLEY 'OLENENSIS,' a Black friar of Warwick; d. 1502, Sept. Suffragan of Worcester, 1482–1501; Hereford, 1480. He was Rector of Powick, 1493, Dec. 5, to 1501; Salwarp, 1486, Oct. 14, to 1502. He is called John in the London Registers of 1497. His will is in the Probate Office, 16 Blamyr. Vid. Wood, *A. O.* i. 551, and *Notes and Queries*, Aug. 1856.

A. D. **1480.** THOMAS CORNISH 'TINENSIS.' Master of S. John's Hospital, Wells, 1483, Aug. Provost of Oriel College, Oxford, elected Feb. 5, 1493. Vicar of S. Cuthbert's, Wells, 1497, July 29. Chancellor of Wells, 1499, Apr. 21; Precentor, 1502, Sept. 4. Vicar of Chewe, 1505, Oct. 8; Axbridge, 1489, Apr. 3; S. Andrew, Ipplepen, 1499–1513. Warden of Ottery, 1489, Dec. 1, to 1511. Suffragan of Wells, 1486–1513; Exeter, 1487, June 3, to 1505; d. 1513, June 3; Wood, *A. O.* i. 555. (Oliver.) His will is in the Probate Office, 18 Fetiplace.

A. D. **1492.** THOMAS WEELL, Bishop of Pavada, assisted at a consecration in 1494. Suffragan of London, 1492–1502. Rector of Thorley, 1493; Thorp, 1495. His will (Thomas Weell, Bishop 'Pavidencis, Suffrygan of Coventrye, of Nun Eaton, Warwickshire') is in the Probate Office, 10 Maynwaring; dated May 1, proved May 16, 1521; to be buried in the chancel of Nuneyton.

A. D. **1493.** AUGUSTINE CHURCH, Bishop of Lydda. Rector of Washingburgh, 1509; Malden, 1504; East Borscombe, 1498–1499. Suffragan of Sarum, 1494, Feb. 27, to 1499; Exeter, 1493; Lincoln, 1501–1511.

A. D. **1498.** RICHARD MARTIN, Bishop of the Catholic Church and Suffragan of Canterbury; d. 1498, Nov. 19. Prior of the Minorites at Canterbury. Rector of Lydd, 1474, and Ickham, 1492. 1474, June 5 : 'dominus contulit Rev. Patr. Ric. Martyn in Universali ecclesia episcopo, vicariam perpetuam Eccl. Paroch. de Lydde, Cant. dioc. post mortem D. Henrici dum vixit Joppensis episcopi ultimi vicarii ibidem, vacantem;' *Reg. Bourchier*, f. 110 A.

A. D. **1502.** EDMUND, Bishop of Chalcedon; Norwich.

A. D. **1503.** EDWARD, Bishop of Gallipoli. Suffragan of London, 1503; Worcester, 1503.

A. D. **1503.** RALPH HEYLESDEN, Bishop of Ascalon, provided 1503, March 8; Wadding. Has a pension of 150 golden ducats from the revenues of Worcester, being still elect; MS. C. C. C. 170. Suffragan of Worcester, 1503–1523; Hereford, 1510.

A. D. **1505.** JOHN UNDERWOOD, Bishop of Chalcedon. Rector of North Creek and Eccles. Suffragan of Norwich, 1531. Prior of Bromholm, 1509, and of Hildebrand's Hospital, Norwich.

A. D. **1505**. THOMAS WELLS, Bishop of Sidon. Prior of S. Gregory's, Canterbury ; d. 1526, Sept. 17 ; Hasted. Suffragan of Canterbury, 1505–1511. Incumbent of Holy Cross, Westgate, Canterbury, 1507, Feb. 8. Rector of Woodchurch, 1519, May 15 ; Adisham, 1523, Dec. 7.

A. D. **1506**. JOHN HATTON, Bishop of Negropont. Prebendary of Givendale, 1503 ; Ulleskelf, 1504. Archdeacon of Nottingham, 1506, Sept., to 1516 ; d. 1516, Apr. 25. Suffragan of York ; Wood, *A. O.* i. 560.

A. D. **1506**. —— SEBASTIENSIS. Suffragan of Exeter, 1506.

A. D. **1506**. JOHN THORNDEN, Bishop of Sirmium, or Cyrene, provided as Syrinensis, 1505, Apr. 4, being Prior of Wallingford ; Brady, i. 110. Commissary at Oxford, 1506–1514. Prior of Dover. Suffragan of Canterbury, 1508–1514. He held Highardys, 1505, Dec. 23 ; Harbledown, 1507, Aug. 30 ; Newington, 1506, Aug. 6 ; Aldington, 1512, July 31 ; Monks Illegh, 1513, Feb. 25 ; Folkestone Priory, 1514, Mar. 4 ; and d. 1516 ; Wood, *A. O.* i. 559.

A. D. **1508**. WILLIAM BARTON 'SALONIENSIS.' Prebendary of Ruscombe, 1509, Sept. 7 ; Beaminster, Nov. 18 ; Grimston, 1515, May 3. Suffragan of Sarum, 1509–1517.

A. D. **1508**. THOMAS CHARD 'SOLUBRIENSIS,' consecrated 1508. Vicar of Torrington Parva, 1508, Sept. 26 ; S. Gluvias ; Holbeton ; Wellington, 1512, June. Warden of Ottery, 1513, Oct. 9 ; resigned 1518. Prior of Montacute, 1515–1525 ; Carswell, 1535. Abbot of Forde, 1521. Vicar of Thorncombe, 1529, Apr. 15 ; Rector of Nothill, 1532, Apr. 10 ; Vicar of Tintenhull, 1521. Minister of Ottery, 1540, Mar. 22 ; resigned, 1543, Oct. 20. He was executor of the will of Bishop Oldham ; as Lord Suffragan of Montacute, was at the funeral of the Countess of Devon in 1527 ; see *Test. Vetust.*, and Green's *Princesses*, iv. 40. (Oliver.)

A. D. **1510**. THOMAS FOWLER, episcopus Lachorensis. Suffragan of Hereford. Vicar of Bosbury.

A. D. **1512**. JOHN 'AVIENSIS,' consecrated 1512 ; *Reg. Warham.*

A. D. **1512**. JOHN TINMOUTH, Bishop of Argos, a Grey friar of Lynn. Rector of Ludgarshall ; resigned 1511. Prebendary of Sarum, 1510. Vicar of Boston, Lincolnshire ; d. 1524. Suffragan of Sarum, 1510–1524 ; Wood, *A. O.* i. 566.

A. D. **1513**. THOMAS WOLF, Bishop of Lacedaemon, prohibited by Bishop Fitz James from officiating in the diocese of London (about 1510). Vicar of East Ham, 1514, May 2 ; d. before 1518, Nov. 6. Suffragan of Wells, 1513, Sept. 30.

A. D. **1513**. JOHN YOUNG, Bishop of Gallipoli, consecrated 1513, July 3 ; d. 1526, Mar. 28. Rector of S. Martin's, Oxford. Warden of New College, 1521. Master of S. Thomas's Hospital, 1510, Sept. 16. Rector of S. Magnus the Martyr, 1514, Mar. 20 ; S. Christopher Stocks, 1514, Jan. 23. Prebendary of Holborn, 1511, Nov. 28 ; Newington, 1513, Feb. 10. Archdeacon of London, 1514, Mar. 28. Dean of Chichester, 1517. Suffragan of London, 1513–1526 ; Wood, *A. O.* i. 567.

A. D. **1513**. RICHARD 'NATURENSIS' (in the province of Heraclea). Suffragan of Durham, consecrated 1513 ; see above, p. 97.

A. D. **1513**. ROGER SMITH, Bishop of Lydda, consecrated 1513 ; d. 1518. Prior of Ronton. Abbot of Dorchester and buried there. Suffragan of Sarum, 1517–1518 ; see above, p. 97.

A.D. **1515.** WILLIAM GRANT, Bishop of Pavada, in the province of Constantinople. Vicar of Redgwell, 1522, Aug. 30, to 1524, Mar. 23. Suffragan of Ely, 1516, Jan. 20; Newcourt, ii. 490.

A.D. **1515.** RICHARD WILSON, Bishop of Negropont. Prior of Drax. Buried at Bingley, Yorkshire. Suffragan of York, 1515–1518; Wood, *A. O.* i. 561. Translated to Meath, 1523; Brady, i. 234.

A.D. **1515.** WILLIAM BACHELOR, a Carmelite of Burnham, Prior of the London Carmelites, Bishop 'Carvahagonensis in Grecia.' Suffragan of Chichester. Buried at Rome, at S. Thomas of Canterbury's, 1515, July 30; Bale, MS. Harl. 1819, and Br. Willis.

A.D. **1518.** JOHN PINNOCK, Bishop of Syene, provided 1518, Nov. 10; Brady, i. 110. Vicar of Inglesham. Prebendary of Dornford, 1519; Chardstock, 1523. Suffragan of Sarum, 1518–1535.

A.D. **1518.** THOMAS VIVIAN, Bishop of Megara provided 1517, May 4; Brady, i. 110. Suffragan of Exeter, 1518–1532. Prior of Black Canons at Bodmin; Wood, *A. O.* i. 554. Rector of Withiel. Vicar of Egloshel. Prebendary of Endellient; d. 1533, June 1.

A.D. **1519.** RICHARD BURGH, provided as Suriensis, for Carlisle; Brady, i. 111. He was Abbot of Thorp.

A.D. **1519.** WILLIAM GILBERT, provided 1519, May 13, as Majorensis under the Archbishop of Nazareth; Brady, i. 111. Abbot of Bruton. Suffragan of Wells, 1519–1526; Wood, *A. O.* i. 568.

A.D. **1520.** THOMAS BELE, Bishop of Lydda, provided 1521, June 7; Brady, i. 112. Prior of S. Mary's, Oxford, 1508; S. Mary's Hospital, Bishopsgate. Vicar of Witham, 1528, Jan. 28. Suffragan of London, 1521–1528. Master of S. John's Hospital, Ely, 1528, Apr. 10; Wood, *A. O.* i. 569.

A.D. **1520.** WILLIAM HOGIESON, a Dominican, provided 1520, Aug. 8, as Dariensis in partibus for Winchester; Brady, i. 112. Suffragan of Winchester, 1520–1525; York, 1530. One William, Suffragan of Winchester, was parson of Chilbolton in 1522, and witnessed the will of John Tutt; Bodfelde, 10.

A.D. **1521.** WILLIAM SUTTON, provided to Pavada, 1521, Aug. 9, in the place of William, defunct, being Prior of Avecote, in the diocese of Lichfield, for Lichfield; Brady, i. 113.

A.D. **1524.** MATTHEW MACKARELL, Bishop of Chalcedon, provided 1524, Apr. 28, for York; Brady, i. 113. He was Abbot of Berling, and hanged for his share in the Pilgrimage of Grace in 1537.

A.D. **1524.** JOHN STANYWELL, Bishop 'Poletensis,' provided 1524, Apr. 28, for York; Brady, i. 113. Called Prior of Tynemouth; ibid. Became Abbot of Pershore in 1527. Prior of Gloucester Hall, Oxford. Subscribed the Royal Supremacy, 1534; d. 1553; buried at Longdon, Staffordshire; Wood, *A. O.* i. 579.

A.D. **1526.** WILLIAM HOW 'AURENSIS'; Wood, *A. O.* i. 567.

A.D. **1526.** ANDREW WHITMAY, Bishop of Chrysopolis; d. 1546. Provided as Gerupolitanus, 1525, Sept. 15; Brady, i. 113. Suffragan of Worcester, 1526–1541; Hereford, 1540; Wood, *A. O.* i. 577.

A.D. **1526.** JOHN SMART, Bishop of Pavada, provided 1526, July 13; Brady, i. 114. Abbot of Wigmore. Suffragan of Hereford, 1526–1535; Worcester, 1526–1531.

A.D. **1526.** ALFONSUS DE VILLA SANCTA, a Franciscan, provided as Sabulensis, 1526, Feb. 21, for S. Asaph; Brady, i. 114.

A.D. **1527.** ROBERT KING, Bishop of Rheon, in the province of Constantinople, provided on a reference of Cardinal Campegio for the aid of the see of Lincoln, 1527, Jan. 7, being then Abbot of Thame; Brady, i. 115. He was the first Bishop of Osney, 1542, Sept. 1; of Oxford, 1545, June 9; Wood, *A. O.* i. 585.

[A.D. **1529.** THOMAS HALLAM, Prior of Newstead by Stamford, an Austin canon. Recommended as Suffragan of Lincoln 1529, May 13. Subscribed the Royal Supremacy, 1534, as Prior, and died or resigned before 1555. Probably confounded with Thomas Swillington, 1532.]

A.D. **1530.** JOHN HOLT, Bishop of Lydda; d. 1540, Aug. 12; buried at S. Mary's, Bury; Wood, *A. O.* i. 569. His will is in the Probate Office, 10 Alenger.

A.D. **1532.** WILLIAM FAWELL, Bishop of Hippo, provided 1532, May 15; Brady, i. 116. Archdeacon of Totness, 1549; d. 1557, July 25; buried at Exeter. Bishop Voysey gave him the advowson of Boseham. d. Chichester, 1540, Feb. 15. Suffragan of Exeter, 1532–1544. He was V. Probus, 1537, Aug. 26; resigned 1550, Jan. He ordained for the last time 1554, Sept. 22. (Oliver.)

A.D. **1532.** THOMAS SWILLINGTON, Bishop of Philadelphia, an Austin friar, provided at Rome, 1532, July 12, for Lincoln; Brady, i. 116. Prebendary of Stow in Lindsey, 1544, Apr. 12; d. 1546. Suffragan of Lincoln, 1533, July 15; London, 1534, Mar. 21; v. Memoir on the Winkburne Seal, *Archaeologia*, vol. vii; *Athenae Cant.* i. 90.

A.D. **1532.** JOHN, Prior of S. Velinus, provided, with title of Majorensis in partibus, for Winchester, 1532, Nov. 13; Brady, i. 117.

A.D. **1533,** Aug. 27. WILLIAM DUFFIELD, provided to the see Ascolensis in partibus infidelium, for S. Asaph; Brady, i. 115. Possibly identical with the Bishop of Ascalon, who was Suffragan of York in 1535.

A.D. **1533–4.** CHRISTOPHER LORD, Bishop of Sidon. Abbot of the Premonstratensian Canons of Newsome in Lincolnshire, sat as such in the Convocation of 1529; *Domestic State Papers*, 1529, No. 6047. He is provided as Bishop of Sidon and Suffragan of Canterbury, and excused his fees at Rome, 1533, Aug. 27; Brady, *Episcopal Succession*, i. 117, ii. 278. Protests that, although he has taken the oath that his predecessor took to the Pope, he does not mean to keep it, being still elect of Sidon, 1534, Jan. 18; MS. Calthorpe (*Register* under Warham and Cranmer). Assists at a consecration, Apr. 19, at Croydon (above, p. 99); is dead before 1534, May 18, when Cranmer recommends his successor; *Domestic State Papers*, 1534, Nos. 685, 686; Cranmer's *Remains*, pp. 290, 291.

A.D. **1534–5.** THOMAS CHETHAM, Bishop of Sidon, an Austin canon of Leeds, Kent. Subscribes the Royal Supremacy, 1534, Dec. 22; *Dep. K. Rep.* vii. App. ii. p. 290. Has a pension of £40 from the priory; *Valor Eccl.* i. 75, 98. Suffragan of Canterbury, 1535; of London also, and Prebendary of S. Paul's, 1553–1558; assists at a consecration, 1535, Apr. 11 (above, p. 99). Vicar of Harleston,

Norfolk, 1555. Rector of Wrotham, 1557. Has his commission renewed, 1558, Mar. 8. His prebend vacant by death, 1558, Oct. 6 ; Cooper, *Ath. Cant.* i. 177 ; Newcourt, i. 196.

. Brady, *Episcopal Succession*, i. 114, gives a note from the Barberini MSS., according to which the Pope, in 1526, Jan. 19, provided, on the reference of Cardinal Campegio, Thomas Chetam to the see of Sidon, and authorized him to exercise his pontificalia in the city and diocese of Canterbury only, with consent of the Archbishop. If the date is right, and there is no confusion of two men of the same name, there must have been two Bishops with the same title, or Chetham must have waited for the declaration of his appointment for eight years. This is improbable.

A.D. **1539**. JOHN DRAPER, Bishop of Neapolis. Prior of Christ Church, Twynham, elected 1520, Jan. 31. Prebendary of Winchester, 1541. Suffragan of Winchester.

A.D. **1545**. RICHARD THORNDEN, or LE STEDE, Bishop of Dover. Bishop Yngworth died in 1515 ; his will is in the Prerogative Court. Thornden must have been consecrated soon after, but no record of the fact is preserved ; hence he has been confounded with his predecessor. He was Warden of Canterbury Hall, Oxford, in 1528. Rector of Wrotham, 1546, Apr. 3 ; and one of the first Prebendaries of Canterbury ; d. 1557 ; Wood, *A. O.* i. 586.

IRISH SUFFRAGANS.

The following are the names of the principal Irish Bishops who had permanent duty in England as Suffragans.

Armagh.

ROLAND DE JORZ, cons. 1311, Nov., by Berenger, Bishop of Tusculum, at Vienne ; resigned 1321. Suffragan of Canterbury, 1311 ; of York, 1332. See Theiner, *Vetera Monumenta Hibernorum*, &c., pp. 183-223.

EDMUND CONISBURGH, Suffragan of Ely, 1477.

Meath (Midensis).

WILLIAM ANDREW, consecrated to Aghadoe by Urban VI in 1373 ; Theiner, p. 350. Prior of Langley ; *Mon. Angl.* ii. 236, d. 1385. Suffragan of Canterbury, 1380, Mar. 29.

Clogher.

FLORENTIUS WOOLLEY, provided as Glowhoriensis or Clocharensis, 1475, Nov. 27 ; Brady, i. 250. Suffragan of Norwich, 1478-1485. Will dated 1500, July 20: to be buried in the Priory Church of S. Mary at Snape. He was Rector of Merston, Norfolk ; Vicar of Codington, Suffolk. Will proved at Ipswich, 1500, Oct. 4.

Down and Connor.

RICHARD WOLSEY, Suffragan of Lichfield, 1452 ; Worcester, 1465-1479. See Wood, *Ath. Ox.* i. 551 ; Brady, i. 261.

THOMAS ——, elect of Down and Connor, 1454 ; Brady, i. 262. Consecrated by John Mey, Archbishop of Armagh, in 1456 ; Ware ; d. 1468. Rector of S. Botolph, Bishopsgate, 1461 ; Vicar of East Ham, 1459 ; Newcourt, i. 312 ; ii. 302. Another, Thomas Pollard, was consecrated at Rome, 1447, Aug. 27 ; Brady, i. 261 ; pref. p. xxiii : as Bishop of Down ; and Thadeus, in 1469, as elect of Down and Connor ; ibid.

ROBERT BLYTH, Suffragan of Ely, 1539–1541. Abbot of Thorney. Will dated 1547, Oct. 19 ; see *Mon. Angl.* ii. 596 ; Brady, i. 262.

Connor.

ADAM, Abbot of Wardon, 1242–1244 ; see Ware, and M. Paris, iv. 227, 247, 250, 390.

SIMON ELVINGTON, Suffragan of Sarum, 1459–1481 ; of Exeter, 1463. Vicar of Gillingham, 1463–1475.

Derry (Derensis).

JOHN DONGAN, Suffragan of London, 1392.

Raphoe (Rathpotensis).

CARBRIC, Suffragan of Canterbury, 1273. Consecrated 1266 ; d. 1275 ; Ware.

Triburna (Kilmore).

JOHN STOKES, Suffragan of Lichfield, 1407 ; Worcester, 1416.

Ardagh (Ardachadensis).

HENRY NONY, Suffragan of Exeter, 1396. Provided at Rome, 1392 ; Brady, i. 288.

Dromore.

NICOLAS WARTRE, provided as Bishop of Dromore, 1419, March 27 ; Brady, i. 297. Suffragan of York, 1420–1445. He has several commissions to consecrate churches, &c., 1424–1445 ; *York Fabric Rolls*, pp. 238, 239.

JOHN, Bishop of Dromore. Suffragan of Canterbury, 1420 ; of London, 1419–1426 ; Rochester, 1423 ; *Reg. Roff.* p. 570. He was Rector of Stisted, and also of S. Mary Somerset, in London. His will is in Chichele's *Register*, dated 1433, Apr. 1, pr. Aug. 14 ; and he desires to be buried in the church of S. Mary Somerset. It is possible that he is the Bishop John Chourles who was provided in 1410 ; Brady, i. 297.

THOMAS RADCLIFFE, consecrated at Florence in the church of S. Ambrose, 1434, Dec. 21, by Andrew of Megara, ' Johanne Libanens.,' and ' Luca Agen.' ; Brady, i. pref. xxv.

DAVID CHIRBURY, provided 1431, June 22, to the see of Dromore, vacant by the death of William ; Brady, i. 298. He was Archdeacon of Brecon, and Suffragan of S. David's, 1437. His will is dated 1456, Nov. 9 ; Hardy, *Le Neve*, i. 311.

THOMAS [BRADLEY], consecrated to Dromore, 1450, Feb. 1, by Angelus, Bishop of Ascoli, Alexius of Chiusi, and Andrew of Bojano, in the church of S. Maria in Aquiro, Rome ; Brady, i. pref. xxv. ' Orate pro anima Thomae Bradley quondam anachoritae in conventu fratrum Carmelitarum Norwic.; et postea A.D. 1448 factus est episcopus Dromorensis in Ybernia et sanctae Romanae ecclesiae legatus, qui obiit 1489;' Harl. MS. 211. His name was Scrope, Bradley being his birthplace, and died 1499, Jan. 25; Bale, *Scriptt.* p. 629. He was Suffragan of Norwich, 1450–1477.

RICHARD MESIN, Suffragan of York, 1460. Pays fees on his provision at Rome, 1457, Aug. 18; Brady, i. 298. *York Corpus Christi Guild* (Surtees Soc.), pp. 291, 292.

WILLIAM EGREMONT, Suffragan of York, 1463–1501. Ordains in Blackfriars, York, 1480, and in other churches there until 1501; see his commissions in the *Fabric Rolls*, p. 240.

GEORGE BRAN, consecrated 1483, May 4, by 'Pet. Nissariensis, R. Anthecaden.,' and John of Lismore at Rome; Brady, i. pref. xxvi. Suffragan of London, 1497; Worcester, 1497.

THADDAEUS IRRIL, appointed 1511, Apr. 30, in succession to George Bran; Brady, i. 299. Celebrated Holy Orders in London diocese when excommunicate; *Reg. Fitz James.*

Kildare (Darensis).

GEOFFREY HEREFORD, consecrated at Easter, 1449; Ware. Rector of S. Margaret, Lothbury, 1454; Newcourt, i. 401. Paid his fees at Rome, 1447, Sept. 1. Suffragan of Hereford, 1449.

RICHARD LANG (Ware), Suffragan of Chichester, 1480; Winchester, 1488.

JAMES WALE, Suffragan of London, 1491. Rector of Great Horkesley, 1488; of Laindon, 1483; and of S. Christopher, Threadneedle Street, 1485; Newcourt, i. 324; ii. 334, 356.

WILLIAM BARNETT, Suffragan of Winchester, 1520–1525; of York, 1530.

Leighlin (Lechlinensis).

RALPH. Has 10 marks salary as Suffragan of York, 1344, Jan. 20.

THOMAS HALSEY, Suffragan of York, 1519; see Brady, i. 385 (citing MS. Rawlinson, 484).

JOHN ——, Bishop of Leighlin, Abbot of Wymondham in 1520; *Mon. Angl.* iii. 327.

Cashel.

RALPH KELLY, Archbishop, Suffragan of Winchester, 1346.

Emly (Imelacensis).

ROBERT WINDEL, provided 1422, Dec. 14; Brady, ii. 33. Suffragan of Norwich, 1424; Sarum, 1435–1441; Worcester, 1433; St. Edmund's, 1430.

ROBERT, consecrated 1444. Suffragan of Winchester, 1456; translated to Tiberias; Brady, ii. 34.

DONATUS O'BRIEN, Suffragan of Worcester, 1500. Paid his fees as elect of Emly in 1494; Brady, ii. 34.

Ferns.

ALBINUS, consecrated the infirmary chapel at Waverley in 1201, and altars in 1214 ; *Ann. Wav.* 167, 180.

NICOLAS COMYN. See above, p. 97.

Limerick.

JOHN DONNOWE, provided 1486 ; Ware. Suffragan of Exeter, 1489 ; see Brady, ii. 41.

Waterford.

RICHARD, Suffragan of Exeter, 1338.

JOHN GEESE, GEEZ, or GOES, Suffragan of London, 1424.   Provided 1422, Dec. 4 ; Brady, ii. 65.

Cloyne (Clonensis).

THOMAS HARTPERRY, Suffragan of Hereford, 1490.

Ross.

STEPHEN BROWN, Suffragan of S. David's, 1408 ; Wells, 1410 ; Worcester, 1420.

RICHARD, Suffragan of Canterbury, 1439–1465 ; London, 1434–1441 ; Sarum, 1454 ; Dean of Shoreham, 1453.   Rector of Saltwood, 1455 ; d. 1465.

JOHN, Suffragan of Norwich, 1466–1469.

JOHN, Bishop of Ross, Suffragan of Wells, 1479–1481. Rector of Broxbourne, 1475 ; S. Andrew Undershaft, 1478 ; Newcourt, i. 267 ; ii. 812.

Killaloe (Laonensis).

ROBERT MULFIELD, Suffragan of Lichfield ; a monk of Meaux. Provided 1409 ; resigned 1418. Has leave from Martin V to become Suffragan of Lichfield, Dec. 2.

Ardfert.

JOHN, Suffragan of Canterbury ; d. 1245 ; see Prynne, iii. 60 ; M. Paris.

JOHN PYGGE, Rector of S. Christopher, Threadneedle Street, 1462–1483.

Tuam.

JOHN BATERLEY, Suffragan of Sarum, 1425 ; cf. Brady, ii. 128, 129.

PHILIP PINSON, Suffragan of Hereford, 1503 ; Ware, *Tuam*, p. 6. Provided and died in 1503, Dec. ; Brady, ii. 131.

Elphin.

ROBERT FORSTER, 1418. Suffragan of Durham, 1426. Provided 1418, Feb. 17 ; Brady, ii. 195.

JOHN MAX or MAXEY. Provided 1525, April 7 ; Brady, ii. 198. Commendator of Titchfield and Welbeck ; Prebendary of York and Southwell ; Visitor of the Premonstratensians in England ; d. 1536 ; *Testamenta Eboracensia,* v. 221, 222 ; *Mon. Angl.* vi. 872.

Clonfert.

ROBERT, Suffragan of Canterbury, 1296–1307.

ROBERT LE PETIT, 1319–1325. Suffragan of Worcester, 1322. Translated to Enaghdun, 1325; Theiner, p. 231.

JOHN HEYNE, Suffragan of London, 1443–1448; Worcester, 1443; Exeter, 1447. Vicar of West Thurrock, 1457; Newcourt, ii. 591; d. 1459. His will is in the Probate Office, 16 Stokton.

Killala (Aladensis).

THOMAS ORWELL or HORWELL, Suffragan of Ely, 1389–1404; see Brady, ii. 70. He had a commission for the Isle of Wight from William of Wykeham. His will, dated 1401 and proved 1404, is in the Probate Office, 7 Marche: to be buried at Grey Friars.

THOMAS ——, provided 1471; Brady, ii. 172.

THOMAS CLARKE, provided 1501, May 4; Brady, ii. 172. Rector of Chedsey, 1505–1508; Wood, *Ath. Ox.* i. 553.

Mayo.

JOHN BELL, provided 1493, Nov. 4; Brady, ii. 154. Suffragan of London, 1499; Sarum, 1501; Exeter, 1501; Lichfield, 1503; Wells, 1519; Canterbury, 1503; d. 1541.

Achonry (Achadensis).

SIMON, a Cistercian of Quarr. Suffragan of Canterbury, 1386; London, 1385; Lichfield, 1387; Winchester, 1387–1395; d. 1398.

RICHARD BELMER, provided 1424, April 12; Brady, ii. 183. Suffragan of Worcester, 1426–1433; Hereford, 1430.

JAMES BLAKEDON, provided 1442, Oct. 15; Brady, ii. 184. Suffragan of Wells, 1443–1451; Sarum, 1443–1449; Worcester, 1443. Made Bishop of Bangor, 1453; d. 1464. See p. 89, above.

THOMAS FORT or FORD, provided 1492, Oct. 5 (Ware) or Oct. 8; Brady, ii. 186. Suffragan of Lincoln, 1496–1504; Lichfield, 1494–1495; see Churton's *Life of Smith*, p. 45. Rector of Southwick, 1504. Prior of S. Mary's, Huntingdon, 1496; Stone, 1493, Aug. 26. Rector of Edgmond, 1494; Abbot of Bourn, 1501. Rector of Willesford, 1501. Has a Bull to hold three benefices with his see, 1500.

Enaghdun (Enachdunensis).

GILBERT ——, Suffragan of Winchester, 1313; Worcester, 1313. Consecrated shortly before 1308, July 15.

JAMES ——, succeeds, and is translated to Connor, 1322; *Papal Letters*, ii. 238; Theiner, p. 229.

ROBERT LE PETIT, Suffragan of Sarum, 1326. Translated from Clonfert. See above.

HENRY TWILLOWE, Suffragan of Exeter, 1395–1398; Sarum, 1397; Winchester, 1399–1401. Provided 1394, Aug. 26; Brady, ii. 150.

John Britt, provided 1402, Jan. 25. Suffragan of Winchester, 1402; York, 1417–1420. One John Wym pays his predecessor's fees, as elect, in 1408; Brady, ii. 150.

John Bonere or Camere, provided 1421, June 9; Brady, ii. 151. Suffragan of Sarum, 1421; Exeter, 1438. Provost of S. Elizabeth, Winchester, and Rector of Cheddington. Presented 1433, Feb., to Melford, Suffolk; exchanges in 1439 for Bromley, d. Rochester.

Thomas Salscot, paid his fees as elect, 1446, July 29; Brady, ii. 152. Suffragan of Lincoln, 1449; Exeter, 1458. Rector of Willoughby, Lincolnshire, 1448, Dec. 6.

Thomas Barrett, Suffragan of Wells, 1482–1485. Paid his fees as elect, 1458, May 17.

Rathlur. [The see was removed to Derry by Innocent IV; Theiner, p. 48.]

Thomas Ingilby, provided 1471, April 3. Consecrated 1471, April 23, in the Church of the English Hospitallers in regione Arenula at Rome, by Peter Othanensis, James, ep. S. Angeli de Lombardis and Anthony Assolicensis; Brady, i. 323. Rector of Sutton Bonnington, 1476. Vicar of Southweald, 1498, Oct. 8. Suffragan of Lincoln, 1484; London, 1489. Died shortly before 1499, July 8; Newcourt, ii. 645.

APPENDIX VI

A List of the Bishops of Sodor and Man, from the Conquest to the Union of the See with the Province of York.

A PERFECT list of the Bishops of Sodor and Man is a desideratum. The common lists contain many names which ought not to be there, e.g. Hildebert, Bishop of Le Mans, Robert Waldby, Adurensis (Aire in Gascony), and others which perhaps belong to Iceland or to the Scottish see of the Isles. The following is founded on the list at the end of the Manx Chronicle down to 1374, edited by Dr. Munch in 1859, and compared with the results of the investigations of Mr. A. W. Moore, *Diocesan History*, 1893.

It must however still be considered as provisional; there may be confusion of the see with the Scottish see of the Isles, and in some cases complications owing to the conflicting claims of the kings of Scotland and England and of the popes during the schism. But a good deal may be accounted for by the competing claims of aspirants to titles which were of little value, and which in the cases of the poor Scottish and Irish sees were looked on, like titles *in partibus*, merely as qualifications for the office of Suffragan.

> ROLWER, buried at Maughold. Before the date of Godred Crovan, A.D. 1066.
>
> WILLIAM, died in the days of Godred Crovan.

A.D. **1113.** WIMUND or AUMUND MAC AULAY, a monk of Savigny and Furness, to which latter Abbey the election of the Bishop belonged, was consecrated by Thomas II, Archbishop of York, 1109 × 1114, and was deposed or died in 1151. W. Newburgh, lib. i. c. 14; above, p. 42.

A.D. **1151.** JOHN, a monk of Savigny or of Seez, was consecrated 1151 × 1153 by Henry Murdac, Archbishop of York; *Hist. Ebor.*; MS. Cotton, Cleopatra, C. 4; M. Paris, ii. 188; R. de Monte, A.D. 1151.

A.D. **1160.** GAMALIEL consecrated by Roger, Archbishop of York, 1154 × 1161. Buried at Peterborough, where his obit was kept, July 13; *Mon. Angl.* ii. 362.

RONALD or REGINALD, a Norwegian, possibly identical with Nemar, mentioned in the Icelandic Annals about 1170.

CHRISTIAN OF ARGYLE, possibly the Bishop of Whithern of that name, 1154–1186. Buried at Benchor in Ulster.

MICHAEL, a Manxman. Buried at Fountains, 1203 (or 1193; Munch, p. 29).

A.D. 1210. NICOLAS OF MEAUX, Abbot of Furness, 'consecratus ad Ebudas ubi tunc per 40 annos episcopus non fuerat ex quo Nemarus (Reinarus) episcopus in vivis erat;' *Ann. Island*. Langebek, iii. 77. He was probably consecrated by the Archbishop of Drontheim; he is said to have d. 1217; Munch, p. 17; but unless there were two of the name, he was alive in 1224 attesting a York charter as 'quondam' Bishop of Man and the Isles; see Archbishop Gray's *Register* (Surtees), pp. 5, 11, 149, 154; and to be buried at Benchor. Compare *Monasticon*, vol. vi. p. 1186; Appendix xlvi; *Chron. de Melsa*, i. 380.

A.D. 1217. REGINALD or RONALD, of the blood royal; d. 1225, and was buried at Rushen; *Chron. Manniae*, p. 29. He was probably appointed by the King of Man, and consecrated in Norway, for we find

A.D. 1219. A Bishop of Man, elected by the monks of Furness and consecrated by the Archbishop of Dublin, unable to get possession of his see owing to the hostility of the King. This was probably John Mac Ivar or Harfare. The see was apparently under Caducan, Bishop of Bangor, as official, when King Reginald wrote to the Pope, 1219, Sept. 22; Theiner, p. 11. In 1219, Nov. 9, Honorius III charges Pandulf and the Bishop of Carlisle to see him righted: and 1224, May 15, the same Pope allows him to resign, retaining the episcopal insignia. It is uncertain whether this was Nicolas or John; *Reg. Gray*, 149, 154; *Vatican Papers*. John, Bishop of Man, is found as late as 1230 attesting a deed of Archbishop Walter Gray (Le Neve). Cf. *Reg. Gray*, p. 225. He was buried at Jervaux.

A.D. 1226. SIMON OF ARGYLE, consecrated at Bergen by the Archbishop Peter of Drontheim. His Statutes, a° 1229, are in the *Concilia*; Wilkins, i. 664. He must be the Bishop of Sodor who has leave from Gregory IX to resign the administration of Lesmore (Argyle) in 1236; see Theiner, *Vet. Mon.* p. 33. He was bishop eighteen years, and d. 1247, Feb. 28 (*Chron. Manniae*), or more probably 1243, as we find in

A.D. 1244, Feb. 15. Innocent IV, at the request of the monks of Furness, allows the Archbishop of York, with permission from the Archbishop of Drontheim, to consecrate the Bishop of Man; see *Papal Letters*, Rolls Series, i. 206; Archbishop Gray's *Register*, p. 198. However, the see was vacant six years after the death of Simon, during which time Laurence, Archdeacon of Man, was elected and sent to Norway for the royal assent and consecration. The latter being delayed from the informality of his election, he returned to be re-elected, and was lost at sea with King Harald and his court, in 1249.

A.D. 1252. RICHARD, an Englishman, consecrated at Rome by Serlo, Archbishop of Drontheim. Consecrated S. Mary's, Rushen, in the fifth year of his pontificate, 1257; ruled twenty-three years; d. 1275, and was buried at Furness, Mar. 25.

A.D. 1275. MARK OF GALLOWAY, intruded by the King of Scots in opposition to Abbot Gilbert of Rushen, who had been elected by the clergy and people of Man; MS. Cleop. A. 1; W. Newb. ed. Howlett, p. 569; and consecrated at Tunsberg (Munch, p. 146) in Norway by John, Archbishop of Drontheim; ruled twenty-four years; then exiled for three, during which time the Isles were under interdict; afterwards he returned, and d. about 1303; buried at S. German's. His Constitutions of 1291 are in the *Concilia*, Wilkins, ii. 175.

A.D. **1305**. ALLAN, consecrated by Jorund of Drontheim; has safe conduct from Edward I; Prynne, iii. 1111; d. 1321, Feb. 13; buried at Rothsay.

A.D. **1321**. GILBERT MAC LELLAN, consecrated by Eilulf of Drontheim; subscribes 1327. According to the *Chron. Manniae* he ruled only two and a half years.

A.D. **1328**. BERNARD DE LINTON, Abbot of Arbroath, elected, 1328; Bishop, 1329; consecrated in Norway; ruled four years, and d. 1333; buried at Kilwinin.

A.D. **1334**. THOMAS, consecrated in Norway; ruled eighteen years, and d. 1348, Sept. 20; buried at Scone.

A.D. **1348**. WILLIAM RUSSELL, elected by the clergy of Man; consecrated at Avignon, 1349, May 3, by Bertrand of Ostia (Munch, p. 167); d. 1374, April 21, and buried at Furness.

A.D. **1374**. JOHN DONKAN, consecrated at Avignon, 1374, Nov. 25, by Simon Langham, Bishop of Praeneste. He is said to have died in 1380, and the see of the Isles to have been separated from Sodor and Man. John Donkan is translated from Sodor ad ecclesiam Cathadensem, and John Sprotton provided to Sodor, at Rome, 1392, Sept. 27; *Bullarium Ordin. Praedicatorum.* Yet as John Donkan, Bishop of Sodor, he proves the will of Andrew Skot, knight, in the Commissary's Court at London in 1391, Dec. 13. He must therefore have been the John 'Sodorensis Episcopus' who has a Suffragan's commission from the Bishop of Salisbury, 1390, Jan. 14. He ordains in London 1391 and 1392, and in 1388, July 14, was sent by Richard II to treat with the sons of the Lord of the Isles; *Foedera*, vii. 592. Possibly he survived until 1408; see Moore, *Dioc. Hist.* p. 78.

A.D. **1410**, July 20. RICHARD PAYL, Bishop of Dromore, translated to Sodor; Brady, *Episcopal Succession*, i. 106; and 1425, July 30, John Burgherlin, a Franciscan, is provided, on a vacancy by death; Wadding, *Ann. Minoritarum*, and Brady, p. 106. Nothing is known of either of these bishops unless Richard be identical with the next named. Brady, however, i. 162, mentions the provision of Michael Anchira to Sodor, 1422, Apr. 20.

A.D. **1429**. RICHARD PULLEY. He held a visitation at Peel in 1429; see Moore, *Dioc. Hist.* pp. 88, 94; *Lex Scripta Manniae* (Douglas, 1819), p. 11.

A.D. **1432**. ANDREW, episcopus Sodorensis, made a payment at Rome, Jan. 24; Brady, i. 107.

A.D. **1441**, Nov. 6. JOHN, elect of Sodor, paid 660 florins; Brady, p. 107.

A.D. **1449**. JOHN GREEN. He held the living of Dunchurch in Warwickshire, 1414, Nov. 22, and had leave to hold it in commendam, 1449, Feb. 9. He exchanged it for Little Billing, 1452, Feb. 6; and the living of Gumchester for Stow Nine Churches, 1459, Mar. 21. In 1462 he resigned Stow; and 1464, Dec. 13, was collated to Merseham in Kent. He acted as Suffragan in Lichfield in 1452, ordaining Dec. 23, and soon after must have resigned his see. 1447, Apr. 17, John Grenei, electus ep. Insulanus in Hibernia, made his payment; Brady, p. 107. Whether the Johannes Insulensis and the Johannes Sodorensis, who ordained in the dioceses of Canterbury and Lichfield, were identical, it is difficult to determine.

A.D. **1455**. THOMAS BURTON, a Franciscan. Provided 1445, Sept. 25 (Wadding). Made his will, 1458, Feb. 18; Le Neve (citing Booth's *Register*), p. 357: ed. Hardy, iii. 326.

A.D. 1458. THOMAS OF KIRKHAM, Abbot of Vale Royal. Provided 1458, June 21 ; Willis, i. 366; was alive in 1472, and d. 1480 (Hardy); d. before 1475 (*Monasticon*, v. 701).

A.D. 1472. ANGUSIUS SODORENSIS, consecrated in the church of S. Bartholomew in Urbe, Sept. 27, by James, Bp. Sanctangeli de Lombardis, John Rossensis, and Ceccantonio of Caserta ; Brady, i. pf. xxii.

A.D. 1480. RICHARD OLDHAM, Abbot of Chester (royal assent, 1453, June 2); d. 1485, Oct. 13, and was buried at Chester. He was Bishop in 1483; elected about 1475 (*Monasticon*, ii. 375).

A.D. 1487, Jan. 19. JOHN, elect of Sodor and the Isles. Pays fees ; Brady, i. 162.

A.D. 1487. HUAN HESKETH or BLACKLEACH, fl. 1487–1521. Richard Hesketh, Esq., of Rufforth, by will dated Aug. and proved Nov. 13, 1520, appoints his brother Hugh, Busshopp of Manne, executor ; Maynwaring, fo. 30.

A.D. 1523, June 18. JOHN HOWDEN, a Dominican, provided in the place of Hugh, Bishop of Sodor and Man ; Brady, i. 170. Signs agreement with the clergy in 1532 ; Moore, pp. 96, 138.

A.D. 1530, Feb. 21. CERTARDUS, provided to the see Sardorensi in Hibernia ; Brady, i. 107.

[A.D. 1530. THOMAS STANLEY, who on the authority of Wood, Kennett, and Willis was supposed to have been consecrated in 1530, deposed in 1544, restored in 1555, and died in 1568 or 1570, has under Mr. Moore's researches disappeared from the list ; *Dioc. Hist.* p. 96 ; Brady, 107 sq.]

A.D. 1546. HENRY MAN ; above, p. 103. The see of Man was united with the province of York by Act of Parliament, 33 Hen. VIII, c. 31, 1542.

A.D. 1555, June 21. THOMAS STANLEY, provided at Rome with dispensation for illegitimacy ; Brady, i. 107 ; ii. 303. Rector of Wigan, 1558; d. 1570; see Bridgeman's *Wigan* (Chetham Soc.), i. 131–141.

APPENDIX VII

Catalogues of British and Welsh Bishops before the Union of the Welsh Sees with the English Province of Canterbury.

The following lists are given in this place in order to clear away at once all questionable legendary matter from the subject. There is probably some little truth in each of them; but so much that is simple fabrication that I have thought it better to insert them whole here, with what remarks I have to make on them, than to mix with undoubtedly true records any portion of what stands on so weak a foundation. Many however of the least impossible names are discussed in the *Dictionary of Christian Biography* with ample references.

I. PROVINCE OF LONDON.

1. List of the Metropolitans of London.

The following list was formed by Jocelin of Furness, a monk of the twelfth century. It may be found in Stow, Ussher, Godwin, and the Fasti of Le Neve. Wharton unhesitatingly rejects the whole, and it is indeed a most uncritical performance. The compiler however evidently acted in good faith, and put down no more than he found in his authorities.

I. Theonus or Theanus.	In the time of Lucius. He built the church of S. Peter, Cornhill.
II. Elvanus.	The messenger of Lucius to Rome; consecrated by Pope Eleutherus.
III. Cadar or Cadoc.	He occurs also at Caer Leon.
IV. Obinus.	Ussher, *Antiqq.* p. 67.
V. Conan.	
VI. Palladius.	Plainly a mistake arising from Palladius's being called a Bishop of Britain.
VII. Stephanus.	
VIII. Iltutus.	He was Abbot of the school of Llandaff; perhaps there is a confusion between Landavensis and Londinensis.
Augulus.	A Saint and Bishop of Augusta; commemorated in *Martyrologies*, Feb. 7; AA. SS. Feb. ii. 16, 17.

IX. Theodwin or Dedwin. X. Theodred.	Both these names have a Saxon look; the latter is evidently a late Bishop who has been misplaced. Perhaps Dedwin may be a mistake for Bedwini, who was King Arthur's Bishop in Cornwall; *Dict. Chr. Biog.* i. 304.
XI. Hilarius.	
XII. Guitelinus.	Mentioned by Nennius (p. 77) as having quarrelled with Ambrosius. Geoffrey of Monmouth says he was sent to Armorica for aid against the Saxons; *Hist.* vi. cc. 2-6.
XIII. Vodinus.	Put to death 453. He opposed the marriage of Vortigern and Rowena.
XIV. Theonus II.	He was translated from Gloucester in 542, and fled into Wales in A.D. 586; Geoffrey, *Hist.* xi. 3, 10.

To these are to be added :—

I. Restitutus.	Bishop of London. He attended the Council of Arles in A.D. 314.
II. Fastidius.	Bishop of Britain in A.D. 431.

One of Merlin's prophecies was that the pall of London should be translated to Dorobernia. Gilbert Foliot, Bishop of London, in the twelfth century attempted to reject the obedience of Canterbury on the ground that London was once the metropolitan see of Britain. S. Gregory seems to have designed that it should continue to be so.

2. Suffragan Sees.

1. Winchester. (*a*) Constans.	Bishop at the second consecration of the cathedral in A.D. 293; Rudborne, *Ang. Sac.* i. 186.
(*b*) Diruvianus.	Appointed by King Arthur in 519; Geoffrey, *Hist.* ix. 15.
2. Gloucester. (*a*) Eldad.	Bishop cir. 488; cf. Geoffrey, *Hist.* viii. c. 7.
(*b*) Theonus.	Translated to London, 542; *Hist.* xi. 3.
3. Congresbury.	A see was founded here by Fagan and Duvian which lasted till 721, when it was removed to a village called Tydenton, now Wells. Daniel, the last bishop, was consecrated in 704; doubtless the same as Daniel, Bishop of Winchester; Can. Well. *Ang. Sac.* i. 553.
4. Silchester. Mauganius.	Made Bishop in A.D. 519; Geoffrey, *Hist.* ix. 15.
5. Cornwall.	Whitaker makes Rumon, Mancus, Barnic, Conoglas, and Elidius, Bishops of Cornwall. Kenstec, Bishop of Dinurrin in Cornwall, made his profession to Archbishop Ceolnoth; see *Councils*, ed. Haddan and Stubbs, i. 674.

II. PROVINCE OF YORK.

1. Metropolitans.

The following list is given by Godwin, and is probably a fabrication of his own age.

(*a*) Sampson.	Godwin says he was appointed by Lucius. William Harrison, quoted by Ussher, names Theodosius; others Faganus; Ussher, *Antiqq.* p. 72.
(*b*) Taurinus.	He was Bishop of Evreux, Ebroicensis. Similarly, Eutropius, Bishop of Saintes, has been placed at Canterbury; Ussher, p. 30.

(c) Eborius.	Was at Arles in A.D. 314.
(d) Sampson or Sanxo.	Was expelled by the Saxons, took refuge in Gaul, and, according to one account, transferred the pall to Dol, in Brittany. He was consecrated in 490, and flourished in A.D. 507; Geoffrey, *Hist.* viii. 12, ix. 8.
(e) Piran.	Was appointed by King Arthur in the place of Sampson at Christmas, A.D. 522; Geoffrey, *Hist.* ix. 8.
(f) Thadiacus Thadiocenus or Cadiocenus.	Retired into Wales in A.D. 586; Geoffrey, *Hist.* xi. 10.

2. Alclud or Dumbarton.

Eledanius.	Appointed by King Arthur in 519; Geoffrey, *Hist.* ix. 15.

3. Candida Casa. (Whithern.)

S. Ninian.	The Apostle of the Picts; Bede, *H. E.* iii. 4; consecrated by the Pope, probably Siricius, in 394; Ailr. V. *Niniani*, ed. Forbes, p. 142. He built a church of stone. Retired to Ireland 420; d. Sept. 16, 432.

4. Man.

(a) Amphibalus. (b) Germanus. (c) Conondrius. (d) Romulus.	447. All consecrated by S. Patrick.
(e) Machutus. (f) Contentus.	498; d. 553 or 554.
(g) Baldus. (h) Malchus. (i) Torkinus. (j) Brandan.	Conan d. 648.

III. PROVINCE OF CAER LEON.

1. Metropolitans.

The following list is from *The Chronicles of the Ancient British Church*, Lond. 1851. It is described as 'taken from a MS. of the late Iolo Morganwg (Edward Williams) as given by the Rev. J. Williams in his Antiquities of the Cymry.'

1. Dyfan. 2. Ffagan. 3. Elldeyrn.	The missionaries of Eleutherus.
4. Edelfeid.	Adelfius, who was at Arles 314. He is claimed also by Colchester and Lincoln.
5. Cadwr. 6. Cynan. 7. Ilan. 8. Llewyr. 9. Cyhelyn.	
10. Guitelin.	He appears also in the list for London.
11. Tremorinus.	Died about 490, and was succeeded by Dubritius of Llandaff; after this time the primacy seems to have wavered between Llandaff and Menevia; Geoff. *Hist.* viii. 10.

2. Bishops of Menevia.

The following list is formed from a collation of the two given by Godwin, one of which is from Giraldus; *Itiner. Kambr.* lib. ii. c. 1 (ed. Dimock, pp. 102 sq.). It will be remarked that there is much repetition of names, that some of them are claimed by Llandaff and Bangor, while others are obvious mistakes and interpolations. From the year 1023 the succession is ascertained from the *Annales Cambriae*; but even here are great difficulties. Freeman and Jones, *Hist. of S. David's*, p. 357, reproduce Giraldus's list with orthographical emendations.

1. S. David, Metropolitan.	Said to have been consecrated at Jerusalem, and elected to the see of Caer Leon on the death or retirement of Dubritius at the synod of Llandewi Brevi in 519. He died in 542. The *Annales Cambriae* place his death in A. D. 601, which seems more likely, as he is not mentioned by Gildas.
2. Kenauc or Cynoc.	Bishop of Llanbadarn, translated to Menevia on S. David's death; Geoffrey, xi. 3. He died 606; *Annales Cambriae*. He was perhaps a Suffragan. Ussher places his death in 597, and makes Teilo succeed him as Metropolitan.
3. Teilo, Metropolitan.	Possibly succeeded to the Metropolitan office on S. David's death. He was Bishop of Llandaff, which he retained, consecrating Ismael to Menevia. Ussher thinks him the same as Sampson who is said to have taken the pall to Dol. He is called also Eliud. ῞Ηλιος = Samson.
4. Ismael.	Consecrated by S. Teilo. Suffragan.
5. Morwal.	(Morfael.)
6. Haernunen.	
7. Elwaed.	Perhaps Metropolitan, with see at Bangor. Flor. 768–807.
8. Gurnueu.	(Gwrnwen.)
9. Lendivord.	See below, under *Lumbert*.
10. Gorwyst.	(Gwrgwyst.)
11. Gogan.	(Gwgan.)
12. Cledauc.	
13. Anian.	
14. Elvoed.	See 7.
15. Elduven.	
16. Elauc or Elvaeth.	See 7.
17. Mascoed.	(Maelsgwyd.)
18. Sadernueu.	Perhaps Satubin, who died 831; *Ann. Cambr.*
19. Catellus.	
20. Sulhaithuay.	
21. Novis.	Regnavit 840, d. 873. The *Brut* says Meuric reigned 840, d. 873.
22. Etwal.	(Idwal.)
23. *Asser.*	A Monk of S. David's, not Bishop of Menevia, but of Sherborne, 889–909.
24. Arthwael.	
25. *Sampson.*	Placed here by Giraldus, who says that he retired to Dol with his pall. One Sampson was really Bishop of Dol, and died, according to Ussher, in 599.
26. Ruelin.	
27. *Rodherich.*	Died 961; *Ann. Cambr.* Misplaced.
28. Elguni.	Elwin, succeeded by Morbiw (Jones and Freeman, p. 357).
29. Lunverd.	Died 942 or 944. Consecrated by Ethelred of Canterbury; above, p. 37.
30. Nergu.	Vercu, a good Bishop, d. 948.
31. Sulhidir.	

32. Eneuris.	Died 944 or 946; *Ann. Cambr.* and *Brut.* (Jones and Freeman insert Hubert and Ivor.)
Ritherch.	Died 961 or 962; ib.
33. Morgeneu.	Slain A.D. 998 or 1000; *Ann. Cambr.* Could he be the same as Tremerinus, who was consecrated by Sigeric or Elfric of Canterbury? above, p. 37.
34. Nathan.	
35. Jeuan.	
36. Argustil.	
37. Morgeneuth.	Died 1023 or 1025.
38. Ervin or Ernun.	Died 1038 or 1040.
39. Tramerin.	(Trahearn) died 1055. He was Suffragan to Ethelstan of Hereford.
40. Joseph.	Died 1061 or 1064.
41. Bleithud.	Died 1071. Consecrated by [Ethelnoth] the Archbishop of Canterbury.
42. Sulghein.	Resigned in 1076, returned in 1078, and died in 1088; *Ann. Menev.*
43. Abraham.	1076–1078.
44. Rithmarch.	1088–1096.
45. Wilfrid or Griffith.	1096. He was suspended, and afterwards restored, by S. Anselm; Eadmer, p. 72. Died 1115.

3. Bishops of Llandaff.

The list of Bishops of Llandaff seems to be the work of Godwin, who was himself Bishop of that see, and to have been drawn from the *Liber Landavensis*, with some attempts at fixing order and dates.

1. Dubritius, Metropolitan.	Consecrated, according to Benedict of Gloucester, by Germanus in 449; according to Geoffrey in 490. He was Bishop of Llandaff, and kept his Metropolitical seat there, as his successor did at Menevia. Resigned in 519, and d. 522, Geoffrey; d. 612; *Ann. Cambr.*
2. Teilo, Metropolitan.	Succeeded to Llandaff, 519, to the Metropolitan dignity in A.D. 542. He was consecrated at Jerusalem with S. David. He retired into France during the prevalence of the *ictericia pestis*, and returned in 596; d. 604; Ussher.
3. Oudoceus.	Succeeded Teilo. He is said to have been consecrated at Canterbury.
4. Ubilwyn or Berthgwin[1].	Contemporary with King Brochmail. One Brocmail was at the massacre of Bangor in 613; one died in A.D. 662.
5. Aidan[1].	
6. Elgistil[1].	
7. Lunapeius[1].	A disciple of S. Teilo in 596; Ussher.
8. Comegern[1].	Contemporary with Ywyr, King of Gwynedd.
9. Argustil[1].	(Aristobulus.)
10. Guodoloiu[1].	(Guitelinus.)
11. Edilfiu.	(Adelfius.)
12. Grecielus.	
13. Berthguin.	
14. Trychan.	Contemporary with King Fernmail. One King of this name died 763, another 775, another flourished 880.
15. Elvogus.	See Menevia, 7, and Bangor.

[1] Mr. Rees, in the notes to the *Liber Landavensis*, makes Ubilwyn, Aidan, Elgistil, Lunapeius, Comegern, Argustil, Guodoloiu, and Gurwan, 'Chorepiscopi.' Other names of Bishops, not to be even conjecturally assigned, occur in the Iolo MSS.

16. Catgwaret.	
17. Cerenhir.	
18. Novis.	Cf. Menevia, 21.
19. Gulfrid.	
20. Nudd.	
21. Cimeliauc.	Consecrated by Ethelred of Canterbury; d. 927.
22. Libiau.	Consecrated by Athelm or Wulfhelm of Canterbury; d. 929.
23. Marchluith.	See Bangor. Died 943. (Marcant, signs a charter in 932; Kemble, *C. D.* 1107.)
24. Pater.	Flor. 955.
25. Gucan or Gucaur.	Consecrated between A.D. 963 and 971 by S. Dunstan, Brihthelm, Alfwold, Ethelwold, Oswald; *Liber Landav.* p. 509.
26. Bledri or Bedreu.	Consecrated after 993 by Alfric of Canterbury; *Liber Landav.* p. 518.
27. Joseph.	Consecrated Oct .1, 1022 or 1027, by Ethelnoth; *Liber Landav.* p. 518. Died 1043 or 1046.
28. Herewald.	Consecrated at Pentecost, 1056, at London, by Kinsy, Archbp. of York; d. 1103. According to the Chapter of S. David's (Giraldus, iii. 57), he was consecrated by Joseph of S. David's.

On both the preceding lists we must remark—

1. That they abound with anachronisms.

2. That the names are repeated in a way that seems to show that there were a few well-known ones, and that these were indefinitely varied to fill up a certain space in the lists.

3. That some names belong to other sees, as Elvod and Asser.

4. Some, as Catellus, may have been Princes, not Bishops.

5. But we must not be too critical; the successive Bishops may have had similar names. The mischief is that the historical portions are so corrupt as to throw suspicion on all that is known from these sources only.

4. Suffragan Sees.

These are given by Godwin as Llandaff, Bangor, Llanelwy, Exeter, Bath, Hereford, and Ferns; from Hoveden as Llandaff, Bangor, S. Asaph, Worcester, Hereford, Chester, and Llanbadarn.

1. S. Asaph or Llanelwy.	
(a) Kentigern.	A Briton, consecrated by an Irish Bishop for Glasgow; was in exile in Wales and founded a see at Llanelwy; cons. 540; 543 came to Llanelwy; d. 612; *Ann. Cambr.*
(b) S. Asaph.	Succeeded Kentigern in A.D. 560.
(c) Chebur.	940; temp. Howel Dha. See also *Ann. Cambr.* ad annum 501.
2. Bangor.	
(a) Daniel.	Consecrated by Dubritius or S. David about 522. He died 584; *Ann. Cambr.*; Geoff. *Hist.* xi. 3.
(b) Elvod.	Or Elbod, Archbishop of Gwynedd; fl. A.D. 768 to 809.
(c) Mordav.	Fl. 940. Perhaps the same as Marchluith of Llandaff, who died in 943.

3. Llanbadarn.
   (a) S. Patern. | Consecrated at Jerusalem with S. David about 518; ruled twenty-one years.
   (b) S. Cynoc. | Succeeded at Menevia, on S. David's death.
   (c) Idnerth. | Slain by his townspeople (date unknown). Was the last Bishop.

4. Anglesey.
   S. Kebius. | Corinnius, son of Solomon, Duke of Cornwall, consecrated by S. Hilary of Poitiers; founded Holy Head, A.D. 369.

APPENDIX VIII

INDEXES OF BISHOPS ARRANGED UNDER THEIR SEES.

CANTERBURY.

	Conse-cration.	Accession.	First Signature.	Last Signature.	Death.
Augustine.........	597	597			604
Laurentius	604	604	604		619
Mellitus	604	619			624
Justus	604	624			627
Honorius	627	627			653
Deusdedit.........	655	655			664
Theodore	668	668	676	686	690
Berchtwald	693	693	693	706	731
Tatwine	731	731	732		734
Nothelm	735	735	736	738	740
Cuthberht.........	736	741	741	758	758
Bregowine	759	759	762	764	765
Jaenberht.........	766	766	765	789	790
Æthelheard	793	793	793	805	805
Wulfred	805	805	805	831	832
Feologild	832	832			832
Ceolnoth	833	833	833	868	870
Æthelred	870	870	875	882	889
Plegmund.........	890	890	895	910	914
Athelm	909	914			923
Wulfhelm.........	914	923	923	941	942
Odo	926	942	942	959	959
Dunstan	957	960	960	988	988
Ethelgar	980	988	988		989
Sigeric	985	990	994		994
Ælfric	990	995	995	1005	1005
Ælfheah	984	1005	1007	1012	1012
Lyfing	999	1013	1015	1019	1020
Æthelnoth	1020	1020	1020	1035	1038
Eadsige.........	1035	1038	1042	1052	1050
Robert	1044	1051			1070
Stigand...........	1043	1052	1052		1072

CANTERBURY (CONTINUED).

	Conse-cration.	Accession.		Conse-cration.	Accession.
Lanfranc	1070	1070	Thomas Bourchier.........	1435	1454
Anselm	1093	1093	John Morton	1479	1486
Ralph d'Escures	1108	1114	Henry Dean	1496	1501
William de Corbeuil	1123	1123	William Warham	1502	1503
Theobald	1139	1139	Thomas Cranmer	1533	1533
Thomas Becket	1162	1162	Reginald Pole.............	1556	1556
Richard	1174	1174	Matthew Parker............	1559	1559
Baldwin	1180	1185	Edmund Grindal............	1559	1576
Hubert Walter	1189	1193	John Whitgift.............	1577	1583
Stephen Langton............	1207	1207	Richard Bancroft	1597	1604
Richard le Grant	1229	1229	George Abbot.............	1609	1611
Edmund Rich	1234	1234	William Laud	1621	1633
Boniface.......................	1245	1245	William Juxon	1633	1660
Robert Kilwardby	1273	1273	Gilbert Sheldon	1660	1663
John Peckham	1279	1279	William Sancroft	1678	1678
Robert Winchelsey.........	1294	1294	John Tillotson.............	1691	1691
Walter Reynolds	1308	1313	Thomas Tenison...........	1692	1695
Simon Mepeham	1328	1328	William Wake	1705	1716
John Stratford	1323	1333	John Potter.................	1715	1737
Thomas Bradwardine	1349	1349	Thomas Herring............	1738	1747
Simon Islip	1349	1349	Matthew Hutton	1743	1757
Simon Langham	1362	1366	Thomas Secker	1735	1758
William Whittlesey.........	1362	1368	Frederick Cornwallis......	1750	1768
Simon Sudbury..............	1362	1375	John Moore.................	1775	1783
William Courtenay	1370	1381	Charles Manners Sutton .	1792	1805
Thomas Arundel	1374	1397	William Howley	1813	1828
Roger Walden	1398	1398	John Bird Sumner.........	1828	1848
Thomas Arundel restored		1399	Charles Thomas Longley	1836	1862
Henry Chicheley............	1408	1414	Archibald Campbell Tait	1856	1868
John Stafford	1425	1443	Edward White Benson...	1877	1883
John Kemp	1419	1452	Frederick Temple	1869	1896

LONDON.

	Conse-cration.	First Signat.	Last Signat.	Death.		Conse-cration.	First Signat.	Last Signat.	Death.
Mellitus	604				Sigheah		772	772	
Cedd..............	654			664	Aldberht		775	786	
Wine	662			675	Eadgar		789		
Earconwald......	675	676	692	693	Coenwalh		793	793	
Waldhere.........	693	694	704		Eadbald				
Ingwald		706	737	745	Heathoberht ...	794	798	799	801
Ecgwulf	745	747	759		Osmund	802	803	805	

LONDON (CONTINUED).

	Conse-cration.	First Signat.	Last Signat.	Death.		Conse-cration.	First Signat.	Last Signat.	Death.
Æthelnoth		811	816		Dunstan	957	959		
Ceolberht.........		824	839		Ælfstan	961	961	995	
Deorwulf.........		860–2			Wulfstan II ...	996	997	1003	
Swithulf					Ælfwin	1004	1004	1012	
Ælfstan				898	Elfwig	1014	1015	1035	
Wulfsige	898	910	910		Elfweard	1035	1035	1044	1044
Heahstan.........					Robert Champart }	1044	1046	1050	
Theodred.........		926	951		William	1051			1075
Wulfstan									
Brihthelm		953	959						

	Conse-cration.	Accession.		Conse-cration.	Accession.
Hugh d'Orivalle	1075	1075	William Barons	1504	1504
Maurice	1086	1086	Richard Fitz James	1497	1506
Richard de Beames	1108	1108	Cuthbert Tunstall	1522	1522
Gilbert Universalis	1128	1128	John Stokesley	1530	1530
Robert de Sigillo	1141	1141	Edmund Bonner...........	1540	1540
Richard de Beames	1152	1152	Nicolas Ridley	1547	1550
Gilbert Foliot	1148	1163	Edmund Grindal...........	1559	1559
Richard Fitz Neal	1189	1189	Edwin Sandys	1559	1570
Wm. de S. Mere l'Eglise...	1199	1199	John Aylmer	1577	1577
Eustace de Fauconberg ...	1221	1221	Richard Fletcher	1589	1595
Roger Niger	1229	1229	Richard Bancroft	1597	1597
Fulk Bassett	1244	1244	Richard Vaughan	1596	1604
Henry de Wengham	1260	1260	Thomas Ravis...............	1605	1607
Henry de Sandwich	1263	1263	George Abbot...............	1609	1610
John Chishull	1274	1274	John King	1611	1611
Richard Gravesend	1280	1280	George Mountain	1617	1621
Ralph Baldock	1306	1306	William Laud...............	1621	1628
Gilbert Segrave	1313	1313	William Juxon	1633	1633
Richard Newport............	1317	1317	Gilbert Sheldon	1660	1660
Stephen Gravesend	1319	1319	Humfrey Henchman	1660	1663
Richard Bintworth	1338	1338	Henry Compton............	1674	1675
Ralph Stratford	1340	1340	John Robinson	1710	1714
Michael Northburgh	1355	1355	Edmund Gibson	1716	1723
Simon Sudbury	1362	1362	Thomas Sherlock	1728	1748
William Courtenay	1370	1375	Thomas Hayter	1749	1761
Robert Braybrook	1382	1382	Richard Osbaldeston......	1747	1762
Roger Walden	1398	1405	Richard Terrick	1757	1764
Nicolas Bubwith	1406	1406	Robert Lowth	1766	1777
Richard Clifford	1401	1407	Beilby Porteus	1777	1787
John Kemp	1419	1421	John Randolph	1799	1809
William Gray	1426	1426	William Howley	1813	1813
Robert Fitzhugh	1431	1431	Charles J. Blomfield	1824	1828
Robert Gilbert	1436	1436	Archibald C. Tait	1856	1856
Thomas Kemp	1450	1450	John Jackson	1853	1869
Richard Hill	1489	1489	Frederick Temple	1869	1885
Thomas Savage..............	1493	1496	Mandell Creighton...... .	1891	1897
William Warham	1502	1502			

WINCHESTER.

	Conse-cration.	First Signat.	Last Signat.	Death.		Conse-cration.	First Signat.	Last Signat.	Death.
Birinus	634			650	Swithun	852	858	862	862
Agilbert	650				Alfred............	862	868	871	
Wine	662				Tunberht			877	879
Leutherius	670		676	676	Denewulf	879	882	904	908
Haeddi............	676	676	701	705	Frithstan	909	909	931	933
Daniel	705	705	737	745	Beornstan	931	931	934	934
Hunferth	744	747	749		Ælfheah.........	934	934	951	951
Cyneheard	754	755	766		Ælfsige	951	952	958	
Æthelheard					Brihthelm	960	960	961	963
Ecgbald		778	781		Æthelwold......	963	964	984	984
Dudd					Ælfheah	984	985	1005	
Cyneberht		786	801		Kenulf	1005			1006
Alhmund	802	803	805		Æthelwold ...	1006	1007	1012	
Wigthen		811	828	833?	Ælfsige	1014	1014	1033	
Herefrith.........	825	825	826	833?	Alwin............	1032	1033	1046	1047
Eadmund	833?	836	838		Stigand	1043	1077	1053	
Helmstan.........	838	838	841						

	Conse-cration.	Accession.		Conse-cration.	Accession.
Walkelin	1070	1070	John White..................	1554	1556
William de Giffard	1107	1107	Robert Horne...............	1561	1561
Henry de Blois.............	1129	1129	John Watson	1580	1580
Richard of Ilchester........	1174	1174	Thomas Cowper............	1571	1584
Godfrey de Lucy	1189	1189	William Wickham	1584	1595
Peter des Roches..........	1205	1205	William Day	1596	1596
William de Raleigh.........	1239	1244	Thomas Bilson	1596	1597
Aylmer de Valence	1260	1260	James Montagu	1608	1616
John Gervais..................	1262	1262	Launcelot Andrewes......	1605	1619
Nicolas of Ely	1266	1268	Richard Neile...............	1608	1628
John of Pontoise	1282	1282	Walter Curll	1628	1632
Henry Woodlock............	1305	1305	Brian Duppa	1638	1660
John Sendale	1316	1316	George Morley	1660	1662
Rigaud Asser	1320	1320	Peter Mews	1673	1684
John Stratford	1323	1323	Jonathan Trelawney......	1685	1707
Adam Orlton..................	1317	1333	Charles Trimnell	1708	1721
William Edendon............	1346	1346	Richard Willis	1715	1723
William of Wykeham	1367	1367	Benjamin Hoadly	1716	1734
Henry Beaufort	1398	1405	John Thomas	1747	1761
William of Waynflete......	1447	1447	Brownlow North	1771	1781
Peter Courtenay	1478	1487	George Pretyman	1787	1820
Thomas Langton	1483	1493	Charles R. Sumner	1826	1827
Richard Fox..................	1487	1501	Samuel Wilberforce	1845	1869
Thomas Wolsey	1514	1529	Edward Harold Browne	1864	1873
Stephen Gardiner	1531	1531	Anthony William Thorold	1877	1892
John Poynet..................	1550	1551	Randall Thomas Davidson	1891	1895

ELY.

	Consecration.	Accession.		Consecration.	Accession.
Hervey	1092	1109	Nicolas West	1515	1515
Nigel	1133	1133	Thomas Goodrich	1534	1534
Geoffrey Riddell	1174	1174	Thomas Thirlby	1540	1554
William Longchamp	1189	1189	Richard Cox	1559	1559
Eustace	1198	1198	Martin Heaton	1600	1600
John of Fountains	1220	1220	Launcelot Andrewes	1605	1609
Geoffrey de Burgh	1225	1225	Nicolas Felton	1617	1619
Hugh Norwold	1229	1229	John Buckeridge	1611	1628
William de Kilkenny	1255	1255	Francis White	1626	1631
Hugh Belsham	1257	1257	Matthew Wren	1635	1638
John Kirby	1286	1286	Benjamin Laney	1660	1667
William of Louth	1290	1290	Peter Gunning	1670	1675
Ralph Walpole	1289	1299	Francis Turner	1683	1684
Robert Orford	1302	1302	Simon Patrick	1689	1691
John Keeton	1310	1310	John Moore	1691	1707
John Hotham	1316	1316	William Fleetwood	1708	1714
Simon Montacute	1334	1337	Thomas Green	1721	1723
Thomas de Lisle	1345	1345	Robert Butts	1733	1738
Simon Langham	1362	1362	Thomas Gooch	1737	1747
John Barnet	1362	1366	Matthias Mawson	1739	1754
Thomas Arundel	1374	1374	Edmund Keene	1752	1771
John Fordham	1382	1388	James Yorke	1774	1781
Philip Morgan	1419	1426	Thomas Dampier	1802	1808
Lewis of Luxemburg	1415	1438	Bowyer E. Sparke	1810	1812
Thomas Bourchier	1435	1443	Joseph Allen	1834	1836
William Gray	1454	1454	Thomas Turton	1845	1845
John Morton	1479	1479	Edward Harold Browne	1864	1864
John Alcock	1472	1486	James Russell Woodford	1873	1873
Richard Redman	1471	1501	Alwyne Compton	1886	1886
James Stanley	1506	1506			

LEICESTER AND DORCHESTER.

	Consecration.	First Signat.	Last Signat.	Death.		Consecration.	First Signat.	Last Signat.	Death.
Cuthwine	680			691	Alcheard			888	897–8
Wilfrid [administered 692–705]	664				Ceolwulf	909			
					Winsige		926	934	
					Oskytel	950	952	956	
					Leofwine			965	
The see was joined to Lichfield 705–737.					Eadnoth		975	975	
					Æscwige		979	1002	
Torhthelm	737	747	758	764	Ælfhelm	1002	1002	1005	
Eadberht	764	764	781		Eadnoth	1006	1012	1012	1016
Unwona		786	799		Æthelric	1016	1020	1032	1034
Werenberht	802	803	814		Eadnoth	1034	1042	1046	1050
Hrethun	816	816	839		Ulf	1050	1050		
Aldred					Wulfwig	1053	1055		1067
Ceolred	840	840	869		Remigius	1067			1092

LINDSEY.

	Conse-cration.	First Signat.	Last Signat.	Death.		Conse-cration.	First Signat.	Last Signat.	Death.
Eadhed.............	678				Ceolwulf	767	767	794	796
Æthelwin	680				Eadulf	796	796	836	
Eadgar		706			Berhtred		838	869	
Cyneberht				732					
Alwig	733	737	747	750	Leofwine		953	965	
Eadulf	750	758			Sigeferth		997	1004	

LINCOLN.

	Conse-cration.	Accession.		Conse-cration.	Accession.
Robert Bloett	1094	1094	John Taylor	1552	1552
Alexander	1123	1123	John White..................	1554	1554
Robert de Chesney	1148	1148	Thomas Watson...........	1557	1557
Walter de Coutances	1183	1183	Nicolas Bullingham	1560	1560
Hugh of Grenoble	1186	1186	Thomas Cowper............	1571	1571
William of Blois	1203	1203	William Wickham	1584	1584
Hugh de Wells...............	1209	1209	William Chaderton	1579	1595
Robert Grosteste	1235	1235	William Barlow	1605	1608
Henry Lexington............	1254	1254	Richard Neile...............	1608	1614
Richard Gravesend	1258	1258	George Monteigne	1617	1617
Oliver Sutton	1280	1280	John Williams	1621	1621
John Dalderby	1300	1300	Thomas Winniffe	1642	1642
Henry Burghersh	1320	1320	Robert Sanderson	1660	1660
Thomas Beck	1342	1342	Benjamin Laney...........	1660	1663
John Gynwell	1347	1347	William Fuller	1663	1667
John Bokyngham............	1363	1363	Thomas Barlow	1675	1675
Henry Beaufort	1398	1398	Thomas Tenison	1692	1692
Philip Repingdon............	1405	1405	James Gardiner	1695	1695
Richard Fleming	1420	1420	William Wake	1705	1705
William Gray	1426	1431	Edmund Gibson	1716	1716
William Alnwick	1426	1436	Richard Reynolds	1721	1723
Marmaduke Lumley........	1430	1450	John Thomas	1744	1744
John Chadworth	1452	1452	John Green............. ...	1761	1761
Thomas Rotherham........	1468	1472	Thomas Thurlow	1779	1779
John Russell................	1476	1480	George Pretyman	1787	1787
William Smith	1493	1496	George Pelham	1803	1820
Thomas Wolsey	1514	1514	John Kaye	1820	1827
William Atwater	1514	1514	John Jackson	1853	1853
John Longlands	1521	1521	Christopher Wordsworth	1869	1869
Henry Holbeche	1538	1547	Edward King	1885	1885

LICHFIELD, CHESTER AND COVENTRY.

	Consecration.	First Signat.	Last Signat.	Death.		Consecration.	First Signat.	Last Signat.	Death.
Diuma	656			658	Herewin		816	817	
Ceollach	658				Æthelwald	818	822	825	828
Trumhere	659			662	Hunberht	828			
Jaruman	662			667	Cyneferth		836	841	
Ceadda	664			672	Tunberht		844	857	
Wynfrid	672				Ella, or Ælfwin		926	935	
Saxulf	675	676		691	Alfgar, or Wulgar		941	948	
Headda	691	693	706		Kinsige		949	963	
Aldwine, Wor...	721	727	736	737	Winsige		964	973	
Hwitta	737	747	749		Ælfheah	973	975	1002	
Hemele	752				Godwine		1004	1008	
Cuthfrith	765		767		Leofgar	1020			
Berhthun	768	774	777		Brihtmær	1026	1026	1033	1039
Hygberht	779	779	801		Wulfsige	1039	1039	1053	1053
Aldulf		803	814		Leofwine	1053			1067

	Consecration.	Accession.		Consecration.	Accession.
Peter	1072	1072	Rowland Lee	1534	1534
Robert de Limesey	1086	1086	Richard Sampson	1536	1543
Robert Peche	1121	1121	Ralph Bayne	1554	1554
Roger de Clinton	1129	1129	Thomas Bentham	1560	1560
Walter Durdent	1149	1149	William Overton	1580	1580
Richard Peche	1161	1161	George Abbot	1609	1609
Gerard la Pucelle	1183	1183	Richard Neile	1608	1610
Hugh Nonant	1188	1188	John Overall	1614	1614
Geoffrey Muschamp	1198	1198	Thomas Morton	1616	1619
William Cornhill	1215	1215	Robert Wright	1622	1632
Alexander Stavenby	1224	1224	Accepted Frewen	1644	1644
Hugh Pateshull	1240	1240	John Hackett	1661	1661
Roger Weseham	1245	1245	Thomas Wood	1671	1671
Roger Longespée	1258	1258	William Lloyd	1680	1692
Walter de Langton	1296	1296	John Hough	1690	1699
Roger Northburgh	1322	1322	Edward Chandler	1717	1717
Robert Stretton	1360	1360	Richard Smallbrooke	1724	1731
Walter Skirlaw	1386	1386	Frederick Cornwallis	1750	1750
Richard le Scrope	1386	1386	John Egerton	1756	1768
John Burghill	1396	1398	Brownlow North	1771	1771
John Catterick	1414	1415	Richard Hurd	1775	1775
William Heyworth	1420	1420	James Cornwallis	1781	1781
William Booth	1447	1447	Henry Ryder	1815	1824
Nicolas Close	1450	1452	Samuel Butler	1836	1836
Reginald Boulers	1451	1453	James Bowstead	1838	1840
John Hales	1459	1459	John Lonsdale	1843	1843
William Smith	1493	1493	George Augustus Selwyn	1841	1867
John Arundel	1496	1496	Wm. Dalrymple Maclagan	1878	1878
Geoffrey Blyth	1503	1503	Augustus Legge	1891	1891

SHERBORNE.

	Conse-cration.	First Signat.	Last Signat.	Death.		Conse-cration.	First Signat.	Last Signat.	Death.
Aldhelm	705			709	Æthelbald				
Forthere	709	712	737		Sighelm		926	932	933
Herewald	736	737	766		Alfred	933	933	943	943
Æthelmod		778	789		Wulfsige		943	958	958
Denefrith	793	794	796		Ælfwold	958	961	975	978
Wigberht		801	816		Æthelsige	978	979	990	
Ealhstan	824	824	862	867	Wulfsige	992	993	1001	
Heahmund	868	868	870	871	Æthelric	1001	1002	1009	
Ethelheah	872		877		Ethelsige		1012	1014	
Alfsige, or ... ⎱ Wulfsige ... ⎰	883	889	892		Brihtwy				
					Ælfmaer	1017	1020	1022	
Asser		900	904	909	Brihtwy	1023	1023	1045	
Æthelweard		910			Elfwold	1045	1046	1050	1058
Waerstan					Herman	1045	1058		1078

RAMSBURY.

	Conse-cration.	First Signat.	Last Signat.	Death.		Conse-cration.	First Signat.	Last Signat.	Death.
Æthelstan	909	910			Wulfgar	981	982	984	
Odo		927			Sigeric	985	985		
Ælfric					Ælfric	990		994	1005
Osulf		952	970	970	Brihtwold	1005	1005	1045	1045
Ælfstan		974	980	981	Herman	1045	1045		1078

SALISBURY.

	Conse-cration.	Accession.		Conse-cration.	Accession.
Osmund	1078	1078	Robert Wyville	1330	1330
Roger	1107	1107	Ralph Erghum	1375	1375
Jocelin de Bohun	1142	1142	John Waltham	1388	1388
Hubert Walter	1189	1189	Richard Mitford	1390	1395
Herbert le Poor	1194	1194	Nicolas Bubwith	1406	1407
Richard le Poor	1215	1217	Robert Hallam	1407	1407
Robert Bingham	1229	1229	John Chandler	1417	1417
William of York	1247	1247	Robert Neville	1427	1427
Giles Bridport	1257	1257	William Aiscough	1438	1438
Walter de la Wyle	1263	1263	Richard Beauchamp	1449	1450
Robert Wickhampton	1274	1274	Lionel Woodville	1482	1482
Walter Scammell	1284	1284	Thomas Langton	1483	1485
Henry Brandeston	1287	1287	John Blyth	1493	1493
William de la Corner	1289	1289	Henry Dean	1496	1500
Nicolas Longespée	1292	1292	Edmund Audley	1480	1502
Simon of Ghent	1297	1297	Lorenzo Campegio		1524
Roger Mortival	1315	1315	Nicholas Shaxton	1535	1535

SALISBURY (CONTINUED).

	Conse-cration.	Accession.		Conse-cration.	Accession.
John Salcot, or Capon......	1534	1539	Richard Willis	1715	1721
John Jewell	1560	1560	Benjamin Hoadly	1716	1723
Edmund Gheast	1560	1571	Thomas Sherlock	1728	1734
John Piers.....................	1576	1577	John Gilbert	1740	1748
John Coldwell	1591	1591	John Thomas	1747	1757
Henry Cotton	1598	1598	Robert Hay Drummond	1748	1761
Robert Abbot	1615	1615	John Thomas	1744	1761
Martin Fotherby	1618	1618	John Hume...................	1756	1766
Robert Townson	1620	1620	Shute Barrington	1769	1782
John Davenant..............	1621	1621	John Douglas	1787	1791
Brian Duppa.................	1638	1641	John Fisher..................	1803	1807
Humfrey Henchman	1660	1660	Thomas Burgess............	1803	1825
John Earle	1662	1663	Edward Denison	1837	1837
Alexander Hyde	1665	1665	Walter Kerr Hamilton ...	1854	1854
Seth Ward	1662	1667	George Moberly............	1869	1869
Gilbert Burnet	1689	1689	John Wordsworth	1885	1885
William Talbot...............	1699	1715			

WELLS.

	Conse-cration.	First Signat.	Last Signat.	Death.		Conse-cration.	First Signat.	Last Signat.	Death.
Athelm	909				Ælfwin	997	997	998	
Wulfhelm	914				Lyfing	999	999	1012	
Ælfheah	923	930	937		Æthelwin ...)	1013	1018	1023	
Wulfhelm	938	938	955		Brihtwin ...)	1013	1018		
Brihthelm	956	956	973	973	Merewit	1027	1031	1032	1033
Cyneward	973	975		975	Duduc	1033	1042	1050	1060
Sigar	975	979	995	997	Giso	1061	1061		1088

BATH AND WELLS.

	Conse-cration.	Accession.		Conse-cration.	Accession.
John of Tours	1088	1088	Walter Hasleshaw.........	1302	1302
Godfrey.......................	1123	1123	John Drokensford	1309	1309
Robert	1136	1136	Ralph of Shrewsbury ...	1329	1329
Reginald Fitz Jocelin	1174	1174	John Barnet	1362	1363
Savaric	1192	1192	John Harewell	1366	1366
Jocelin	1206	1206	Walter Skirlaw	1386	1386
Roger..........................	1244	1244	Ralph Erghum	1375	1388
William Button...............	1248	1248	Henry Bowett	1401	1401
Walter Giffard	1265	1265	Nicolas Bubwith............	1406	1407
William Button...............	1267	1267	John Stafford	1425	1425
Robert Burnell..............	1275	1275	Thomas Beckington	1443	1443
William of March...........	1293	1293	Robert Stillington	1466	1466

BATH AND WELLS (CONTINUED).

	Conse-cration.	Accession.		Conse-cration.	Accession.
Richard Fox	1487	1491	William Piers	1630	1632
Oliver King	1493	1495	Robert Creighton	1670	1670
Hadrian de Castello	1502	1504	Peter Mews	1673	1673
Thomas Wolsey	1514	1518	Thomas Ken	1685	1685
John Clerk	1523	1523	Richard Kidder	1691	1691
William Knight	1541	1541	George Hooper	1703	1704
William Barlow	1536	1549	John Wynne	1715	1727
Gilbert Bourne	1554	1554	Edward Willes	1743	1744
Gilbert Berkeley	1560	1560	Charles Moss	1766	1774
Thomas Godwin	1584	1584	Richard Beadon	1789	1802
John Still	1593	1593	George Henry Law	1812	1824
James Montagu	1608	1608	Richard Bagot	1829	1845
Arthur Lake	1616	1616	Robert John Eden	1847	1854
William Laud	1621	1626	Arthur Charles Hervey	1869	1869
Leonard Mawe	1628	1628	George Wyndham } Kennion	1882	1894
Walter Curll	1628	1629			

CREDITON.

	Conse-cration.	First Signat.	Last Signat.	Death.		Conse-cration.	First Signat.	Last Signat.	Death.
Eadulf	909	926	934	934	Ælfwold	988	988	1008	
Æthelgar	934	934	953	953	Eadnoth		1012	1019	
Ælfwold		953	970	972	Lyfing	1027	1027	1045	1046
Sideman	973	974	975	977	Leofric	1046	1046	1065	1072
Ælfric	977	979	985						

CORNWALL.

	Conse-cration.	First Signat.	Last Signat.	Death.		Conse-cration.	First Signat.	Last Signat.	Death.
Conan		931	934		Ealdred		993	1002	
Daniel		955	959		Burwold		1018		
Comoere					Lyfing		1027		
Wulfsige		967	980						1046

EXETER.

	Conse-cration.	Accession.		Conse-cration.	Accession.
Osbern	1072	1072	John the Chantor	1186	1186
William Warelwast	1107	1107	Henry Marshall	1194	1194
Robert Chichester	1138	1138	Simon of Apulia	1214	1214
Robert Warelwast	1155	1155	William Briwere	1224	1224
Bartholomew	1162	1162	Richard Blondy	1245	1245

EXETER (CONTINUED).

	Consecration.	Accession.		Consecration.	Accession.
Walter Bronscomb	1258	1258	William Cotton	1598	1598
Peter Wyville	1280	1280	Valentine Cary	1621	1621
Thomas Button.............	1292	1292	Joseph Hall................	1627	1627
Walter Stapleton	13 8	1308	Ralph Brownrigg	1642	1642
James Berkeley	1327	1327	John Gauden	1660	1660
John Grandison	1327	1327	Seth Ward	1662	1662
Thomas Brentingham	1370	1370	Antony Sparrow	1667	1667
Edmund Stafford	1395	1395	Thomas Lamplugh	1676	1676
John Catterick	1414	1419	Jonathan Trelawney	1685	1689
Edmund Lacy	1417	1420	Offspring Blackall	1708	1708
George Neville.............	1458	1458	Launcelot Blackburn......	1717	1717
John Booth	1465	1465	Stephen Weston	1724	1724
Peter Courtenay	1478	1478	Nicolas Claggett...........	1732	1742
Richard Fox	1487	1487	George Lavington	1747	1747
Oliver King	1493	1493	Frederick Keppel	1762	1762
Richard Redman	1471	1496	John Ross	1778	1778
John Arundel	1496	1502	William Buller	1792	1792
Hugh Oldham	1505	1505	Henry Reg. Courtenay..	1794	1797
John Harman, or Voysey	1519	1519	John Fisher.................	1803	1803
Miles Coverdale	1551	1551	George Pelham	1803	1807
James Turberville	1555	1555	William Carey	1820	1820
William Alley	1560	1560	Christopher Bethell	1824	1830
William Bradbridge.........	1571	1571	Henry Phillpotts	1831	1831
John Wolton	1579	1579	Frederick Temple	1869	1869
Gervas Babington	1591	1595	EdwardHenryBickersteth	1885	1885

DUNWICH.

	Consecration.	First Signat.	Last Signat.	Death.		Consecration.	First Signat.	Last Signat.	Death.
Felix..............	630			647	Aldberht				
Thomas	647			652	Ecglaf...........				
Boniface	652			669	Heardred		781	789	
Bisi	669				Aelhun	790	790	793	797
Æcci..............	673				Tidferth	798	798	816	
Æscwulf					Waeremund ..		824		
Eadulf		747			Wilred	825	825	845	
Cuthwine........					Æthelwulf				

ELMHAM.

	Consecration.	First Signat.	Last Signat.	Death.		Consecration.	First Signat.	Last Signat.	Death.
Baduvine.........	673	693			Eanferth.........		758		
Nothbert		706			Æthelwulf.....		781		
Heatholac					Alcheard		786	811	
Æthelfrith	736				Sibba		814	816	

ELMHAM (CONTINUED).

	Conse-cration.	First Signat.	Last Signat.	Death.		Conse-cration.	First Signat.	Last Signat.	Death.
Hunferth					Ælfgar		1001	1018	1021
Humbert		824	838	870	Ælfwine.........	1016	1019	1022	
Eadulf		956	964		Ælfric...........				1038
Ælfric					Ælfric...........	1038			
Theodred.........		975			Stigand	1043		1046	
Theodred.........			995		Æthelmaer......	1047		1055	
Ælfstan	995	997	1001						

THETFORD AND NORWICH.

	Conse-cration.	Accession.		Conse-cration.	Accession.
Herfast	1070	1070	John Parkhurst	1560	1560
William de Beaufeu.........	1086	1086	Edmund Freke	1572	1575
Herbert Losinga	1091	1091	Edmund Scambler	1561	1585
Everard of Montgomery ...	1121	1121	William Redman	1595	1595
William de Turbe...........	1146	1146	John Jegon	1603	1603
John of Oxford.............	1175	1175	John Overall	1614	1618
John de Gray	1200	1200	Samuel Harsnett	1609	1619
Pandulf Masca	1222	1222	Francis White	1626	1629
Thomas Blunville...........	1226	1226	Richard Corbett...........	1628	1632
William de Raleigh	1239	1239	Matthew Wren	1635	1635
Walter Suffield, or Cal-thorp	1245	1245	Richard Montagu	1628	1638
			Joseph Hall..................	1627	1641
Simon de Wauton	1258	1258	Edward Reynolds	1661	1661
Roger Skerning	1266	1266	Antony Sparrow...........	1667	1676
William Middleton	1278	1278	William Lloyd...........	1675	1685
Ralph Walpole..............	1289	1289	John Moore	1691	1691
John Salmon	1299	1299	Charles Trimnell	1708	1708
William Ayermin............	1325	1325	Thomas Green	1721	1721
Antony Bek	1337	1337	John Leng	1723	1723
William Bateman...........	1344	1344	William Baker	1723	1727
Thomas Percy	1356	1356	Robert Butts	1733	1733
Henry Spenser	1370	1370	Thomas Gooch	1737	1738
Alexander Tottington	1407	1407	Samuel Lisle	1744	1748
Richard Courtenay	1413	1413	Thomas Hayter	1749	1749
John Wakering	1416	1416	Philip Young	1758	1761
William Alnwick	1426	1426	Lewis Bagot	1782	1783
Thomas Brown..............	1435	1436	George Horne..............	1790	1790
Walter le Hart	1446	1446	Charles Manners Sutton ..	1792	1792
James Goldwell	1472	1472	Henry Bathurst	1805	1805
Thomas Jane.................	1499	1499	Edward Stanley...........	1837	1837
Richard Nykke.............	1501	1501	Samuel Hinds..............	1849	1849
William Repps, or Rugg...	1536	1536	John Thomas Pelham ...	1857	1857
Thomas Thirlby	1540	1550	John Sheepshanks.........	1893	1893
John Hopton..................	1554	1554			

WORCESTER.

	Conse-cration.	First Signat.	Last Signat.	Death.		Conse-cration.	First Signat.	Last Signat.	Death.
Bosel	680				Æthelhun	915			922
Oftfor	692	693			Wilferth.........	922			929
Æcgwine.........	693		716	717	Cynewold	929	930	957	957
Wilfrid	717	718	743	743	Dunstan	957	958		
Milred	743	743	774	775	Oswald	961	961	991	992
Waeremund ...	775	775			Aldulf............	992	994	1001	1002
Tilhere............	777	777	780	781	Wulfstan	1003	1004	1022	1023
Heathored	781	781	798	798	Leofsin	1016	1016	1022	1033
Deneberht	798	801	817	822	Brihteah.........	1033	1033		1038
Eadberht	822	822	845	848	Lyfing (succ. 1038)		1027	1045	1046
Aelhun	848	848	869	872	Ealdred	1044	1044		
Werefrith	873	873	904	915	Wulfstan	1062			1095

	Conse-cration.	Accession.		Conse-cration.	Accession.
Samson	1096	1096	Tideman of Winchcomb	1393	1395
Theulf	1115	1115	Richard Clifford............	1401	1401
Simon........................	1125	1125	Thomas Peverell	1397	1407
John of Pageham	1151	1151	Philip Morgan............	1419	1419
Alfred......	1158	1158	Thomas Polton	1420	1426
Roger........................	1164	1164	Thomas Bourchier	1435	1435
Baldwin......................	1180	1180	John Carpenter	1444	1444
William Northall	1186	1186	John Alcock	1472	1476
Robert Fitz Ralph	1191	1191	Robert Morton	1487	1487
Henry de Soilli	1193	1193	John de Gigliis	1497	1497
John of Coutances	1196	1196	Silvester de Gigliis..... ...	1498	1498
Mauger	1200	1200	Julius de Medicis	adm.	1521
Walter Gray................	1214	1214	Jerome Ghinucci	1512	1522
Silvester of Evesham	1216	1216	Hugh Latimer............	1535	1535
William of Blois	1218	1218	John Bell	1539	1539
Walter Cantilupe............	1237	1237	Nicolas Heath............	1540	1543
Nicolas of Ely	1266	1266	John Hooper	1551	1552
Godfrey Giffard	1268	1268	Richard Pates..............	1541 ?	1554
William Gainsborough ...	1302	1302	Edwin Sandys	1559	1559
Walter Reynolds	1308	1308	Nicolas Bullingham	1560	1571
Walter Maidstone	1313	1313	John Whitgift..............	1577	1577
Thomas Cobham	1317	1317	Edmund Freke	1571	1584
Adam Orlton........	1317	1327	Richard Fletcher	1589	1593
Simon Montacute............	1334	1334	Thomas Bilson	1596	1596
Thomas Hemenhale	1337	1337	Gervas Babington	1591	1597
Wulstan Bransford	1339	1339	Henry Parry	1607	1610
John Thoresby................	1347	1350	John Thornborough	1593	1616
Reginald Brian...............	1350	1352	John Prideaux	1641	1641
John Barnet	1362	1362	George Morley	1660	1660
William Whittlesey.........	1362	1364	John Gauden	1660	1662
William de Lynn	1362	1368	John Earle	1662	1662
Henry Wakefield............	1375	1375	Robert Skinner	1637	1663

WORCESTER (CONTINUED).

	Consecration.	Accession.		Consecration.	Accession.
Walter Blandford	1665	1671	Brownlow North	1771	1774
James Fleetwood	1675	1675	Richard Hurd	1775	1781
William Thomas	1678	1683	Ffolliot H. W. Cornewall	1797	1808
Edward Stillingfleet	1689	1689	Robert James Carr	1824	1831
William Lloyd	1680	1699	Henry Pepys	1840	1841
John Hough	1690	1717	Henry Philpott	1861	1861
Isaac Maddox	1736	1743	John James Stewart Perowne	1891	1891
James Johnson	1752	1759			

HEREFORD.

	Consecration.	First Signat.	Last Signat.	Death.		Consecration.	First Signat.	Last Signat.	Death.
Putta (succ. 676)	669			688	Beonna	823	824	825	
Tyrhtel	688		693		Eadulf		836		
Torhthere	710		727		Cuthwulf	837	838	857	
Wahlstod					Mucel				
Cuthberht	736	737			Deorlaf		866	884	
Podda	741		747		Cynemund	888			
Hecca		758			Eadgar		901	930	
Ceadda			770		Tidhelm		930	934	
Aldberht	777	777	781		Wulfhelm		939	940	
Esne		785			Ælfric		941	951	
Ceolmund		788	793		Athulf		973	1012	
Utel		798	799		Æthelstan	1012	1012	1052	1056
Wulfheard	800	801	822		Leofgar	1056			1056
					Walter	1061			1079

	Consecration.	Accession.		Consecration.	Accession.
Robert Losinga	1079	1079	Richard Swinfield	1283	1283
Gerard	1096	1096	Adam Orlton	1317	1317
Reinhelm	1107	1107	Thomas Charlton	1327	1327
Geoffrey de Clive	1115	1115	John Trilleck	1344	1344
Richard	1121	1121	Lewis Charlton	1361	1361
Robert de Bethune	1131	1131	William Courtenay	1370	1370
Gilbert Folliot	1148	1148	John Gilbert	1372	1375
Robert de Maledon	1163	1163	John Trevenant	1389	1389
Robert Folliot	1174	1174	Robert Mascall	1404	1404
William de Vere	1186	1186	Edmund Lacy	1417	1417
Giles de Bruce	1200	1200	Thomas Polton	1420	1420
Hugh de Mapenore	1216	1216	Thomas Spofford	1422	1422
Hugh Folliot	1219	1219	Richard Beauchamp	1449	1449
Ralph Maidstone	1234	1234	Reginald Boulers	1451	1451
Peter d'Aigueblanche	1240	1240	John Stanbery	1448	1453
John Breton	1269	1269	Thomas Milling	1474	1474
Thomas Cantilupe	1275	1275	Edmund Audley	1480	1492

HEREFORD (CONTINUED).

	Conse-cration.	Accession.		Conse-cration.	Accession.
Hadrian de Castello.........	1502	1502	Gilbert Ironside	1689	1691
Richard Mayew	1504	1504	Humfrey Humphries......	1689	1701
Charles Booth	1516	1516	Philip Bisse................	1710	1713
Edward Fox	1535	1535	Benjamin Hoadly	1716	1721
John Skip	1539	1539	Henry Egerton	1724	1724
John Harley	1553	1553	James Beauclerk............	1746	1746
Robert Parfew, or Wharton	1536	1554	John Harley	1787	1787
John Scory	1551	1559	John Butler.................	1777	1788
Herbert Westfaling........	1586	1586	Ffolliott H. W. Cornewall	1797	1803
Robert Bennett.............	1603	1603	John Luxmore	1807	1808
Francis Godwin	1601	1617	George Is. Huntingford...	1802	1815
Augustine Lindsell	1633	1634	Edward Grey	1832	1832
Matthew Wren...............	1635	1635	Thomas Musgrave	1837	1837
Theophilus Field	1619	1635	Renn D. Hampden.........	1848	1848
George Coke.................	1633	1636	James Atlay	1868	1868
Nicolas Monk	1661	1661	John Percival	1895	1895
Herbert Croft	1662	1662			

SELSEY.

	Conse-cration.	First Signat.	Last Signat.	Death.		Conse-cration.	First Signat.	Last Signat.	Death.
Eadberht	709				Beornege	909	926	929	
Eolla..............		714			Wulfhun		931	940	
Sigga	733	737	747		Ælfred		944	953	
Aluberht					Ealdhelm		963	979	
Osa		765	770		Æthelgar	980	980	987	
Gislehere.........		780	781		Ordbriht........	989	990	1008	1009
Tota		785			Ælfmaer.........	1009	1012	1031	
Wiohthun		789	805		Æthelric.........	1032	1032	1033	1038
Æthelwulf		811	816		Grimketel	1039	1042	1046	1047
Coenred		824	838		Hecca...........	1047	1050		1057
Gutheard		860	862		Æthelric	1058			

CHICHESTER.

	Conse-cration.	Accession.		Conse-cration.	Accession.
Stigand	1070	1070	Simon de Wells	1204	1204
Gosfrid	1087	1087	Richard le Poor............	1215	1215
Ralph Luffa	1091	1091	Ralph of Wareham	1218	1218
Seffrid d'Escures	1125	1125	Ralph Neville	1224	1224
Hilary	1147	1147	Richard Wych	1245	1245
John Greenford	1174	1174	John Climping	1254	1254
Seffrid II	1180	1180	Stephen Berksted	1262	1262

CHICHESTER (CONTINUED).

	Conse-cration.	Accession.		Conse-cration.	Accession.
Gilbert de S. Leofard	1288	1288	Antony Watson	1596	1596
John Langton	1305	1305	Launcelot Andrewes	1605	1605
Robert Stratford	1337	1337	Samuel Harsnett	1609	1609
William de Lynn	1362	1362	George Carleton	1618	1619
William Reade	1368	1368	Richard Montagu	1628	1628
Thomas Rushook	1383	1385	Brian Duppa	1638	1638
Richard Mitford	1390	1390	Henry King	1642	1642
Robert Waldby	1387	1396	Peter Gunning	1670	1670
Robert Reade	1394	1397	Ralph Brideoake	1675	1675
Stephen Patrington	1415	1417	Guy Carleton	1672	1678
Henry de la Ware	1418	1418	John Lake	1683	1685
John Kemp	1419	1421	Simon Patrick	1689	1689
Thomas Polton	1420	1421	Robert Grove	1691	1691
John Rickingale	1426	1426	John Williams	1696	1696
Simon Sydenham	1431	1431	Thomas Manningham	1709	1709
Richard Praty	1438	1438	Thomas Bowers	1722	1722
Adam Moleyns	1446	1446	Edward Waddington	1724	1724
Reginald Pecocke	1444	1450	Francis Hare	1727	1731
John Arundel	1459	1459	Matthias Mawson	1739	1740
Edward Story	1468	1478	William Ashburnham	1754	1754
Richard Fitz James	1497	1503	John Buckner	1798	1798
Robert Sherborn	1505	1508	Robert James Carr	1824	1824
Richard Sampson	1536	1536	Edward Maltby	1831	1831
George Day	1543	1543	William Otter	1836	1836
John Scory	1551	1552	Phil. N. Shuttleworth	1840	1840
John Christopherson	1557	1557	Ashurst T. Gilbert	1842	1842
William Barlow	1536	1559	Richard Durnford	1870	1870
Richard Curteis	1570	1570	Ernest Roland Wilberforce	1882	1895
Thomas Bickley	1586	1586			

ROCHESTER.

	Conse-cration.	First Signat.	Last Signat.	Death.		Conse-cration.	First Signat.	Last Signat.	Death.
Justus	604	604			Waeremund		785	803	
Romanus	624			627	Beornmod		805	842	
Paulinus (succ. 633)	625			644	Tatnoth	844	844		
					Badenoth				
Ithamar	644				Waeremund		860	862	
Damian	655			664	Cuthwulf	868			
Putta	669				Swithulf			880	897
Cuichelm	676				Ceolmund		904	909	
Gebmund	678		693		Cyneferth		926	931	
Tobias	693	706		726	Burrhric		934	946	
Eadulf	727	735	738		Ælfstan		964	995	
Dunn	741		747		Godwine	995	995		
Eardulf	747	747	765		Godwine			1046	
Diora		775	781		Siward	1058	1058		1075

ROCHESTER (CONTINUED).

	Consecration.	Accession.		Consecration.	Accession.
Arnostus	1076	1076	John Fisher	1504	1504
Gundulf	1077	1077	John Hilsey	1535	1535
Ralph d'Escures	1108	1108	Nicolas Heath	1540	1540
Ernulf	1115	1115	Henry Holbeche	1538	1544
John	1125	1125	Nicolas Ridley	1547	1547
Ascelin	1142	1142	John Poynet	1550	1550
Walter	1148	1148	John Scory	1551	1551
Waleran	1182	1182	Maurice Griffin	1554	1554
Gilbert Glanville	1185	1185	Edmund Gheast	1560	1560
Benedict de Sansetun	1215	1215	Edmund Freke	1572	1572
Henry Sandford	1227	1227	John Piers	1576	1576
Richard Wendene	1238	1238	John Young	1578	1578
Laurence de S. Martin	1251	1251	William Barlow	1605	1605
Walter de Merton	1274	1274	Richard Neile	1608	1608
John Bradfield	1278	1278	John Buckeridge	1611	1611
Thomas Ingaldsthorpe	1283	1283	Walter Curll	1628	1628
Thomas of Wouldham	1292	1292	John Bowle	1630	1630
Haymo Hethe	1319	1319	John Warner	1638	1638
John Sheppey	1353	1353	John Dolben	1666	1666
William Whittlesey	1362	1362	Francis Turner	1683	1683
Thomas Trilleck	1364	1364	Thomas Spratt	1684	1684
Thomas Brinton	1373	1373	Francis Atterbury	1713	1713
William Bottlesham		1389	Samuel Bradford	1718	1723
John Bottlesham	1400	1400	Joseph Wilcocks	1721	1731
Richard Young	1400	1404	Zachary Pearce	1748	1756
John Kemp	1419	1419	John Thomas	1774	1774
John Langdon	1422	1422	Samuel Horsley	1788	1793
Thomas Brown	1435	1435	Thomas Dampier	1802	1802
William Wells	1437	1437	Walker King	1809	1809
John Lowe	1433	1444	Hugh Percy	1827	1827
Thomas Rotherham	1468	1468	George Murray	1814	1827
John Alcock	1472	1472	Joseph Cotton Wigram	1860	1860
John Russell	1476	1476	Thomas Legh Claughton	1867	1867
Edmund Audley	1480	1480	Anthony William Thorold	1877	1877
Thomas Savage	1493	1493	Randall Thomas Davidson	1891	1891
Richard Fitz James	1497	1497	Edward Stuart Talbot	1895	1895

OXFORD.

	Consecration.	Accession.		Consecration.	Accession.
Robert King	1527	1545	John Howson	1619	1619
Hugh Curwen	1555	1567	Richard Corbet	1628	1628
Vacant 1568–1589.			John Bancroft	1632	1632
John Underhill	1589	1589	Robert Skinner	1637	1641
Vacant 1592–1604.			William Paul	1663	1663
John Bridges	1604	1604	Walter Blandford	1665	1665

OXFORD (CONTINUED).

	Conse-cration.	Accession.		Conse-cration.	Accession.
Nathaniel Crewe	1671	1671	John Butler....................	1777	1777
Henry Compton	1674	1674	Edward Smallwell	1783	1788
John Fell	1676	1676	John Randolph	1799	1799
Samuel Parker	1686	1686	Charles Moss	1807	1807
Timothy Hall	1688	1688	William Jackson	1812	1812
John Hough	1690	1690	Edward Legge	1816	1816
William Talbot..............	1699	1699	Charles Lloyd	1827	1827
John Potter	1715	1715	Richard Bagot	1829	1829
Thomas Secker	1735	1737	Samuel Wilberforce	1845	1845
John Hume	1756	1758	John Fielder Mackarness	1870	1870
Robert Lowth	1766	1766	William Stubbs	18ⁿ4	1889

PETERBOROUGH.

	Conse-cration.	Accession.		Conse-cration.	Accession.
John Chamber	1541	1541	White Kennett	1718	1718
David Poole	1557	1557	Robert Clavering	1725	1729
Edmund Scambler	1561	1561	John Thomas	1747	1747
Richard Howland	1585	1585	Richard Terrick..........	1757	1757
Thomas Dove	1601	1601	Robert Lambe	1764	1764
William Piers	1630	1630	John Hinchcliffe	1769	1769
Augustine Lindsell	1633	1633	Spencer Madan	1792	1794
Francis Dee	1634	1634	John Parsons	1813	1813
John Towers	1639	1639	Herbert Marsh	1816	1819
Benjamin Laney	1660	1660	George Davys..............	1839	1839
Joseph Henshaw............	1663	1663	Francis Jeune..............	1864	1864
William Lloyd	1675	1679	William Connor Magee...	1868	1869
Thomas White	1685	1685	Mandell Creighton........	1891	1891
Richard Cumberland	1691	1691	Edward Henry Carr Glyn	1897	1897

BRISTOL.

	Conse-cration	Accession.		Conse-cration.	Accession.
Paul Bush	1542	1542	Thomas Howell	1644	1644
John Holyman	1554	1554	Gilbert Ironside............	1661	1661
Richard Cheyney............	1562	1562	Guy Carleton	1672	1672
John Bullingham	1581	1581	William Gulston............	1679	1679
Richard Fletcher	1589	1589	John Lake	1683	1684
Vacant 1593–1603.			Jonathan Trelawney	1685	1685
John Thornborough.........	1593	1603	Gilbert Ironside	1689	1689
Nicolas Felton	1617	1617	John Hall	1691	1691
Rowland Searchfield	1619	1619	John Robinson	1710	1710
Robert Wright...............	1623	1623	George Smallridge.........	1714	1714
George Coke..................	1633	1633	Hugh Boulter.............	1719	1719
Robert Skinner	1637	1637	William Bradshaw	1724	1724
Thomas Westfield	1642	1642	Charles Cecil	1733	1733

BRISTOL (CONTINUED).

	Conse-cration.	Accession.		Con-e-cration.	Accession.
Thomas Secker	1735	1735	Ffoll. H. W. Cornewall	1797	1797
Thomas Gooch	1737	1737	George Pelham	1803	1803
Joseph Butler	1738	1738	John Luxmoore	1807	1807
John Conybeare	1750	1750	William L. Mansel	1808	1808
John Hume	1756	1756	John Kaye	1820	1820
Philip Young	1758	1758	Robert Gray	1827	1827
Thomas Newton	1761	1761	Joseph Allen	1834	1834
Lewis Bagot	1782	1782	James Henry Monk	1830	1836
Christopher Wilson	1783	1783	Charles Baring	1856	1856
Spencer Madan	1792	1792	Charles John Ellicott	1863	1863
Henry R. Courtenay	1794	1794			

GLOUCESTER.

	Conse-cration.	Accession.		Conse-cration.	Accession.
John Wakeman	1541	1541	Richard Willis	1715	1715
John Hooper	1551	1551	Joseph Wilcocks	1721	1721
James Brooks	1554	1554	Elias Sydall	1731	1731
Richard Cheyney	1562	1562	Martin Benson	1735	1735
John Bullingham	1581	1581	James Johnson	1752	1752
Godfrey Goldsborough	1598	1598	William Warburton	1760	1760
Thomas Ravis	1605	1605	James Yorke	1774	1779
Henry Parry	1607	1607	Samuel Hallifax	1781	1781
Giles Thompson	1611	1611	Richard Beadon	1789	1789
Miles Smith	1612	1612	George Is. Huntingford	1802	1802
Godfrey Goodman	1625	1625	Henry Ryder	1815	1815
William Nicolson	1661	1661	Christopher Bethell	1824	1824
John Pritchett	1672	1672	James Henry Monk	1830	1830
Robert Frampton	1681	1681	Charles Baring	1856	1856
Edward Fowler	1691	1691	Charles John Ellicott	1863	1863

S. DAVID'S.

	Conse-cration.	Accession.		Conse-cration.	Accession.
Bernard	1115	1115	Henry Gower	1328	1328
David Fitzgerald	1148	1148	John Thoresby	1347	1347
Peter de Leia	1176	1176	Reginald Brian	1350	1350
Geoffrey Henlaw	1203	1203	Thomas Fastolf	1352	1352
Gervas	1215	1215	Adam Houghton	1362	1362
Anselm le Gras	1231	1231	John Gilbert	1372	1389
Thomas Wallensis	1248	1248	Guy de Mona	1397	1397
Richard de Carew	1256	1256	Henry Chicheley	1408	1408
Thomas Beck	1280	1280	John Catterick	1414	1414
David Martin	1296	1296	Stephen Patrington	1415	1415

S. DAVID'S (CONTINUED).

	Conse-cration.	Accession.		Conse-cration.	Accession.
Benedict Nicolls	1408	1418	Laurence Womock	1683	1683
Thomas Rudborne	1434	1434	John Lloyd	1686	1686
William Lindwood	1442	1442	Thomas Watson	1687	1687
John Langton	1447	1447	George Bull	1705	1705
John De la Bere	1447	1447	Philip Bisse	1710	1710
Robert Tully	1460	1460	Adam Ottley	1713	1713
Richard Martin	1482	1482	Richard Smallbrooke	1724	1724
Thomas Langton	1483	1483	Elias Sydall	1731	1731
Hugh Pavy	1485	1485	Nicolas Claggett	1732	1732
John Morgan	1496	1496	Edward Willes	1743	1743
Robert Sherborn	1505	1505	Richard Trevor	1744	1744
Edward Vaughan	1509	1509	Antony Ellis	1753	1753
Richard Rawlins	1523	1523	Samuel Squire	1761	1761
William Barlow	1536	1536	Robert Lowth	1766	1766
Robert Ferrar	1548	1548	Charles Moss	1766	1766
Henry Morgan	1554	1554	James Yorke	1774	1774
Thomas Young	1560	1560	John Warren	1779	1779
Richard Davies	1560	1561	Edward Smallwell	1783	1783
Marmaduke Middleton	1579	1582	Samuel Horsley	1788	1788
Antony Rudd	1594	1594	William Stewart	1794	1794
Richard Milbourne	1615	1615	George Murray	1801	1801
William Laud	1621	1621	Thomas Burgess	1803	1803
Theophilus Field	1619	1627	John B. Jenkinson	1825	1825
Roger Mainwaring	1636	1636	Connop Thirlwall	1840	1840
William Lucy	1660	1660	William Basil Tickell Jones	1874	1874
William Thomas	1678	1678	John Owen	1897	1897

LLANDAFF.

	Conse-cration.	Accession.		Conse-cration.	Accession.
Urban	1107	1107	William Bottlesham		1386
Uhtred	1140	1140	Edmund Bromfield	1389	1389
Nicolas ap Gurgant	1148	1148	Tideman de Winchcomb	1393	1393
William Saltmarsh	1186	1186	Andrew Barrett	1395	1395
Henry of Abergavenny	1193	1193	John Burghill	1396	1396
William of Goldclive	1219	1219	Thomas Peverell	1397	1398
Elias of Radnor	1230	1230	John de la Zouch	1408	1408
William de Burgh	1245	1245	John Wells	1425	1425
John de la Ware	1254	1254	Nicolas Ashby	1441	1441
William of Radnor	1257	1257	John Hunden	1458	1458
William de Bruce	1266	1266	John Smith	1476	1476
John of Monmouth	1297	1297	John Marshall	1478	1478
John Eaglescliffe	1318	1323	John Ingleby	1496	1496
John Pascall		1347	Miles Salley	1500	1500
Roger Cradock	1350	1361	George de Athequa	1517	1517
Thomas Rushook	1383	1383	Robert Holdegate	1537	1537

LLANDAFF (CONTINUED.)

	Consecration.	Accession.		Consecration.	Accession.
Antony Kitchin, or Dunstan	1545	1545	Robert Clavering	1725	1725
Hugh Jones	1566	1566	John Harris	1729	1729
William Blethin	1575	1575	Matthias Mawson	1739	1739
Gervas Babington	1591	1591	John Gilbert	1740	1740
William Morgan	1595	1595	Edward Cressett............	1749	1749
Francis Godwin	1601	1601	Richard Newcome.........	1755	1755
George Carleton	1618	1618	John Ewer	1761	1761
Theophilus Field	1619	1619	Jonathan Shipley	1769	1769
William Murray	1622	1627	Shute Barrington	1769	1769
Morgan Owen	1640	1640	Richard Watson............	1782	1782
Hugh Lloyd	1660	1660	Herbert Marsh	1816	1816
Francis Davies	1667	1667	William Van Mildert......	1819	1819
William Lloyd	1675	1675	Charles R. Sumner	1826	1826
William Beaw	1679	1679	Edward Copleston.........	1828	1828
John Tyler	1706	1706	Alfred Ollivant	1849	1849
			Richard Lewis	1883	1883

BANGOR.

	Consecration.	Accession.		Consecration.	Accession.
Hervey	1092	1092	John Stanbery..............	1448	1448
David the Scot	1120	1120	James Blakedon............	1442	1453
Maurice	1140	1140	Richard Edenham	1465	1465
Guy Rufus	1177	1177	Henry Dean	1496	1496
Alan	1195	1195	Thomas Pigott	1500	1500
Robert of Shrewsbury ...	1197	1197	John Penny	1505	1505
Martin or Cadogan	1215	1215	Thomas Skirvington	1509	1509
Richard	1237	1237	John Salcot.................	1534	1534
Anian	1267	1267	John Bird	1537	1539
Griffin ap Yorwerth........	1307	1307	Arthur Bulkeley............	1542	1542
Anian Seys	1309	1309	William Glynne	1555	1555
Matthew Englefield	1328	1328	Roland Meyrick............	1559	1559
Thomas Ringsted	1357	1357	Nicolas Robinson	1566	1566
Gervas de Castro...........	1366	1366	Hugh Bellott	1586	1586
Howel ap Grono	1371	1371	Richard Vaughan	1596	1596
John Gilbert	1372	1372	Henry Rowlands	1598	1598
John Swaffham	1363	1376	Lewis Bayly	1616	1616
Richard Young..............	1400	1400	David Dolben	1632	1632
Benedict Nicolls [1]..........	1408	1408	Edmund Griffith...........	1634	1634
William Barrow	1418	1418	William Roberts	1637	1637
John Cliderow	1425	1425	Robert Morgan	1666	1666
Thomas Cheriton...........	1436	1436	Humfrey Lloyd	1673	1673

[1] Lewis Bifort was appointed Bishop of Bangor by the interest of Owen Glendower soon after 1400, but was never recognized by the English Church. The Pope is said to have translated him to another see in 1408, but he appeared as 'Ludovicus Bangorensis' at the Council of Constance, and may have been the Bishop of Bangor translated to Ross in Scotland in 1418; see Brady, *Epis. Succ.* i. 80; Godwin, ed. Richardson, p. 623.

BANGOR (CONTINUED).

	Conse-cration.	Accession.		Conse-cration.	Accession.
Humfrey Humphries	1689	1689	John Ewer	1761	1769
John Evans	1702	1702	John Moore..................	1775	1775
Benjamin Hoadly...........	1716	1716	John Warren	1779	1783
Richard Reynolds	1721	1721	William Cleaver............	1788	1800
William Baker..............	1723	1723	John Randolph	1799	1807
Thomas Sherlock..........	1728	1728	Henry W. Majendie	1800	1809
Charles Cecil	1733	1734	Christopher Bethell	1824	1830
Thomas Herring	1738	1738	James Colquhoun Camp- bell	1859	1859
Matthew Hutton	1743	1743			
Zachary Pearce	1748	1748	Daniel Lewis Lloyd	1890	1890
John Egerton	1756	1756			

S. ASAPH.

	Conse-cration.	Accession.		Conse-cration.	Accession.
Gilbert	1143	1143	Richard Davies	1560	1560
Geoffrey Arthur	1152	1152	Thomas Davis..............	1561	1561
Richard	1154	1154	William Hughes...........	1573	1573
Geoffrey.....................	1160	1160	William Morgan...........	1595	1601
Adam	1175	1175	Richard Parry	1604	1604
John	1183	1183	John Hanmer..............	1624	1624
Reiner	1186	1186	John Owen.................	1629	1629
Abraham	1225	1225	George Griffith	1660	1660
Hugh	1235	1235	Henry Glemham	1667	1667
Howel ap Ednevet	1240	1240	Isaac Barrow	1663	1670
Anian	1249	1249	William Lloyd	1680	1680
John	1267	1267	Edward Jones...	1683	1692
Anian Schonaw	1268	1268	George Hooper	1703	1703
Leoline Bromfield	1293	1293	William Beveridge........	1704	1704
David ap Blethyn...........	1315	1315	William Fleetwood	1708	1708
John Trevor	1352	1352	John Wynne	1715	1715
Leoline ap Madoc	1357	1357	Francis Hare	1727	1727
William Spridlington	1376	1376	Thomas Tanner	1732	1732
Laurence Child	1382	1382	Isaac Maddox..............	1736	1736
Alexander Bache............	1390	1390	Samuel Lisle •.............	1744	1744
John Trevor	1395	1395	Robert H. Drummond ...	1748	1748
Robert Lancaster............	1411	1411	Richard Newcome.........	1755	1761
John Lowe	1433	1433	Jonathan Shipley	1769	1769
Reginald Pecocke	1444	1444	Samuel Hallifax............	1781	1789
Thomas Knight	1451	1451	Lewis Bagot	1782	1790
Richard Redman	1471	1471	Samuel Horsley	1788	1802
Michael Deacon	1496	1496	William Cleaver............	1788	1806
David ap Yorwerth	1500	1500	John Luxmoore	1807	1815
David ap Owen	1504	1504	William Carey	1820	1830
Edmund Birkhead	1513	1513	Thomas Vowler Short ...	1841	1846
Henry Standish	1518	1518	Joshua Hughes	1870	1870
Robert Wharton	1536	1536	Alfred George Edwards...	1889	1889
Thomas Goldwell...........	1555	1555			

TRURO.   SOUTHWELL.

	Conse-cration.	Accession.		Conse-cration.	Accession.
Edward White Benson ...	1877	1877	George Ridding	1884	1884
George Howard Wilkinson	1883	1883			
John Gott	1891	1891			

S. ALBANS.

	Conse-cration.	Accession.		Conse-cration.	Accession.
Thomas Legh Claughton...	1867	1877	John Wogan Festing ...	1890	1890

YORK.

	Conse-cration.	First Signat.	Last Signat.	Death.		Conse-cration.	First Signat.	Last Signat.	Death.
Paulinus	625				Wulfhere	854			900
Ceadda............	664				Æthelbald	900			
Wilfrid............	664			709	Rodewald		928	930	
Bosa	678			705	Wulfstan		931	955	956
John of Bever-ley (succ. 705)	687			721	Oskytel (succ. 958)	950	958	969	971
Wilfrid II.........	718			732	Oswald (succ. 972)	961		991	992
Ecgberht	734			766	Aldulf............	992	995	1001	1002
Æthelberht or Cœna	767			780	Wulfstan II ...	1003	1004	1022	1023
Eanbald	780			796	Ælfric............	1023	1033	1049	1051
Eanbald II	796		808		Kinsige	1051			1060
Wulfsige					Ealdred (succ. 1061)	1044			1069
Wigmund.........	837								

	Conse-cration.	Accession.		Conse-cration.	Accession.
Thomas	1070	1070	John Romanus	1286	1286
Gerard	1096	1101	Henry Newark	1298	1298
Thomas II	1109	1109	Thomas Corbridge	1300	1300
Thurstan	1119	1119	William Greenfield	1306	1306
William Fitz Herbert	1143	1153	William de Melton.........	1317	1317
Henry Murdac	1147	1147	William de la Zouch	1342	1342
Roger of Pont l'Evêque ...	1154	1154	John Thoresby	1347	1352
Geoffrey Plantagenet	1191	1191	Alexander Neville	1374	1374
Walter Gray.................	1214	1215	Thomas Arundel	1374	1388
Sewall de Bovill	1256	1256	Robert Waldby	1387	1397
Godfrey de Ludham........	1258	1258	Richard le Scrope	1386	1398
Walter Giffard	1266	1265	Henry Bowet	1401	1407
William Wickwane.........|	1279	1279	John Kemp	1419	1426

YORK (CONTINUED).

	Conse-cration.	Accession.		Conse-cration.	Accession.
William Booth	1447	1452	Accepted Frewen	1644	1660
George Neville	1458	1464	Richard Sterne	1660	1664
Laurence Booth	1457	1476	John Dolben	1666	1683
Thomas Rotherham..... ...	1468	1480	Thomas Lamplugh.........	1676	1688
Thomas Savage	1493	1501	John Sharpe	1691	1691
Christopher Bainbridge ...	1507	1508	William Dawes	1708	1714
Thomas Wolsey	1514	1514	Launcelot Blackburn. ...	1717	1724
Edward Lee	1531	1531	Thomas Herring............	1738	1743
Robert Holdegate	1537	1545	Matthew Hutton	1743	1747
Nicolas Heath	1540	1555	John Gilbert	1740	1757
Thomas Young...............	1560	1561	Robert H. Drummond ...	1748	1761
Edmund Grindal	1559	1570	William Markham	1771	1777
Edwin Sandys	1559	1577	Edward V. Vernon	1791	1808
John Piers	1576	1589	Thomas Musgrave	1837	1847
Matthew Hutton	1589	1595	Charles Thomas Longley	1836	1860
Tobias Matthew	1595	1606	William Thomson	1861	1862
George Monteigne	1617	1628	William Connor Magee...	1868	1891
Samuel Harsnett	1609	1628	William Dalrymple Maclagan	1878	1891
Richard Neile	1608	1632			
John Williams	1621	1641			

LINDISFARNE.

	Conse-cration.	Death.		Conse-cration.	Death.
Aidan...........................	635	651	Æthelwold	724	740
Finan..........................	651	661	Cynewulf.....................	740	782
Colman	661	676	Hygbald	781	802
Tuda	664	664	Ecgbert	803	
Eata	678		Heathored	821	
Cuthberht	685	687	Ecgred	830	
Eadberct	687	698	Eanbert	845	
Eadfrith	698	721	Eardulf	854	899

CHESTER-LE-STREET. 883.

	Conse-cration.	Death.		Conse-cration.	Death.
Cutheard	900		Sexhelm	947	
Tilred..........................	915		Ealdred	957	968
Wigred	928	944	Elfsige........................	968	990
Uhtred	944				

HEXHAM.

	Conse-cration.	Death.		Conse-cration.	Death.
Eata	678	686	Alhmund	767	781
Tunbert	681		Tilberht	781	789
Eata (restored 685)		686	Æthelberht (succ. 789)	777	797
John of Beverley	687		Heardred	797	797
Wilfrid (succ. 705)	664	709	Eanbert	800	
Acca	709	740	Tidferth	806	821
Friothoberht	734	766			

DURHAM.

	Conse-cration.	Accession.		Conse-cration.	Accession.
Aldhun	990	990	William Senhouse	1496	1502
Eadmund	1020	1020	Christopher Bainbridge	1507	1507
Eadred	1041	1041	Thomas Ruthall	1509	1509
Æthelric	1042	1042	Thomas Wolsey	1514	1523
Æthelwin	1056	1056	Cuthbert Tunstall	1522	1530
Walcher	1071	1071	James Pilkington	1561	1561
William of S. Carileph	1081	1081	Richard Barnes	1567	1577
Ralph Flambard	1099	1099	Matthew Hutton	1589	1589
Geoffrey Rufus	1133	1133	Tobias Matthew	1595	1595
William de S. Barbara	1143	1143	William James	1606	1606
Hugh de Puiset	1153	1153	Richard Neile	1608	1617
Philip of Poitou	1197	1197	George Monteigne	1617	1628
Richard Marsh	1217	1217	John Howson	1619	1628
Richard le Poor	1215	1229	Thomas Morton	1616	1632
Nicolas Farnham	1241	1241	John Cosin	1660	1660
Walter Kirkham	1249	1249	Nathaniel Crewe	1671	1674
Robert Stichill	1261	1261	William Talbot	1699	1721
Robert of Holy Island	1274	1274	Edward Chandler	1717	1730
Antony Beck	1284	1284	Joseph Butler	1738	1750
Richard Kellaw	1311	1311	Richard Trevor	1744	1752
Lewis de Beaumont	1318	1318	John Egerton	1756	1771
Richard of Bury	1333	1333	Thomas Thurlow	1779	1787
Thomas Hatfield	1345	1345	Shute Barrington	1769	1791
John Fordham	1382	1382	William Van Mildert	1819	1826
Walter Skirlaw	1386	1388	Edward Maltby	1831	1836
Thomas Langley	1406	1406	Charles T. Longley	1836	1856
Robert Neville	1427	1438	Henry Montague Villiers	1856	1860
Laurence Booth	1457	1457	Charles Baring	1856	1861
William Dudley	1476	1476	Joseph Barber Lightfoot	1879	1879
John Sherwood	1484	1484	Brooke Foss Westcott	1889	
Richard Fox	1487	1494			

CARLISLE.

	Conse-cration.	Accession.		Conse-cration.	Accession.
Adelulf	1133	1133	Owen Oglethorpe	1557	1557
Bernard	1189	1203	John Best	1561	1561
Hugh	1219	1219	Richard Barnes	1567	1570
Walter Mauclerc	1224	1224	John May	1577	1577
Silvester Everdon	1247	1247	Henry Robinson	1598	1598
Thomas Vipont	1255	1255	Robert Snowden	1616	1616
Robert Chause	1258	1258	Richard Milbourne	1615	1621
Ralph Ireton	1280	1280	Richard Senhouse	1624	1624
John Halton	1292	1292	Francis White	1626	1626
John Ross	1325	1325	Barnabas Potter	1629	1629
John Kirkby	1332	1332	James Ussher	1621	1642
Gilbert Welton	1353	1353	Richard Sterne	1660	1660
Thomas Appleby	1363	1363	Edward Rainbow	1664	1664
Robert Reade	1394	1396	Thomas Smith	1684	1684
Thomas Merks	1397	1397	William Nicholson	1702	1702
William Strickland	1400	1400	Samuel Bradford	1718	1718
Roger Whelpdale	1420	1420	John Waugh	1723	1723
William Barrow	1418	1423	George Fleming	1735	1735
Marmaduke Lumley	1430	1430	Richard Osbaldeston	1747	1747
Nicolas Close	1450	1450	Charles Lyttelton	1762	1762
William Percy	1452	1452	Edmund Law	1769	1769
John Kingscote	1462	1462	John Douglas	1787	1787
Richard le Scrope	1464	1464	Edw. Venables Vernon	1791	1791
Edward Story	1468	1468	Samuel Goodenough	1808	1808
Richard Bell	1478	1478	Hugh Percy	1827	1827
William Senhouse	1496	1496	Henry Montagu Villiers	1856	185
Roger Layburn	1503	1503	Samuel Waldegrave	1860	186
John Penny	1505	1509	Harvey Goodwin	1869	186
John Kite	1513	1521	John Wareing Bardsley	1887	1892
Robert Aldrich	1537	1537			

CHESTER.

	Conse-cration.	Accession.		Conse-cration.	Accession.
John Bird	1537	1541	John Wilkins	1668	1668
George Coates	1554	1554	John Pearson	1673	1673
Cuthbert Scott	1556	1556	Thomas Cartwright	1686	1686
William Downham	1561	1561	Nicolas Stratford	1689	1689
William Chaderton	1579	1579	William Dawes	1708	1708
Hugh Bellott	1586	1595	Francis Gastrell	1714	1714
Richard Vaughan	1596	1597	Samuel Peploe	1726	1726
George Lloyd	1600	1605	Edmund Keene	1752	1752
Thomas Morton	1616	1616	William Markham	1771	1771
John Bridgman	1619	1619	Beilby Porteus	1777	1777
Brian Walton	1660	1660	William Cleaver	1788	1788
Henry Fern	1662	1662	Hen. W. Majendie	1800	1800
George Hall	1662	1662	Bowyer E. Sparke	1810	1810

CHESTER (CONTINUED).

	Conse-cration.	Accession.		Conse-cration.	Accession.
George Henry Law	1812	1812	William Jacobson	1865	1865
Charles J. Blomfield	1824	1824	William Stubbs	1884	1884
John Bird Sumner	1828	1828	Francis John Jayne	1889	1889
John Graham	1848	1848			

RIPON.   MANCHESTER.

	Conse-cration.	Accession.		Conse-cration.	Accession.
Charles T. Longley	1836	1836	James Prince Lee	1848	1848
Robert Bickersteth	1857	1857	James Fraser	1870	1870
William Boyd Carpenter ..	1884	1884	James Moorhouse	1876	1886

LIVERPOOL.   WAKEFIELD.

	Conse-cration.	Accession.		Conse-cration.	Accession.
John Charles Ryle	1880	1880	William Walsham How..	1879	1888

NEWCASTLE.

	Conse-cration.	Accession.		Conse-cration.	Accession.
Ernest Roland Wilberforce	1882	1882	Edgar Jacob	1895	1895

SODOR AND MAN.

	Conse-cration.	Accession.		Conse-cration.	Accession.
Henry Man	1546	1546	Richard Richmond	1773	1773
Thomas Stanley (p. 213)..	1555	1555	George Mason	1780	1780
John Salisbury	1536	1571	Claudius Crigan	1784	1784
John Meyrick	1576	1576	George Murray	1814	1814
George Lloyd	1600	1600	William Ward	1828	1828
John Philips	1605	1605	James Bowstead............	1838	1838
William Forster	1634	1634	Henry Pepys	1840	1840
Richard Parr................	1635	1635	Thomas Vowler Short ...	1841	1841
Samuel Rutter	1661	1661	Walter A. Shirley	1847	1847
Isaac Barrow	1663	1663	Robert John Eden	1847	1847
Henry Bridgman	1671	1671	Horace Powys	1854	1854
John Lake....................	1683	1683	Rowley Hill	1877	1877
Baptist Levinz	1685	1685	John Wareing Bardsley...	1887	1887
Thomas Wilson	1698	1698	Norman Dumenil John } Straton	1892	1892
Mark Hildesley	1755	1755			

WHITHERN IN GALLOWAY.

	Conse-cration.		Conse-cration.
Pecthelm	730	John	1189
Friothwald	735	Walter	1209
Pehtwine	763	Gilbert	1235
Æthelberht	777	Henry	1255
Bealdwulf	791	Thomas Dalton	1294
		Simon of Wedehale	1327
Gilaldanus	1133	Michael Malconhalgh	1355
Christian	1154	Thomas of Kirkton	1358

APPENDIX IX.

INDEX TO APPENDIX I.

INDEX TO APPENDIX I (CONTINUED).

INDEX TO APPENDIX VIII.

THE END

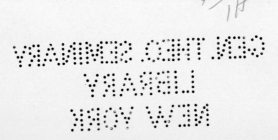